Residence and Economic Substance of Subsidiary Corporations in International and European Tax Law

Series on International Taxation

VOLUME 88

Series Editors

Prof. Ruth Mason, University of Virginia School of Law
Prof. Dr Ekkehart Reimer, University of Heidelberg

Introduction & Contents

The Series on International Taxation deals with a wide variety of topics in the global tax arena. The authors include many of the field's leading experts as well as talented newcomers. Their expert views and incisive commentary have proven highly useful to practitioners and academics alike.

Objective

The volumes published in this series are aimed at offering high-quality analytical information and practical solutions to international tax practitioners.

Readership

Practitioners, academics and policy makers in international tax law.

Frequency of Publication

2-3 new volumes published each year.

The titles published in this series are listed at the end of this volume.

Residence and Economic Substance of Subsidiary Corporations in International and European Tax Law

Savvas Kostikidis

Wolters Kluwer

Published by:
Kluwer Law International B.V.
PO Box 316
2400 AH Alphen aan den Rijn
The Netherlands
E-mail: lrs-sales@wolterskluwer.com
Website: www.wolterskluwer.com/en/solutions/kluwerlawinternational

Sold and distributed by:
Wolters Kluwer Legal & Regulatory U.S.
920 Links Avenue
Landisville, PA 17538
United States of America
E-mail: customer.service@wolterskluwer.com

ISBN 978-94-035-3858-7

e-Book: ISBN 978-94-035-3868-6
web-PDF: ISBN 978-94-035-3878-5

Για σένα μπαμπά.
Μου λείπεις.
Σ' αγαπώ.

Table of Contents

List of Abbreviations

AC	Appeal Cases
AG	Advocate General
ALP	Arm's Length Principle
AOA	Authorised OECD Approach
ATAD	Anti-Tax Avoidance Directive
BEPS	Base Erosion and Profit Shifting
BFH/NV	Sammlung Amtlich Nicht Veröffentlichter Entscheidungen des Bundesfinanzhofes
BNB	Beslissingen in Belastingzaken
BO Clause	Beneficial Ownership Clause
BStBl.	Bundessteuerblatt
CBDT	Central Board of Direct Taxes
CCA	Cost Contribution Agreement
CFC	Controlled Foreign Corporation
CJEU	Court of Justice of the European Union
CLR	Commonwealth Law Reports
CMC	Central Management and Control
DTC	Double Tax Convention
ECHR	European Convention on Human Rights
ECtHR	European Court of Human Rights
EFG	Entscheidungen der Finanzgerichte
EWHC	England and Wales High Court
FCA	Federal Court of Appeal
FCA	Federal Court of Australia

FTT	First-Tier Tribunal
GAAR	General Anti-avoidance Rule
HCA	High Court of Australia
HMRC	Her Majesty's Revenue and Customs
IP	Intellectual Property
IRD	Interest-Royalty Directive
ITLR	International Tax Law Reports
LOB	Limitation on Benefits
LoN	League of Nations
MAP	Mutual Agreement Procedure
MD	Merger Directive
MLI	Multilateral Instrument
MNE	Multinational Enterprise
OECD	Organisation for Economic Co-operation and Development
OECD MTC	OECD Model Tax Convention
OECD TPG	OECD Transfer Pricing Guidelines
OEEC	Organisation for European Economic Co-operation
PE	Permanent Establishment
POEM	Place of Effective Management
POI	Place of Incorporation
POM	Place of Management
PPMC	Primary Place of Management and Control
PPT	Principal Purpose Test
PSD	Parent-Subsidiary Directive
R&D	Research and Development
RPM	Resale Price Method
RStBl.	Reichssteuerblatt (Germany)
SARS	South African Revenue Service
SCD	Special Commissioners Decisions
SCR	Supreme Court Reports
SPF	Significant People Functions
SPV	Special Purpose Vehicle
STC	Simon's Tax Cases
T.C.	Reports of the US Tax Court
TAG	Technical Advisory Group on Monitoring the Application of Existing Treaty Norms for the Taxation of Business Profits

TC	Tax Cases
TCC	Tax Court of Canada
TEU	Treaty on European Union
TFEU	Treaty on the Functioning of the European Union
TNMM	Transactional Net Margin Method
USCIB	United States Council for International Business
VC	Venture Capital

List of Figures

List of Tables

Acknowledgements

This dissertation has been written during the author's time as a research associate at the Max-Planck-Institute for Public Finance. I would first like to thank my supervisor, professor Wolfgang Schön, for initiating this book, accompanying the whole process with interest, and inspiring me to do academic work.

I would also like to thank professor Peter Kindler for accepting to write the second evaluation of the dissertation and professor Klaus-Dieter Drüen for accepting to attend the defensio.

The heroes of the institute, Ms Auer and Ms Golombek, who made my life so easy, have gained my utmost respect. My colleagues and friends at the institute have also contributed enormously to my emotional well-being during the hard process of writing the book in the middle of the pandemic.

This book would not have been possible without the practical and emotional help of my friends, family, and wife. My dear Nikos, thank you for just being there, all the time. My dear Paul, thank you for understanding me and reading the manuscript. Mama, Stella, and Iliana thank you for giving me the feeling that no matter what happens I have you.

Finally, my beloved wife, Katharina, my rock, my everything, I thank you for bearing with me, supporting me, calming me down.

This book is dedicated to my father who left us too early.

Introduction: Combating Tax Arbitrage via Subsidiary Corporations with Substance-Oriented Rules

A WHY A SUBSIDIARY?

Have you ever considered who your contract partner really is when purchasing something from the famous online platform Amazon? A look at the receipt brings about an astonishing finding, at least for consumers with no legal background. Indeed, it is a well-known fact that Amazon was founded and incorporated in the United States where its headquarters is still located. Therefore, again the layperson would expect that the seller of the purchased good would be headquartered in the US. However, Amazon is not selling goods within the European Union directly from its headquarters but through a subsidiary corporation[1] ('subsidiary'; alternatively reference is made to the 'taxpayer') that is established in Luxembourg and entrusted with the distribution activities of the Multinational Enterprise (MNE) in Europe.

In fact, almost all MNEs nowadays use this organizational model, not just Amazon.[2] And, admittedly, subsidiaries are not only established as entities engaged in the distribution of goods but can also be involved in manufacturing goods, Research and Development (R&D), or a conjunction of such activities. But it is not the *role* of the subsidiary within the MNE that is of interest at this point.[3] Rather, the question we are faced with reads '*why* a subsidiary?' This question has two prongs.

1. One first remark as to the scope of the work can be made here. The work is restricted to subsidiary *corporations*. The research questions presented later on (s. C. of this chapter) are not related to partnerships.
2. 'In 2010, the one hundred US public companies with the highest annual revenues reported an average of 245 major subsidiaries, with 114 as the median. Only five reported fewer than five major subsidiaries.' *See* Squire (2011), p. 606, n. 1.
3. *See* one of the most influential articles on the roles of subsidiaries by Bartlett/Ghoshal (1986), according to whom subsidiaries can be strategic leaders, contributors, implementers and black holes. For an overview of the literature *see* Daniel (2010), pp. 13 et seq.

First, one could ask why a subsidiary and not an independent contractor or a franchisee. This question was first raised in 1937 by Ronald Coase in a seminal article where he pointed to transaction costs as the key aspect when deciding between, on the one hand, internalizing, i.e., 'making' through self-owned subsidiaries or partnerships, and, on the other, outsourcing,[4] i.e., 'buying' from independent contractors ('theory of the firm').[5] The Coase article gave birth to a whole discipline of economics, i.e., institutional economics. Nevertheless, for the purposes of this work, the question 'make or buy' around which institutional economics revolve is set aside.

Second, one could ask the question why Amazon set up a subsidiary in the legal form of a corporation and not a branch.[6] In order to answer this question we need to be familiar with the characteristics of the corporate legal form and the advantages these may convey to investors compared to partnerships.

Corporate law discerns 'five core structural characteristics of the business corporation ...: (1) legal personality, (2) limited liability, (3) transferable shares, (4) centralised management ..., and (5) shared ownership by contributors of equity capital'.[7] What do these characteristics mean with respect to the establishment of subsidiaries in the legal form of a corporation?

The analysis commences with the characteristic that corporations possess legal personality. Just like in the case of natural persons, corporations are juridical persons, which means, *inter alia*, that they have the ability to own assets in their own right.[8] Hence, the shareholders furnish the corporation with assets and these assets are owned by it; we have two distinct asset pools ('separation of assets'), i.e., one comprising the shareholder assets and the other consisting of the corporation's assets.[9] This is an important feature of the corporation in the case of subsidiaries. By creating a subsidiary and not simply integrating an activity into its own business, the controlling shareholder[10] ('parent') reduces the cost of credit for the business of the subsidiary[11] and of course insulates the subsidiary (and its creditors) from claims of the parent's creditors.

4. 'With outsourcing, firms contract with outside firms for some activities and only the most central activities remain within the ownership chain. In the 1990s, the shift to offshoring occurred when activities were specialized in the countries best suited to them. Today, outsourcing represents a similar specialization of activities across firms so that not every firm undertakes all activities.' Desai (2009), pp. 1275-1276.
5. Coase (1937), p. 395: 'a firm will tend to expand until the costs of organising an extra transaction within the firm become equal to the costs of carrying out the same transaction by means of an exchange on the open market or the costs of organising in another firm'. For a plead to take the theory of the firm into account in the tax (transfer pricing) realm, Schön (2012), passim.
6. The term 'branch' refers to PEs for tax purposes. *See* Zanotti (2004), p. 496.
7. Armour et al. (2017), p. 5.
8. In German law, partnerships also have this ability, without, however, possessing legal personality. *See* the critique by Lehmann (2007), pp. 240 et seq.
9. Fleckner (2010), p. 39.
10. 'Jurisdictions may differ on what constitutes "control" of a foreign subsidiary. To simplify the analysis, I take the case here of a wholly-owned foreign subsidiary.' Kane (2006), p. 888. This work follows this approach and also refers to wholly-owned subsidiaries henceforth.
11. As to the elucidation of this assertion, the reader is referred to Hansmann/Kraakman (2000), pp. 810-811. For the purposes of this work, this assertion is taken as a given.

The limited liability characteristic of corporations also helps explain why the corporation form is so popular when establishing a subsidiary. That is, shareholders, in contrast to partners of a partnership, cannot, in principle, be held liable for debts of the corporation. Limited liability of the subsidiary protects its parent from being held liable for its subsidiary's losses. In this way, the parent can be sure that even if its investment fails, its assets are protected.

So, the separation of assets as well as the limited liability characteristic of the corporation form constitute the sole reason corporate law provides to explain the expansion of subsidiaries in the legal form of a corporation. The use of corporations to limit the claims of creditors of the corporation to its assets and not to the property of its shareholders (and vice versa) is known as *asset partitioning*.[12] Still, economic literature points to the costs of asset partitioning, e.g., high accounting costs, rendering it an unfavourable solution.[13] Worth mentioning are also reputational/prestige gains from choosing the corporate form in a specific jurisdiction which promises high-quality corporate law standards (corporate surplus).[14] Finally, literature provides another explanation for the expansion of subsidiaries and thus the election of the corporate form: tax considerations.[15] Since tax considerations are at the heart of this dissertation, they will be analysed at length.

B SUBSIDIARIES AS A MEANS OF TAX ARBITRAGE

I Preliminary Remarks

It has been indicated that the first characteristic of a corporation is the recognition of the corporate body's legal personality.[16] This also has tax implications: corporations are separate taxpayers for tax purposes[17] – in contrast to partnerships, which are subject to transparent taxation, that is, tax is levied directly at the shareholder and not at the company. And as a rule of thumb taxpayers (individuals as well as legal persons) are taxable in their state of residence (or 'residence state') with their worldwide income.[18] In contrast, foreign, i.e., non-resident, taxpayers are taxable in a state other

12. Hansmann/Kraakman (2000), p. 810: 'by "asset partitioning" we mean the division of a fixed pool of assets into subpools, each of which is separately pledged as security to a different creditor or group of creditors'.
13. Hansmann/Squire (2018), pp. 263 et seq.
14. Shaviro (2011), pp. 407 et seq.
15. Hansmann/Squire (2018), p. 266.
16. The landmark case in this respect is House of Lords, 16 Nov. 1897, *Salomon v. Salomon*, AC (1897), p. 22.
17. German jurisprudence underlines the necessity that corporate taxation must 'maintain the structural order of civil law consistently', and therefore it must be linked to the corporate legal form. *See* German Federal Tax Court ('Bundesfinanzhof'), 25 Jun. 1984, GrS 4/82, BStBl. II (1984), p. 751 (author's unofficial translation).
18. France constitutes a notable exception to that rule, applying a territorial system. According to s. 209(1) of the French Tax Code, only business carried on within the French territory is subject to taxation in France. Accordingly, a corporation incorporated in France is not taxable there with income derived from operations taking place outside its territory. Respectively, a foreign corporation is taxable in France for profits arising within French territory.

than the residence state ('source state' or 'state of source') if they demonstrate a territorial nexus[19] to that state (e.g., conveyed through immovable property in that state). The taxation in the case of non-residents, though, is limited to the income accruing within the territory of the source state.

Now, imagine that you had the choice to be taxed on a 15% or a 25% basis on your total income. What would you prefer? Probably the former option. That is exactly what may incentivize MNEs to set up subsidiaries in low-tax states. Additionally, they may try to take advantage of their status as separate taxpayers in that state and shift as much profit as possible to this subsidiary which is taxed at a lower rate.[20] In that way, their worldwide tax burden may be reduced.

In fact, empirical evidence from the field of economic research has provided the assertion made above with some backing in recent years.[21] Subsidiaries can be set up, for instance, in low-tax countries with the sole purpose of holding Intellectual Property (IP) and licensing it to other subsidiaries and/or to the parent. By paying the royalties from the license agreement, the taxable income of the parent and/or the other subsidiaries possibly located in high-tax countries is reduced, while the income shifted to the foreign subsidiary is taxed at a low rate, thereby reducing the worldwide tax burden of the MNE ('milking effect').[22] For example, a corporation in a high-tax state (assume a 20% tax rate) with a total gross profit of EUR 20 and paying EUR 10 in royalties has at the end of the day a total net profit of EUR 10 which is taxable in its residence state, since the royalties are deductible from the tax base (20–10 = EUR 10). If EUR 20 were taxed in the high-tax state, the tax burden would be EUR 4. Now that

19. The terms 'nexus', 'connection' and 'allegiance' are considered synonymous for the purposes of this work.
20. Admittedly, it is not only the behaviour of MNEs that leads to profit shifting. 'The other side of the coin' lies in the behaviour of states 'which gives the incentive for, and makes possible, tax arbitrage' *see* Pichhadze (2015), p. 103. This side of the coin is not subject of investigation in this work.
21. Huizinga/Laeven (2008), p. 1174, who suggest that 'there is evidence of profit shifting between subsidiaries and their parent firms as well as among the subsidiaries themselves'. In particular, the authors show in their study that a 1% decrease in the tax rate at the level of the subsidiary results in an increase of its pre-tax profits of 0.98% (*see* column 4 of Table 4). A similar conclusion is reached by Dischinger (2010), p. 10 and Dharmapala (2016), p. 6 both suggesting other figures, though (0.74% and 0.8%, respectively).

    According to Egger et al. (2010), p. 103, foreign-owned subsidiaries set up in high-tax jurisdictions pay considerably less taxes than comparable domestic-owned ones, which is due to profit shifting engaged in by the MNE. In the same sense, Alfons Weichenrieder shows that a 10% increase in the tax rate at the level of the foreign parent results in half a percentage point increase in the profitability of the German subsidiary. This implies that when the parent jurisdiction is not a low-tax jurisdiction, more profit remains in the hands of the high-taxed German subsidiary. *See* Weichenrieder (2009), p. 292. Unlike the other studies cited, this one does not show that a subsidiary is set up in order to decrease the overall tax burden. Nevertheless, it shows the profit shifting potential arising from such structures.

    Finally, *see* the meta-analyses by Heckemeyer/Overesch (2017) and Beer et al. (2018).
22. Dischinger/Riedel (2011), p. 698, who argue that a decrease in the tax rate differential by one percentage in the subsidiary jurisdiction raises the subsidiary's level of IP ownership by 2.2%. In other words, subsidiaries holding IP are more prone to be established in low-tax jurisdictions.

only EUR 10 are taxed the tax burden amounts to EUR 2. If the subsidiary's state of residence receiving the royalties taxes EUR 10 on a 10% basis, the tax burden is EUR 1, which makes the worldwide tax burden of the group EUR 1 instead of EUR 2, without the interposition of the subsidiary and the licensing of the IP.

Furthermore, subsidiaries can also be established in order to amass profits in low-tax jurisdictions. In particular, as already noted, the separate legal personality of the subsidiary for civil law purposes is respected by tax law, which generally ascribes the status of a separate taxpayer to corporations. This has the effect that profit gained by the subsidiary can be taxed at the level of the parent only after it is distributed to the shareholders/parent in the form of dividends; a phenomenon commonly known as *deferral*. If the profit is taxed both at the level of the subsidiary before distribution and at the level of the parent after receiving it, economic double taxation arises.[23] Since double taxation creates an investment barrier, states are interested[24] in avoiding both the economic and the juridical double taxation, the latter being double taxation suffered by the same person because of the same amount of profit being taxed by two different states.

They do so by applying two methods (either unilaterally or, as will be shown below, bilaterally):[25] the exemption method, which exempts foreign income from the domestic tax base, and the credit method, which offsets foreign taxes against the domestic ones. The latter method has the following outcome: if the parent's state of residence has a tax rate higher than the subsidiary's, then the dividend is taxed at that higher rate. If the subsidiary, for example, is taxed on a EUR 10 distribution with a 10% rate (amounting to EUR 1 creditable tax) and the parent jurisdiction taxes the same amount on a 20% basis (amounting to a tax burden of EUR 2), then the difference (2–1 = EUR 1) is taxable in the parent jurisdiction.

So, it follows that if the parent's state of residence applies the credit method, the dividend is subject to its level of taxation (e.g., 20% instead of 10% in the example above). Of course, if this level of taxation is high, the subsidiary has an interest in collecting profits and not repatriating them (i.e., distributing them in the form of dividends to the parent) until conditions for doing so become advantageous.[26] An

23. One can distinguish economic double taxation from juridical double taxation by looking whether the subject suffering the double taxation is the same or not. In the case of the former, different persons (i.e., the subsidiary and the parent) are taxed on the same amount of income. On that distinguishing criterion, *see* Bühler (1964), p. 32.
24. Interested but not obliged. Neither international customary law nor EU law obliges states to eliminate double taxation. *See* Valta (2014), p. 227; Hongler (2019), pp. 168-171 and 403 et seq. The opposite opinion is expressed by the proponents of the 'single tax principle'; on its normative justification *see* the argument by Avi-Yonah (1997), pp. 517-520.
25. Beyond the credit and the exemption method presented here, conceivable is also the unilateral deduction of foreign taxes from the domestic tax base treating foreign taxes as the cost for doing business abroad. *See* Schön (2021), p. 372 with references to authors explaining the rationales behind such policy. *See also* the critique on the deduction method in Valta (2014), p. 284.
26. For a demonstration of the effect on the after-tax profit on the investment via a low-tax subsidiary in a longer period of time, *see* Rust (2007), pp. 12-13; Rust (2008), pp. 492-493.

example would be that the parent jurisdiction changes to an exemption system[27] or sufficient credits have been accumulated in order to completely offset the tax burden in the parent jurisdiction[28] ('parking effect').[29] Even if such advantageous conditions for repatriation do not occur, 'the multinational will have the benefit of the initial tax savings in the interim. This benefit is equivalent to an interest-free loan from the [tax administration] in the amount of the residual ... tax liability'.[30]

These milking and parking tactics have incited reactions on both a unilateral and a bilateral level. The meaning of the term unilateral is intuitive: measures taken by domestic legislatures. In contrast, explaining the term bilateral requires some further analysis.

In particular, cross-border activities take place by definition in more than one state and may have some kind of attachment to all these states. For example, a German resident selling their apartment situated in Greece has a connection to both these states, i.e., Germany and Greece. Although Germany does not demonstrate a connection to the source of the income, i.e., the apartment, it is able to tax it, since, as already noted, it taxes the worldwide income of its residents. If both these states tax the income arising from the sale, double taxation will occur. For this reason,[31] states conclude Double Tax Conventions (DTCs) to prevent juridical[32] double taxation and allocate taxing rights between the source state, i.e., Greece, and the residence state, i.e., Germany.

However, as shown below in further detail (section B.III. of this chapter),[33] DTCs do not only serve these two purposes and take account of the use of subsidiaries described above by containing measures addressing these kind of structures. This fact is also heavily influenced by the work of the Organisation for Economic Co-operation and Development (OECD). The latter, and its predecessor the Organisation for European Economic Co-operation (OEEC), have been a major driver in shaping international tax policy. The OECD's first achievement was to provide the first Model Tax

27. Egger et al. (2015), who prove that the system-switch adopted by the UK in 2009 from the worldwide system applying the credit method on foreign income to a territorial system accompanied by exemption of foreign dividends led to an increase of dividend repatriation.
28. Desai et al. (2001). Regarding strategies for tax-free repatriation (e.g., investment by the low-tax subsidiary in passive assets or in other high-tax subsidiaries), *see* Altshuler/Grubert (2002).
29. The terminology 'milking' and 'parking' is based on Kane (2013).
30. Green (1993), p. 34. In a similar vein, Rust (2007), pp. 12-13; Quilitzsch (2013), p. 42; Devereux et al. (2021), p. 61; Fleming et al. (2009), p. 86. Fleming et al. also mention another reason to employ parking tactics, namely the 'avoidance of the limitations on foreign tax credit carry-overs'. Fleming et al. (2009), p. 85, n. 19.
31. Not only for this reason. In fact, 'tax treaties may provide the signatory countries with a number of supplementary advantages, including: improved compatibility between the tax rules of the signatory countries, assistance in tax enforcement, reinforcement of investor certainty, and strengthened general cooperation in tax enforcement among nations'. *See* Dagan (2000), pp. 983 et seq.
32. Economic double taxation is left for the states to deal with unilaterally. *See* para. 51 of the Commentary (2017) on Article 23A and 23B.
33. References to sections and chapters of this work are made in the text in order to enable a better reading flow.

Convention (OECD MTC)[34] in 1963, which since then has formed the basis for DTC negotiations between states.[35]

Admittedly, the OECD did not stop its work in 1963. On the contrary, we have become witnesses in recent years to a staggering number of reports and policy recommendations. One of the most recent and the most important for this work, to which recurrent reference is made, is the Base Erosion and Profit Shifting (BEPS) Project.[36] The BEPS Project was released in 2015 in 15 'Actions'. Certain Actions centred their attention on strategies put forward by MNEs like the milking and parking of profits, which is why the measures to be discussed are based to a great extent on policies adopted therein.

In the next section, it will be demonstrated based on a case study how subsidiaries may be interposed to achieve the milking and parking effects. Subsequently, both unilateral and bilateral measures against that kind of use of subsidiaries are presented.

II A Case Study[37]

Assume that a parent corporation ('PaCo') in a high-tax country possesses a series of valuable intangibles which it intends to use in order to develop some new IP and do so in the most tax-efficient way. For this purpose, it sets up a subsidiary ('SubCo') in a low-tax country and injects equity capital into SubCo. PaCo and SubCo enter into a cost contribution agreement (CCA). Pursuant to this agreement, PaCo and SubCo are to jointly develop the new IP. PaCo contributes to the CCA all the services related to the development of the new IP and its existing intangibles. SubCo contributes to the funding of the whole project (with the capital injected by PaCo). PaCo will be the legal

---

34. Currently, OECD, *Model Tax Convention on Income and on Capital* (OECD 2017).
35. 'It is estimated ... that about 75 percent of the language of all bilateral tax treaties is identical to the language of the OECD model.' Brauner (2014), p. 62.

    Note here two issues: first, when reference is made to bilateral measures, DTC measures are meant and therewith measures stipulated in the OECD MTC because of the importance of the latter as a basis for DTC negotiations. Second, exactly because most DTCs are based on the OECD MTC, its Articles as well as the OECD Guidelines on transfer pricing are referred to as legal rules. The OECD is an international organization merely providing for recommendations to the states. The OECD Council merely *recommends* the Members 'when concluding new bilateral conventions or revising existing bilateral conventions, to conform to the Model Tax Convention, as interpreted by the Commentaries thereon'. *See* Annex to the OECD Model, Recommendation of the OECD Council Concerning the Model Tax Convention on Income and on Capital (1997). And recommendations are, according to Article 5(b) in conjunction with Article 5(a) of the OECD Convention, not binding upon the Members.

    However, upon the implementation of these recommendations and incorporation by the states into their DTCs and national law they receive the status of a legal rule. So, here it is not asserted that the rules of the OECD MTC form international customary law, but only that they become ('hard') law upon implementation. Denying that OECD practices can be crystallized into international customary law, Schön (2015), p. 118; Schön (2021), p. 363 with abundant references, also to the opposite opinions of Avi-Yonah (2007), pp. 4-8 and Kofler (2007). The OECD works form, thus, soft law. *See* Pistone (2010), p. 102.
36. OECD, *Action Plan on Base Erosion and Profit Shifting* (OECD 2013).
37. Readers familiar with the tax-planning industry may know that this structure resembles the 'Double Irish Arrangement'. On the structuring elements of the arrangement, *see* Benshalom (2013), pp. 445-446; Pinkernell (2013), pp. 181-182; Screpante (2019), pp. 436-438.

owner of the new IP, whereas SubCo will be its economic owner for a certain region (e.g., Asia).

Assume further that after five years of operating this structure, PaCo develops the new IP. The following tax-relevant results arise:

(1) The new IP is legally attributable to SubCo as its economic owner although it has been developed solely by PaCo. If SubCo licenses the new IP to another highly taxed subsidiary of the group ('SubSub'), which needs it for its manufacturing activities, it can achieve both the milking and the parking effect in the following way.

(2) SubSub will need to pay royalties for the licensed IP, say EUR 10 for five years. These EUR 10 milk the tax base in the residence state of SubSub ('SubSub state'), since royalties are deductible from the total income of SubSub, and the SubSub state cannot tax the outflowing royalty payments. This is because the DTC between the state of residence of SubCo ('SubCo state') and the SubSub state, in accordance with Article 12 of the OECD MTC, stipulates that the taxing right regarding royalty income lies only with the state of residence of the recipient of that income (i.e., the SubCo state). In addition, the state of the payer (i.e., the SubSub state) is not allowed to impose withholding taxes on the royalty.[38] All in all, the high-taxing SubSub state cannot get its hands on the royalty income which is favourably taxed in the SubCo state.

(3) SubCo parks the royalty income received by SubSub. SubCo holds on to the accumulated profits until favourable conditions of distributing them to PaCo arise; that can be, for example, a DTC between the state of residence of PaCo ('PaCo state') and SubCo state relieving dividends paid by entities residing in these two jurisdictions (in our example dividends paid by SubCo to PaCo) from withholding taxes. So, SubCo keeps the profits parked until the DTC is concluded.

(4) The overall tax burden of the group is reduced. This is not only because SubCo milks profit from the high-taxed SubSub but also because it is SubCo which licenses the IP to SubSub and not PaCo. Had PaCo not set up SubCo and entered into the CCA with it, PaCo would be the sole owner of the new IP and, thus, it would be the one licensing it to SubSub. Now, if the PaCo state taxes the SubSub royalties on a 40% rate the tax burden is EUR 4 (10*0.4 = EUR 4), whereas if SubCo taxes it on a 10% rate the tax burden is EUR 1 (10*0.1 = EUR 1).

38. Withholding taxes are withheld from a gross payment and paid to the government directly by the payer. It is assumed that SubSub is not resident in an EU Member State. Otherwise, if SubCo is an EU resident too, withholding taxes on inter-company dividends would be, all requirements fulfilled, limited pursuant to Directive 2003/49/EC of the European Parliament and of the Council of 3 Jun. 2003 on the common system of taxation applicable to interest and royalty payments made between associated companies of different Member States, OJ L157 (2003), as amended. *See* above s. B.III.4. of this chapter where the assumptions on which the case study is based are changed and it is assumed that SubCo and SubSub are residents in two different EU Member States.

The following figure illustrates the structure underlying the case study.

Figure 1 Milking and Parking Through Low-Taxed Subsidiaries

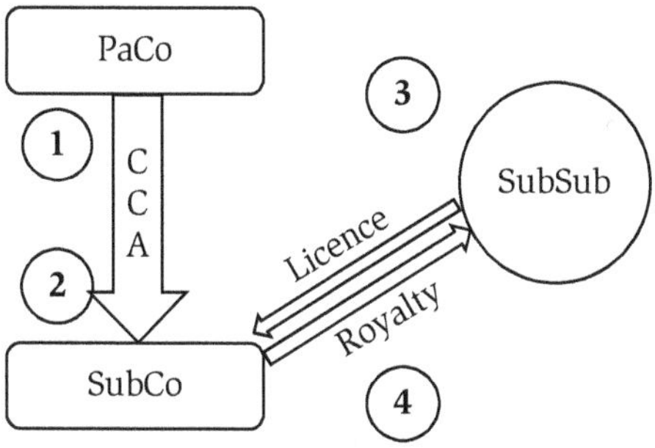

1. High-taxed PaCo enters into CCA with its low-taxed subsidiary, SubCo
2. SubCo becomes the economic owner of the developed IP
3. SubCo licenses the IP to other high-taxed subsidiaries of the group like SubSub
4. Tax-related results:
a) 'milking' of the profits of SubSub
b) 'parking' of the profits in the low-taxed jurisdiction

It can be inferred from the above that by applying this structure, PaCo implements its business plan, i.e., creating a new IP, and at the same time reduces the overall tax burden that would incur without the interposition of SubCo.

In the final analysis, SubCo is solely responsible for holding the new IP and receiving the royalties from the license agreement with SubSub. For that purpose, it rents an office where one part-time employee is responsible for day-to-day tasks in relation to these activities. For the sake of clarity, it is noted that the employee does not perform any task of any nature whatsoever with respect to the licensed IP; she merely controls whether royalty payments are made correctly and on time and is responsible for the communication with PaCo and SubSub. It is PaCo's technical staff who are entrusted by SubCo with the development, enhancement, maintenance, and use of the new IP, whereas with regard to the legal protection of the new IP, a legal firm is engaged by SubCo. Still, all strategic decisions rest formally with SubCo's manager, who is also a member of the executive board of PaCo and a resident of the PaCo state. She conducts a yearly day trip to the SubCo state in order to formally sign some core decisions for the business of SubCo (e.g., control whether litigation has to be initiated because of a breach of the patent belonging to SubCo, control and sign the accounts of SubCo, etc.).

It seems that SubCo gets a lot for doing too little. Now, the question is whether such a business structure is accepted for tax purposes. The next section deals with this issue.

III Unilateral and Bilateral Substance-Oriented Responses

From the above case study, it becomes evident that two states are losing a part of their tax base: the PaCo and the SubSub state. Further states will join if/when SubCo licenses the new IP to (and thereby milks the income of) other subsidiaries of the group residing in the region for which it is the economic owner of the new IP. The 'losers' in this game are interested in protecting their domestic tax-base from being eroded through milking and parking enabled by the interposition of subsidiaries. Moreover, tackling these issues helps to promote social welfare and competition between enterprises.[39] Unilateral and bilateral responses address milking and parking on four levels, all of which have something in common: they concentrate on the *substance* of the subsidiary.

1 Treaty Corporate Residence

First, the PaCo state may raise a fundamental question: is SubCo resident in the PaCo state? The answer to that question is crucial for tax purposes. As has already been mentioned (section B.I. of this chapter), persons resident in a state are subject to taxation in that state on their worldwide income. Accordingly, states adopt specific criteria determining residence thereby leading to taxation of a taxpayer's worldwide income. With regard to corporations, there are, in principle, two criteria which determine residence: a formal and a *substantive* one.[40] The first one refers to the place where the civil law act giving existence to the legal person of the corporation took place, i.e., the place of incorporation (POI). The second one refers to the place from which the corporation is managed.

Returning to the case study, it has been shown that SubCo is not incorporated in the PaCo state but in the SubCo state. Accordingly, the formal criterion cannot create tax residence of SubCo in the PaCo state. Still, maybe the management of that corporation takes place in the PaCo state. Answering that question leads to another question, namely whether the place of management (POM) of SubCo is located in the PaCo state (and not in its incorporation state, i.e., in the SubCo state). Remember, the sole manager of SubCo is also a member of the executive board of PaCo and a resident of the PaCo state, only visiting the SubCo premises once a year. If this question is answered in the affirmative, that would lead to SubCo being resident in the PaCo state for tax purposes. Consequently, if the POM of SubCo is in the PaCo state, that state may claim the worldwide profits attributable to SubCo (EUR 10 from the royalty payments received by SubSub, consisting of the sole source of income for SubCo, and potentially further profits arising from licensing the new IP to other subsidiaries).

So, according to the PaCo state, SubCo would be taxable with its worldwide profits in its jurisdiction, whereas, according to the SubCo state, it is taxable in the SubCo state (either because that is the state of incorporation or because the SubCo state maintains that the POM of SubCo is located therein since the sole manager formally

39. Tax-planning generates welfare loss because it leads to inefficient allocation of resources by MNEs, since MNEs invest therein resources that could be invested elsewhere. Such resource can be also immaterial, for instance, talent. *See* Dharmapala (2014), p. 12. Furthermore, tax-planning leads to distortions in competition, as smaller enterprises are not able to save taxes and thus have a disadvantage compared to MNEs. *See* OECD, *Addressing Base Erosion and Profit Shifting* (OECD 2013), p. 8.
40. Regarding the dichotomy between formal and substantive criteria, *see* Marian (2013a), pp. 1619 et seq.; Ismer (2018), pp. 43 et seq.; Devereux et al. (2021), p. 96.

finalizes all company decisions there). SubCo would be at once dual resident; both the PaCo and the SubCo state may claim taxation of SubCo's worldwide profits and therefore double taxation is imminent ('residence-residence conflict'). In the final analysis, it is the DTC between the PaCo state and the SubCo state that is decisive in defining where SubCo is resident and resolving the residence-residence conflict and therewith the double taxation issue. If it is assumed that the DTC in question follows the OECD MTC in its 2014 version,[41] Article 4(3) of the 2014 version of the OECD MTC applies in order for the conflict to be solved. Accordingly, SubCo is resident in the state of its place of effective management (POEM). This is the place 'where key management and commercial decisions that are necessary for the conduct of the entity's business as a whole are *in substance* made'.[42] Accordingly, tax administration and courts in the PaCo state and SubCo state need to investigate when applying Article 4(3) of the DTC between them whether SubCo has enough *substance* in the SubCo state in order for it to be managed in that state and thus not from the PaCo state?

2 Transfer Pricing Rules

This brief discussion of the residence response has made apparent that residence rules attribute persons to territories (e.g., SubCo to either the PaCo state or the SubCo state).[43] But one should keep in mind that it is *the income*, or, to put it more accurately, the positive net income, i.e., *the profit* of a person that is subject to income tax; the same applies with respect to corporate income tax, the corporation being a separate taxable person. To put it simply, the more positive net income a person has, the more its state of residence can tax. It follows that attributing income to a person indirectly influences the claim of its state of residence.[44]

Returning to the case study, if the PaCo state could not make the residence claim and access SubCo's worldwide profits, it could conceivably argue that the royalties paid by SubSub to SubCo (constituting its worldwide profits) should not be attributable to SubCo but to PaCo. The same holds true with regard to future royalties arising from the licensing of the new IP by SubCo to other subsidiaries of the group. The allocation of the royalty income to PaCo would increase the tax base taxable in the PaCo state. But what would be the legal basis for such an income allocation?

---

41. As explained in detail below in s. A.III. of Ch. 1, reference is made to the 2014 version of the OECD MTC and not the latest one regarding the POEM, because Article 4(3) has been amended in the 2017 version of the OECD MTC.
42. Paragraph 24 second sentence of the Commentary (2014) on Article 4 (emphasis added). *See* Lipniewicz (2020), p. 610: 'The POEM concept is an expression of the "substance over form" doctrine. Substance over form regimes are prevalent in many countries, and they purport to let the taxation of transactions follow their economic substance. In the case of the POEM, this economic substance concerns management processes that are crucial for managing the company.'
43. Schön (2010b), p. 555.
44. In the words of Wolfgang Schön: 'the territorial allocation of an item of income follows the personal attribution of the same income'. Schön (2010b), p. 561. *See also* Schoueri/Galendi (Jr.) (2020), p. 155.

The legal basis could be Article 9 of the DTC between the PaCo and the SubCo state which (is assumed that) is based on Article 9 of the OECD MTC incorporating the arm's length principle (ALP) into the DTC.[45] This principle[46] governs the personal attribution of profit[47] to different parts of an MNE. However, Article 9 of the OECD MTC is not self-executing.[48] That is, states cannot use it directly as a legal basis to justify profit attribution. Thus, the ALP needs to be implemented by the states in their domestic law via so-called transfer pricing rules, which are, again, based on an OECD recommendation, namely the *Transfer Pricing Guidelines for Multinational Enterprises and Tax Administrations* (OECD TPG)[49,50] Without going into detail, the OECD approach in the latest revision of the OECD TPG following the mandate of BEPS Actions 8-10[51] has been to endorse the attribution of profit to a person who 'in *substance*: performs and controls all of the functions ... provides all assets ... assumes all of the risks'.[52]

Returning to the case study, the PaCo state may maintain that the profit arising from licensing of the new IP to SubSub is not attributable to SubCo, despite it being legally the economic owner of the intangible. Remember, the development, enhancement, maintenance, and use of the software have been outsourced by SubCo to PaCo. Accordingly, the PaCo state could argue that the profit from the IP should be allocated

45. As to the origins of the ALP in US tax policy *see* Avi-Yonah (1995), pp. 95 et seq.; Koomen (2015a), pp. 142-143.
46. It is debatable whether the ALP constitutes a (hard law) principle. It is not the right place to take position on this debate. In this regard, *see* most prominently Avi-Yonah (2007), pp. 4-8; Baistrocchi (2022), s. 6.2.5.1. *Contra,* Hongler (2019), pp. 175 et seq.; Braumann (2020), pp. 767-768; Mosquera Valderrama (2020), p. 756.
47. Words are chosen carefully here. The ALP governs the allocation of *profit* to persons and thereby to territories. It does *not* govern the allocation of (items of) *income* to persons. To put it bluntly, the ALP does not dictate: 'You, company A, should not be allocated this item of income (e.g., a dividend payment), but company B should.' This is the function of income attribution which takes place according to domestic law. *See* Rust (2007), p. 67; Canè (2017), p. 534; Navisotschnigg (2022), p. 107. By contrast, the ALP is not an income allocation rule; it only says: 'You, company A, are entitled to 10 EUR profit and you, company B, to 5 EUR profit out of the total 15 EUR that is to be attributed to you both.' On this distinction, *see* Wittendorff (2010), p. 151. Indirectly, however, the ALP may be employed as an income allocation rule. For example, if it dictates: 'You, company A, are entitled to 15 EUR profit and you, company B, to 0 EUR profit', then the ALP practically excludes income allocation to company B and functions as a see-through provision, i.e., it negates the existence of company C.
48. For references *see* below n. 11 in Ch. 2.
49. OECD, *Transfer Pricing Guidelines for Multinational Enterprises and Tax Administrations* (2022) (hereinafter 'OECD TPG').
50. Brauner (2015), p. 76. *See also* Calderón (2007), pp. 9 and 15, first clarifying that 'these Guidelines, like the OECD MC and its Commentaries, do not legally integrate a binding law for the Member States of the OECD. They constitute recommendations issued by the OECD Council' and then affirming, though, that '[t]he OECD Transfer Pricing Guidelines have become the international standard or the internationally agreed principles that govern the distribution of tax power between the states on the income flow and expenses between associated enterprises'. It must be reminded (*see* above n. 35 in this chapter) that recommendations of the OECD Council are, pursuant to Article 5(b) in conjunction with Article 5(a) of the OECD Convention, not binding upon the Members of the OECD; this applies, of course, all the more to non-Members. *See also* with abundant references from state practice Monsenego (2015), pp. 32-33.
51. OECD, *Aligning Transfer Pricing Outcomes with Value Creation,* Actions 8-10 - 2015 Final Report.
52. OECD TPG, para. 6.71 (emphasis added).

to PaCo. This could take place by asserting that PaCo and not SubCo in substance performs and controls all of the functions, provides all assets, and assumes all of the risks with regard to the new IP; the only thing that SubCo does is to offer IP administration services to PaCo.[53] So, tax administration and courts in the PaCo state need to ask more or less exactly the same question in order to change the attribution of income in its favour: does SubCo have enough *substance* in order for the profit arising from the new IP to be able to be attributed to it?[54]

3 *DTC Anti-abuse Rules*

The third response addresses the erosion of the tax base originally attributable to the SubSub state. Remember that the tax base of the SubSub state is milked due to the royalty payments, these being taxable pursuant to the DTC between the SubCo state and the SubSub state in the former state, whereas the latter state must refrain from imposing withholding taxes on those payments. Nevertheless, the latter restriction could cease to exist. In particular, the DTC between the SubCo state and the SubSub state could include rules which allow the denial of all or certain benefits included in the DTC (e.g., the benefit of royalty payments not being subject to withholding taxes in the source state) ('anti-abuse rules').[55] This also applies to the future royalty payments by other subsidiaries of the group to whom the new IP may be licensed by SubCo. Their states of residence may also want to levy withholding taxes on the royalties paid from their territory, which would necessitate recourse to the application of anti-abuse rules.

The OECD MTC contains in its current version a series of such rules in Article 29, introduced into the OECD MTC as a consequence of the policies adopted in Action 6 of the BEPS Project.[56] One of these rules is the Limitation on Benefits (LOB) clause, which was also first adopted in US DTC policy in the 1980s.[57]

The LOB includes numerous tests and is characterized in the literature as a rule of 'mind-numbing complexity'.[58] Interestingly for this stage of the work, parts of that rule ask the same question that the sets of rules already dealt with above also ask: does the recipient of the royalty income claiming the DTC benefits (in our case study SubCo claiming exemption from withholding taxes imposed from the SubSub state on the royalty income it receives) have enough *substance*? In particular, Article 29(3) of the OECD MTC lays down the active conduct of a business test according to which companies engaged in the active conduct of a business are entitled to (certain) treaty

53. This solution corresponds to the one given in Example 1 in OECD TPG, para. 4 of Annex to Ch. VI.
54. Hoor (2019), p. 604: 'the functional analysis focuses on functions performed, assets used, and risks assumed, which are clearly features of substance'. In detail *see* below s. A.II.1. of Ch. 2.
55. As to which these benefits are *see* OECD, *Preventing the Granting of Treaty Benefits in Inappropriate Circumstances*, Action 6 – 2015 Final Report, p. 24 (hereinafter 'OECD Action 6').
56. OECD Action 6.
57. Kornikova (2008), p. 279; Fleming (2012), p. 245; Jiang (2015), p. 139-140.
58. Fleming (2012), p. 249.

benefits. This test 'implies economic substance in terms of premises, personnel and activities'.[59]

In addition to this substance test, Article 29(5) of the OECD MTC stipulates the headquarters company test. Like the active conduct of a business test, a company regarded as a headquarters company is entitled to (all)[60] treaty benefits. In order for a company to be regarded as a headquarters company, it is required that '[the] company's primary place of management and control is in the Contracting State of which it is resident'. This provision is also regarded by tax scholars as a criterion to assess the substance requirement, as it 'takes the fact that the company must develop certain sound activities from the activity test'.[61]

Apart from the LOB, the OECD MTC contains in Article 29(9) the Principal Purpose Test (PPT), which may also be invoked to deny DTC benefits. The PPT, a product of Action 6 of the BEPS Project like the LOB clause, is also 'substance-oriented' according to the literature.[62] Overall, having enough substance could ensure SubCo is compatible with the LOB and the PPT and therefore entitled to treaty benefits (i.e., exemption from withholding taxes).

4 *CFC Rules and the Shell Entities Directive in the EU Tax Law Context*

Assume that the PaCo state cannot prove that SubCo's substance is insufficient for it to be managed in the SubCo state because the core decisions are officially taken when the manager of SubCo visits its premises. This would result in SubCo actually being both incorporated and managed in the SubCo state, which has the rightful claim on the worldwide profit gained by SubCo. Hence, making the residence claim according to the substance criterion and subjecting the worldwide profit of SubCo to taxation does not come into question for the PaCo state.

Remember, SubCo is interposed in order to park profits in the SubCo state. The PaCo state may want to try to extend its tax base to these profits in another way. A well-known unilateral measure to do so are Controlled Foreign Corporation (CFC) rules. In short, these rules were first enacted by the United States in the 1960s and since then many other states have also adopted them.[63] They apply under three fundamental requirements:[64]

59. De Broe/Luts (2015), p. 130; *see also* Jiang (2015), p. 146; Stewart (2015), p. 404.
60. It needs to be noted here that the one test (active conduct of a business test) provides for entitlement to certain, whereas the other test (headquarters company test) to all treaty benefits. On the mechanism of the LOB *see* below s. A.I.2. of Ch. 3.
61. Vega Borrego (2017), p. 187; *see also* Monsenego (2014), p. 21; van Weeghel (2019), p. 39.
62. Danon (2018a), p. 48; Petruzzi/Myzithra (2020), p. 431; Hoor et al. (2022), p. 229.
63. Avi-Yonah (2004), pp. 486 et seq.; Arnold (2012), p. 478; Quilitzsch (2013), pp. 46-47; Dahlberg/Wiman (2013), p. 25; Blum (2018), p. 297; Arnold (2019), p. 638. The enactment of uniform CFC rules by states has been one of the Actions of the BEPS Project. *See* OECD, *Designing Effective Controlled Foreign Company Rules*, Action 3 – 2015 Final Report (hereinafter 'OECD Action 3').
64. Based on Kofler (2008), p. 728 and Arnold (2019), p. 635.

(1) there is a controlling shareholder who can influence the distribution of income of a controlled (subsidiary) corporation;[65] in other words, when the controlling shareholder says 'park', the subsidiary corporation will not distribute any profits, whereas when the controlling shareholder says 'distribute', the controlled corporation will distribute dividends to them;
(2) the controlled corporation receives passive income, e.g., interest, dividends, royalties and capital gains;[66] and
(3) that income is subject to low taxation.

The legal consequence of the application of the CFC rule is that, in principle, the attributable income of the subsidiary corporation[67] is added to the tax base of the parent corporation although it has not in fact been distributed to it yet.[68]

In the case study, all requirements are met so the CFC rule of the PaCo state should apply. The EUR 10, consisting of royalty payments, is in fact passive income earned by a controlled person, which should result in that amount being attributed to the tax base of PaCo. However, an additional requirement for the application of CFC rules was introduced in 2006. In that year, the Court of Justice of the European Union (CJEU) held in its seminal *Cadbury Schweppes* judgment that in order for CFC rules to be compliant with EU law they have to be restricted only to 'wholly artificial arrangements'.[69] And, in order to determine which arrangements are wholly artificial, the following question needs to be answered: does the controlled corporation have enough substance?[70] If it does not have enough substance, then CFC rules may apply.

65. For some CFC regimes, it suffices that more than one, also unrelated, shareholders reach a participation threshold. There, it is not the rationale of the CFC rule that there is a controlling shareholder who may influence the distribution policy of the subsidiary, but the so-called control theory. *See* Schönfeld (2004), p. 447; Schönfeld (2005), pp. 160 et seq.; Quilitzsch (2013), pp. 49 et seq.; Schönfeld (2017), p. 146. *Avi-Yonah* rejects the compatibility of the control theory with public international law. *See* Avi-Yonah (2004), pp. 489 et seq.
66. In more generic terms, the nature of the income earned by the CFC plays a role. Here, either a specific nature of income is targeted (transactional approach), mostly passive income, or the entity as such is considered 'tainted' because of the low level of taxation it is subjected to and thus all of its income falls under the CFC rule (entity approach). *See* Maisto/Pistone (2008), p. 510; Arnold (2012), pp. 487 et seq.
67. Depending on whether the transactional or the entity approach is applied, either the tainted income only or the (whole) income of the tainted subsidiary is attributed to the parent. *See* Maisto/Pistone (2008), pp. 511-512; Dahlberg/Wiman (2013), p. 39.
68. This may take place in the following ways. Either by disregarding the legal personality of the subsidiary (piercing the corporate veil), or treating the income of the CFC as deemed dividends or taxing the shareholder on a basis of the fair value of the shares. *See* Schönfeld (2005), pp. 138 et seq.; Rust (2008), p. 493; Quilitzsch (2013), pp. 62 et seq.; Blum (2018), p. 307.
69. CJEU, 12 Sep. 2006, C-196/04, *Cadbury Schweppes plc and Cadbury Schweppes Overseas Ltd v. Commissioners of Inland Revenue,* EU:C:2006:544, para. 55.
70. CJEU, C-196/04, *Cadbury Schweppes,* at para. 64: 'In order to find that there is such an arrangement there must be ... objective circumstances showing that ... the objective pursued by freedom of establishment, as set out in paragraphs 54 and 55 of this judgment [the actual establishment of the company concerned in the host Member State and the pursuit of genuine economic activity there], has not been achieved' and para. 67 suggests that the objective circumstances refer to 'the extent to which the CFC physically exists in terms of premises, staff and equipment'.

Further, the Anti-Tax Avoidance Directive (ATAD)[71] includes a CFC rule which also involves rules that suggest the adoption of a substance requirement. In particular, Article 7(2)(a) of the ATAD stipulates that '[the CFC rule] shall not apply where the controlled foreign company carries on a *substantive* economic activity supported by staff, equipment, assets and premises, as evidenced by relevant facts and circumstances'. (Emphasis added).

Further, Article 7(2)(b) of the ATAD only targets *non-genuine arrangements*. And non-genuine is defined as 'an arrangement or a series ... [where] the entity or permanent establishment would not own the *assets* or would not have undertaken the *risks* which generate all, or part of, its income if it were not controlled by a company where the *significant people functions*, which are relevant to those assets and risks, are carried out and are instrumental in generating the controlled company's income'. (Emphasis added).

Therefore, future CFC rules in the European Union based on the ATAD are bound to contain either substance requirement. Hence, if we assume that the PaCo state is an EU Member State, it is bound to ask the question: does SubCo have enough *substance*? Only if the PaCo state answers that question negatively can it apply its CFC rule and tax the EUR 10 royalty income.

The enquiry referring to the substance of SubCo could be made by the SubSub state. Remember that SubSub pays royalties to SubCo. Assume that both SubSub and SubCo are residents of two different EU Member States.[72] The SubSub state would not be allowed to impose withholding tax on the royalty payments because of the Interest-Royalty Directive (IRD). The benefit arising from the IRD (i.e., the non-imposition of withholding tax on outflowing royalty payments), however, could be denied if SubCo does not have substance. In particular, in December 2021 the European Commission (Commission) presented a Directive proposal laying down rules to prevent the misuse of shell entities for tax purposes ('Shell Entities Directive').[73] This directive identifies shell entities, payments to which are disallowed tax advantages arising from the application of the IRD, the Parent-Subsidiary Directive (PSD),[74] and DTCs (Articles 11 and 12 of the Shell Entities Directive) by making use of a *substance test*.

The first step of the substance test consists of reporting on substance in order to differentiate between entities that are at risk for lacking substance and those with low risk. The second step consists of the substance test itself. 'The third step of the test prescribes the appropriate assessment of the information that the undertaking reported

71. Council Directive 2016/1164 of 12 Jul. 2016 laying down rules against tax avoidance practices that directly affect the functioning of the internal market, OJ L 193/1 (2016) (Anti-Tax Avoidance Directive).
72. Up until this point it was assumed that SubSub is not an EU resident. *See* above n. 38 in this chapter.
73. Proposal for a Council Directive laying down rules to prevent the misuse of shell entities for tax purposes and amending Directive 2011/16/EU. Available at: https://eur-lex.europa.eu/legal-content/EN/TXT/?uri=CELEX:52021PC0565.
74. Directive 2003/49/EC of the European Parliament and of the Council of 3 Jun. 2003 on the common system of taxation applicable to interest and royalty payments made between associated companies of different Member States, OJ L157 (2003), as amended.

in the second step in terms of substance.'[75] 'An undertaking that is a risk case, since it has crossed the gateway, and whose reporting also leads to the finding that it lacks at least one of the relevant elements on substance, should be presumed to be a 'shell' for the purposes of the Directive, i.e., lacking substance and being misused for tax purposes.'[76] However, this presumption can be rebutted.

So in order for SubCo to receive the royalties without the imposition of withholding tax it needs to have substance pursuant to the Shell Entities Directive.

5 *Synthesis*

In total, MNEs may use subsidiaries as means of milking and/or parking profits in order to reduce their worldwide tax liability. Four sets of bilateral and unilateral measures (the latter stemming from EU jurisprudence and legislation) address that kind of use of subsidiary corporations by asking the exact same question: does the subsidiary have enough substance? The substance requirements in these four sets of legal rules function as *presumptions* of substance.[77] For example, if a subsidiary has 'substance in terms of premises, personnel and activities', it is presumed that it has enough substance for it to be eligible for treaty benefits. And '[l]egal presumptions can be classified as (i) rebuttable (iuris tantum); or (ii) irrebuttable or conclusive (iuris et de iure), depending on whether the legal inference from the manifestation of appearance and the conclusion can or cannot be withdrawn'.[78]

C RESEARCH QUESTIONS, STATUS QUO AND SCOPE

The above case study demonstrates that the notion of substance is essential in applying all four sets of legal rules to that case. But are all substance requirements in these rules the same or are they different? For example, does a subsidiary having substance for the purposes of DTC residence also have substance for the purposes of CFC rules? In order to answer this question, one needs to analyse the content of each of the four substance requirements discussed. This is the first research question of this work:

(1) What is the content of the substance requirement in DTC residence, transfer pricing, DTC anti-abuse rules, and in the EU tax law context?
At the same time, the outcome of the research regarding the content of the substance requirement in these four sets of legal rules may provide an answer to the ultimate research question dealt with in this work. In particular, by understanding the content of the substance requirements in these four sets of legal rules, one can ask the ultimate question.

75. Shell Entities Directive, *Explanatory Memorandum*, p. 10.
76. *Ibid.*
77. Pistone et al. (2021), pp. 11-12.
78. *Ibid.*

(2) What is the relationship between the substance requirements in the four sets of legal rules at hand? Are they the same or are they different?[79] And if they are different, how is this justified?

Of course, this work would not be justified if there had been enough legal doctrine dealing with the research questions raised here. It must be conceded that tax literature has touched upon the matter, although maybe not in a comprehensive way.[80] Comprehensive studies that do exist have a different scope from that of this work: they analyse substance requirements in unilateral legal rules.[81] By contrast, this work is confined to legal rules containing substance requirements in the DTC context. Not extending the scope of the work by investigating the notion of substance of subsidiaries with respect to unilateral measures (e.g., domestic residence rules, unilateral anti-abuse rules denying treaty benefits, and unilateral transfer pricing rules) has a justification.

First, practicability issues have to be taken into account. It is almost impossible to conduct research on four sets of legal rules and their application both in a DTC context and unilaterally. Second, it has already been said that academic work already exists on the notion of substance at a unilateral level. Third, and most importantly, the ultimate goal of this work is to find the relationship between four substance-oriented legal rules. This relationship can only relate to an overarching legal system within which these legal rules exist and interact. If unilateral measures are added, then this system will always refer only to one country. For example, if German unilateral substance-oriented measures are analysed, the conclusions drawn should therefore apply solely with respect to the German international tax law system. Admittedly, other states may make use of the conclusions drawn with respect to that system, i.e., the

79. Commentators have already argued exactly that, however without going into detail, which is what this work intends to do. *See* Chand/Malek (2019), p. 418; concurring Arnold (2021), p. 48, although both articles refer to slightly different rules from the ones that are dealt with in this work (Action 5 instead of DTC residence is included in the scope of the analysis of these articles).

80. *See, e.g.*, Schönfeld (2014); Martín Jiménez (2020a), p. 208: 'it is legitimate to question the relationship between the "value creation concept or framework" of BEPS Actions 8-10 and the OECD Transfer Pricing Guidelines (2017) on the one hand, and GAARs and article 29(9) of the OECD Model (2017) on the other'.

Monsenego (2014), Petruzzi/Myzithra (2020) and Arnold (2021) deal (only) with the content of the substance requirement in transfer pricing. Similarly, Picciotto (2016).

Robert/Tof (2011), Haase (2016), Schmidtmann (2019), Müller (2021) and Bärsch/Schneider (2022) attend to the issues arising from the substance requirement in CFC rules. Chand/Malek (2019), not dealing with substance for the purposes of the POEM and the LOB.

From the perspective of EU tax law, Pistone et al. (2021). On the Shell Entities Directive, Benz/Böhmer (2022), Graßl/Kemmer (2022), Hoor et al. (2022), Offermanns (2022), Pistone et al. (2022) and von Brocke (2022).

81. *See*, from the perspective of German tax law, Leukefeld (2018). Dealing only with substance in the German CFC rules, Ekinci (2023). Regarding only anti-abuse rules, also at a unilateral level, *see* McMechan (2012). *See also* the country reports in Issues 5 and 6 of the International Transfer Pricing Journal (2014) on 'Substance in International Taxation'. One exception is the work from Navisotschnigg (2022), still dealing only with substance in transfer pricing, Action 5, and the beneficial ownership and only in the context of intangibles.

German international tax law system, and apply them to their domestic legal system, but in the final analysis, no uniform conclusions eligible for global use can be drawn.

By contrast, limiting the work to the DTC context may provide such an outcome. As already outlined in section B.I. of this chapter, DTCs are based on the work of the OECD, an international institution with massive significance regarding the formation of international tax policy. Especially current developments like the Inclusive Framework containing over 140 states demonstrate the global reach of OECD tax policy.[82] Therefore, assessing, interpreting and finding the relationship of substance-oriented legal rules with reference only to the works of the OECD has the enormous advantage that the conclusions drawn in this work may attain a global reach and are not confined, for instance, to the international tax law system of Germany or the UK.

This last argument also applies with regard to CFC rules and the Shell Entities Directive. Although they constitute a unilateral measure, the substance requirement therein has an EU origin (section B.III.4. of this chapter). So the conclusions drawn as to the content of the substance requirement in this respect are applicable across the EU, albeit not globally. Thus, CFC rules and the substance test in the Shell Entities Directive, again although unilateral measures are, within the scope of the work, also explore substance requirements in the EU tax law context. In total, the research questions relate to substance requirements in the DTC and EU tax law context.

Finally, and again with regard to the scope of the work, it must be underlined that: (1) The work remains strictly within the realm of tax law. Whether substance plays a role in accounting, for example, for the ownership of assets, is not examined here. (2) The work specifically targets the content of substance requirements as applied to subsidiary corporations; it is accepted that different results may arise when these rules (e.g., the POEM) are applied to parent corporations. (3) The work is not related to a specific industry or type of subsidiary (e.g., holdings). It offers a general framework which can be tested from case to case and industry to industry.

D DEFINING 'SUBSTANCE'

Before delving into the main part of the work dealing with the research question therein, the reader must be familiar with the meaning of the most important term for the purposes of the work: the term 'substance'. In this section, it is first shown that the definition of the day-to-day term (section D.I.), as well as the definition of substance for corporate law purposes (section D.II.1.), are inadequate for the purposes of this work. Then the author analyses the substance-oriented rules presented so far and draws therefrom the definition of substance for the purposes of this work (section D.II.2.), based on which the content of the substance-oriented rules presented so far will be analysed in the next chapters.

82. https://www.oecd.org/tax/beps/about/.

I Day-to-Day Term

According to the *Oxford Advanced Learner's Dictionary*, the word substance can either refer to the 'quality of being based on facts or the truth' or 'the most important or main part of something'.[83] So, for example, on the one hand, the statement of a person who has not even finished their bachelor studies that they hold a PhD title is of no substance. On the other hand, human organs make the substance of the human body; they imbue it with life. The most prominent legal dictionary refers to the substance term only in the second sense, i.e., as '[t]he essence of something; the essential quality of something as opposed to its mere form'.[84]

So let us explore which is the essence of a subsidiary; and which are its essential qualities. 'Companies are a legal construct and exist insofar as the law recognizes them. Accordingly, it is difficult, if not impossible, to identify the substance of companies in the sense of identifiable elements beyond the text of the law that have to be taken into account despite the text of the law.'[85] So what does the law say?

II Definition Based on Legal Interpretation

1 Corporate Law

As has already been stated in section A. of this chapter, corporate law discerns 'five core structural characteristics of the business corporation …: (1) legal personality, (2) limited liability, (3) transferable shares, (4) centralized management …, and (5) shared ownership by contributors of equity capital'. But are these elements also the constituent elements of the term substance with regard to subsidiaries in the particular context of this work? This proposition needs to be explored on the basis of the legal interpretation of the four sets of legal rules referred to making use of this notion.

2 International and EU Tax Law

Citing the legal rules each laying down a substance requirement may provide a first insight. In the case study in section B.III.1. of this chapter, it has been shown that residence at a DTC level is determined by the POEM criterion, which also entails a substance requirement. The Commentary on the Articles of the OECD MTC (2014) ('the Commentary') offers at first a negative distinction with regard to the POEM. In particular, the Commentary on the 2014 version of the OECD MTC states that the POEM has been elected as a rule for determining residence at a DTC level because '[i]t would

83. https://www.oxfordlearnersdictionaries.com/definition/english/substance. There are also other usages of the term in everyday language referring to 'a type of solid, liquid or gas that has particular qualities'. However, they are not discussed further because they cannot support the notion of substance in the legal systems presenting the scope of this work.
84. Garner/Black (2014). Here, again, the meaning of substance as 'any matter; esp[ecially] addictive drug' is not further explored. *See also* the philosophical analysis by Pistone et al. (2021), p. 10 reaching the same conclusion.
85. Pistone et al. (2021), p. 10.

not be an adequate solution to attach importance to a purely formal criterion like registration'.[86] In this sense, the POEM introduces a substance requirement as opposed to formal requirements. The fact that the substance and not the formal requirement has been chosen by the OECD implies that substance requirements have priority over formal ones, and they are the ones that determine the allocation of persons to territories.[87]

A look at the substance requirement in the OECD TPG confirms this inference. Indeed, it has been affirmed in section B.III.2. of this chapter that pursuant to the OECD TPG profits are allocated to the legal owner of an asset only if it 'in substance performs and controls all of the functions (…) provides all assets (…) and assumes all of the risks'.[88] In other words, if legal ownership does not follow substance, the latter prevails. If the legal owner of an asset does not have the necessary substance, then returns[89] related to that asset are allocated to the member 'of the MNE group *other than the legal owner* [that in substance] performs functions, uses assets, or assumes risks'.[90] From that, it follows, first, that substance requirements are to be distinguished from formal requirements (e.g., incorporation and legal ownership of an asset), and, second, they prevail over them and lead, or may lead, to an allocation of persons and profits to territories different from the one that formal requirements may prescribe. So, the first part of the substance definition for the purposes of this work is as follows:

> Substance requirements stipulated in the DTC context are requirements distinguishable from formal requirements of that system. They lead, or may lead, to an allocation of persons and/or profits to territories different from the one that formal requirements would lead to.

The first part of this definition also fulfils in part the functions that every definition of a term entails. A definition must, first, assign the term to more general categories and, second, delineate it from other terms by determining its constituent elements.[91] The above passage, first, delineates substance from form. Second, it puts the substance term into the general category of criteria that determine the allocation of persons and profits to territories. Therefore, the following sentence is added to the definition:

> Together with the formal requirements, substance requirements belong to the criteria determining the allocation of persons and profits to territories.

86. Paragraph 22 first sentence of the Commentary (2014) on Article 4 (emphasis added).
87. It has already been stressed that this is the function of the residence criterion. *See* above s. B.III.1. of this chapter.
88. OECD TPG, para. 6.71 (emphasis added). *See also* Australian Taxation Office, *Taxation Ruling 2014/6 – Income Tax: Transfer Pricing – The Application of Section 815-130 of the Income Tax Assessment Act 1997*, para. 39 (hereinafter 'ATO, TR 2014/6'): 'The "substance" of the commercial or financial relations describes the economic reality or essence of those dealings and is determined by examining all of the relevant facts and circumstances.'
89. The terms 'profit' and 'return' are synonymous and will be henceforth used alternatively.
90. OECD TPG, para. 6.71 (emphasis added).
91. Hart (1961), p. 14.

But delineating a term is only possible by determining its constituent elements. However, this has not taken place in the analysis of the term substance so far. Again, at the outset, the substance requirement in the POEM may provide some insight. By distinguishing the POEM test from the primary place of management and control (PPMC) test used in the headquarters company test of the LOB (Article 29(5) of the OECD MTC), the Commentary focuses on a common element that both tests share, which appears in different forms in both legal rules:

> The concept of 'place of effective management' was interpreted by some States as being the place where the most senior *person or group of persons* (for example a board of directors) made the key management and commercial decisions necessary for the conduct of the company's business. The concept of the primary place of management and control, by contrast, refers to the place where the day-to-day responsibility for the management of the company or entity (and its direct and indirect subsidiaries) is exercised.[92]

Accordingly, both legal rules connect the substance of a corporation to a *personal element*. In turn, this personal element can take different forms and support different legal rules having regard to criteria like the position of the person in question (e.g., board of directors) and their responsibilities (e.g., key management or day-to-day responsibilities). So the content of the personal element of the term substance is dependent on other criteria.

Likewise, the OECD TPG also emphasize the personal element when determining to which corporation the profits arising from an asset should be allocated. In particular, the OECD TPG emphasize *inter alia*, the control over functions and risks when determining the person to whom profits are to be allocated.[93] Control is exercised by making decisions regarding the respective function or risk; decisions which are taken by persons, or, as the OECD TPG call them, 'decision-makers'.[94] Therefore, the personal element of the substance requirement also has a central role with regard to the allocation of profits to persons: profits follow functions, assets, and risks; functions, assets, and risks follow decisions; decisions are taken by persons. The personal element for the purposes of the OECD TPG is also dependent on another criterion attached to it: the capability or competence of a person to make a decision.[95] Hence, it may not be the position of a person or their responsibilities that is critical for the notion

92. Paragraph 149 third sentence of the Commentary (2017) on Article 29 (emphasis added).
93. Regarding the requirement of control over functions, *see* above nn. 51-52 in this chapter. Risk assumption is interpreted as control over the respective risk in OECD TPG, para. 1.60: '[in order] to interpret the information and determine whether the contractual assumption of risk is consistent with the conduct of the associated enterprises and other facts of the case [it needs to be analysed] (i) whether the associated enterprises follow the contractual terms under the principles of Section D.1.1; and (ii) whether the party assuming risk, as analysed under (i), *exercises control over the risk* and has the financial capacity to assume the risk' (emphasis added).
94. OECD TPG, para. 1.66.
95. Regarding the capability requirement, *see* OECD TPG, para. 1.65: '[c]ontrol over risk involves … the capability to make decisions'. Regarding the competence requirement, *see* OECD TPG, para. 1.66 '[d]ecision-makers should possess competence and experience'.

of substance but their capabilities/competences that determine whether they come into question as persons giving substance to the corporation.

All in all, the substance requirements involve the existence of a personal element; this personal element, in turn, can have a different content depending on: (a) who these persons are (is it the directors or simple employees and other staff making day-to-day decisions that determine the substance of a corporation?); and (b) which capabilities these persons have (do they have the necessary education and training, for example, to assess risk?). (a) is called the *personal element stricto sensu* because it aims at identifying which persons are the significant ones for the respective substance requirement. (b) is called the *qualitative sub-element* because it refers to the qualities of the pertinent persons. Introducing these findings into the definition of substance for the purposes of this work leads to the following formulation of them:

> They [substance requirements] consist of a personal element. The personal element consists of the personal element stricto sensu and the qualitative sub-element.

Nevertheless, by making use of the substance requirement the POEM and the OECD TPG refer not only to the personal element but also to another element: the existence of physical assets/objects in the state of residence. In particular, it has already been maintained in section B.III.2. of this chapter that, apart from the control over functions and risks, it is the provision of assets that determines the allocation of profits to persons (and so indirectly to territories). Moreover, concerning the allocation of persons to territories, the POEM, which is responsible for that kind of allocation, can be located 'where the person's headquarters are located'.[96] Hence, assets and premises (e.g., headquarters) may furnish a corporation with substance; they are therefore an element of it, which is called the objective element.

Furthermore, the qualitative sub-element of the personal element may also be used for the purposes of the objective element. What qualities should the physical objects have in order to provide substance to a corporation? Should they have the form of premises or does the use of mere physical assets (e.g., the use of a machine outside of any kind of premise) suffice? Introducing these new elements into the definition of substance for the purposes of this work leads to the following additions to the previous sentence:

> They [substance requirements] consist of a personal and an objective element. The personal element consists of the personal element stricto sensu and the qualitative sub-element. *The objective element consists of a qualitative sub-element.*

But one of the provisions presented in section B.III. of this chapter containing a substance requirement has not been addressed in this section yet: the active conduct of a business test of the LOB. A look at that provision could provide some further elements of the term substance with respect to its use in the DTC context.

First of all, the fact that the activities of a corporation are a factor in determining its substance for the purposes of providing DTC benefits could provide for a third

96. Paragraph 24.1 fourth sentence of the Commentary (2014) on Article 4.

element, in addition to the personal and the objective element: 'a functional element (with regard to the exercise of certain activities)'.[97] Therefore, '[substance requirements] consist of a personal, *a functional*, and an objective element'.[98]

Second, the Commentary on the active conduct of a business test reveals a sub-element of the functional element. In particular, for the purposes of the active conduct of a business test, only activities of the corporation invoking DTC benefits in its residence state are taken into account. However, Article 29(3)(b) of the OECD MTC stipulates that activities of the corporation invoking DTC benefits as well as those of other group corporations in another state may also be taken into account. However, this is only the case 'if the business activity carried on by the resident [in their residence state] to which the item [of income with respect to which DTC benefits are invoked] is related is *substantial* in relation to the same or complementary business activity carried on by the resident or such connected person in the other [state]'.

According to that passage, a corporation claiming DTC benefits based on the functional element of the substance requirement must prove that the functional element is 'substantial'. The Commentary accompanying this term relates the term substantial to 'the size of the business activity'.[99] Accordingly, the functional element contains a *quantitative sub-element.*

This sub-element may also exist with regard to the other two main elements of the substance term, i.e., the personal and the objective elements. It may be asked, for example, with respect to the personal element, how many persons and/or how many decisions are necessary for a company to have substance. Likewise, the number and value of assets or the size of premises may be critical. Hence, the quantitative sub-element applies also for the purposes of the personal and the objective element. These new findings lead to a further specification of the term substance for the purposes of this work:

> They [substance requirements] consist of a personal, a functional and an objective element. The personal element consists of the personal element stricto sensu, *the quantitative* and the qualitative sub-element. The objective element consists of a qualitative and *a quantitative* sub-element. *The functional element consists of a quantitative sub-element.*

Finally, the fact that the conduct of business must be *active* for a corporation to comply with the LOB shows that the nature/*quality* of the activities/*functions* performed is also relevant. Therefore, the qualitative sub-element also has significance for the purposes of the functional element of our substance definition. So, the last two defining sentences are modified and consolidated into one:

> Both the objective and the functional element consist of a qualitative and a quantitative sub-element.

97. Leukefeld (2018), p. 24 (author's unofficial translation).
98. *Ibid.*
99. Paragraph 79 second sentence of the Commentary (2017) on Article 29.

So, at this point, the pieces of the puzzle can be put together. The definition of substance for the purposes of this work is the following:

> Substance requirements stipulated in the DTC context are requirements distinguishable from formal requirements of that system. They lead, or may lead, to an allocation of persons and/or profits to territories different from the one that formal requirements would lead to. Together with the formal requirements, substance requirements belong to the criteria determining the allocation of persons and profits to territories. They consist of a personal, a functional, and an objective element. The personal element consists of the personal element stricto sensu, the quantitative, and the qualitative sub-element. Both the objective and the functional element consist of a qualitative and a quantitative sub-element.[100]

The following figure illustrates the definition of substance and its components.

Figure 2 The Definition of Substance and Its Constituent Elements

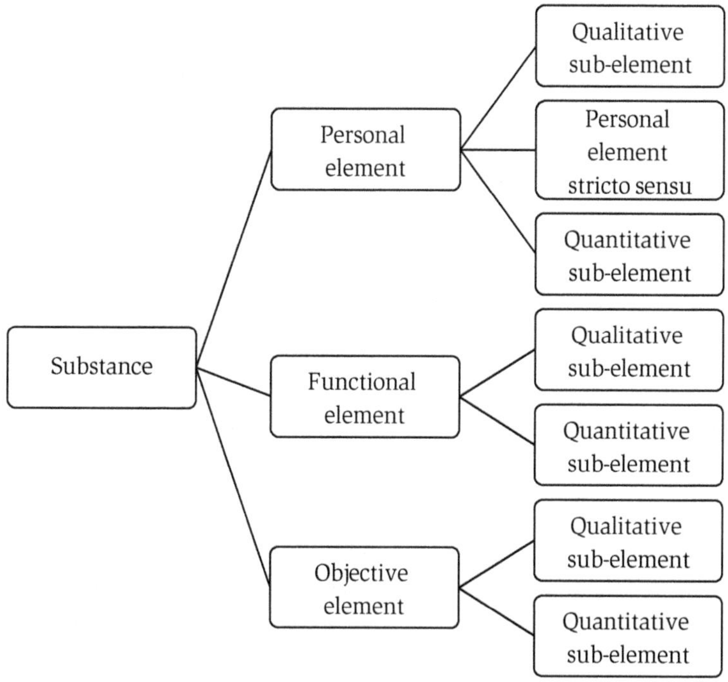

Lastly, it should be highlighted that, for the sake of simplicity and uniformity of the work, the same definition applies to the EU tax law context. This is in line with the

100. For another approach on the elements of substance *see* Hoor (2019), pp. 593-594; Hoor et al. (2022), pp. 226-227.

CJEU jurisprudence[101] and tax scholars[102] who support an interpretation of terms in the EU tax law context may follow OECD practice. A problem exists here, though. The definition given above is not included in any OECD document. This problem could be solved if the definition of substance that this work adopts is added to Article 3 ('General definitions') of the OECD MTC. The substance-oriented rules in the DTC context then could make recourse to this definition and expand upon its elements. And the CJEU could do the same when interpreting substance-oriented rules in the EU tax law context.

E STRUCTURE OF THE WORK AND METHODOLOGY

The structure of the work follows the line of the research questions raised. Chapters 1-4 answer the first research question, referring to the content of the substance requirements in the four sets of legal rules in the DTC and EU tax law context. Each substance requirement of the four sets of legal rules is covered in one chapter (Chapters 1-4) whereby each chapter contains three sections:

(1) The first one (A.) includes preliminary remarks, especially dealing with the functions and mechanism of the legal rule in question including a substance requirement (A.I.), clarifying the scope of the investigation (A.II.) and pointing to the relevance of the investigation regarding the respective substance requirement (A.III.).
(2) After these preliminary remarks, section B. of Chapters 1-4 proceeds to the analytical part of the work where the first research question is partially answered, i.e., the content of the substance requirement in each rule is elucidated. Section B. consists of one section with some opening remarks (B.I.) and section B.II. analysing each element of the substance requirement in one separate section.
(3) The third section (C.) of these four chapters sums up the findings as to the content of the substance requirement in question and illustrates them by means of a 'substance checklist'.

Sometimes the order of the sections is different in the pertinent chapter in order to enable a better flow of the text,[103] but the basic structure presented remains the same throughout the work. In the last chapter the author summarizes the findings of the

101. CJEU, 26 Feb. 2019, C-115/16, C-118/16, C-119/16 and C-299/16, *N Luxembourg 1, X Denmark, C Danmark I and Z Denmark v. Skatteministeriet*, ECLI:EU:C:2019:134, para. 90, where the CJEU interpreted the BO Clause in the IRD based on the OECD MTC and the Commentary thereon.
102. Schön (2020a), p. 294: 'Whenever European directives do not contain specific definitions for those terms and whenever the particular purpose of EU legislation does not require otherwise, there is plenty of room for a common understanding built on OECD work.'
103. This is the case, for instance, in Ch. 2 where, in the preliminary remarks, the scope of the investigation is dealt with after the relevance of the investigation.

work and answers the second research question regarding the relationship between the substance requirements in the four sets of legal rules dealt with in this work.

With regard to the methodology applied, as already elaborated in section C., this work does not deal with substance requirements in domestic laws. This does not exclude, however, recourse to domestic legal systems and, especially, the relevant case law to ascertain how they interpret the substance requirements introduced in section B.III. The work does not hold itself out to be a comparative work of different legal systems; it simply refers to domestic administrative practice and case law to shed light on issues arising in relation to the particular substance requirements.

Now, the question arises as to which administrative practice and which case law has been chosen to serve the aforementioned purpose. Upon which criteria have the jurisdictions dealt with been chosen? First, German case law and administrative practice have been chosen simply because the writer is more familiar with this jurisdiction. Therefore, German administrative practice and case law are ubiquitous in this work. Second, jurisdictions have also been chosen depending on the legal rule in question and the availability of information. For example, the United States does not use the POEM in their DTCs. Thus, it does not come into question as a jurisdiction to be dealt with for the purposes of this rule simply because it does not use it and, thus, no information can come from this jurisdiction. On the contrary, as already seen in section B.III.4., transfer pricing rules are a 'US product', making this jurisdiction very important with regard to substance for the purposes of transfer pricing rules.

Finally, the work follows a descriptive-analytical method. Remember that answering the research questions raised require analysing the content of the four substance-oriented legal rules dealt with and their relationship. The work thus confines itself to describing and analysing and not ascertaining how the rules ought to be, for example, proposing changes to the current legal regime. That is, the work does not follow a normative approach. Of course, due to the author's background, the work is a legal one. Sometimes reference is made to economic knowledge and sources, without, however, raising the claim that the work follows an interdisciplinary approach.

CHAPTER 1

The Substance Requirement for the Purposes of Treaty Corporate Residence

A PRELIMINARY REMARKS

I Functions and Mechanism of Treaty Corporate Residence

The analysis of the content of the substance requirements in the DTC and EU tax law context commences with the substance requirement in treaty corporate residence. This is because residence is logically the first question that a state poses when intending to levy tax on a corporation. Again, if the corporation is resident in a state, then this state may tax its worldwide profits (section B.I. of the introduction). But before delving into the core of the work, namely the analysis of the substance requirement, it is important to talk about the function and mechanism of treaty residence in general. That is because the function of residence in the DTC context informs its mechanism; and the mechanism of the residence definition, in turn, influences the scope of the investigation.

In particular, residence has three main functions within a DTC, which, as elaborated further below in this section, also inform its mechanism: (1) residence defines the personal scope of DTCs; (2) it defines the source of some types of income; and (3) it resolves residence-residence conflicts:

(1) The very first provision of the OECD MTC underlines the importance of residence for the application of a DTC: 'This Convention shall apply to persons who are residents of one or both of the Contracting States.' E contrario, a non-resident person may not fall under the (personal scope of the) DTC and enjoy benefits therefrom. Remember that DTCs govern the allocation of taxing rights between source and residence states (section B.I. of the introduction). Thus, they are based upon the premise that a residence state exists which taxes the worldwide income of a person and thus threatens

to double tax items of income that have an attachment also to another state, i.e., the source state.[1] If no such residence state exists, the application of a DTC is neither required nor conceivable.[2]

It is important to underline that the personal scope of the DTC must only comprise taxpayers with some kind of economic connection to the taxing state's territory. This notion refers to the principle of economic allegiance enunciated by the four economists Gijsbert Bruins, Luigi Einaudi, Edwin Selgman and Sir Josiah Stamp in the very first Report on Double Taxation under the auspices of the League of Nations (LoN).[3]

(2) Second, other provisions of the OECD MTC also refer to the residence state of a person as the state of source of income. That is the case, for example, with respect to dividends and interest which determine as source of that type of income the residence of the payer (Articles 10(1) and 11(5) sentence 1). Moreover, pursuant to Article 13(1), the source of capital gains is the residence of the seller of the asset in question.[4] In a similar vein, profits from active business are taxed pursuant to Article 7(1) sentence 1 in the residence state. 'By this process the residence country of the corporation collects what is effectively a source tax on the operations of the firm in that country.'[5] So residence also functions as a sourcing rule in DTCs.[6]

(3) Finally, the third role of the residence rule in DTCs has already been made clear (section B.III.1. of the introduction). Returning to the introductory case

1. Obuoforibo (2020), s. 1.1.2.1.
2. Provisions that do not need to make this distinction and allocate taxing rights with respect to an item of income do not require the residence of a person invoking them. That is the case, for instance, in Article 24(1) addressing the discrimination based on the nationality of a person.
3. *See* the recent decision UK First-Tier Tribunal, 8 Jun. 2021, *GE Financial Investments v. HMRC*, UKFTT (2021), p. 210 (TC) (at paras 36 et seq.) conducting an in depth analysis dissecting case law and literature. Judge *Brooks* concludes at para. 62: 'the construction of Article 4 advanced by HMRC requires both worldwide taxation and a connection or attachment to the contracting state concerned. In my judgment, this is the correct approach as it takes into account the common feature or similarity of domicile, residence, citizenship etc, in the context of the Convention, ie that they are all criteria providing, in addition to the imposition of a worldwide liability to tax, a "connection" or "attachment" of a person to the contracting state concerned'. *Contra* Canadian Federal Court of Appeal, 12 Feb. 2020, *Alta Energy Luxembourg S.A.R.L. v. Her Majesty the Queen*, FCA (2020), p. 43 (at para. 65): 'There is no distinction in the Luxembourg Convention between residents with strong economic or commercial ties and those with weak or no commercial or economic ties.' But *see* the dissenting opinion: 'Contracting states extend the benefits of the tax treaties only to their residents (that is, persons liable to pay tax in their state) because residence is an appropriate criterion to ensure that the treaty will, cover only persons who had an economic allegiance to one or both of the contracting states.' *Alta Energy Luxembourg S.A.R.L. v. Her Majesty the Queen*, FCA (2020), p. 43, at para. 152. In favour of the majority opinion, Lavez (2022), s. 3.1.2.

   Generally, on the economic allegiance requirement for the assertion of taxing rights, Bruins, G.W.J./et al., *Report on Double Taxation*, E.F.S.73. F.19 (April 1923), pp. 20[4024] et seq. This principle had already been enunciated by von Schanz (1892), p. 368. The parallel has already been detected by scholars, *see* Vogel (1988), pp. 219-220 with critical remarks on how the Four Economists comprehended Georg von Schantz's observations on international taxation.
4. *See* Marian (2013b), p. 474, who points to this function of residence to contest scholarship claiming that tax residence is unimportant.
5. Vann (2010), p. 310.
6. *Ibid.* Although Richard Vann uses the term 'sourcing device'.

study, there is a dispute between two states, i.e., the PaCo state and the SubCo state, regarding which of the two is the state of residence of a subsidiary (residence-residence conflict). It has been shown when discussing the case study that the POEM in Article 4(3) of the 2014 version of the OECD MTC is the legal rule resolving residence-residence conflicts. It is because of this function that Article 4(3) is known, and is referred to also in this work, as the *tiebreaker* rule in DTCs.

Indeed, if the OECD MTC, and by following it DTCs, defined the term residence expressly, residence-residence conflicts like the one described above would not occur (except for divergent interpretations of the DTC's residence definition). The states in question would apply the residence definition in order to determine whether a person is resident or not. Instead, the OECD opted for another mechanism for the residence definition, i.e., a two-step approach.[7] In short, the OECD MTC pursuant to Article 4(1) sentence 1 does not define residence for DTC purposes. Instead, it refers, at the first stage, to the domestic legal rules on residence of the states applying the DTC ('any person who, *under the laws of [a Contracting State]*'), merely listing a host of connecting criteria ('domicile, residence, place of management or any other criterion of a similar nature'). This is because the mechanism of the residence definition is informed by the first function of residence rule in DTCs.

As already stressed, DTCs are based upon the premise that there is a residence state and that this state taxes the worldwide income of its residents.[8] But if a DTC (autonomously) would define a state as the residence state, whereas the same state does not define itself (for domestic tax purposes) as the residence state, then the premise upon which the DTC is based cannot be fulfilled. That is, the state which was designated by the DTC as the residence state does not tax the taxpayer's worldwide income which leads to double non-taxation. In particular, the source state would forfeit its taxing right on income generated within its territory in favour of the residence state, which would be supposed to tax that income (since it would tax the worldwide income of its residents). If the latter were not to do so because it would not consider itself as the residence state, then it would also not tax income generated outside its territory, i.e., in the source state. The income generated in the source state would remain untaxed. Summing up, the first function of residence for the purposes of DTCs, which consists

7. This has not always been the case. Within the LoN, residence was expressly defined for DTC purposes. The 1925 LoN Report was the first LoN Report in this respect. *See* Technical Experts, *Report on Double Taxation and Tax Evasion*, F.212 (1925), p. 34[4094] (hereinafter 'LoN 1925'). Commentators evaluating the succeeding LoN Reports inform us that they all follow the same approach, i.e., define residence autonomously, and thus preferred a one-tier approach to the two-tier one which has been adopted by the OEEC and follows us until now. *See* Ismer (2018), pp. 57 et seq.
8. A look at the very first Report of WP2 of the OEEC, commissioned with the concept of fiscal domicile, affirms this assertion: 'The Concept of Fiscal Domicile, that is the application of the taxpayer's circumstances *as a criterion to determine whether full tax liability exists*' (emphasis added). WP2, *Report on the Concept of Fiscal Domicile* (October 1956), p. 1 (hereinafter 'FC/WP2(56)1').

of determining the personal scope of DTCs, calls for a reference to the domestic definition of residence and excludes an autonomous one.

Since DTCs do not include an autonomous residence definition but rather refer to the domestic definition of residence, two things may happen: either states use different residence criteria (for instance, in the introductory example the PaCo state uses the POM and the SubCo state uses the POI) or they interpret the same domestic residence criterion differently (e.g., both the PaCo and the SubCo state maintain that the POM of SubCo is within their jurisdiction). For this reason, the OECD MTC, at a second stage, resolves such kinds of conflicts by means of the tiebreaker rule. So, the mechanism of the residence definition described above results in two 'residence terms' with regard to corporations:[9] the one in Article 4(1) sentence 1 and the other one in Article 4(3) of the 2014 version of the OECD MTC.

This begs the question of which of the two 'residence terms' is relevant for this work. The one in Article 4(1) sentence 1 or the other one in Article 4(3) of the 2014 version of the OECD MTC? Or maybe both? The next section focuses on the relevance of Article 4(1) sentence 1 for this work since Article 4(3) of the 2014 version of the OECD MTC has already been identified and considered one including a substance requirement. In the next section, it is shown that the scope of this work is restricted to the latter provision.

II Scope of the Investigation

Article 4(1) sentence 1 defines residence for DTC purposes by referring to 'any person who, under the laws of [a Contracting State], is liable to tax therein by reason of his domicile, residence, place of management or any other criterion of a similar nature'. At first glance, it can be concluded that from the connecting factors establishing residence for domestic tax purposes, to which the OECD MTC attaches residence for DTC purposes, only the POM refers to corporations and is, as already discussed in section B.III.1. of the introduction, a substance-oriented rule, thus relevant for the purposes of this work. Notwithstanding this fact, the POM is not investigated in this work.

That is because, as already analysed in the previous section, for the POM to become part of a DTC, recourse to domestic law is necessary ('any person who, *under the laws of [a Contracting State]*' (emphasis added)). By contrast, in Article 4(3) of the 2014 version of the OECD MTC, which contains the POEM, no such reference to domestic law interpretation can be found; the term 'POEM', according to the prevailing opinion in the literature[10] which is followed in this work, must be interpreted autonomously and not according to domestic law at the DTC level. This is why only the latter term must be interpreted uniformly. Thereby, only regarding that term, uniform conclusions eligible for global use can be drawn, which is the main reason why this

9. The tiebreaker in case of a residence-residence conflict with regard to individuals is stipulated in Article 4(2) of the OECD MTC and is not dealt with in this work owing to the scope thereof.
10. *See, e.g.*, Großmann (1995), p. 77; Vogel (1997), p. 262; Staringer (1999), p. 148; Haslinger (2008), p. 195; Sepúlveda Ramirez (2016), p. 187; Maisto et al. (2018), pp. 27 et seq. with references to jurisprudence and tax administration.

work has been limited to the DTC and EU tax law context (section C. of the introduction). In contrast to the POEM, the POM is defined by each state unilaterally. This means that conclusions related thereto may have application only with reference to the domestic legal system containing this residence criterion. So, if, for example, the term POM is analysed with respect to the German legal system, the findings of the analysis are relevant only within the boundaries of that system. Their usefulness beyond that point is constrained solely to comparative law research. Such an approach would fail the aim of this work to attain the most global reach possible. In sum, only the content of the substance requirement in Article 4(3) of the 2014 version of the OECD MTC is investigated.

Now that these issues have been clarified, an important issue that every book has to take into account must be discussed: its relevance for the reader.

III Relevance of the Investigation

The reader may have already noticed that each time reference has been made to the POEM and Article 4(3), the clarification has been made that reference is made to the 2014 version of the OECD MTC. Nevertheless, a more recent version of the OECD MTC exists, i.e., the 2017 version, to which all other OECD MTC provisions in this work refer. Consequently, the question arises as to why this inconsistency in citing the OECD MTC provisions occurs.

A brief examination of Article 4(3) in its current version is enough to answer this question: the POEM is no longer the tiebreaker rule in the OECD MTC. Since 2017, Article 4(3) of the OECD MTC provides for a mutual agreement procedure (MAP) as the proposed tiebreaker rule and not the POEM. Action 6 of the BEPS Project mandated that amendment as early as 2015.[11] In November 2016, another fundamental development occurred having an impact on the application of the POEM as a tiebreaker: the OECD adopted the Multilateral Instrument (MLI).[12] The MLI is meant to swiftly implement the measures put forward in the BEPS Project by transposing its results into DTCs worldwide. So, a state signing the MLI is able to add new provisions to their extant DTCs or replace already existing provisions with the ones contained in the MLI. One of the new provisions that may replace the old ones is Article 4(1) of the MLI providing for a MAP instead of the POEM as a tiebreaker. This development enables states to replace the POEM with the MAP in all their DTCs quickly and easily compared to negotiating each DTC anew.

So the question arises whether an investigation of the substance requirement in the POEM is still relevant for the reader. This question must be answered in the affirmative for the following reasons. First, even the MAP introduced in the current version of Article 4(3) refers to the POEM as one of the relevant criteria when determining residence in the MAP (*'having regard to its place of effective management'*

11. OECD Action 6, p. 72.
12. OECD, *Multilateral Convention to Implement Tax Treaty Related Measures to Prevent BEPS* (OECD 2017).

(emphasis added)).[13] Second, both academic literature and international tax law practitioners have been hostile to the replacement of the POEM with the MAP.[14] Third, and most importantly, many DTCs still use the POEM as the tiebreaker rule. Of course, the MLI has had an impact on its application, but the POEM is still, according to empirical studies, the most widely used tiebreaker rule.[15] So this legal rule containing a substance requirement is still a part of the current DTC network.

Consequently, the first research question laid down in section C. of the introduction must also be answered with respect to the POEM: what is the content of the substance requirement in the POEM? Section B. of this chapter answers this question.

B THE CONTENT OF THE SUBSTANCE REQUIREMENT IN TREATY CORPORATE RESIDENCE

I Opening Remarks

1 Purpose of the Substance Orientation in the POEM

The purpose of a legal rule informs its content. Accordingly, delineating the purpose of the POEM contributes to understanding why the POEM is substance-oriented. Understanding both later on contributes to explaining some features of the substance requirement in the POEM.

Article 4(3) of the 2014 version of the OECD MTC is the tiebreaker rule for solving residence-residence conflicts; it is, as history informs us, a *preference criterion*.[16] This leads to a preliminary conclusion regarding its purpose: the tiebreaker must point only to one residence state. It thus follows an *all-or-nothing approach*: either you are the POEM state or you are not.[17] Because of that function of the tiebreaker, it has been contended in tax literature that the POI is a more appropriate tiebreaker than the

13. Cerioni/Eden (2018), p. 685. Commentators have also pointed to the similarity between the factors determining the POEM and the additional factors that the competent authorities are expected to take account of in the MAP process. In fact, para. 24.1 of the Commentary (2017) on Article 4 denotes factors 'such as where the meetings of the person's board of directors or equivalent body are usually held, where the chief executive officer and other senior executives usually carry on their activities, where the senior day-to-day management of the person is carried on, where the person's headquarters are located'. *See* Sepúlveda Ramirez (2016), p. 209.
14. This has also been acknowledged, albeit at the end ignored, by the OECD. *See* OECD, *BEPS Action 6: Preventing Treaty Abuse – Revised Discussion Draft* (22 May 2015), para. 100: '[C]omments mostly focussed on the alleged uncertainty, unpredictability and risks of double taxation that would be created by a move away from the longstanding place of effective management criterion in Article 4(3). … Almost all commentators felt that the tie-breaker rule for determining the treaty residence of dual-resident persons other than individuals should not be changed.'
15. *See* Gerlach/Niemeyer (2018), pp. 756 et seq. *See also* Bräumann (2019), p. 190, according to whom 21 EU Member States have opted against Article 4(1) of the MLI. Obuoforibo (2020), s. 5.2.3., who stresses 'the lasting power of the PoEM tiebreaker provision *and the attendant need for a clear definition of the "place of effective management"*' (emphasis added). Such statements make the conduct of this research all the more apparent.
16. FC/WP2(56)1, p. 2 (emphasis added).
17. *See* Elkins (2022), p. 172 referring to the concept of residence as a 'binary' one.

substance-oriented POEM.[18] The POI is easy to administer and, most importantly, results in each case in a resolution of the residence-residence conflict. In contrast, the POEM is much more difficult to administer for several reasons (e.g., peripatetic decision-makers, decisions that are not easily localizable because they are taken, for instance, during a video call, etc.) which jeopardizes its results as the test may point to more than one POEM.[19]

It is, however, important to bear in mind that, although the residence-residence conflict solution constitutes the primary purpose of the POEM, the results that are dictated by this solution must be in line also with the other functions of residence for the purposes of a DTC. The first function of residence for DTC purposes is to define the personal scope of a DTC. Here the reader is reminded (section A.I. of this chapter) that in doing so, one should take into account the principle of economic allegiance, according to which the taxpayer or the item of income taxed must have some economic connection with the territory of the state intending to levy the tax in order for it to do so justifiably.

By including a substance requirement, the POEM reconciles the purpose of functioning as a preference criterion with the requirement of pointing to a state where the tiebreaker winner has economic allegiance. History teaches us exactly that. WP2 of the OEEC stresses the rationale behind choosing the POEM: 'The Working party considered that it was natural not to attach importance to a purely formal criterion like registration.'[20] So the POEM, the substance-oriented POEM, has been chosen as the tiebreaker because it is not formal but substantive. It points to a state where the corporation has economic connections and not only purely formal ones.

So it can be concluded that the POEM is a preference criterion that must point to only one state but it must also point to a state to whose territory the taxpayer has some economic connection. That is why it is substance-oriented.

2 *Structure of the Analysis*

Having said that, the main part of the investigation follows, i.e., the analysis of the content of the POEM. For this purpose, the elements of substance presented in the definition given in section D. of the introduction are examined. Remember the substance definition that this work laid down in section D. of the introduction comprises three elements: a personal, a functional, and an objective element.

It is submitted that the POEM concentrates on the personal element of substance, i.e., the persons making decisions for the subsidiary. In particular, the Commentary informs us that the POEM is located in 'the place where key management and

18. Breuninger/Krüger (1999), p. 111; van Weeghel (2008), p. 967; van Weeghel (2009), p. 307.
19. *See* OECD, *The Impact of the Communications Revolution on the Application of 'Place of Effective Management' as a Tie Breaker Rule*: Discussion Draft (2001), paras 34 and 37 (hereinafter 'OECD, TAG Discussion Draft'); Board of Taxation, *Review of Corporate Tax Residency* (2020), pp. 24-25 (hereinafter 'Board, Review') and from the literature Burgstaller/Haslinger (2004), pp. 381 et seq.
20. Working Party 2, *Report on the Concept of Fiscal Domicile* (May 1957), p. 6 (hereinafter 'FC/WP2(57)1').

commercial decisions that are necessary for the conduct of the entity's business as a whole are in substance made'.[21] This passage of the Commentary to the OECD MTC 2014 offers some first insight regarding the content of the POEM, namely that in order to localize the POEM one needs to identify the place where *decisions* are made.[22] And of course, decisions are made by persons. So identifying the decision-makers is key to determining where the POEM is located.

Furthermore, it needs to be underlined that the requirement of the POEM that persons making decisions must exist in the residence state does not only fulfil the personal element of substance. The fact that persons exist (personal element) who perform decision-making *functions* for the subsidiary also fulfils the functional element of substance. Thus, these two elements of substance are merged into one for the purposes of the analysis of the substance requirement in the POEM (section B.II.). The role of the third element of substance, i.e., the objective element, is discussed in section B.III.

II The Personal and Functional Elements of the Substance Requirement in Treaty Corporate Residence

In the previous section, it has been ascertained that decision-making functions play the most important role when determining in which state the POEM is. But that oversimplifies a much more complex enquiry. In particular, one may first ask what kind of decision-making functions are required. In other words, what qualities should they have (section B.II.1.)? For example, one person may argue that low-level management is relevant, while the other would respond that high-level management is more important and should thus be relevant. Another issue relates to detecting the persons that make the relevant decisions (section B.II.2.). Should they be employees of the subsidiary? And which hierarchical position and qualities should they have? Finally, not only the quality of the decisions and the persons may play a role but also the quantity thereof (section B.II.3.). Sections B.II.1.-B.II.3. explore these issues.

1 Qualitative Sub-element of Both the Personal and the Functional Element of Substance: What Kind of Decision-Making Functions Are Required?

When referring to the qualities that the decision-making functions of a subsidiary should have in order for it to have its POEM in a specific state, one needs to elaborate on three things:

(1) As already quoted above, the POEM is located in 'the place where key management and commercial decisions that are necessary for the conduct of

21. Paragraph 24 second sentence of the Commentary (2014) on Article 4.
22. UK First-Tier Tribunal, 7 Apr. 2017, *Richard Lee and Nigel Bunter v. HMRC*, 19 ITLR (2017), p. 279 (at para. 74). *See also* from the management literature Fama (1980), p. 290.

the entity's business as a whole are in substance made'. This implies that not all kinds of decisions are relevant when determining where the POEM is located but only those that are business-related.[23] Section B.II.1.a. explores which relationship should exist between the business of the subsidiary and the decision-making functions it is required to make.

(2) As already alluded to above, there are many different categories of decisions (e.g., low- and high-level), so the question arises which decision category is relevant for the purposes of the POEM (section B.II.1.b.).

(3) And finally, decision-making contains many stages, from preparing the decision to implementing it. Which stage is the relevant one for the purposes of the POEM (section B.II.1.c.)?

Let us delve into these issues.

a Relationship Between the Business of the Subsidiary and the Decision-Making Functions Required

aa Whose Business and Which Business?

The first issue when elaborating on the role of business activities and their relevance for the POEM is whose business is relevant. In particular, the relevant decision-making functions refer to '*the entity's* business *as a whole*'[24] so that arguably the question could arise whether it is the subsidiary's business ('stand-alone perspective') or the one of MNE group's as a whole ('group perspective') that is relevant for the purposes of the POEM.[25]

---

23. Courts interpreting domestic substance-oriented residence criteria confirm that approach. *See*:

    Germany: Bundesfinanzhof, 3 Aug. 1977, I R 128/75, BStBl. II (1977), p. 857; Tax Court ('Finanzgericht') of Munich, 5 Nov. 2020, 10 V 1479/20, EFG (2021), p. 429 (at para. 70).
    The Netherlands: Dutch Supreme Court ('Hoge Raad'), 14 Oct. 2005, No. 41.050, BNB 2006/79. *See* Burgers (2007), p. 381, who in commenting the decision states that 'it is decisive whether or not top management had such a steering role *in respect of the key activities of the taxpayer*' (emphasis added).
    Italy: Italian Supreme Court ('Corte Suprema di Cassazione'), 28 Dec. 2016, No. 27113, which, according to Beretta (2017), p. 257, stated that 'it is important to consider whether or not the managerial functions *related to the nature and object* of a passive holding company, although limited, are truly performed by that entity'. (Emphasis added).
    Australia and the United Kingdom: Australian Taxation Office, Taxation Ruling 2018/5 – Income Tax: Central Management and Control Test of Residency, para. 18 (hereinafter 'ATO, TR 2018/5'), referring to Australian and UK case law.
    Switzerland: Maraia (2009), p. 807: 'The specific purpose and the activity of the company should be taken into account.'

24. Paragraph 24 second sentence of the Commentary (2014) on Article 4 (emphasis added).
25. This question is not a theoretical one at all. John Avery Jones summarizing the discussion at the joint IFA/OECD Seminar at the IFA Congress in Vienna in 2004 affirmed that '[o]ne member considered that one should ignore the management of each office and look for the management of the company as a whole, but another pointed out that the Commentary does not say this'. Avery Jones (2005), p. 23.

However, notice that the passage refers to '*the entity's* business' as the relevant one. Is there a contradiction here? Does 'as a whole' mean that it is not the entity's but the group's business that determines which decisions are relevant? The answer is no. The addition of 'as a whole' does not relate solely to the business but to the entity's business. It is the entity's business and not that of the MNE group which is relevant for the purposes of the POEM; the stand-alone perspective applies.[26]

Another question would be whether the POEM ascertains residence by examining only a part of the entity's business, for example, single transactions ('transactional approach') or whether the whole business of the entity should be examined ('holistic approach'). If, for example, a subsidiary is responsible for the general administration and finance of the group, should both the decisions related to the administration and the finance (e.g., the granting of loans to sub-subsidiaries) be relevant (that would be the holistic approach) or should residence be determined for each transaction on its own? It is submitted that, applying the POEM prerequisites, one must indicate all the activities that the subsidiary carries out and determine which decisions attach to these activities; the holistic approach applies.

Of course, all of these findings are somehow intuitive. It is the subsidiary's residence that is at stake. Consequently, the decisions forming its business are the ones that matter. The business and business-related decisions of other group members do not play a role in determining the POEM of a subsidiary. And since residence controls the attachment of the taxpayer, i.e., the subsidiary, to a territory and not the attachment of a certain type of income to a territory, e.g., the income from the loans granted by the subsidiary in the above example, the whole spectrum of decisions must be taken into consideration and therewith the whole business pertaining to these decisions. Of course, this may lead to a spill over effect: although a subsidiary does not have substance for an individual transaction (e.g., granting loans), it may have substance for another transaction (e.g., rendering administrative services) and, thus still be considered to have enough substance for the purposes of the POEM.

In conclusion, the decisions related to a (single) entity's business (stand-alone perspective) as a whole, meaning all the business activities conducted by the entity (holistic approach), must be taken into account when determining the POEM. But decision-making is only one aspect of carrying on business. An interesting question would thus be whether, besides the decisions in themselves,[27] other functions, i.e., the

26. This is also accepted for the purposes of the German POM. *See* Bundesfinanzhof, 7 Dec. 1994, I K 93, BStBl. II (1995), p. 175.
27. Decision-making is in itself business. *See* High Court of Australia, 8 Apr. 1946, *Malayan Shipping Co Ltd v. Federal Commissioner of Taxation*, CLR (1946), p. 156 (at p. 159). *See also* ATO, TR 2018/5, para. 8: 'the central management and control of a business is factually part of carrying on that business'. From the literature, *see* Kostikidis (2022), pp. 146-147. *Contra* Heinrich (2008), pp. 211-212: 'It should also be noted that the fact that each legal entity has a place of effective management does not mean that it also operates an enterprise within the meaning of Article 7 OECD MTC.' (Author's unofficial translation). Although Heinrich does not deny the fact that decisions may be business activities, by denying that they may give rise to an enterprise he also denies that business activities are conducted, since it is the enterprise that conducts the business activities; if no enterprise exists no business activities are conducted.

business operations taking place in the state of the POEM (e.g., construction or distributive activities, R&D, etc.), play a role when determining which that state is. The next section deals with this problem.

bb Role of Business Operations in Determining the State of the POEM

The only inference that can be made by looking at the Commentary to the OECD MTC 2014 as regards the importance of the existence of business operations in the POEM state is an argument e contrario. In particular, Italy's reservation, according to which 'the place where the main and substantial activity of the entity is carried on is also to be taken into account when determining the place of effective management of a person other than an individual'[28] demonstrates, e contrario, that the OECD does not accept such an interpretation.

Moreover, the Technical Advisory Group on Monitoring the Application of Existing Treaty Norms for the Taxation of Business Profits (TAG), established under the auspices of the OECD, in 2001 released a Discussion Draft dealing with the future of the POEM. In its Discussion Draft, the TAG considered the possibility of replacing the POEM with '[t]he place where economic nexus' exists, whereby the latter 'may be characterised by the extent that land, labour, capital and enterprise (the factors of production) are used by the company in deriving its profits'.[29] E contrario, the POEM does not take account of these factors. Actually, these factors are taken into account for the purposes of another sourcing rule,[30] namely the permanent establishment (PE) threshold, which, pursuant to Article 5(1) of the OECD MTC, 'means a fixed place of business through which the business of an enterprise is wholly or partly carried on'.[31]

It must be highlighted that domestic courts interpret domestic substance-oriented residence in exactly the same way. The German Bundesfinanzhof ruled that it is not the place where the decisions are implemented, but the one in which these are made that is important when determining the POM for domestic law purposes.[32] Consequently, the place where the decisions are made (e.g., decisions are taken by the board in Germany) and the one where the decisions are executed (e.g., they are executed by staff in a distribution centre in Luxemburg) may differ. Common law jurisprudence shares that viewpoint. In fact, the very first case that established the central management and control (CMC) as the substance-oriented domestic residence test for common law countries, i.e., *De Beers*,[33] related to a corporation set up in South Africa, where all its business operations (diamond mines) took place. Regardless of this state of facts, the House of Lords maintained that 'the real business', referring to the CMC, was

28. Paragraph 25 of the Commentary (2014) on Article 4.
29. OECD, TAG Discussion Draft, paras 50 and 59.
30. Remember residence in DTCs functions also as a sourcing rule. *See* above s. A.I. of this chapter.
31. On the PE threshold in DTCs *see* in detail Kostikidis (2023), pp. 180 et seq.
32. Bundesfinanzhof, 3 Jul. 1997, IV R 58/95, BStBl. II (1998), p. 86.
33. House of Lords, 30 Jul. 1906, *De Beers Consolidated Mines Limited v. Howe*, AC (1906), p. 455.

carried on in the UK.[34] Australian jurisprudence has also interpreted the CMC as 'the place of the personal control over and not of the physical operations of the business'.[35]

In sum, the POEM does not account for business operations conducted in the residence state; to do so would require either the replacement of the POEM by a test examining the presence of business activity other than decision-making or the existence of both the POEM and such a test in the tiebreaker. Business operations are taken into account, though, when determining whether a PE exists in a state.

cc Role of the Scale and Nature of the Business Operations in Relation to Which Decisions Are Made

A different question relates to whether the subsidiary must carry out a certain degree or nature of operations in relation to which decisions are made in the POEM state, irrespective of whether these operations take place within the borders of the residence state or not. For example, do decisions related to passive investments also suffice for the purposes of the POEM? And what if the scale of the subsidiary's operations is so low that only one or two decisions, for instance, suffice for it to be properly managed?

The Commentary is silent on this matter. Still, an argument e contrario may again provide a satisfactory solution. As already seen in section B.III.3. of the introduction, a new provision has been introduced into the OECD MTC to deny DTC benefits for corporations, namely the LOB. So, a subsidiary with its POEM in a state and thereby falling under the personal scope of its DTC with another state may, in a second step, see DTC benefits withdrawn because of the application of the LOB. In relation to the questions raised in this section, the LOB contains a provision that could be of interest: the active conduct of a business test in Article 29(3) of the OECD MTC. In a nutshell, this provision requires that a corporation claiming DTC benefits must pursue an economic activity either in its residence state or, when it does so in the other contracting state (i.e., the source state), that the economic activity in the residence state must be substantial in relation to the activity in the source state (Article 29(3)(b) of the OECD MTC). Furthermore, passive activities are not considered economic activities pursuant to Article 29(3)(a).

These provisions are interesting because of the fact that the LOB requires business operations in the residence state to be substantial in relation to the activity in the source state and that it disregards passive activities implies that these aspects are not important for the purposes of the POEM. If they played a role under the POEM, then a subsidiary would not be considered a resident of the state the DTC of which is invoked in the first place because it would neither have substantial business operations

34. *Ibid.*, at p. 458. This is underlined by subsequent UK case law, *see* UK High Court, 8 Apr. 2005, *Wood v. Holden*, EWHC (2005), p. 547 (at para. 21).
35. High Court of Australia, 16 Nov. 2016, *Bywater Investments Limited v. Commissioner of Taxation*, HCA (2016), p. 45 (at para. 116) citing High Court of Australia, 21 Apr. 1941, *Koitaki Para Rubber Estates Ltd v. Federal Commissioner of Taxation*, 64 CLR (1941), p. 241 (at pp. 248 et seq.). *See also* ATO, TR 2018/5, para. 8, according to which '[i]t is not necessary for any part of the actual trading or investment operations of the business of the company to take place in Australia'.

nor pursue activities other than those of a passive nature. Courts and tax administrations confirm this viewpoint.

In particular, the UK Court of Appeal in the case *Wood v. Holden* provided insightful guidance regarding the scale and duration of business operations that need to be conducted by a corporation in order for it to have its CMC in the UK. In this case, the Court of Appeal upheld the decision of the High Court judge and maintained that 'it is not the law that that test is superseded by some different test if the business of a company is such that *not a great deal is required for central control and management of its business to be carried out*'.[36] Accordingly, even a special purpose vehicle (SPV), to which this judgment refers, may have a CMC. An SPV is, in simple terms, a subsidiary set up by the parent in order to perform very limited functions, for instance, to buy another company. After it has fulfilled this 'special purpose' (e.g., the acquisition of another company), it is normally liquidated. So, the scale and duration of the business operations underlying the decision-making are not decisive when determining the POEM, as even subsidiaries with very limited business operations and, in most cases, short life term like SPVs 'are not necessarily shorn of independent existence'[37] and thus may also have a POEM.

As to the nature of the subsidiary's activities, the Australian Practical Compliance Guideline 2018/9 also deals with the CMC of SPVs. There it is stated that '[t]he decisions to enter into the buy and sell transactions and wind up the company are the key high-level decisions that amount to the exercise of the SPV ... central management and control'.[38] So, a subsidiary whose business is of merely a passive nature (implement an investment decision of the parent) may also claim residence on the basis of the CMC for domestic tax law purposes.

The fact that the nature of the business activity is not relevant in determining the POEM is not problematic. Remember that the primary function of residence in DTCs is to open the personal scope of the DTC to a taxpayer by taking into account the principle of economic allegiance (section A.I. of this chapter). And the tiebreaker, especially, functions as a preference criterion when more than one state claims to be the residence state and therewith the one to which the subsidiary in question is more economically attached (section B.I.1. of this chapter). In order to do so, the tiebreaker does not need to take account of the nature of the subsidiary's business. Take, for example, a finance subsidiary incorporated in state A whose board meets and acts on premises in state B where it takes substantial decisions (e.g., on which other group companies it will grant loans to). In this case, the subsidiary does not demonstrate any active operations. Still, one could argue that its *strongest* ties (and that is what the tiebreaker examines) are in

36. UK Court of Appeal, 26 Jan. 2006, *Wood v. Holden*, EWCA Civ 26, para. 35 (emphasis added), referring to para. 65 of the High Court decision and para. 42 where it is stated that because of the very limited business operations of the subsidiary '[t]here was nothing else to manage'. *See also* Beretta (2017), p. 257 commenting on the decision of the Italian *Corte Suprema di Cassazione* according to which a passive holding company with limited activities can have a POEM.
37. UK Court of Appeal, 8 Jul. 2010, *Revenue and Customs Commissioners v. Smallwood & Anor*, STC (2010), p. 2045 (at para. 68).
38. Australian Taxation Office, *Practical Compliance Guideline 2018/9*, para. 26 (hereinafter 'ATO, PCG').

state B. So, the function of the tiebreaker is fulfilled by applying the POEM here although the subsidiary does not carry out any active business.

More problematic is the fact that the tiebreaker does not take account of the scale and the duration of the subsidiary's business activity. What is to be managed when no activity exists? Do the decisions to buy an asset and then liquidate the subsidiary, for example, in the case of the SPV, suffice in order to ascertain that the state in which these decisions were made is economically attached to the subsidiary? Well, the answer is probably no, but *in a first step*, it can be maintained that the ties in that state are stronger than in any other state so that the POEM still does its job again quite well. It is only when the subsidiary has substantial activities in a state or states other than the state of the POEM that one should ask whether the subsidiary's ties are closer to the other state and not the POEM state. Consider, for example, a subsidiary managed from state A and incorporated in state B where all its staff and assets are located and functions are executed. Is the subsidiary resident in state A or B? The POEM would only take account of the decision-making and thus point to state A.[39,40]

39. In contrast, the HMRC, for example, would grant residence to state B. *See* HMRC, *International Manual: Company Residence: Standard Treaty Tie-Breakers* (2016), at example 2. *See also* Loomer (2011), p. 143 interpreting the older HMRC, Statement of Practice 1 (1990), para. 22 as suggesting 'that POEM lies closer to the productive operations of the business'.

    The Indian tax authorities consider business operations only as a secondary factor when determining the POEM. *See* Central Board of Direct Taxes, 24 Jan. 2017, *Circular No. 6 – Guiding Principles for Determination of Place of Effective Management (POEM) of a Company*, para. 7 and para. 8.3 (hereinafter 'CBDT, Circular No. 6').

    The SARS considers the economic nexus as 'irrelevant in the determination of its place of effective management. However, this factor may be considered circumstantial and given some weight in cases where other factors are inconclusive'. *See* SARS, *Interpretation Note 6 (Issue 2), Resident – Place of Effective Management (Companies)* (2015), p. 12 (at s. 4.2.8.) (hereinafter 'SARS, Interpretation Note 6(2)').

40. There have been proposals in the academic literature trying to address exactly these situations. *See*, as to residence for domestic tax purposes, Marian (2014), pp. 181 et seq. proposing using the mechanics of formulary apportionment, that is, 'a formula that takes into account number of employees, tangible assets, and sales figures'. According to him '[if such a formula] is used to determine the residency of a corporation, a corporation will have very little chance to end up a resident in a jurisdiction where it has no economic activity'. Rosenzweig (2015), p. 507: 'the term domestic corporation shall mean any entity treated as a corporation for US tax purposes for which (1) 50 percent or more of the gross income of such corporation for the taxable year is income from sources within the United States, or (2) the average percentage of assets held by such corporation during the taxable year which produce income from sources within the United States or which are held for the production of income from sources within the United States is at least 50 percent'. With regard to the POEM, *see* Maisto et al. (2018), pp. 32 et seq. resorting to the place 'in which the business or such activity ... is primarily carried on' but only if the POEM cannot be defined; Escribano (2019a), pp. 202-204 referring to the criterion of the 'strongest economic connection' as the tiebreaker.

    There are also domestic residence tests that require similar connections of the taxpayer with the residence state like the Italian 'principle economic activity' test. *See* Escribano (2019a), p. 79. Recently the Australian Board of Taxation proposed that the Australian domestic residence test is changed. In particular: 'It is the view of the Board that there must be a sufficient economic connection between Australia and a company that has been incorporated overseas for that company to be considered an Australian tax resident. A sufficient economic connection exists for these purposes where both the company conducts its core commercial activities in Australia and has its central management and control in Australia.' *See* Board, Review, pp. 35-39. The difference between a test merely based on the CMC and one requiring both the existence of the CMC and a sufficient economic connection of the taxpayer with the residence

Of course, *in a second step*, for example, by applying the LOB, one may question whether such a subsidiary crossing the threshold of the POEM but having important economic connections to other states should have access to DTC benefits; or one could attribute more profits to the place where business operations occur than to the POEM. The latter could take place by, first, accepting that the state(s) where the subsidiary's business operations are carried out has a taxing right (e.g., because the subsidiary has a PE there), and, second, by attributing to these activities the lion's share of the profits.

Summing up, there exists no threshold regarding the scale and the duration of the business operations carried on by the subsidiary; the same holds true regarding the nature of its business. Admittedly, this can lead to locating the POEM in a state other than the state where business operations primarily take place. However, this flaw of the POEM can be eliminated if one takes business operations into account in a second stage when applying the LOB and transfer pricing rules.

b What Kind of Decisions Are Relevant?

So if decision-making functions are determinative for the POEM, naturally, the question arises as to which decisions are the decisive ones. A decision can relate to the very future of a corporation (e.g., the decision to liquidate the corporation or sell its shares) or to the most simple tasks performed by its employees (e.g., the decision to answer rudely to a client email). Further, and similarly, decisions may either refer to the business operations themselves and have a technical nature (e.g., the decision to switch from one manufacturing process to another one) or be of a commercial nature (e.g., the decision to invest in a specific product).

In order to specify which decisions are relevant for the purposes of determining the POEM, first the categories of decisions taken in a corporation are presented and the peculiarities that exist with respect to subsidiaries are underlined (section B.II.1.b.aa.). Then, it is explored which of the decision categories introduced are the relevant ones when determining the POEM (sections B.II.2.b.bb. and B.II.2.b.cc.).

aa Decision Categories in the Corporation

Management literature distinguishes decisions made in the corporation from an institutional and a functional perspective. On the one hand, the institutional perspective refers to the persons within the corporations that take pertinent decisions;[41] on the other, the functional perspective differentiates with regard to the nature of the decisions to be made.[42] The following analysis is limited to the decision categories from a solely functional perspective.

---

country is illustrated by way of examples in Board, Review, at pp. 59 et seq.

41. From an institutional perspective, management is divided into top-level management (normally consisting in the board of directors), middle-level management, and lower-level management. *See* Daum et al. (2016), p. 225.
42. Daum et al. (2016), p. 225.

From a functional perspective, three kinds of decisions may be distinguished according to the following four criteria:

(1) the degree of certainty of the decisions with regard to their realization;
(2) the complexity of the decisions with regard to their realization;
(3) the degree of detail of the decisions; and
(4) the time range within which the decisions need to be implemented.[43]

Accordingly, three categories arise:

(1) Strategic decisions: these are decisions concerning the long-term future of an enterprise. They are the most complex since they need to take into account many factors outside of the business of the corporation itself (e.g., customer demand, competition, scarcity of raw materials, etc.), and the degree of uncertainty regarding the realization of the decision is high, too. Because of the uncertainty and complexity, they do not offer concrete 'numbers' but are restricted to abstract qualitative statements (e.g., 'In the next five years, our aim is to expand production by 10%'). It is submitted that the business of a corporation exerts influence as to which decisions are considered strategic.[44] For example, a corporation operating in an unstable environment may make strategic decisions extending over three years, whereas another one operating in a safe business environment can make strategic decisions with reference to the next seven years, that is, in general, '[i]ncreased volatility of the business environment makes systematic strategic planning more difficult'.[45] For this reason, it is preferable to adhere to the characteristics of a strategic decision, and not define it by providing concrete statements (e.g., strategic decisions are the ones referring to a period of time over five years). The business activities of each corporation must be assessed based on the four criteria presented above and only then can it be determined which decisions are the strategic ones.

Now, taking into account the fact that subsidiaries are controlled persons, the question arises whether they can convey strategic decisions at all or whether these are taken by the controlling parent for them.[46] In this respect, one has to distinguish between what is here denoted as strategic decision-making and the formulation of parent policy.[47] The latter, containing, for example, the market sectors in which the whole enterprise operates

43. Horváth (2020), p. 85. Other factors analysed there like the formality of the decisions are not adopted.
44. Kreikebaum (2018), p. 21.
45. Grant (2003), p. 491 and in more detail pp. 493 et seq.
46. Milewska (2017), p. 51, informing us that '[g]enerally, no single employee of a subsidiary is entitled to take a strategic decision regarding business in Mexico and put capital at risk, even though he or she makes day-to-day decisions regarding the implementation of strategic decisions made by the parent company'.
47. Wöhe et al. (2016), p. 74.

and the capital structure at the outset of a venture, are reserved for the parent to outline. The parent makes, for example, the decision to set up a distribution subsidiary in Germany in order to be in close proximity to the German customers and conquer the respective market. And the parent is the one that provides the subsidiary with start-up capital to reach the goal set above. But it is the subsidiary which still makes long-term, abstract, complex, and uncertain as to their realization strategic decisions with regard to *its* business.

An easy way, which has already been considered in German literature[48] and by tax authorities,[49] to distinguish between strategic decisions from the principle guidelines that are reserved for the parent to formulate is to take a look at what the corporate law provides to which the subsidiary is subject.[50] There, as well as in the articles of association, these decisions are laid down precisely.

Finally, again, the business activities of the subsidiary of course have an impact on how these strategic decisions look. MNEs with many different products or with operations in different continents divide management with regard to the specific product or region. It is then a holding subsidiary that plays the role of the parent regarding the specific product or region.[51] Of course, this subsidiary's strategic decisions are completely different from the ones that its sub-subsidiaries have to take. Still, its sub-subsidiaries also have to make decisions that in relation to the other decisions referring to their operations bear the characteristics of a strategic decision.

(2) The long-term, abstract and uncertain decisions need to be specified in order for the corporation to be able to run its business operations without the risk of having made only rough estimations. This task is fulfilled by making tactical decisions. These are medium-term decisions and a very important characteristic thereof is that they are bound to respect the framework that the strategic decisions have laid down.[52] This is how one can distinguish them from the strategic decisions, since they, just like the strategic decisions, can also be abstract, or at least not concrete enough, accompanied with uncertainty regarding their realization, and highly complex. Furthermore, it has already been ascertained that a decision taken for a time horizon of three years, for example, may be long-term for one corporation, whereas for another one it pertains to the medium-term decisions. Thus, the time criterion

48. Schröder (1980), pp. 98 et seq.
49. *India:* Central Board of Direct Taxes, 24 Jan. 2017, *Circular No. 6 – Guiding Principles for Determination of Place of Effective Management (POEM) of a Company*, para. 8.2(f) (hereinafter 'CBDT, Circular No. 6').
    South Africa: SARS, Interpretation Note 6(2), p. 9 (at s. 4.2.5.).
50. The Indian tax authorities also adopt an interesting approach. They discern whether the board of the subsidiary merely follows policies which apply to the whole group per se or whether they refer specifically to the entity in question. *See* CBDT, Circular No. 6, para. 7.1.
51. For example, the well-known energy MNE RWE AG has divided its operations into production segments. One of these segments relating to nuclear energy is controlled by a subsidiary, RWE Power. *See* RWE, Annual Report (2018), p. 19. Available at: RWE-annual-report-2018.pdf.
52. Hahn (2018), p. 374. Although Ulrich Hahn calls them operational decisions.

is also not conclusive. All in all, tactical decisions are the ones that adhere to the strategic decisions and specify them.

(3) The last category relates to the operational decisions. These are the most short-term, detailed, concrete and certain as to their realization decisions in relation to the other decisions referring to the operations of the corporation in question.

Management literature acknowledges that it is difficult to differentiate between these categories of decisions.[53] To illustrate this take, for example, in a small manufacturing subsidiary, the production officer's decision to change to another production method within the next year. What kind of decision is this? One can only apply the four criteria presented above and produce a result. This decision could certainly not be a strategic one. It is quite concrete and lacks complexity (taking into account non-business considerations, etc.). However, it is not easy to tell whether it is a tactical or an operational one. It could be a mid-term decision, and thus a tactical one, when taking into account the peculiarities of the business of the pertinent subsidiary. But it could just as well be an operational one. For this reason, in line with management literature,[54] this work only differentiates between strategic and operational decisions. Tactical decisions are classified either as strategic or as operational ones after applying the four criteria presented above for the purposes of this work.

In sum, this work divides decisions in the corporation into two categories: strategic and operational. The criteria that help in this process are the degree of certainty and complexity of the decisions with regard to their realization, the degree of detail of the decisions, and the time range within which the decisions need to be implemented. Examining whether a decision is taken within a given framework laid down at the entity level is also helpful when distinguishing the operational from the strategic decisions. The strategic decisions provide the framework within which the operational ones have to remain. Finally, in order to distinguish strategic decisions from parent policy-making, the corporate law to which the subsidiary is subject may provide insightful guidance.

So, which of these decision categories is decisive in determining the POEM?

bb The Relevant Decision Category for the Purposes of the POEM

The Commentary on Article 4 is not conclusive regarding the decision category that is decisive in order to ascertain where the POEM is located. It refers only to 'key management and commercial decisions'.[55] Now, both a strategic and an operational decision can be viewed as 'key'.[56] The decision by the production officer dealt with above is certainly a 'key' one; production may, namely, collapse if the decision proves

53. Jung (2016), p. 174.
54. Horváth (2020), p. 85.
55. Paragraph 24 second sentence of the Commentary (2014) on Article 4.
56. *See, e.g.*, Vann (2010), p. 330; Padia/Maroun (2012), p. 123.

to be wrong. Reputational damage may ruin the subsidiary or at least be difficult to contain.

The confusion grows if one examines the Commentary further. Until 2017, the alternative provision to the POEM was the MAP. The Commentary suggested a quite similar provision to the one adopted in the 2017 OECD MTC, mentioning the POEM as one of the factors to be taken into account. But the Commentary states that the '[c]ompetent authorities having to apply such a provision ... would be expected to take account of various factors, such as where *the meetings of its board of directors or equivalent body are usually held*, where the chief executive officer and other senior executives usually carry on their activities, where the *senior day-to-day management of the person is carried on*, where the person's headquarters are located'.[57]

Taking this passage at face value would mean that both strategic and operational decisions are of relevance. While the board, as we *see* below in this section, takes strategic decisions for the corporation, the day-to-day management corresponds to the operational (short-term) management. Courts interpreting the POEM provided an answer in this respect. The French Supreme Administrative Court ('Conseil d'État') in the *Paupardin* case[58] ruled that the POEM is the place, 'where the persons exercising the highest functions in the enterprise make the *strategic decisions* that determine the conduct of the business of this enterprise as a whole'.[59] Commentators find it interesting that 'no reference is made to (French) domestic law or to the Commentaries on Article 4(3)'.[60] Apparently, the court did not address why the strategic decisions in particular are relevant, and not the operational or perhaps both of them.

UK case law also seems to emphasize strategic decisions when ascertaining the POEM. In *Wensleydale's Settlement Trustees*,[61] the Special Commissioner cited Klaus Vogel's Commentary on DTCs, which posited that the POEM is 'the centre of top level management'.[62] And, in fact, it can be assumed that the 'top level management' points

---

57. Paragraph 24.1 fourth sentence of the Commentary (2014) on Article 4 (emphasis added).
58. Conseil d'État, 16 Apr. 2012, No. 323592, *Paupardin*, FR:CESSR:2012:323592.20120416.
    In *Paupardin* the *Conseil d'État* had to interpret the term POEM of an *enterprise* (and not a single entity). The POEM of an enterprise can be in a different place from that of a single entity. If one applies the economic meaning of the term 'enterprise' and puts it next to the term 'entity' to which the POEM in Article 4(3) of the 2014 version of the OECD MTC refers, it becomes apparent that the POEM of an enterprise refers to the POEM of the group as a whole, comprising the parent and all subsidiaries, sub-subsidiaries, etc., whereas the POEM of an entity refers to the POEM of that specific entity. Arguably, the POEM can be found in diverging places in these two cases. For example, the POEM of the Siemens group as a whole is, undoubtedly, in Germany, but the POEM of its subsidiaries as such may be in the state where these subsidiaries are incorporated.
    Still, this problem does not reduce the value of the ruling of the court regarding the issue discussed here. The term enterprise only changes the subject to whom the POEM test is to be applied, i.e., the enterprise as a whole and not the entity as such. It does not have any impact on the category of decisions that is relevant for the purposes of the POEM. Both strategic and operational decisions can be taken both at the level of the group as a whole and at the level of an entity as such.
59. Gooijer (2019), p. 191.
60. *Ibid.*, at pp. 191-192.
61. Special Commissioners, 14 Mar. 1996, *Wensleydale's Settlement Trustees v. Commissioners of Inland Revenue*, STC (1996), p. 241.
62. *Ibid.*, at para. 6.

to the strategic decisions. Moreover, both parties involved, i.e., the counsel for the applicants and the Crown's representative, cited case law which referred to the domestic CMC test.[63] The latter is located in the place where strategic decisions are taken.[64] But why are the strategic decisions and not the operational ones relevant with regard to the POEM (and not the CMC!)? Is the court's argumentation sufficient to justify its ruling? With all due respect, the quotation of a legal commentary, even one as authoritative as Vogel's, and of case law not even referring to the POEM but to the CMC is not an adequate elucidation as to why the strategic decisions are the decisive ones when determining the POEM.

Subsequent case law could provide an explanation for connecting the POEM to the place where the strategic decisions are made. In *Smallwood*, the UK Court of Appeal held that the POEM is where the 'real top-level management' is located.[65] The citation of *Wensleydale's Settlement Trustees*[66] shows that the court espouses the interpretation made in this decision. The court derives its reasoning not only by referring to this previous case law but also by citing the Commentary on Article 4. Accordingly, '[t]he place of effective management will ordinarily be the place where the most senior person or group of persons (for example a board of directors) makes its decisions'.[67] Pursuant to this passage, meetings of the most senior persons, i.e., the board of directors, who according to management literature consist the top-level management,[68] are decisive.[69] In fact, strategic decisions are only taken by the board of directors – although the latter may also delegate them to other persons.[70] So, at first glance, this passage locates the POEM in the place where the board of directors makes decisions; the board is the only organ of a corporation making strategic decisions; thus the POEM is located in the place where strategic decisions are taken. Literature has also pointed to the strategic decisions, again following this line of argument.[71]

This argument is not conclusive. In particular, the board of directors may take also operational decisions, especially in small subsidiaries.[72] Moreover, if the subsidiary has a two-board structure, i.e., one management board and one supervisory board, the management board will 'not only manage[s] the company's affairs, but also sets up

63. The counsel for the applicants cited *De Beers*. The Crown's representative cited *Bullock v. Unit Construction Co Ltd. See ibid.*, at para. 6.
64. Panayi (2009), pp. 834-835; Cerioni/Eden (2018), p. 672.
65. UK Court of Appeal, *Revenue and Customs Commissioners v. Smallwood & Anor*, at paras 48 et seq.
66. *Ibid.*, at para. 48.
67. Paragraph 24 third sentence of the Commentary (2000) on Article 4.
68. *See* above n. 41 in this chapter.
69. Sasseville (2009), p. 294.
70. High Court of Australia, *Bywater Investments Limited v. Commissioner of Taxation*, at para. 41.
71. Haslinger (2008), pp. 196 et seq.
72. ATO, TR 2018/5, para. 13: 'For example, for a small passive investment company with a very small number of investments, the decision to make, hold and dispose of those investments, would be both the day-to-day management and the central management and control of the company.' Admittedly, the opposite case is also possible where not the board but other persons make both strategic and operational decisions. *See* SARS, *Discussion Paper on Interpretation Note 6 Place of Effective Management* (September 2011), p. 11. On this problem generally, Valta (2022), p. 71.

long term goals and guidelines [i.e., the strategic decisions]'.[73] Thus, stating that the decisions taken by the board are the decisive ones does not necessarily mean that these decisions are the strategic ones.

Furthermore, the fact that the above-quoted Commentary passage was deleted in the 2008 amendment of the Commentary deprives the abovementioned argumentation of its basis. In fact, one could even argue that the deletion of this passage from the Commentary may indicate a step back to the previous status under which an interpretation 'that assigns equal significance to both day-to-day [what is here called operational management] and strategic decisions' is conceivable.[74]

From that, it follows that it should not come as a surprise that commentators assign the POEM to the place where the operational decisions are taken.[75] Moreover, it appears logical that states like Germany, although they accept that the POEM has to be interpreted autonomously, make recourse to their domestic substance-oriented residence criteria in order to interpret the POEM.[76] If the provision underlying the POEM and the accompanying Commentary do not provide any guidance as to the content of the term, how can states interpret the term in an appropriate way?

Of course, this can lead to unpleasant situations. Imagine a subsidiary with its strategic management in the UK and its operational management in Germany. Both states would reasonably argue that the POEM is located on their territory. The UK, on the one hand, emphasizes the strategic decisions, the German interpretation of the POEM, on the other hand, in line with the interpretation of the domestic substance-oriented residence test, i.e., the POM, gives priority to the operational decisions. In this case, the primary purpose of the POEM, i.e., to solve the residence-residence conflict between the UK and Germany, has failed. And this is not only because states apply

73. Jungmann (2006), p. 433.
74. Englisch (2009a), p. 511, who supports this interpretation for DTCs based on the OECD MTC prior to the 2000 update. Actually, what the OECD intended with the deletion of the passage referring to the board of directors was to dispel the confusion that this reference created. It is not only the place where the board of directors meets that is relevant. In other words, the OECD wanted to clarify that the POEM is not equated with and does not always correspond to the place in which the board of directors meets and decides. *See* Plakhin (2009), p. 91.
75. Burgstaller/Haslinger (2004), pp. 380 and 383. On this issue, *see also* Lipniewicz (2020), p. 608.
    This is also the *Austrian* viewpoint. *See* Simader (2009), p. 368. Seemingly so partly *Indian* case law *see* Sharma/Cardozo (2012), p. 42: 'In the cases of *DLJMB Mauritius Investment Company* and *Integrated Container Feeder Service,* it was observed that a "place of effective management" refers to the place from where, factually and effectively, day-to-day affairs of the companies are carried on and not at the place in which the ultimate control of the company resides.' *Contra* subsequent case law as well as the Indian tax authorities. As to the case law *see* Gooijer (2019), p. 193 commenting on the *Saraswati Holding v. Deputy Director of Income-tax* and coming to the conclusion that '[a]pparently, to establish POEM it is insufficient that a power of attorney "empowered the persons in India to conduct the day-to-day affairs of the company."' *See also* CBDT, Circular No. 6, para. 8.2(g).
    This interpretation was also accepted in *South Africa* by the SARS until 2015. *See* SARS, *Interpretation Note 6, Resident – Place of Effective Management* (2002), s. 3.2. (2002). *See also* Padia/Maroun (2012), pp. 123 et seq.
    In the same vein, the *Swiss* Federal Supreme Court ('Bundesgericht'). *See* Bundesgericht, 16 May 2013, 2C_1086/2012, 2C_1087/2012, at para. 2.2.
76. Pötgens et al. (2014b), p. 425; Avery Jones (2005), p. 21; Traversa (2018), p. 7; Valta (2022), p. 71.

their own domestic substance-oriented residence criteria but also because the OECD in Article 4(3) of the 2014 version of the OECD MTC and in its Commentary do not provide states with sufficient guidance in order to use the concept in a comprehensible way. Were sufficient guidance to exist, recourse to the interpretation of the domestic substance-oriented residence test would not be necessary.

Finally, even if we accept that the Commentary clearly refers to the strategic decisions, as literature and case law have partly asserted, although on the basis of a passage that only lasted eight years, the question continues to exist: on what grounds has this option been chosen? Why should the strategic decisions be relevant and not the operational ones? The OECD is silent with regard to this issue.

cc Proposed Interpretational Approach

The previous section has shown that both strategic and operational decisions can be decisive in determining the POEM depending on which state is interpreting Article 4(3) of the 2014 version of the OECD MTC owing to the lack of OECD guidance in this respect. The consequence can be that the POEM fails in its purpose, i.e., to function as a preference criterion. The need to provide guidance is apparent. Here, the author argues in favour of an interpretation pointing to the strategic decisions.

The analysis commences with a systematic argument. Article 4(1) sentence 1 and Article 5(2)(a) of the OECD MTC use a pretty similar expression to the one in Article 4(3) of the 2014 version of the OECD MTC, namely the POM (so only the word 'effective' is added into the wording of Article 4(3) of the 2014 version of the OECD MTC). Similar is, however, not the same. The POEM and the POM are not the same terms. First, if the POM in Article 4(1) sentence 1 of the OECD MTC and the POEM meant the same thing, the tiebreaker would fail in its purpose. Of the two states claiming to be the POM states and thus the residence states for the purposes of the DTC in question, only one is the POEM state. If the POM is equated with the POEM, then in case of a POM-POM conflict both states would also be the POEM state and the tiebreaker would fail in its purpose since no 'winner' would arise.

Second, if the POM in Article 5(2)(a) of the OECD MTC, giving rise to a PE and thus to source taxation, and the POEM in Article 4(3) of the 2014 version of the OECD MTC were the same thing, Article 5(2)(a) would be redundant. The state in which the POM is located would always be the residence state since it would always win the tiebreaker (because POM and POEM would be the same thing). Thus, it would not need to tax profits arising within its territory based on source. It could tax the worldwide profit based on residence. For example, Article 7(1) sentence 1 of the OECD MTC grants the taxing right with regard to business profits to the state of residence, unless the business profits are gained through a PE in another (source) state.[77] In other words, the

77. Vann (2010), p. 315: 'The PE definition is critical for tax and statistics purposes because it sets the boundary of the firm in the sense that it determines to what extent the firm has FDI in a country *when a legal entity which is (part of) the firm is not resident there*' (emphasis added).

POM in Article 5(2)(a) intends to grant the taxing right based on source to a state that does not have the taxing right otherwise, i.e., based on the residence. This suggests that the connecting factors POM in Article 5(2)(a) and POEM in Article 4(3) of the 2014 version of the OECD MTC are distinguishable.[78]

A final argument can be brought forward supporting the difference between the terms POM and POEM. The POEM is not only used in Article 4(3) but also in Article 8(1) of the 2014 version of the OECD MTC,[79] the provision regarding the taxing right of income from shipping, inland waterways transport and air transport. 'The effect of Art. 8(1) is to prevent a charge to tax on the permanent establishment of a shipping or air transport enterprise because of the difficulty of apportioning its profits to numerous permanent establishments.'[80] If the POEM is used in Article 8(1) exactly in order to avoid PE taxation of the pertinent income, then it could not fulfil its purpose if it were identical to the term POM, the latter inducing PE taxation.

So, if the connecting factors POM in Article 5(2)(a) of the OECD MTC and POEM in Article 4(3) of the 2014 version of the OECD MTC are distinguishable, the question arises as to how the POM can be distinguished from the POEM. A distinction between the place where strategic decisions are made and the one where operational decisions are made could be useful in this respect and give these terms a rational-systematic position in the OECD MTC. Systematically, it makes sense to locate the POEM in the place where strategic decisions are made, whereas the POM should be in the place where operational decisions are made. In this way, the state where operational decisions are taken loses the tiebreaker but may tax profits arising within its jurisdiction as source state (for instance, because the operational decision-making gives rise to a PE there).[81] By contrast, the state where strategic decisions are taken is the residence state. But why should the strategic decisions point to the residence state and the operational ones to the source state and not, for example, the other way around? The following arguments underpin this proposition.

It can be maintained that the operational decisions are the ones closer to the operations of a corporation. So, operational decisions require that business operations and decision-making are close to each other, probably in the same state. And as has been shown in section B.II.1.a.bb. of this chapter, the POEM does not include such a requirement. It suffices if only decisions amounting to management activities are taken in the POEM state, and no business operations must take place therein. Since strategic decisions must not be – at least in every case – close to the operations of the corporation and they just form the framework within which these operations have to take place, they should be the ones that must be decisive for the purposes of the POEM. In other

78. In a similar vein, *see* Heinrich (2008), p. 212.
79. Like Article 4(3), the POEM has been deleted in the 2017 amendment from Article 8, which now reads: 'Profits of an enterprise of a Contracting State from the operation of ships or aircraft in international traffic shall be taxable only in that State.'
80. Avery Jones et al. (2006), p. 242.
81. Fett (2014), p. 423; Hoor (2019), p. 594, n. 3: 'The country where a company's effective management is located should be considered the state of residence (which may tax all the income realized by a company), whereas the other contracting state may exercise tax rights only over income sourced in its territory (if it has a right to tax under the tax treaty).'

words, the strategic decisions should be relevant for the purposes of the tiebreaker, since they are the ones that take place without a certain proximity to the operations of the corporation being necessary. In contrast, operational decisions are a suitable candidate for the purposes of the POM. In fact, and as already stated in section B.II.1.a.bb. of this chapter, a prerequisite for a PE is always that business operations take place in the source state since it is defined in Article 5(1) of the OECD MTC as 'a fixed place of business through which the business of an enterprise is wholly or partly carried on'.

Moreover, the POEM's telos justifies an interpretation placing emphasis on the strategic decisions instead of the operational ones. Since the POEM is the preference criterion for solving a residence-residence conflict and thus needs to offer a clear answer as to which state wins the conflict, clear evidence is needed in order to determine where the relevant decisions have been made. And it is the strategic decisions that are always – or at least with high probability – documented and can be attributed to a place and a person, not the operational ones. Strategic decisions must be documented, especially so that the persons taking the operational decisions know within which framework they can exercise their discretion.[82] In contrast, operational decisions, especially in small subsidiaries, may not be documented or they may not be clearly attributable to a person or a place. It is therefore in accordance with the POEM's purpose to emphasize the strategic decisions since it is more probable that these decisions are documented than the operational ones and thus concentrating on them is more likely to lead to a clear result than focusing on the operational decisions.

Finally, examining the POEM's history strengthens this interpretation. It has already been stated[83] that the 1925 LoN Report provided for an autonomous definition of residence:

> The State which has the right to levy the tax is the State in which the head office is situated or, if that office is not the *real centre of management and control* of the undertaking, the State in which this centre is situated.[84]

So the 1925 LoN Report equated residence with the *real centre of management and control.* And in the minds of the authors of the 1925 LoN Report, the real centre of management and control took place in the corporation's headquarters:

> In the case of legal entities (joint-stock companies), we propose that the *fiscal domicile* should be the place where the concern has its *effective centre*, i.e., the place where the 'brain', *management and control* of the business are situated. If this definition is accepted, businesses will be prevented from nominally transferring their *headquarters*.[85]

At the time of the 1925 LoN Report referring to the real centre of management and control as the headquarters of a corporation, firms were *free-standing*. That means that

82. *See*, however, noting the increasing informality of strategic planning, Grant (2003), p. 507.
83. *See* above n. 7 in this chapter.
84. LoN 1925, p. 34[4094] (emphasis added).
85. *Ibid.*, at p. 21[4081] (emphasis added).

operations and therewith operational decisions took place outside the investor state. In the investor state, the headquarters were located where the strategic decisions were taken which were the beacon for the operational management to follow. The whole business in the state of production was highly dependent on the decisions taken in the headquarters, which had the necessary knowledge for the project carried out in the production state, and the equity finance provided by the shareholders who were also residents in that state.[86] Thus, according to the 1925 LoN Report, the real centre of management and control was the place in which strategic decisions were taken and the state in which the former took place was the residence state. From all that, it follows that the POEM's predecessor treated the state in which strategic decisions were taken as the residence state.

To summarize, operational and strategic decisions can be used as an element to distinguish the POM from the POEM. The POEM points to the residence state and should be the place where the strategic decisions are taken (irrespective of whether the operational decisions are also taken there). In contrast, the POM points to the state of the source pursuant to Article 5(2)(a) of the OECD MTC and should be the place where the operational decisions are taken.[87]

c Which Stage in the Decision-Making Process Is Relevant?

The author took the decision to move to Germany for his PhD in the summer of 2015 in Thessaloniki. However, this decision had been massively influenced by his Erasmus experience in the winter of 2014 in Frankfurt. And he thoroughly assessed the correctness of his decision during his military service in the winter of 2016 in Limnos by comparing it with other alternatives, etc. Decision-making is a process;[88] and parts of this process may take place in different countries, by different persons, etc. In our

86. Hennart (1994), at p. 120, who, although arguing for the second factor as the decisive one for the emergence of free-standing firms, accepts the fact that 'it is quite possible that free-standing firms arose to internalize the market for other inputs besides financial capital, including property-development know-how'. According to Wilkins (1988), p. 267: 'typically, the board of directors of a free- standing company contained a man (or men) active in the same or in a closely associated economic sector. The board membership (and often stockholdings) was based on familiarity with the industry and capability in assessing opportunities'. *See also* Wells/Lowell (2013), p. 10: 'When we examine the origins of current tax treaty policy, we need to imagine the world as it was in the 1920s. The paradigm of commerce and international taxation was a company resident in a residence country (let's call it "ImperialCo") with an affiliate in an under-developed source country that was a colony of the residence country ("ColonyCo"). A global war just ended, with the residence country having enormous debt. There was a material flow of commerce between the ImperialCo and ColonyCo. For the most part, the former transferred to the latter capital, technology, and access to global markets. ColonyCo responded by producing commodities and goods for ImperialCo and its global markets. The residence country was a creditor and the source country a debtor.'
87. An additional argument is that for the purpose of other substance requirements (in transfer pricing) also the strategic decisions are the relevant ones. In that way both substance requirements are in harmony. *See* the argument mounted in s. B.II.1.a.aa. of Ch. 2.
88. Collier/Dykes (2020), p. 711; Collier/Dykes (2022), p. 27.

example, the question arises as to where the decision in question has been made since the decision process spanned different places (Thessaloniki, Frankfurt, and Limnos) with equally tenable arguments speaking for each one as being the place where the decision has been made. This section raises this question with regard to the POEM. For this purpose, the author will first summarize/present which steps a corporate decision-making process consists of (section B.II.1.c.aa.). Thereafter, the guidance that Article 4(3) of the 2014 version of the OECD MTC and the accompanying Commentary are explored (section B.II.1.c.bb.). It is shown that additional guidance in this respect is necessary, which is provided in this work after interpreting the POEM (section B.II.1.c.cc.).

aa Steps in the Decision-Making Process in the Corporation

The management of a corporation comprises three stages:

(1) the planning stage;
(2) the implementation stage; and
(3) the monitoring stage.[89]

During the planning stage, several sub-stages can also be distinguished: first, the management has to set goals (e.g., increase sales by 5% within the next three years);[90] second, alternative ways to reach the goals set must be identified; third, it must be anticipated which outcomes each alternative entails (sub-steps 1-3 are considered 'preparatory measures'); fourth, and lastly, the alternatives must be evaluated on the basis of the results they are anticipated to produce in order to come up with a decision ('decision-making stricto sensu').

After the decision has been taken, the management has to make sure that its decisions are successfully implemented. In order to do so, the management has to lay down the organization of the corporation. Admittedly, by doing so the management has to take further decisions (e.g., the division into sectors, which executive officers supervise which sectors, etc.). Lastly, decisions taken and implemented must be monitored. In this last stage, the result anticipated is compared with the result reached. The following figure summarizes the findings of this short examination of the steps in the decision-making process in the corporation.

89. Hahn (2018), p. 369. Admittedly, this categorization is contentious. Daum et al. (2016), p. 226 detect, for example, two stages, whereby the implementation stage pertains to the monitoring stage. Wöhe et al. (2016), p. 151 consider the setting of goals, which according to the distinction made here pertains to the planning stage, as a separate stage and therefore point to the existence of four stages of management.

90. Daum et al. (2016), pp. 229 et seq. identify here a separate sub-stage, which they call 'problem ascertainment'. Since setting goals already includes identifying problems with the goal to solve them, the categorization by *Daum et al.* is not adopted here.

Figure 3 Steps in the Decision-Making Process in the Corporation

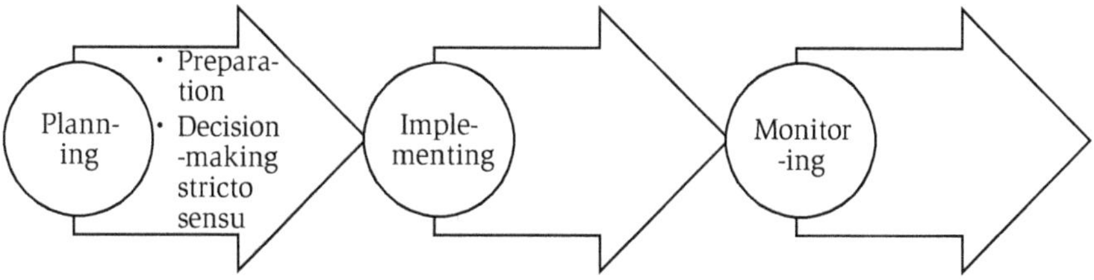

So, it can be ascertained that a decision is preceded by a number of preparatory measures and followed by an implementation and a monitoring stage. However, the complexity does not stop here. Even the sub-stage of decision-making stricto sensu can comprise sub-sub-stages.

Consider, for example, the board of a subsidiary incorporated in state X. Its managers must decide whether the subsidiary will venture to sell its products in a new market. Employees of the subsidiary in state X have explored all the alternatives and outlined them to managers A, B, and C who are entrusted with the decision. Managers A and B meet unofficially during a business trip in state Y, which happens to be the state of incorporation and the POEM of the parent.[91] They choose one of the alternatives and inform the third manager (C) of the subsidiary per email so that the latter will be ready to vote in state X, i.e., the state of incorporation of the subsidiary, where the decision is officially made during a board meeting.

Where has the decision been taken? In state X or in state Y? Does it make a difference that the decision has been prepared in state X? And assume that the implementation of the decision is controlled with the help of an external provider,[92] who processes, compares, and evaluates the data anticipated in relation to the actual data occurred, and this external provider is resident in state W. The external provider then gives the outcomes of the monitoring process to managers A, B, and C in whose discretion it is to decide whether further action (e.g., amendments as regards the content of the decision) is necessary. Is this stage of the decision-making process relevant so that one could argue that the decision-making has been transferred to state W?

The next section analyses and evaluates the OECD guidance in this respect.

bb The Relevant Step in the Decision-Making Process for the Purposes of the POEM

The Commentary on Article 4 provides some pointers regarding the stage of the decision-making process that should be decisive when determining the POEM. The

91. According to the SARS such a pre-meeting 'could impact on the place of effective management'. *See* SARS, Interpretation Note 6(2), p. 9 (at s. 4.2.3.).
92. Management literature informs us that this kind of 'outsourcing of intelligence activities and analysis to consulting companies' is a rising trend, at least in the oil industry. *See* Grant (2003), p. 508.

Commentary states that the POEM is located where the decisions 'are in substance *made*'.[93] It does not say prepared, nor implemented, or controlled. It does, however, say 'made'. It follows from a strict interpretation of the Commentary's wording that out of the three decision-making stages described above, i.e., the planning stage, the implementation stage, and the monitoring stage, the planning stage is the decisive one. In particular, within the planning stage, it is the decision-making stricto sensu that is decisive, and not that referring to the preparation of the decision (e.g., where staff is researching possible alternatives).

However, legal terms, just like words in general, may have more than one meaning. There may be a 'core' meaning, like in our case the core meaning of the term 'make a decision' refers to decision-making stricto sensu, but other possible meanings of the term may also exist.[94] By extensively or restrictively interpreting the term according to the telos or the system in which the term is found to be, other meanings may be preferable in the particular context than the core meaning.[95] This could also be the case with respect to the word 'made'. Arguably, the phrase 'make a decision' can certainly include both the preparation and the monitoring of an already made decision. When we say 'decisions are being made', we may both mean that decisions are being prepared and are upcoming, but we can just as well mean that we monitor the effect of decisions already made and possibly tweak them. So, what do the POEM's history and telos tell us regarding the determinative decision-making stage?

It is submitted that the history of the Commentary on Article 4 does not provide a clear answer in this matter. In particular, mention has already been made in section B.II.1.b.bb. of this chapter as regards the amendment of the Commentary on Article 4 in 2008, which resulted in the deletion of the following passage: '[t]he place of effective management will ordinarily be the place where the most senior person or group of persons (for example a board of directors) makes its decisions'.[96] This passage clearly supported the viewpoint that the preparation and execution of the relevant decisions are not decisive.

That is because the board of directors mentioned in the previous passage, even in the smallest corporations, is rarely entrusted with actively preparing a decision. Further, the execution of the strategic decisions – which is the relevant foundation for the purposes of the POEM (section B.II.1.b.cc. of this chapter) – is delegated from the board to executive officers, etc. Even if we take very small corporations where the functions of executive officers rest with the board members (since executive officers simply do not exist), then the execution of these decisions is attributable to the lowest

93. Paragraph 24 second sentence of the Commentary (2014) on Article 4 (emphasis added).
94. H.L.A. Hart, uses the terms 'core' and 'penumbra'. *See* Hart (1958), p. 607. It was, however, the German jurist Philipp Heck who, long before Hart talked about the core of a term (*Begriffskern*) and the surroundings of the term (*Begriffshof*). *See* Heck (1914), p. 46. The author owes the observation of this parallel to Auer (2008), p. 528, n. 56.
95. Canaris (1964), p. 22. As Claus-Wilhelm Canaris explains, this is not to say that by interpreting terms extensively we find ourselves outside the law (praeter legem).
96. Paragraph 24 third sentence of the Commentary (2000) on Article 4.

staff level.[97,98] So, both the preparation and implementation stages should be, according to the passage of the Commentary quoted above, excluded as the relevant stages in the decision-making process for the determination of the POEM. Regarding the monitoring stage, this also involves the participation of the board of directors. It may be carried out by the lowest level of staff, but the evaluation of the findings and the decision for (further) action rests with the board of directors.[99]

But this Commentary passage was deleted in 2008. Accordingly, it could be speculated that the OECD has detached the Commentary from the interpretation according to which the preparation and the execution of a decision are not relevant for the purposes of determining the POEM. This assertion would mean that all stages of the decision-making process may be relevant when determining the POEM; neither Article 4(3) of the 2014 version of the OECD MTC nor the Commentary differentiate in this respect.

Accordingly, one could posit that, in the aforementioned example, the POEM is divided among states X (where the decision is formally taken and prepared), Y (where the decision is informally taken), and W (where the implementation of the decision is monitored). Nevertheless, an interpretation according to which three POEMs arise would not be in line with the telos of the provision, which is to provide for a preference criterion pointing to one and only one state (section B.I.1. of this chapter). But this barrier is easy to overcome. One could claim, further, that the POEM is a purely factual test. All the facts and circumstances must be weighed, and the result is not contingent on the stage to which a step of the decision-making process pertains. Accordingly, the POEM may just as well not only be in the place where decisions are formally made but also in the place where these decisions are monitored; the facts of the case may lead to a different result each time.

The system of the rule, or to be more accurate of the Commentary accompanying the rule, endorses its indifference regarding the stage of the decision-making process. In particular, the Commentary refers to the following factors as relevant proxies when determining the residence of a corporation in the MAP: 'where the meetings of its board of directors or equivalent body are usually held, where the chief executive officer and other senior executives usually carry on their activities, where the senior day-to-day management of the person is carried on'.[100] While the place of the board's meetings

97. This cannot apply if a corporation is so small that only the directors exist. In this case the directors decide and execute at the same time. In these cases, however, one does not even need to differentiate between decision-making stages. Since all decision-making stages are concentrated in the hands of the directors one only needs to pinpoint them and the place from which they make the decisions.
98. The OECD also sees the board as an organ entrusted with top level management. This can be confirmed by referring to Article 16 of the OECD MTC covering directors' fees. This provision covers '[d]irectors' fees and other similar payments derived by a resident of a Contracting State in his capacity as a *member of the board of directors of a company*' (emphasis added). And the term 'board of directors' is interpreted as not including 'every type of mere "day-to-day" management activities, but only top-level functions' (emphasis omitted). Cordewener (2021), para. 37.
99. According to management literature, the board is involved in both forming corporate strategy and evaluating, albeit in the latter to a lesser degree. *See* Judge/Zeithaml (1992), p. 781.
100. Paragraph 24.1 fourth sentence of the Commentary (2014) on Article 4.

would suggest that the formal stage of the decision-making process is determinative, the reference to the day-to-day management clearly points to the execution of the strategic decisions made.

And of course, the POEM's purpose does not influence which stage of the decision-making process should be relevant. Again, the POEM's purpose is to provide a preference criterion in cases of residence-residence conflict which points to the state with which a corporation is mostly connected (section B.I.1. of this chapter). A corporation can be more connected to the territory in which decisions are formally taken, but it can just as well be more connected to the territory in which these decisions are controlled. Imagine a corporation having all its operations in state A. This is also the place in which the preparation, execution, and monitoring of the business decisions of the respective corporation are taken. However, decisions are formally taken during board meetings in state B. Is state B the state with which the corporation in question is most closely connected?

If it is neither Article 4(3) of the 2014 version of the OECD MTC nor the accompanying Commentary that solves the puzzle, the weight falls on domestic courts to interpret the provision. The Former German Federal Tax Court ('Reichsfinanzhof') ruled in 1934 that for the purposes of the domestic substance-oriented residence test, the place where decisions are enunciated by the management is decisive and not the place of their implementation.[101] Subsequent case law and literature adhere to this finding.[102] Furthermore, recent French case law on the POM for the purposes of the establishment of a PE (Article 5(2)(a) of the OECD MTC) also emphasizes the place in which decisions are formally taken. Since decisions were formally taken during board meetings taking place in France, the *Conseil d'État* found that the company in question had a POM and therewith a PE in France. Importantly for this stage of the study, the court also underlined as a factor in its reasoning the fact that the decisions made during board meetings in France had also been prepared in France.[103]

However, neither the German nor the French case law provides reasons explaining their rulings. Why is the place where the decision is formally made the decisive one and not the one in which this decision is executed?[104] And why should the preparation of a decision not matter? Why is the monitoring stage not decisive? For example, the common law developed substance-oriented residence test, i.e., the CMC, focuses on the management *and* control of a corporation. Consequently, the test is a unified one, meaning that both management (i.e., decision-making stricto sensu) and control (i.e., the monitoring stage of the decision-making process) must coincide.[105] However, if the

101. Reichsfinanzhof, 3 Jul. 1934, I A 129/33, RStBl. (1934), p. 1078. *See* more recent German case law: Finanzgericht of Munich, 5 Nov. 2020, 10 V 1479/20, EFG (2021), p. 429 (at para. 79).
102. *See* the references by Musil (2020), para. 31.
103. Conseil d'État, 7 Mar. 2016, No. 371435, *Société Compagnie internationale des wagons lits et du tourisme*, FR:CESSR:2016:371435.20160307. *See* Gooijer (2019), p. 192.
104. *See* Padia/Maroun (2012), p. 123: 'the place of effective management is where the board decisions are actually implemented'. In a similar vein, focusing on where the economic activity of a corporation takes place and not where the decision-makers are, Lampert (2018), para. 2.72.
105. 'Note that "management" and "control" in his formula are joined by the conjunctive "and", and followed by the singular verb "abides". "Management and control" is expressed as unitary and must be located collectively.' *See* Couzin (2002), p. 42; in a similar vein, Dirkis (2003), p. 407.

board performs the monitoring, whereas executive managers perform the decision-making stricto sensu, this suffices for the purposes of the CMC.[106]

It can be concluded from this excursus on domestic viewpoints that states can regard all stages in the decision-making process as decisive in determining substance-oriented residence. If neither Article 4(3) of the 2014 version of the OECD MTC nor the Commentary on Article 4 differentiate between the steps in the decision-making process to determine the POEM, all decision-making stages presented here may be relevant within the fact analysis for the purposes of ascertaining the POEM. This complete lack of guidance may lead to different interpretations and result in the POEM not fulfilling its purpose.

In the example discussed in the previous section, what prevents all states involved, i.e., X (where the decision is formally taken and prepared), Y (where the decision is informally taken), and W (where the implementation of the decision is controlled) from claiming that the POEM is in their territory? Both Article 4(3) of the 2014 version of the OECD MTC and the accompanying Commentary permit all possible interpretations. Although commentators had already noticed this point before the 2008 update,[107] the OECD did not seem to have considered the possibility of providing guidance in this respect. On the contrary, the sole reference which seemed to point to the place in which decisions are formally made has been deleted, leaving the provision completely open to every interpretation.

cc Proposed Interpretational Approach

The previous section has illustrated how important it is to determine exactly which stage in the decision-making process is the decisive one for the purposes of the POEM. This section endeavours to come up with a tenable interpretation and provide answers in this respect. For this purpose, the exclusion method is put into use. That is, first the stages of the decision-making process that cannot and should not underlie the POEM are excluded in order to discuss the ones that can and should do so.

First, it is submitted that the preparatory stage in the decision-making process should not be decisive for the purposes of the POEM. Systematically, it makes sense to exclude preparatory activities as a connection point for the allocation of taxing rights, i.e., for the purposes of the POEM and thereby of DTC residence which, again (section B.III.1. of the introduction), allocates persons to territories. This is because preparatory or auxiliary activities do not give rise to a PE and thus to source taxation according to

106. *See* the example in ATO, PCG, paras 51 et seq. There, the board members are residing and meeting in a state other than Australia (Ostasia). The board during its meetings 'reviews' the decisions/performance of a manager located in Australia where the operations of the corporation in question are also carried out. So, the decision-making stage has been transferred to the manager in Australia, and the board has reserved for itself the reviewing process which takes place in Ostasia. Still, this reviewing, or as it is called here the monitoring stage, suffices for the corporation in question to have its CMC in Ostasia and not in Australia. In this respect, *see also* below s. B.II.2.c.hh. of this chapter and especially the case law in n. 209.

107. Burgers (2007), p. 386.

Article 5(4) of the OECD MTC. If preparatory activities cannot give rise to source taxation,[108] then a fortiori the same should hold true for the purposes of residence.[109]

However, one could respond to this a fortiori argument that, since the preparatory activities do not give rise to a PE, then e contrario they should justify residence taxation. But the a fortiori argument brought forward here can be confirmed by another systematic argument: the fact that the OECD MTC explicitly excludes preparatory activities as ones that give rise to PE means that they could only give rise to a PE but they do not do so. If preparatory activities play a role for the purposes of the POEM, the exclusion in Article 5(4) of the OECD MTC would be redundant or, to put it more accurately, out of place.[110]

A further systematic argument underpins this position and provides grounds for a teleological argument as well. In particular, as elaborated below,[111] in principle the decisions of the board of directors are relevant for the purposes of the POEM. In other words, the personal element stricto sensu of this provision refers to the persons of the directors. And it can be assumed that the board of directors rarely prepares a decision; others make the preparations for them and they decide upon the alternatives presented to them.[112] Thus, if the preparatory stage were the decisive one, a curious situation could arise where the qualitative sub-element points to the persons preparing decisions and the personal element stricto sensu to the board of directors. If the persons preparing the decisions and the ones comprising the board of directors act from different states, there would be two POEMs, one based on the qualitative sub-element and the other based on the personal element stricto sensu. It becomes apparent that this would not only be systematically erroneous but would also run counter to the telos of the POEM, this being a preference criterion needing to point to one and only one state. In sum, the preparatory stage should not be relevant when determining the POEM.

But what about the implementation stage of decisions; couldn't that be relevant? As has been previously described (section B.II.1.b.cc. of this chapter), the strategic decisions are the relevant ones for the purposes of the POEM. In section B.II.1.b.aa. of this chapter, the characteristics of the strategic and operational decisions have been identified. The first ones set up the framework within which the second ones can move

108. Note that the argument is systematic and thus *de lege lata*. It is not contended that preparatory activities as a matter of policy should not, *de lege ferenda*, give rise to a PE. In fact, scholars have made exactly this argument. *See* Arnold (2003), pp. 486-487; Valta (2014), pp. 402-404; Castelon (2018), p. 207.

109. *See also* CBDT, Circular No. 6, para. 9(v): 'The existence in India of support functions that are preparatory and auxiliary in character will not be conclusive evidence that the conditions for establishing POEM in India have been satisfied.' By contrast, another OECD document, namely the OECD TPG, seem to connect the POEM to the place where the preparation of decisions takes place. In paras 9.123 and 9.124 the fact that 'decisions are prepared by Company A's head office in Country A before the meetings take place in Country Z [where company Z is located]' may give rise to 'the question about Company Z's place of effective management.'

110. So it seems that, according to the OECD, preparatory and auxiliary activities are so unimportant that they do not provide sufficient grounds for establishing a nexus both based on source and residence.

111. *See* above s. B.II.2.b.aa. of this chapter.

112. *See* above the previous section.

by implementing them. So, the implementation of strategic decisions amounts to making operational decisions. Consequently, if the implementation of strategic decisions is the relevant stage of decision-making, then the operational decisions (again, which constitute the implementation of strategic decisions) would be relevant. This would lead to an ad absurdum: we would exclude for the purposes of the relevant decision category the operational decisions only to come back to (what we have already excluded!) them for the purposes of the relevant stage in the decision-making process.

Through this exclusion method, it can be concluded that the preparatory and implementation stages in the decision-making process should not be relevant for the purposes of the POEM. What remains is the decision-making stricto sensu and the monitoring stage. Selecting any of them would not contradict the findings up until this point as well as with the proposition, which again is supported below, that the legally appointed directors are the relevant persons for the purposes of the POEM.

Directors are involved in the decision-making stricto sensu; in fact, they are the ones who, in principle, make the decisions. And they are the ones who monitor the state of affairs and may amend decisions.[113] Hence, both the decision-making stricto sensu and the monitoring stage in the decision-making process should be relevant for the purposes of the POEM. This begs the question of what happens when these decision-making stages take place in different states. For example, the decision-making part is delegated by the board to executive managers and the board reserves for itself the monitoring part. The board acts from state A, whereas the executive managers act from state B. Where is the POEM? In this case, the qualitative sub-element cannot provide an answer. One should turn to the personal element stricto sensu for an answer.[114] Section B.II.2.b.bb. of this chapter analyses this substance element. But first, the next section sums up the conclusions reached so far.

d Synthesis

In section B.II.1., the question of which decision-making functions are relevant for the purposes of the POEM, and in particular which quality should they have, has been dealt with. The following conclusions have been drawn:

- Business-related decisions are the relevant decision-making functions of the subsidiary, whereby the stand-alone perspective and a holistic approach are applied (section B.II.1.a.aa.).

113. *See* above n. 99 in this chapter.

114. Take the following case: Decision-making stricto sensu and monitoring are divided between two states and are taken by the same persons, which are also the relevant ones for the purposes of the POEM, i.e., the board of directors (*see* above s. B.II.2.b.aa. of this chapter). In this case the personal element cannot provide an answer. In such cases, the stage of decision-making is immaterial. What is important is from which place the most important decisions are taken. For example, if in one state decisions that influence the subsidiary's economic well-being more than the decisions taken in the other state, then the POEM is in the former state. *See also* the analysis in s. B.II.3.a. of this chapter and the example in n. 231.

- The existence of business operations in the state where these decision-making functions take place is not necessary (section B.II.1.a.bb.).
- The scale and nature of the business operations do not play a role in the purposes of the POEM. As for the scale of activities, it is problematic that the POEM does not take account of them, but this problem can be solved by applying, at a second stage, other rules that should do so, like the LOB and transfer pricing rules (section B.II.1.a.cc.).
- In this work, the interpretation of the POEM has shown that the strategic decisions should be the relevant ones for the purposes of the rule (sections B.II.1.b.aa.-B.II.1.b.cc.).
- The stages of decision-making stricto sensu and the monitoring stage are the relevant stages in the decision-making process for the purposes of the POEM (sections B.II.1.c.aa.-cc.).

2 Personal Element Stricto Sensu: Which Persons Carry Out the Necessary Decision-Making Functions?

One of the sub-elements of the personal element of substance is, according to the definition given in section D. of the introduction, the personal element stricto sensu which refers to the identification of the relevant persons for the purposes of the personal element. The next sections endeavour to find out who these persons are for the purposes of the POEM.

a Economic Reality: Peculiarities in the Case of Subsidiaries

Normally, the owner of an asset vests also has control over the asset. 'To "own land" usually means to have the right to till (or not to till) the soil, to mine the soil, to *offer* those rights for sale, etc. ... It is not *the* resource itself which is owned; it is a bundle, or a portion, of rights to *use* a resource that is owned.'[115] But to own corporate shares does not give their owner the right to decide how this corporation 'is used'. It has already been established in section A. of the introduction that one of the basic features of a corporation is that it has centralized management. It is up to a corporation's management to determine its 'use'. What is being referred to here is the separation of ownership (shareholders) and control (managers) that takes place in the corporation.[116] But why is that? Economists offer answers to this question.[117]

115. Alchian/Demsetz (1973), p. 17.
116. This argument has first been made by Berle/Means (1932) in their ground-breaking work. *See* there, for instance, at p. 118 the conclusion that '[f]ormerly assumed to be merely a function of ownership, control now appears as a separate, separable factor'.
117. The following analysis as to the reasons leading to the separation of ownership and control in the corporation is based on Bainbridge (2018), pp. 293 et seq.

First, shareholders do not possess the necessary expertise to manage a corporation.[118] Their agenda consists of minimizing the risk of their investment by diversifying it, i.e., investing in as many different corporations in as many different sectors as possible.[119] Of course, they are probably not able to manage the corporation's business successfully. So, they leave this task to specialized managers.[120] Second, they do not possess the necessary information on the corporation's business in order to manage it, and, to the extent they do so, significant information asymmetries exist between them. It is cheaper for them to gain a general overview before their investment, but going deeper than that would result in enormous costs which investors would not be willing to bear. Third, shareholders have different interests. Arguably, de facto all of them want to make money but there may exist completely diverging views as to how, when, and where the corporation ought to make money. Fourth, and lastly, it is difficult and inefficient for, possibly, thousands of shareholders to come together and manage a corporation ('collective action problem'). Again, a centralized player is the best solution to this problem.

The four grounds upon which separation of ownership and control in the corporation is based are challenged in the case of subsidiary corporations. First, the parent sets up the subsidiary with a specific plan in mind[121] and it knows exactly how the subsidiary is to be used to fulfil this plan. Of course, certain peculiarities of the region, language, culture, etc., in the subsidiary jurisdiction necessitate the existence of an independent management which has the knowledge to cope with them.[122] But control by the parent can be more intense than in the case of 'rationally apathetic'[123] investors who diversify risk and change shareholdings every other day. Second, the problem of information asymmetries does not exist in the case of subsidiaries. The parent is (possibly) the only shareholder. And its interest in controlling its subsidiary is antecedent to its interest in acquiring information about its business. For example, and as will be dealt with in detail below (section B.II.2.c.gg. of this chapter), the parent may even give management positions in the subsidiary to its own managers so as to intensify this effect. Third, there are no different interests; the subsidiary needs to be managed in one way; and that is the parent's way.[124] Fourth, collective action problems do not exist in the case of subsidiaries by definition, where only, or primarily, the parent exists as a shareholder.

118. Fama/Jensen (1983), p. 330.
119. Porter (1987), p. 46.
120. Fama (1980), p. 295.
121. It is because of this fact that 'head office managers think in terms of assigning roles to their subsidiary companies and how to control them', while 'subsidiary managers frequently think in terms of autonomy and strategic choice'. These diametrically different perceptions in the subsidiary role may lead to conflict. Birkinshaw et al. (2000), p. 324.
122. This goal is called 'local responsiveness'. It may be incompatible with the goals set by the headquarters for the group as a whole which also leads to conflict. *See* Schotter/Beamisch (2012), pp. 204 et seq.
123. Bainbridge (2018), p. 294; in detail Fleckner (2010), p. 84.
124. Birkinshaw et al. (2006), p. 688 'In such cases [subsidiaries whose shares are concentrated in the hands of one person], concerns about agency costs do not really apply: either the owners and the managers are one and the same; or the owner is viewed as being an "insider" who is potentially working in collaboration with the firm's managers.'

From this analysis, it follows that in the corporation a central decision-maker exists which does not coincide with the owner of the 'asset' corporation,[125] as is in the case of other goods where ownership and control coincide. However, in the case of subsidiaries, the autonomy of this separate authority is challenged because the owner of the subsidiary can successfully vest control over it.[126] The question is now how this economic reality affects the concept of the POEM.

b *The Relevant Persons from an Institutional Perspective*

aa The Rule: Legally Appointed Directors as the Relevant Persons

Corporate residence takes into account the economic reality surrounding the management of corporations. Principally, both for the purposes of domestic residence tests and for the purposes of the POEM, reliance is placed upon the persons who, pursuant to corporate law or the articles of association, are entrusted with the management of the corporation whose residence is in question ('legally appointed directors'). So, corporations adopting a one-board structure are *regularly* managed for the purposes of domestic substance-oriented tests by that one board.[127] In contrast, in the case of a two-board structure, things can become more complicated.

In short, as already mentioned in section B.II.1.b.bb. of this chapter, the two-board structure comprises a management and a supervisory board. Consequently, the question arises as to which of the two boards is the relevant one for the substance-oriented residence criterion. Or are maybe both relevant?[128] What happens if the managing board meets and acts in state A, while the supervising board acts from

125. Note that referring to the corporation as an asset and to its shareholders as owners of the asset is legally not correct and used only for euphoric/illustrative purposes. *See* Stout (2007), p. 804.
126. If one takes the typology of control structures propounded by Berle and Means, it becomes apparent that the greater the degree of ownership, the greater the power to control. They saw five stages of control: '(1) control through almost complete ownership, (2) majority control, (3) control through legal device without majority ownership, (4) minority control, and (5) management control'. *See* Berle/Means (1932), p. 70. The control over a subsidiary's operations falls under categories (1) and (2) which demonstrates that in this case ownership and control are separated in the least possible degree.
127. *Australia:* High Court of Australia, *Bywater Investments Limited v. Commissioner of Taxation*, at para. 41.
    Canada: Supreme Court of Canada, 12 Apr. 2012, *Fundy Settlement v. Her Majesty The Queen*, SCR (2012), p. 520 (at para. 9).
    India: CBDT, Circular No. 6, para. 8.2.
    South Africa: SARS, Interpretation Note 6(2), p. 8 (at s. 4.2.3.).
    As to the *United Kingdom see* below in text.
128. This could be argued based on the following reasoning: the board of directors is entrusted both with managerial and supervisory activities. So if the POEM refers to the board as the relevant organ, then in cases where two organs exist, the one entrusted with the managerial activities while the other with the supervisory one, both organs 'equal' one board and thus both are relevant. *See*, in the context of Article 16 of the OECD MTC, Cordewener (2021), para. 35; Orlet/Schuch (2017), s. 7.4.2.

state B? Granted, this case does not exist empirically, or it can at least be asserted that it has not been observed by jurisprudence.[129]

It must be said that the supervisory board may have according to law - which is the case in Germany - or the articles of association a veto right regarding decisions made by the management board which renders it a 'co-manager' of the corporation.[130] If this is the case, according to Joachim Englisch, 'it would ... typically be relevant where the members of the supervisory board discuss and decide about the company's commercial strategy together with the chairman of the management board, rather than where the board of management regularly meets or from which location its members coordinate the day-to-day business'.[131] So depending on the circumstances of the case[132] either the management board only or the management board together with the 'co-managing' supervisory board are relevant in two-board structures.

bb The Exception: Management Usurpation

However, the legally appointed directors present only the starting point when it comes to defining the place from which a corporation is managed. And this holds true all the more in the case of subsidiaries. In particular, as early as 1959, the peculiarities governing the management of subsidiaries led to refutation of the aforementioned rule. In the landmark case *Unit Construction*, the House of Lords enunciated an exception to that rule.[133]

In this case, the taxpayer, Unit Construction Co Ltd, a subsidiary of the ultimate UK parent Alfred Booth & Co Ltd, made subvention payments to three co-subsidiaries with residence (based on their POI) in Kenya. Unit Construction Co Ltd claimed a deduction of these payments. Section 20 of the Finance Act (1953) gave it the right for subvention payments between associated companies, whereby only companies resident in the UK (section 20(9)) qualified for this rule. For this purpose, Unit Construction Co Ltd also claimed that the subsidiaries incorporated in Kenya were UK residents because their CMC was in the UK. The UK Revenue rejected this claim since the Kenyan subsidiaries' articles of association contained provisions placing the management and control of their business in the hands of their directors who resided and met in Kenya. According to the rule stipulated above, the CMC of the subsidiaries should also be found to be in Kenya, where the legally appointed directors of the subsidiaries met and acted.

129. *See* the two major studies on this subject where no case law is cited: Maisto et al. (2018), p. 23; Pötgens et al. (2014a), pp. 378-380.
130. Cools (2016), pp. 566-567.
131. Englisch (2009a), pp. 509-510. *Contra* Ismer/Blank (2021), para. 279.
132. *See* Hoge Raad, 23 Sep. 1992, No. 27.293, BNB 1993/79. *See* Pötgens et al. (2014a), p. 380: 'Although the Supreme Court's starting point was that effective management in the context of a two-tier board system is normally exercised by the board of directors, it offered sufficient flexibility in taking into account circumstances in which other persons or bodies actually pursue the company's policy and make the relevant strategic decisions.'
133. House of Lords, 30 Nov. 1959, *Unit Construction Co Ltd v. Bullock*, TC (1959), p. 712.

The House of Lords, reversing the Court of Appeal's decision, did not accept this formal approach. A passage of *Viscount Simonds'* judgment in this decision is illustrative: 'The business is not the less managed in London because it ought to be managed in Kenya. Its residence is determined by the solid facts, not by the terms of its constitution, however imperative.'[134]

In a case where 'truly no precedent can be found',[135] the House of Lords demonstrated that law takes economic reality into account. The analysis in section B.II.2.a. of this chapter has shown that a parent is able to exert excessive control over the business of its subsidiary in which case the parent may *usurp* the management from the persons who are by law entrusted with it. In such a case, domestic substance-oriented residence tests following the UK paradigm give priority to what is actually happening over the legal assignment of management powers.[136] It is noteworthy that the German Reichsfinanzhof had already propounded this axiom in 1936,[137] although it cannot be assumed that this judgment somehow influenced the House of Lords' judgment in *Unit Construction* since the German judgment was not cited therein.

In the same vein, courts have interpreted the POEM as a factual test, whereby legal and factual decision-makers can coincide, but when they do not, the factual decision-makers are decisive. Again, UK case law has paved the way for others to follow. In *Laerstate*,[138] the First-Tier Tribunal (FTT) had to deal with the residence of a taxpayer incorporated in the Netherlands ('Laerstate'). Since 1992, Laerstate had held shares in a UK corporation ('Lonrho'). The only shareholder of Laerstate, an individual referred to as Mr Bock, was also one of its directors. The other director of Laerstate, Mr Trapman, was a close business partner of Mr Bock and succumbed to Mr Bock's wishes when it came to making decisions regarding the business of Laerstate. Mr Bock became director in Lonrho in 1993 and since then he resided in the UK. In 1996, Laerstate sold

134. House of Lords, *Unit Construction Co Ltd v. Bullock*, at p. 736.
135. *Ibid.*
136. *Australia:* High Court of Australia, 31 May 1972, *Esquire Nominees Ltd v. Federal Commissioner of Taxation*, CLR (1972), p. 177 (at para. 27).
Canada: Supreme Court of Canada, *Fundy Settlement v. Her Majesty The Queen*, at para. 9.
India: CBDT, Circular No. 6, para. 8.
Italy: Corte Suprema di Cassazione, 28 Dec. 2016, No. 27113, which, according to Beretta (2017), pp. 256 and 257, ruled that '[t]he of effective management is a *factual* criterion' and 'the managerial functions [have to be] ... *truly* performed by th[e] entity' (emphasis added).
South Africa: SARS, Interpretation Note 6(2), p. 7 (at s. 4.2.).
Switzerland: Bundesgericht, 16 May 2013, 2C_1086/2012, 2C_1087/2012, at para. 2.5.4.; and more recently Bundesgericht, 1 Feb. 2019, 2C_627/2017, at para. 2.3.2.
The Netherlands: Hoge Raad, 23 Sep. 1992, No. 27.293, BNB 1993/79. *See* Pötgens et al. (2014a), p. 380.
137. *See* Reichsfinanzhof, I A 150/36, p. 805: '[w]hile the term "domicile" is generally defined by law, the question of where the center of the business management (the place of management) is located must be answered according to the actual circumstances of the individual case'. And: '[t]he fact that the key management may not only be in the hands of persons who are legally appointed to represent a company (board of directors or managing director), but may also be exercised by any other person, has rightly been established by the tax court'. (Author's unofficial translations). *See also* more recent German case law: Finanzgericht of Munich, 10 V 1479/20, at paras 70-71.
138. UK First-Tier Tribunal, 11 Aug. 2009, *Laerstate BV v. Commissioners for Her Majesty's Revenue and Customs*, UKFTT (2009), p. 209 (TC).

the shares in Lonrho. In 1997, Her Majesty's Revenue and Customs (HMRC) viewed Laerstate as a UK resident and assessed the company accordingly as subject to corporation tax in respect of the gain arising from the disposal of the shares. This was because its CMC was considered to be in the UK, since 'the board [of Laerstate] did not function as a board of management but ... one dominant director, who was at all relevant times the 100% shareholder [Mr Bock] ... made the business decisions'.[139] The FTT upheld HMRC's viewpoint and regarded Laerstate as a UK resident.[140]

The POEM of Laerstate was in question because it was stipulated as the tiebreaker in Article 4(3) of the DTC between the UK and Netherlands (1980). Since Laerstate was a resident in the UK because of its CMC being located there and was also a resident of the Netherlands because of it being incorporated there, the residence-residence conflict had to be solved. The FTT, citing the Special Commissioners' decision on the POEM of a trustee in *Smallwood*, ruled that the adjective '"effective" should be understood in the sense of the French "effective" (siége de direction effective) which connotes *real*'.[141] 'Accordingly, having regard to the ordinary meaning of the words in their context and in the light of their object and purpose' the FTT approached 'the issue of POEM as considering in which state the *real* management of the [company] is found'.[142]

The FTT's argumentation is not compelling. In particular, the word 'effective' does not have to be interpreted as meaning the 'real' management. One could argue, for instance, that the POEM is the place in which decisions take effect, i.e., where they are implemented. This would also bring clarity to the question of which stage in the decision-making process is relevant for the purposes of the POEM.[143] However, interpreting the POEM as the place where 'real' management takes place can be underpinned by other arguments.

First, this interpretation is in line with the Commentary, which underlines that '*facts and circumstances* must be examined' and the decisions must be made 'in substance' in the POEM.[144] Second, it is submitted that this interpretation is in line with the POEM's telos. In particular, the OECD's intention when choosing the POEM as a tiebreaker was to depart from 'a purely formal criterion'.[145] Adhering to the persons who are legally the decision-makers of the subsidiary and not taking into account the facts of the case would frustrate the purpose of the rule. For example, a parent company could set up a corporation in a low-tax state and appoint as its director an accountant residing in that state who has nothing to do with the business of the subsidiary. It becomes apparent that interpreting the POEM in a strictly formalistic way

139. *Ibid.*, at para. 26(2).
140. *Ibid.*, at paras 27 et seq.
141. *Ibid.*, at para. 48 (emphasis added).
142. *Ibid.*
143. This is an approach taken by Robert Couzin. He recommends that '[c]orporate residence under a management and control test could be determined by reference to *effective* rather than strategic management, on the theory that it is more difficult to shuttle *executives* about than directors'. (Emphasis added). *See* Couzin (2002), p. 262.
144. Paragraph 24 second and third sentence of the Commentary (2014) on Article 4 (emphasis added).
145. FC/WP2(57)1, p. 6.

would run counter to the telos of the rule. Consequently, the grounds upon which the substance-oriented POEM is justified would be eliminated if it were not to refer to the 'real' decision-makers.

It is concluded that both domestic substance-oriented and the POEM have a common starting point but also a common aim when determining which person makes the decisions with regard to the corporation whose residence or POEM is in question. Their starting point is the law, but their aim is to find the real, factual, substantive, etc., decision-makers. Of course, placing emphasis on substance over form has a great disadvantage: it is much more difficult for the taxpayer, in our case the subsidiary, to assess whether form and substance coincide. The following section presents criteria to determine where form and substance can diverge with respect to the POEM of subsidiaries.

c *When Do Outsiders Actually Manage the Subsidiary?*

It has become clear that the POEM is amenable to different interpretations in every respect. Countries interpret it differently as regards almost all aspects of its qualitative sub-element, as already seen in section B.II.1. of this chapter. Andrés Báez Moreno has called it an 'indeterminate legal concept'.[146] The fact that the POEM has since its creation remained an indeterminate legal concept is attributable to two basic factors: frequency and heterogeneity.

In particular, economic literature differentiates between rules and standards according to these two factors.[147] Rules are imbued with content *ex ante* because it is far more efficient for the legislature to do so instead of leaving this task to adjudication. It is cheaper, first, because they regulate frequent individual behaviour and, second, because this behaviour is not heterogeneous. The POEM is a standard according to this distinction.[148] It regulates, at least in the eyes of the OECD,[149] a phenomenon that does not occur often (lacking frequency) and a highly heterogeneous series of facts: defining residence can be immensely different when we deal with an active subsidiary with thousands of employees, on the one hand, and an SPV, on the other.

The POEM being a standard, or an indeterminate legal concept, means that it needs to be filled with life *ex post* by the judiciary.[150] The next sections demonstrate how courts have interpreted the POEM with regard to the special issue of the *usurpation of management* (i.e., the act of outsiders taking control of the management) of a subsidiary. Thus, an inductive method is followed to 'make a rule out of the standard' or, as Frederik Schauer calls this process, to 'rulify' the standard.[151]

146. Báez Moreno (2020), p. 824.
147. Kaplow (1992), pp. 563-564; Korobkin (2000), p. 42.
148. On the OECD Model in general as a standard-based regime, *see* Baistrocchi (2008), pp. 386 et seq.
149. *See* FC/WP2(56)1, p. 4: 'That a corporation is regarded as fully liable to tax by two states as a consequence of attachment to each of them may be a *rare occurrence in practice*' (emphasis added).
150. Schauer (2005), p. 814.
151. *Ibid.*

aa The Starting Point: Distinguishing Merely Influencing from Dictating

If one takes into consideration that the rule is that the subsidiary is managed for the purposes of both the POEM and domestic substance-oriented residence criteria by the organ legally entrusted with this task (section B.II.2.b.aa. of this chapter), every person outside of this group of persons is an 'outsider' for the purposes of these tests. Not only persons not possessing an employee relationship or a management position in the subsidiary, such as accountants, lawyers, etc., are considered outsiders but also the parent itself, its directors and staff, the CEO of the subsidiary, etc., are also 'outsiders' so long as they do not pertain to the constitutional organ entrusted with the management of the subsidiary. In fact, that is also how case law has understood this term: 'an "outsider" is a person who is not, himself, a participant in the formal process (a board meeting or a general meeting) through which the relevant constitutional organ fulfils its function'.[152] So, the question arises as to when these outsiders actually manage the subsidiary instead of its legally appointed directors.

Taking into account that directors take advice from many persons (e.g., executive staff, accounting firms, external business advisors, etc.), there must be cases which are not suspicious and ones that cross the border to the usurpation of management. This is actually the starting point of the analysis: dividing the harmless cases from the ones where the suspicion of usurpation by outsiders exists. Only after it has been established that a case bears the mark of suspicion can it be ascertained whether the suspicion can be crystallized into a fact based on the criteria that are henceforth presented.

This approach is derived from UK case law on the CMC. In *Wood v. Holden*, the UK Court of Appeal stipulated that 'it is essential to recognize the distinction (in concept, at least) between the role of an "outsider" in *proposing, advising and influencing* the decisions which the constitutional organs take in fulfilling their functions and the role of an outsider who *dictates* the decisions which are to be taken'.[153] Accordingly, one has to draw a dividing line distinguishing the cases where the outsiders merely influence the board of the subsidiary from the ones where they factually decide on its behalf.

The overt case is the one where the board completely stands by and lets the outsiders do its job, i.e., the outsiders take 'every decision of any importance that concern[s] the running of the businesses [of the subsidiary]'.[154] This is an extreme and therefore rare case, as the board of the subsidiary can easily pretend that it makes all the decisions by formally signing them and pretending that they took place during board meetings. What happens then? How can one distinguish the mere influencing from dictating when the subsidiary board officially makes all decisions? The following sections present criteria developed by case law to distinguish merely influencing from dictating (and thus usurping the management from the legally appointed directors).

152. UK Court of Appeal, *Wood v. Holden*, at para. 27.
153. *Ibid.*
154. This has been in the case in House of Lords, *Unit Construction Co Ltd v. Bullock*, at p. 737.

bb The Role of the Existence of an Enforceable Right and Managerial Liability

One could argue that in order for the outsiders to dictate and not merely influence the decisions of the legally appointed directors of the subsidiary, the former must have an enforceable right ensuring that the latter follow suit. In fact, this argument was raised by the counsels of taxpayers in the *Bywater* case,[155] litigated before the High Court of Australia (HCA), in order to contest that the management of the subsidiary in question, Bywater Investments Ltd, was usurped by the sole director of the parent who also was its sole shareholder.[156] The HCA rejected this argument, stating that 'the absence of legal power to control a board of directors is not determinative of whether that board is actually itself exercising central management and control'.[157] Canadian[158] and UK[159] case law also refer to the effective (and not legal) enforceability of an agreement.[160]

It is submitted that this is a consequent approach. If substance-oriented residence criteria are not dependent on the formalities of the articles of association and the legal provisions regarding the persons entrusted with the management, then they should not be dependent on the legal enforceability of the agreement that the subsidiary's management has with the outsiders. This would only transmit the problem to another level. In other words, the POEM would still be a formal test because in order for an outsider to usurp the management from the legally appointed directors, a formal agreement would be necessary. So, the legal enforceability of the right of the outsider to usurp the management of the subsidiary is not a relevant criterion; it suffices that the outsider factually does usurp the management from the legally appointed directors.

A similar problem relates to the role of managerial responsibility. One could argue that '[t]he personal attribution of management activities is effected based on ... who can be held accountable for actions, in particular by the enterprise, its stakeholders and/or others'.[161] In the author's opinion, this argument must be rejected. As the Tax Court of Münster ruled, albeit in another context, 'th[e] purely formal liability cannot replace the substantive responsibility for the entrepreneurial decisions characterising the business objective of C Ltd. [the subsidiary in this case]'.[162] Taking into

155. High Court of Australia, *Bywater Investments Limited v. Commissioner of Taxation.*
156. *Ibid.*, at paras 31 et seq.
157. *Ibid.*, at para. 69.
158. Tax Court of Canada, 9 Sep. 2009, *Garrons et. al. v. Her Majesty the Queen*, TCC (2009), p. 450 (at para. 191).
159. UK First-Tier Tribunal, *Richard Lee and Nigel Bunter v. HMRC*, at para. 75.
160. *See also* the Indian tax authorities, including de facto control, CBDT, Circular No. 6, para. 8.2(a).
161. Töben/Birk (2016), p. 523.
162. Finanzgericht of Münster, 20 Nov. 2015, 10 K 1410/12 F, EFG (2016), p. 453 (at para. 60) (author's unofficial translation). Agreeing with this finding, Haase (2016), p. 769. This case concerned the application of the CJEU doctrine on wholly artificial arrangements. On this doctrine, *see* below s. B.II. of Ch. 4.

account that the POEM is a factual test, by concentrating on who can be held liable for corporate decisions one would make a formal criterion out of the POEM.[163]

cc Ill-Informed Managers

The first criterion to determine whether the legally appointed directors are the ones that in fact make the decisions offers us the *Wood v. Holden* saga. In particular, the Special Commissioners underscored for the first time the significance of the information upon which the legally appointed directors make their decisions: '[t]he decisions must at least to some extent be informed decisions'.[164] Although the level of information that the legally appointed directors possess has been dismissed by the Court of Appeal which asserted that '[i]ll-informed or ill-advised decisions taken in the management of a company remain management decisions',[165] subsequent case law accepted and expanded upon this criterion.

In *Laerstate*, the Tribunal judges developed a four-step test that concentrated on the information that the decision-makers possess.[166] In step 1, the decision-makers have no information and thus are 'mindless[ly] signing' documents. In step 2, 'the directors have the absolute minimum amount of information that a person would need to have in order to be able to make a decision at all'. In step 3, 'the directors have … at least the absolute minimum information referred to in the previous [sentence] but less information than a reasonable director would require in order sensibly to decide'. Finally, '[a]t the other extreme is where the directors have sufficient information to make an informed decision'. In steps 3 and 4, the decision-makers possess sufficient information in order to make a decision and thus it can be assumed that, regardless of whether they decide in accordance with the influence of outsiders, they are the persons managing the subsidiary's affairs. By contrast, in steps 1 and 2 the situation is the other way around; the legally appointed persons are either mindlessly signing or they simply do not have enough (although they have some) information to decide, but do so anyway.

Apart from this decision, no other case law could be found where this step approach requiring sufficient and not only minimum information has been adopted. In the author's opinion, a minimum amount of information should suffice. It would put enormous pressure on courts to ascertain and discern a minimum amount of information from a sufficient level of information. The fact that no future case law follows the step approach is illustrative in this respect. Against this background and since, as shown in the next sections, there are also other criteria pointing to the usurpation of management, the existence of a minimum of information should suffice in order to

163. Similar would be a criterion attached to whose decisions bind the company which should also be rejected. *See*, referring to the CMC, Avery Jones (2021), pp. 53-54: 'the correct test is who really made the decision, not whether the actions of the directors bound the company'.
164. Special Commissioners, 18 May 2004, *Wood v. Holden*, STC (2004), p. 416 (SCD) (at para. 145).
165. UK Court of Appeal, *Wood v. Holden*, at para. 43.
166. UK First-Tier Tribunal, *Laerstate BV v. Commissioners for Her Majesty's Revenue and Customs*, at paras 34-37.

regard the relevant decision-makers as informed for the purposes of determining where the POEM is located.[167]

The question is why, to begin with, information should be such a strong indicator for management usurpation. Examining the findings regarding the stages of decision-making could shed light on this issue. In section B.II.2.c.aa. of this chapter, it has been laid down that decision-making consists, in principle, of looking at multiple alternative ways of approaching a problem and choosing one of them as the appropriate solution to the problem. How can managers decide in favour of an alternative if they do not even know what these alternatives mean for the business of the company they manage? So, decision-making prerequisites really knowing what is being decided; and knowing prerequisites having the appropriate information. Consequently, the UK Court of Appeal's judgment in the *Wood v. Holden* case was a cacophony in an otherwise well-established and elaborated case law according to which the legally appointed directors must have sufficient information regarding the issues upon which they decide.

dd The Role of Managerial Knowledge/Expertise

In order to 'know' something, one does not only need the appropriate information, as stated above. If you give the author the appropriate information to fly an aeroplane, he still will not know how to do it because he will be missing something essential: knowledge and expertise.[168] Exactly the same applies with regard to directing the affairs of a company. The persons entrusted with this task do not only need appropriate information but they also need to have the knowledge and expertise to do so.[169] This criterion is accepted by courts[170] and tax authorities[171] interpreting domestic substance-

167. An additional argument is that for the purpose of other substance requirements (in transfer pricing; *see* below s. B.III.2.a. of Ch. 2), where information plays a role, also only a minimum of information is required. So interpreting the POEM substance as requiring only a minimum of information leads to an alignment of these two substance requirements.
168. What is being said here is that knowledge and information are not synonymous. Knowledge prerequisites information but also understanding and skills that are gained through education or experience which then lead to a more refined processing of the information at hand.
169. In fact, it is one of the basic assumptions of the transaction costs theory of the firm (on this theory, *see* s. A. of the introduction) 'that economic actors have the capacity to look ahead, recognize potential hazards, and factor these into the organizational design'. *See* Williamson (1999), p. 311.
170. *Canada:* Tax Court of Canada, 17 Jul. 2018, *Landbouwbedrijf Backx BV v. Her Majesty the Queen*, TCC (2018), p. 142 (at para. 43) referring to the lacking experience of the sole director appointed by the shareholders confirmed by Canadian Federal Court of Appeal, 12 Dec. 2019, *Landbouwbedrijf Backx BV v. R*, FCA (2019), p. 310 (at para. 10). The FCA referred the case back to the Tax Court but the residence in Canada and the application of the CMC was not at issue so that the latest decision of the Federal Court of Appeal is not relevant for this work.

    Germany: Finanzgericht of Munich, 10 V 1479/20, at para. 78, where the low management compensation pointed to the existence of management only on paper. And low management compensation could be related to unqualified managers.

    The Netherlands: Hoge Raad, 17 Dec. 2004, No. 39.720, BNB 2005/105 and BNB 2005/106. *See* Gooijer (2019), p. 94: 'the court referred to the lack of the relevant expertise of the statutory board'.

oriented criteria and could be also a useful pointer when determining which persons exercise 'real' management.

Nevertheless, the *Wood v. Holden* saga again puts forward a dissenting viewpoint. According to the High Court judge, 'no-one would suggest that the central control and management ... [does] not rest with [the] board' simply 'because of inadequacies in [the directors'] performance'.[172] In fact, there is some truth to that statement. Tax law cannot 'punish' MNEs for choosing the wrong directors. But the fact that the director does not have any idea about the business of the group (information) and cannot add value to the subsidiary's performance simply because they are incapable thereof is at least a pointer or constitutes, more accurately, a *rebuttable presumption* that this person may not run the company, but someone else is doing it for them.

Consider, however, the case that the subsidiary's business is so 'simple' that all that is required in order for the legally appointed directors to do their jobs is to follow the directions of an outsider, e.g., the parent. This argument was raised by the counsels of taxpayers in *Bywater*.[173] The HCA rejected the argument on the grounds that the business operations of the subsidiary in question were not comparable to the one of an SPV 'that exist[s] for the purpose of only one transaction'.[174] E contrario, the High Court is implying here that if the subsidiary in question were an SPV or a similar subsidiary with very limited business operations, this argument would apply. In other words, in the case of SPVs and subsidiaries with similarly limited operations, it should not matter whether the legally appointed persons have enough information and expertise regarding the operations of the company they manage since the only thing they have to do is follow the instructions given by an outsider who has the information and expertise required.

This line of reasoning cannot be followed. If a subsidiary is to be managed by an outsider in the first place (e.g., the parent) because its operations are simple and the directors are only designated to create a false pretence, then how can it be tenably asserted that the directors run the company? Put another way, why does the parent pay the directors if someone behind the scenes is making the decisions anyway? For example, why does the parent not manage the subsidiary directly from its headquarters? What is being said here is the fact that the business of a subsidiary demands its management to follow the directions of an outsider does not exclude the fact that this outsider is in reality making the decisions; the directors are merely puppets who purport to act in a certain place for tax purposes, *inter alia*, for the purposes of the POEM.

United Kingdom: UK First-Tier Tribunal, *Richard Lee and Nigel Bunter v. HMRC*, at para. 76.

171. *Australia:* ATO, TR 2018/5, para. 29.
South Africa: SARS, Interpretation Note 6(2), p. 8 (at s. 4.2.3.).
172. UK High Court, *Wood v. Holden*, at para. 68.
173. High Court of Australia, *Bywater Investments Limited v. Commissioner of Taxation*, at para. 36.
174. In fact, the Judges compared the taxpayer with the SPV from the *Wood v. Holden* case. *See ibid.*, at para. 87.

A last issue to be clarified relates to the type of knowledge that is expected from the legally appointed directors in order for them to manage a subsidiary. Should they have technical, economic (i.e., knowledge that enables them to evaluate business decisions as to their profit potential), or both types of knowledge? In the author's opinion, it makes sense to require that the legally appointed directors possess both types of knowledge. Even if they are only entrusted with the strategic decisions related to the subsidiary's business, which, as already submitted in section B.II.1.b.bb. of this chapter, is predominantly the case, at least some of them[175] need to be able to control the activities of the lower levels of management taking the operational decisions, which are often of a technical nature.[176] And it goes without saying that they need to be able to evaluate business decisions as to their profit potential since their performance is measured according to the profits the subsidiary generates for the shareholders.[177] From this, it follows that it suffices that the legally appointed directors are lacking either technical or economic knowledge in order for the presumption of usurpation to kick in.

In summary, lack of knowledge and expertise as well as insufficient information are tenable rebuttable presumptions that the legally appointed directors are only managing the company in pretence; instead, the persons having the knowledge/ expertise and information are doing so. As far as knowledge is concerned, in the author's opinion both technical and economic knowledge must be found to exist within the board of the subsidiary. If one of the knowledge types is missing, the usurpation presumption takes effect.

ee Directors Deciding Against the Interests of the Subsidiary They Manage

Another pointer as to the usurpation of management, propounded in the *Untelrab* judgment of the Special Commissioners, 'is whether the directors would ... [decline] to do something improper or inadvisable; if they would then this would point towards the conclusion that there [is] no control by the parent'.[178] Put another way, if the legally

175. So not all directors need to be experts in everything. It should suffice that some directors possess economic, while some others possess only technical knowledge (in relation to the business of the subsidiary). *See* Grant (2003), p. 493: 'strategic planning is a process where decision makers share and synthesize their different knowledge sets and surface their implicit assumptions and the mental models'.
176. It must be said, though, 'that at lower levels of administrative responsibility, the principal need is for technical and human skills. At higher levels, technical skill becomes relatively less important'. *See* Katz (1955).
177. Referring to corporations from the oil industry, Grant (2003), pp. 502 and 506: 'Macroeconomic forecasts provided the basis for predictions of the demand, supply, and prices of oil and refined products upon which outputs, revenues, profits, and capital investment requirements were projected. Hence, all the planning departments included an economics unit typically headed by a professional economist.' Although '[d]uring the 1980s and 1990s, all the companies reduced their forecasting efforts and downsized or eliminated their economist staff'.
178. Special Commissioners, 22 Nov. 1995, *Untelrab Ltd & Ors v. McGregor*, STC (1996), p. 1 (SCD) (at para. 75); *see*, however, prior to this decision Australian jurisprudence had already placed some emphasis on this criterion High Court of Australia, *Esquire Nominees Ltd v. Federal Commissioner of Taxation*, at para. 28: 'If ... [the company's accountants] had instructed the

appointed directors enter into transactions to the detriment of the company they manage, it is again rebuttably presumed that the management does not rest with them.

It is quite interesting how this criterion has been interpreted by subsequent decisions. In *Development Securities*,[179] the UK Upper Tribunal overturned the decision of the FTT basically by refuting an argument based on the grounds of the criterion presented above. In particular, the residence of subsidiaries incorporated in Jersey was in question in this case. The subsidiaries incurred capital losses by entering into uncommercial transactions (acquisition of capital assets at a loss) in order to implement a tax avoidance scheme intended by their parent resident in the UK, i.e., Development Securities plc. It was important for the purposes of the tax avoidance scheme that the subsidiaries were deemed residents of Jersey and not the UK at the time of entering into the aforementioned transactions. Thus, the central question dealt with in this decision was whether the management of the subsidiaries was usurped by their UK parent, which instructed them to enter into the deleterious transactions for the purposes of the scheme. The FTT found that the management of the Jersey subsidiaries was in the hands of their parent because 'the Jersey directors were acting under what they considered was an "instruction" or "order" from the parent'.[180]

The Upper Tribunal misinterpreted the FTT's reasoning. In simple terms, it pointed out that the FTT argued in favour of the management's usurpation because of the improper or inadvisable nature of transactions and the breach of directors' duties.[181] As the Court of Appeal subsequently clarified, what the FTT actually said was that the directors entered into uncommercial transactions from the perspective of the subsidiary and did so 'without any engagement with the substantive decision'.[182] So, the Court of Appeal espouses the *Unterlab* judicature but enriches it with some new elements: the transaction must not be abstractly speaking improper, but uncommercial from the perspective of the subsidiary, and the directors must not have been actively engaged in the decision-making process. If these conditions are fulfilled, then management can be seen as having been usurped. The author agrees with the commerciality test, as formed by the Court of Appeal, but wishes to introduce another consideration/requirement for its use.

In particular, there may be cases where entering into an uncommercial transaction is dictated by law. This has been the case in *Development Securities*. In particular, as the Upper Tribunal ruled, the Jersey directors did a good job by entering into the

directors to do something which they considered improper or inadvisable, I do not believe that they would have acted on the instruction.'

179. UK Upper Tribunal, 5 Jun. 2019, *Development Securities plc and others v. HMRC*, 21 ITLR (2019), p. 801.
180. UK First-Tier Tribunal, 14 Jul. 2017, *Development Securities plc and others v. HMRC*, UKFTT (2017), p. 565 (TC) (at para. 412).
181. UK Upper Tribunal, *Development Securities plc and others v. HMRC*, at paras 45-46. The Court of Appeal found that the Upper Tribunal misinterpreted the FTT's reasoning because it neither argued that 'the directors had failed to decline to do something that was improper or inadvisable' nor did it 'consider that the transactions were entered into by the Jersey directors in breach of their duties as directors'. *See* UK Court of Appeal, 15 Dec. 2020, *Development Securities plc and others v. HMRC*, STC (2021), p. 84 (at paras 73 and 75).
182. UK Court of Appeal, *Development Securities plc and others v. HMRC*, at paras 72-73.

uncommercial transactions in order to implement the scheme in favour of the parent. In order to reach this conclusion, the Upper Tribunal considered the duties vested in the directors of a corporation pursuant to Article 74 of the Companies (Jersey) Law 1991.[183] This provision stipulates that directors have to take into account the interests of shareholders, creditors, and employees when performing their duties. Since in the case at hand no creditors and employees existed, only the parent's interests had to be taken into account. And it was in the parent's interests to enter into the transactions upon which the legally appointed directors 'gave detailed consideration'.[184] What follows from this judgment is that there are cases where the management of a subsidiary must make decisions with disadvantageous consequences for the subsidiary in order to comply with other laws.

Overall, if the legally appointed directors take uncommercial decisions from the perspective of the subsidiary, without being actively engaged in the decision-making process and without being forced to do so by law, a rebuttable presumption of the management's usurpation can be established.

ff Limitation of Authority

Imagine that you want to build a house. Since you do not have the time and knowledge to do that, you entrust a construction company with this task. A typical principal-agent relationship[185] is engendered whereby you are the principal and the construction company is your agent. Now, the agent has an interest in taking care of their own interests; as with every economic actor, their behaviour is characterized by self-interested action.[186] For example, if you pay the agent EUR 100 up front to build the house, they have an incentive to buy the cheapest material in order to maximize their profit (i.e., EUR 100 - material costs = profit for the services of the agent). The efficiency costs arising (in this example the fact that the house is built with low-quality material) are called agency costs. One of the ways to reduce these costs, apart from, for example, providing incentives to the agent, is introducing efficient monitoring mechanisms (e.g., in our example by contractually laying down that the principal has to approve the use of material chosen by the agent).

Exactly the same course of affairs exists between self-interested directors and shareholders:

183. UK Upper Tribunal, *Development Securities plc and others v. HMRC*, at para. 50(1).
184. *Ibid.*, at para. 50(3).
185. *See* Jensen/Meckling (1976), p. 308: '[w]e define an agency relationship as a contract under which one or more persons (the principal(s)) engage another person (the agent) to perform some service on their behalf which involves delegating some decision making authority to the agent'.
186. This is the principle first enunciated by *Adam Smith* in his An Inquiry into the Nature and Causes of the Wealth of Nations (1776). George Stigler underlines the importance of this assumption for the work of economists and in particular for Adam Smith's work by stating that 'the Wealth of Nations is a stupendous palace erected upon the granite of self-interest'. *See* Stigler (1971), p. 265.

> The directors of such [joint-stock] companies, however, being the managers rather of other people's money than of their own, it cannot well be expected, that they should watch over it with the same anxious vigilance with which the partners in a private copartnery frequently watch over their own. Like the stewards of a rich man, they are apt to consider attention to small matters as not for their master's honour, and very easily give themselves a dispensation from having it. Negligence and profusion, therefore, must always prevail, more or less, in the management of the affairs of such a company.[187]

It is therefore logical that the shareholder, i.e., the parent, develops mechanisms to monitor the behaviour of its agents, i.e., the subsidiary's directors. One of these mechanisms is limitation of authority. Accordingly, the directors of the subsidiary have to get the parent's approval in order to take certain actions.

As early as 1935, the German Reichsfinanzhof decided that the principal shareholder and head of the supervisory board of a company usurped its management because 'his influence on the [company] is so great that *nothing important* happened without his approval'.[188] Eleven years later, in 1946, the HCA underscored in *Malayan Shipping* the fact that 'the articles of association … provided that *any* resolution of the directors was to be of no effect unless [the sole shareholder and managing director] or his alternate director concurred therein'.[189] The importance of this criterion can be detected in subsequent case law[190] and in rulings of tax authorities.[191]

The careful reader may have already noticed a difference in the approach of the Reichsfinanzhof and the one of the HCA. In the case presented before the Reichsfinanzhof, a limitation of authority as regards only the important (*see* the word 'important' in italics above) decisions was sufficient for the court to deduct a usurpation of management by the principal shareholder and head of the supervisory board. In stark contrast, in *Malayan Shipping* sole shareholder approval was not only required for decisions regarding important matters. Instead, every decision (*see* the word 'any' in italics above) was under such a reservation. The question is which approach is the most favourable one. The one of the Reichsfinanzhof, resulting in a usurpation of management even in cases of reservation of power by the shareholder regarding only the important decisions, or the one of the HCA, where only a complete reservation of power by the parent signals a usurpation of management by its side?

---

187. *See* the seminal article by *Jensen* and *Meckling* quoting *Adam Smith*, Jensen/Meckling (1976), p. 305.
188. Reichsfinanzhof, 25 Jul. 1935, III A 98/35, RStBl. (1935), p. 1366 (emphasis added) (author's unofficial translations).
189. High Court of Australia, *Malayan Shipping Co Ltd v. Federal Commissioner of Taxation*, at p. 158 (emphasis added).
190. *Australia:* High Court of Australia, *Bywater Investments Limited v. Commissioner of Taxation*, at para. 68.
    The Netherlands: Hoge Raad, 19 Jan. 2018, No. 16/03321, BNB 2018/68. *See* Gooijer (2019), pp. 99 et seq.
191. *South Africa:* SARS, Interpretation Note 6(2), p. 11 (at s. 4.2.5.); seemingly *contra Australia:* ATO, PCG, para. 39: 'The Commissioner accepts that the directors of a subsidiary company do not cease to exercise its central management and control merely because in making decisions they conclude that it is in the best interest of the company to: … make decisions only after receiving approval from its parent to do so.'

If we examine the case law and the tax authorities' rulings cited above, it can be deduced that the approach of the HCA is to be preferred. In particular, the South African Revenue Service (SARS)[192] gives in its Interpretation Note (2015) on the POEM an example where a limitation of authority leads to usurpation of management. The subsidiary's directors need the approval of the parent for every contract that exceeds ZAR 10 million. It turns out that 90% of the contracts exceed ZAR 10 million. So, the SARS views only such a case where almost every ('any') decision of the subsidiary's directors is dependent on the approval of the parent as a usurpation of management.

In a similar vein, the Dutch Hoge Raad[193] ruled that the management of an investment company was usurped by its parent because it was stipulated in the articles of association that every investment decision of its board of directors exceeding EUR 4.540 needed to be approved by the general meeting of shareholders. Although it cannot be ascertained how many such decisions there were, it can be assumed that they consisted, like in the example presented by the SARS, a significant amount of the subsidiary's business. In other words, here we can also assume that almost every investment decision had to be approved by the parent.

However, if it is accepted that the strategic decisions are the relevant ones, as the interpretation of the POEM advocated here does (section B.II.1.b.cc. of this chapter), then it should not matter whether the parent is taking the day-to-day/operational decisions.[194] What should matter would be whether the approval of the parent is required for every *strategic* decision with regard to the business of the subsidiary. And it would not be in line with the behaviour of a prudent principal, i.e., the parent, to not monitor in some way strategic decisions of its agent, i.e., the subsidiary, that can make or break the parent's investment. It is no coincidence that the majority of the German DAX 30 follow a top-down/bottom-up planning model.[195,196] That is, strategic decisions are circulated within the group, meaning that a decision taken at a lower level, i.e., with the subsidiary, goes up to the higher level, i.e., the parent, in order for it to be approved or modified there and come back to the subsidiary level. Moreover, corporate law acknowledges the principal-agent relationship between the subsidiary and the parent and quite often obliges the parent to instal control mechanisms like limitations of authority.[197]

From these arguments, it follows that it should not be a criterion whether the parent needs to approve all strategic decisions taken by the legally appointed directors of the subsidiary. Otherwise, the POEM would completely ignore basic economic principles (i.e., the principle-agent theorem) as well as business reality and corporate

192. SARS, Interpretation Note 6(2), p. 11 (at s. 4.2.5.).
193. *See* above n. 190 in this chapter.
194. In this vein, although with regard to the German POM, Bundesfinanzhof, 29 Nov. 2017, I R 58/15, BFH/NV (2018), p. 684 (at para. 21).
195. Pörner (2003), p. 9. More generally *see* Horváth (2020), p. 108.
196. For this argument in another context (the Shell Entities Directive) *see* Benz/Böhmer (2022), p. 1031.
197. *See* Maisto et al. (2018), p. 24.

law obligations. This seems to also be the approach of the Australian tax authorities[198] and current UK case law[199] with regard to the CMC.

In cases where all strategic decisions are subject to the approval of the supervisory board, the latter co-manages the company (section B.II.2.b.aa. of this chapter). Thus, both the place where the management board makes decisions as well as the one where the supervisory board approves them are relevant. This can be problematic in cases where these two places differ. However, to the author's knowledge, there is no court case in this respect. The author would like to argue, though, that in such cases the POEM should be in the state where the supervisory board approves the strategic decisions. It is its judgment that makes or breaks the corporation; there is the 'brain' of the corporation.

All in all, a consequent approach suggests that it should not matter whether the parent's approval is required with respect to operational decisions since these decisions are not relevant for the purposes of the POEM. The same applies with regard to strategic decisions this time, however, taking into account the nature of the parent-subsidiary relationship as a principal-agent relationship and the business reality, which shows that such a model is widespread without meaning that the parent usurps the subsidiary's management. Only in cases where the supervisory board must approve all strategic decisions and it does so in a place other than the one in which the management board makes the respective decisions should the place of approval be the decisive one.

gg Identity of Board Members

Recall the case study presented in section B.II. of the introduction. There, the subsidiary in question (SubCo) is managed by a manager who is also a member of the parent's executive board (PaCo). Now, in this scenario (or in a similar one)[200] where the subsidiary is managed by persons pertaining also to the management of the company, the question arises whether the parent usurps the subsidiary's management in that way. Case law[201] and tax authorities[202] reject such a claim.

---

198. *See* above n. 191 in this chapter.
199. UK Upper Tribunal, *Development Securities plc and others v. HMRC*, at para. 50(7): 'The problem with the FTT's approach is that it confused an instruction from a parent company ... with the authorisation or ratification of a course of conduct by the shareholders.' The decision has been overturned but not because this distinction is not a valid but because the Court of Appeal reasoned '[t]hat the FTT was alive to the distinction between authorization and instruction'. *See* UK Court of Appeal, *Development Securities plc and others v. HMRC*, at para. 80.
200. With 'similar scenario' cases are meant where not all subsidiary managers, but the majority thereof, also pertain to the parent's management so that it can be said that the decisions are taken by this majority and thus indirectly by the parent.
201. *Belgium:* Belgian Court of Appeal ('Hof van beroep'), 20 September, No. 2011/928. *See* Obuoforibo (2020), s. 5.2.2.2.3., n. 546.
   The Netherlands: Hoge Raad, No. 41.050. *See* Gooijer (2019), pp. 96-97.
   United States: US Tax Court, 21 Sep. 1983, *Hospital Corporation of America v. Commissioner*, 81 T.C. (1983), p. 520 (at p. 586) although this case regarded, *inter alia*, the question

The cases and guidelines cited show, however, that 'there may be something wrong' in such scenarios or, as the saying goes, 'there's no smoke without fire'. In particular, the US Tax Court in *Hospital Corporation of America* states that '[t]he fact that these same individuals were also officers and directors of [the parent] is not sufficient reason'.[203] E contrario, the fact that these same individuals are officers and directors of both the parent and the subsidiary may provide sufficient reason under other circumstances, i.e., if other criteria are also fulfilled. Similarly, the Australian Taxation Office states in its *Practical Compliance Guideline 2018/9* that '[a] foreign incorporated subsidiary of an Australian resident company may also have employees of its parent as directors. This is not, *of itself*, conclusive of where the subsidiary's central management and control is exercised'.[204] Even if it is not itself conclusive, it may be, combined with other factors. In fact, in a Swiss case on the beneficial ownership clause (BO clause) ruled by the Swiss Administrative Federal Court ('Bundesverwaltungsgericht') this factor has played a decisive role, as commentators inform us.[205,206]

This work rejects this approach. It is maintained that this scenario resembles the one dealt with in the previous section. Instead of limiting the authority of the subsidiary's management, the parent's managers take the authority into their own hands. The argumentation brought forward in the previous section can, thus, be equally applied to this situation. Accordingly, the fact that members of the board of (or persons working for) the parent also comprise the board of the subsidiary does not constitute a criterion when determining whether the parent has usurped the subsidiary's management.

hh Outsourcing of Managerial Functions

Now take the, not at all theoretical,[207] case that management tasks, normally resting with the legally appointed directors, are delegated by them, for example, to executive directors (henceforth referred to as 'agents'). The former simply oversee the decision-making carried out by the latter. Does this influence their capacity as decision-makers for the purposes of the POEM?

Here, once more[208] different interpretations exist, at least as far as the domestic substance-oriented residence criteria are concerned. According to the interpretation

---

whether the subsidiary was a sham and not its POEM. As to this case *see* Avi-Yonah (1995), pp. 122-123.

Contra Germany: Finanzgericht of Köln, 22 Sep. 2022, 6 K 2661/18, EFG (2023), p. 89 (at para. 35) (on the German CFC rules).

202. ATO, PCG, para. 40.
203. US Tax Court, *Hospital Corporation of America v. Commissioner,* at p. 586.
204. ATO, PCG, para. 40 (emphasis added).
205. Danon/Malek (2020).
206. Bundesverwaltungsgericht, 28 Feb. 2018, A-7299/2016, at para. 7.2.4. Critical against the reasoning of the Swiss Bundesverwaltungsgericht Danon (2020a), s. 15.2.5.6.
207. *See* Maisto et al. (2018), p. 19.
208. *See* above ss B.II.1.b.bb. and B.II.1.c.bb. of this chapter where different interpretations as regards the relevant decision category and the relevant stage in the decision-making process.

preferred by a number of common law countries,[209] such a delegation would not influence the CMC of the subsidiary so long as the legally appointed directors retain control over the decisions taken by the agents. Again,[210] this is a consequent approach in the case of a test that calls itself CMC, i.e., a case where management and control must coincide. Since delegation and control of the agents themselves constitute acts of management,[211] the legally appointed directors remain behind the wheel. In contrast, German case law[212] as well as the SARS[213] advocate that in this case, for the purposes of their domestic substance-oriented criteria, management is performed by the agents. The question arises as to which approach is more suitable for the purposes of the POEM.

It all boils down to the decision category that is delegated and to the stage in the decision-making process that the legally appointed directors reserve for themselves. We can easily assert that if both operational and strategic management are delegated to outsiders and no powers are reserved by the legally appointed directors, then the outsiders are running the company. But what happens when only operational management is delegated, or when both strategic and operational management are delegated but the legally appointed directors must first, for instance, approve the decision taken by the agents in order for it to have validity?

Let us take first the relevant decision category. In section B.II.1.b.cc. of this chapter, it has been maintained that the appropriate interpretation of the POEM emphasizes the strategic and not the operational decisions. E contrario, if operational decisions are taken by persons other than the legally appointed directors, no usurpation of management occurs, the operational decisions not even being relevant in the first place. Now, what if the legally appointed directors of the subsidiary delegate the (for the purposes of the POEM relevant) strategic decisions to outsiders? It then comes up to whether the legally appointed decision-makers are involved in the decision-making process. But which stage of this process is relevant? Do the directors have to be involved in all stages in order for management not to be taken away from them?

In section B.II.2.c.cc. of this chapter, it has been found that both the decision-making stricto sensu stage and the monitoring stage are relevant for the purposes of the POEM. Furthermore, it has been concluded that in cases where these two are separated between more than one state, the personal element stricto sensu should provide answers.[214]

---

209. *Australia:* ATO, TR 2018/5, para. 24.
 United Kingdom: House of Lords, 6 Feb. 1913, *American Thread Company v. Joyce*, TC (1913), p. 163 (at p. 164); Special Commissioners, 6 Sep. 2006, *News Datacom Ltd v. Atkinson*, SpC (2006), p. 561 (at para. 65); UK Upper Tribunal, *Development Securities plc and others v. HMRC*, at para. 63, n. 38.
210. *See* above s. B.II.1.c.bb. of this chapter and the text accompanying n. 105 as well as the n. itself.
211. Schwarz (2018), p. 204. Harold Demsetz puts it on the spot in his 'theory of the firm': '[In the case of outsourcing] [m]anaged transfer of inputs between the departments of (a now larger) firm is substituted for managed buying and selling. One type of management substitutes for another.' *See* Demsetz (1988), p. 147. In a similar vein, Dziurdź (2014), p. 155.
212. Bundesfinanzhof, IV R 58/95.
213. SARS, Interpretation Note 6(2), p. 8 (at s. 4.2.2.).
214. And again if this is also unable to do so, then the qualities of the decisions should be looked at. *See* above n. 114 in this chapter.

Since the legally appointed directors are the relevant persons in this respect, the POEM should be in the state in which these persons act, even if their only action is monitoring decisions made by other persons. At the end of the day, the final decision is their decision. By espousing the decision made by the agents, they adopt the content of this decision and accept the consequences that come with it. If they fail in their monitoring function, the internal (i.e., the executive managers) and external (i.e., other managers looking for employment) managerial market is there to replace them.[215]

And if we take one step back and look one moment before the legally appointed directors get to control the decisions of the agents, the former will first have to prudently choose the latter. And it can be maintained that even selecting the agents is a fundamental decision for the subsidiary and, of course, for the legally appointed directors too. Pick the wrong persons and you will have the wrong outcomes.[216]

It can be concluded that in case of delegating authority to other persons retaining the monitoring of the decision-making process suffices for the legally appointed directors to be on the wheel for the purposes of the POEM.[217]

ii Relationship Between the Criteria

The previous sections have indicated criteria that may be taken into account when determining whether the management of a subsidiary has been usurped. Now, the question arises whether these criteria are alternative or cumulative and if they are alternative, is there some kind of meta-rule arranging the priority order between them?

It must be remembered that the criteria introduced here are not determined by the legislature. Rather, they have been promulgated through years of judicial practice. And in the decisions commented upon in the previous sections, the criteria arising did not all exist in each and every case. Their weight in the respective case was sufficient enough to lead the courts to uphold usurpation. So, like in other areas where case law determines the criteria for the applicability of a standard,[218] at the outset, one needs to adopt a separate approach. That is, the existence of even only one criterion (for instance, lacking expertise) could induce management usurpation if the criterion has sufficient intensity. In terms of legal logic, each criterion may constitute a *sufficient*

215. Eugene Fama has resorted to the managerial market to account for firm growth. *See* Fama (1980), p. 295: 'The viability of the large corporation with diffuse security ownership is better explained in terms of a model where the primary disciplining of managers comes through managerial labor markets, both within and outside of the firm.'
216. In fact, as management literature informs us, 'the board's responsibility for delegated decisions is exercised primarily through its choice of the senior-most executives and formulation or ratification of the firm's mission and strategy.' *See* Useem/Zelleke (2006), p. 8.
217. Concurring Schön (2013a), p. 16.
218. Reference is being made to the so-called Engel criteria developed by the European Court of Human Rights (ECtHR). These criteria have been developed in order to ascertain whether a tax penalty can constitute a 'criminal charge' within the meaning of Article 6(1) of the ECHR. In detail, Maisto (2011), p. 375.

condition for the usurpation of management. However, it is *not a necessary condition*, that is, management may be usurped, even though a criterion is not fulfilled (e.g., the managers are well-informed).[219] But, again, a criterion *may* constitute a sufficient condition *if* it has sufficient intensity just as well as it may not be a sufficient condition in the opposite case.[220]

From these statements, it follows that the first stage of the judicial control as regards the usurpation of the management of a subsidiary amounts to laying down the criteria fulfilled and establishing their intensity. According to the doctrine of variable intensity of judicial review,[221] the more intense the fulfilment or the non-fulfilment of a criterion is, the more argumentation and evidence are needed from the other party to counterbalance it.

Finally, and again in accordance with other areas where case law determines the criteria about the applicability of a standard,[222] 'a cumulative approach may be adopted where the separate analysis of each criterion does not make a definitive conclusion possible'.[223] This seems to also be accepted by the OECD Commentary stressing that '[a]ll relevant facts and circumstances must be examined to determine the place of effective management'.[224]

d *Synthesis*

This section has analysed the personal element stricto sensu of the substance requirement in the POEM with particular reference to subsidiaries. The key findings can be summarized as follows:

- The reasons leading to the separation of ownership and control in corporations do not apply, or at least not with the same intensity, in the case of subsidiaries (section B.II.2.a.).
- This peculiarity is taken into account by the POEM that not only focuses on the legally appointed directors (rule) but also accepts that the corporation may be run by an outsider (exception), who, in the case of subsidiaries especially, may be the parent (section B.II.2.b.).
- The starting point when determining whether the management has been usurped from the legally appointed directors is delineating between cases of

219. As to sufficient and necessary conditions in legal reasoning *see* Klug (1982), pp. 42 et seq.
220. So it must be stressed that these criteria are, strictly speaking, also no sufficient conditions of the usurpation of management. If a sufficient condition is fulfilled, then the outcome *always* arises. In our case, the sufficient condition must sufficiently exist for the outcome to arise.
221. Rivers (2006), pp. 202 et seq.
222. *See* ECtHR, 8 Jun. 1976, Nos 5100/71; 5101/71; 5102/71; 5354/72; 5370/72, *Engel and others v. the Netherlands*.
223. Maisto (2011), p. 375. *See also* Alexy/Peczenik (1990), p. 136: 'It is well known that in judicial practice the decision is often justified by a cluster of reasons, which are not sufficient in themselves, but provide fairly good evidence when taken along with others.'
224. Paragraph 24 third sentence of the Commentary (2014) on Article 4.

mere influence and the ones where the legally appointed directors are puppets following instructions given by an outsider (section B.II.2.c.aa.).

- The existence of a *legally* enforceable right to shape certain decisions is not required so long as the outsiders can *factually* enforce their positions. Managerial liability according to corporate law also does not play a role (section B.II.2.c.bb.).
- Missing information and knowledge/expertise of the legally appointed decision-makers creates a rebuttable presumption that the legally appointed directors do not really run the company, thus the POEM is located where the outsiders that do so are also located. This appraisal is not influenced by the fact that some subsidiaries' business is so simple that the legally appointed directors only need to pay heed to the outsiders' instructions (section B.II.2.c.cc. and section B.II.2.c.dd.).
- If the legally appointed directors' actions detract from the subsidiary's position, without even having been actively engaged in the decision-making process, then it can be rebuttably presumed that they are acting in accordance with the outsiders' instructions and thus that the POEM is located where these outsiders are located. A limitation to this finding must be made in cases where the legally appointed directors make deleterious decisions, but do so in order to comply with their legal rules (e.g., environmental or corporate law rules) (section B.II.2.c.ee.).
- Limitations of authority should not influence the POEM except for cases where the supervisory board must approve all strategic decisions and it does so in a place other than the one in which the management board makes the respective decisions should the place of approval be the decisive one. (section B.II.2.c.ff.).
- Similarly, the fact that members of the board of (or persons working for) the parent also comprise the board of the subsidiary is irrelevant when determining whether the parent has usurped the subsidiary's management (section B.II.2.c.gg.).
- Lastly, if the legally appointed directors delegate their powers, we first need to establish exactly which powers they are delegating. If they delegate the power to make operational decisions, this should not affect the POEM, while if they delegate the power to make strategic decisions, then it all boils down to whether they have kept the monitoring of the decision-making process for themselves (section B.II.2.c.hh.).
- The criteria developed by case law and presented here are not cumulative, hence they are not necessary conditions for usurpation. One needs to, first, ascertain which criteria are fulfilled and, then, establish their intensity. The more intense the fulfilment or the non-fulfilment of a criterion is, the more argumentation and evidence are needed from the other party to counterbalance it (section B.II.2.c.ii.).

3 *Quantitative Sub-element of Both the Personal and the Functional Element of Substance: How Many Decisions and How Many Decision-Makers Are Necessary?*

According to the substance definition for the purposes of this work, all substance elements (objective, functional, and personal) contain a quantitative sub-element. This section explores the role of this sub-element for the purposes of the two basic substance elements dealt with so far, i.e., the personal and the functional elements. As the title of the section implies, it explores whether the number of decisions (quantitative sub-element of the functional element; section B.II.3.a.) or the number of decision-makers or employees (quantitative sub-element of the personal element; section B.II.3.b.) is relevant for the purposes of the POEM.

a *Quantitative Sub-element of the Functional Element*

As regards the quantitative sub-element of the functional element of substance, it can easily be asserted that the POEM does not raise any threshold requirement. In particular, when elaborating on the relationship between the business of the subsidiary and the decision-making functions required for the purposes of the POEM, the conclusion has been drawn that the scale of the subsidiary's business operations is immaterial for the purposes of the POEM (section B.II.1.a.cc. of this chapter). This means two things.

First, the quantity of the business operations performed by the subsidiary is irrelevant for the purposes of the POEM; second, the number of decisions pertaining to these operations is also irrelevant for the purposes of the POEM. In fact, even an SPV may have enough substance in order for it to have a POEM, although only a few decisions are taken due to its short existence. In other words, there is no *absolute* threshold in this sense.[225] For instance, if for the operation of an SPV only two decisions are necessary and these two decisions are taken in state A, then state A is the state of the POEM, without questioning whether a quantitative threshold has been reached.

Admittedly, the quantitative sub-element of the functional element can be more relevant when decisions are taken in different states. Imagine in this respect a subsidiary whose board meets and decides two times in State A and five times in State B. The question arises as to where its POEM is located; in State A or in State B? In fact, German literature has underlined the importance of this sub-element: 'Here, too, the general rule is that the place where *most* managerial decisions are taken is decisive.'[226] Thus, there is a *relative* threshold in this respect. The place where the most decisions are taken is the POEM.

But imagine that these five decisions only concern operational matters. Then, they are not even relevant decisions for the purposes of the POEM (section B.II.1.b.cc. of this chapter) so if the other two decisions taken in State A are strategic, then the

225. On substance requirements as absolute and relative requirements, *see* Pistone et al. (2021), p. 15.
226. Felix (1962/63), p. 422 (emphasis added) (author's unofficial translation).

POEM is in State A. Therefore, one first needs to refer to the qualitative sub-element and only in the second stage apply the quantitative one.[227]

Cases in which the exact same amount of qualitatively equal decisions are taken in more than one state pose more challenges. In the aforementioned example, imagine that two strategic decisions have been made both in State A and B. Is State A or State B the state where the POEM is located? In such cases, only a case-by-case analysis can break the tie, taking into account the business of the subsidiary in question.[228]

Keeping in mind the modified example from above, if the two decisions taken in State A influence, for example, to a greater extent the financial interests of the subsidiary than the other two taken in State B, then State A should be seen as the state of the POEM.[229] Furthermore, it can also be that in State A two strategic decisions are taken, whereas in State B only one which is, however, qualitatively far more important, as far as its economic ramifications are concerned. In this case, the dilemma exists as to the weight of quality versus quantity. In the author's opinion, quality must have priority over quantity when the qualitative sub-element would prevail also in a quantitative sense.[230] That is, a qualitatively more important decision is also quantitatively predominant since it influences the subsidiary's financial situation to a greater extent than the quantitatively less significant decisions.[231] Finally, it must be considered that quantity is far easier to manipulate. It is easier to create decisions out of nowhere and thus increase the quantity of decisions in a certain state than to move the managers taking the decisions that make and break the subsidiary's business to another state.

In sum, there is no absolute threshold as regards the quantitative sub-element of the functional element of substance. This sub-element becomes relevant when strategic decisions are taken in more than one state. In these cases, the quantitative sub-element *may* play a role, since there is a relative threshold: the POEM *may* be in the place where the most decisions are made. However, quality must take precedence over

227. This approach is followed in German-speaking case law and literature. *See* Finanzgericht of Munich, 10 V 1479/20, at para. 70; Kessler/Müller (2003), p. 365.
228. Kessler/Müller (2003), p. 365.
229. Imagine, however, that the POEM has been for the last five years in State B. Now, unintentionally the POEM is relocated to State A, although State B still remains a decision-making centre. It just happened in this 'snapshot moment' for State A to assume some importance. The question is whether a snapshot approach is to be applied (then State A is the legitimate POEM) or whether a, time-related, more overall approach is taken. This overall approach has the advantage that unintentional relocations are avoided. It has the disadvantage, though, that it is a lot more susceptible to manipulation. This issue is not an issue of substance, but one of the role of time in the application of DTC provisions and thus will not be further pursued. *See,* for example, the Indian tax authorities rejecting the 'snapshot approach' CBDT, Circular No. 6, para. 10.
230. Actually, the OECD also espouses this reasoning, however not in the guidance regarding the POEM but in the OECD TPG. *See* OECD TPG, para. 1.51 in fine: 'While one party may provide a large number of functions relative to that of the other party to the transaction, it is the economic significance of those functions in terms of their frequency, nature, and value to the respective parties to the transactions that is important.'
231. For example, one decision referring to a profit opportunity of EUR 100 affects the financial interests of a subsidiary more than five decisions referring to transactions with a profit potential of EUR 10 each. Thus, the one decision is also quantitatively more important than the other five.

quantity when the qualitative sub-element also prevails in a quantitative sense, that is, the qualitatively superior decision(s) affect the financial interests of the subsidiary more intensely than the quantitative superior decisions.

b *Quantitative Sub-element of the Personal Element*

The quantitative sub-element of the personal element of substance may relate to two things. First, it may relate to the number of employees the subsidiary deploys in order to carry out its activities and, second, it may relate to the number of the decision-makers of the subsidiary.

As regards the first aspect, i.e., whether the number of employees of the subsidiary plays a role for the purposes of the POEM, it is clear that it does not play any role when determining the POEM. In particular, since the scale of business operations in the state of the POEM is immaterial (section B.II.1.a.cc. of this chapter) and the only thing that is relevant for its purposes is the place from which the decision-makers act, it is also immaterial whether the subsidiary has employees in its POEM state. For example, the POEM can be in state A, although the business operations are executed, and thus the employees are located, in state B. This was the state of facts in the landmark House of Lords case *De Beers*, where the House of Lords concentrated on the decision-makers who were primarily acting from the UK and not the business operations and therewith the number of employees in South Africa. Put another way, it does not matter whether thousands of workers carry out mining operations in state B: so long as the decision-makers act in state A, this state is the POEM state.

But maybe the number of decision-makers does play a role. In this regard, and similarly to the previous section, two questions arise:

(1) Does it suffice if, for example, the subsidiary is only managed by one person? In other words, is there an absolute threshold in this respect that needs to be exceeded?
(2) And what if three out of the five decision-makers act from state A, while the other two act from state B? Does the fact that more decision-makers act from state A than from state B result in the POEM being located in the former? In other words, is there a relative threshold in this respect?

As regards the first question, case law informs us that even subsidiaries with a sole director can claim resident status.[232] Put another way, the fact that the only kind of connection with a territory is just one person making decisions does not exclude this

232. *Australia:* Board, Review, pp. 65-67 where examples are given where a corporation is an Australian resident, although the sole shareholder was also the sole director of the company in question.

Canada: Tax Court of Canada, *Landbouwbedrijf Backx BV v. Her Majesty the Queen*, where the fact that there was only a sole director did not play a role in ascertaining whether the management has been usurped.

Ireland: High Court of Justice, 18 and 19 Jun. 1918, *John Hood & Company, Limited v. W.E. Magee (Surveyor of Taxes)*, 7 TC (1918), p. 350.

territory from being the one in which the POEM is located; there is no absolute threshold in this respect. As far as the second question is concerned, the answer is the same as the one given in the previous section. There may be a relative threshold in this respect, but the quality of the decisions taken should matter more than the quantity of those decisions or the number of persons making them when the qualitative sub-element also prevails in a quantitative sense.

c *Synthesis*

With regard to the quantitative sub-element of both the functional and the personal elements, similar conclusions can be drawn. First, there is no absolute quantity threshold. That is, even one decision (functional) or one decision-maker (personal) may suffice for a subsidiary to have its POEM in a contracting state. Second, there is a relative threshold in the quantitative sub-element, but both in the functional and personal respect, quality takes precedence over quantity. That is, first, the quantity of decisions or decision-makers only plays a role if strategic decisions are taken in more than one state; second, even in such a case, the qualitative importance of decisions trumps their quantitative amount or the number of the persons taking them when the qualitative sub-element also prevails in a quantitative sense (i.e., the qualitatively superior decision(s) affect the financial interests of the subsidiary more intensely than the quantitatively superior decisions).

III Content of the Objective Element of Substance in Treaty Corporate Residence

Section B.II. dealt with the functional and personal elements of substance in the POEM. Remember, though, that the definition of substance contains three constituent elements, the third one being the objective element. This section deals with the latter.

Recall the case study in section B.II. of the introduction. There, the subsidiary in question (SubCo) rents an office in which an employee dispatches tasks connected with the daily operations of SubCo. The manager of SubCo lives in the state of residence of the parent (PaCo) and only travels once a year to the premises of SubCo to formally sign documents conveying strategic decisions. Let us assume that it can be proven that these decisions are taken (again the decision-making stage stricto sensu is relevant) in the PaCo state. Does it still play a role that in the SubCo state some 'substance' exists in the form of the office where the employee conducts her work? Could it be said that the objective element trumps the personal and functional elements for the purposes of the POEM?

The Netherlands: Hoge Raad, 3 Feb. 2012, Nos 10/05383, 10/05385; 10/05386, BNB 2012/126 cited in Gooijer (2019), p. 97 where also the fact that the sole shareholder was also the sole director of the company in question did not play any role as to its residence. On this decision where actually the important legal issue was a different one (i.e., whether in case of fiscal unities residence is determined for each company separately or for the group as a whole) *see* Mooij (2012).

Another question relates to the existence of some kind of a quantitative threshold with regard to the objective element of substance that needs to be exceeded so that the subsidiary claims residence different from the one of its parent (quantitative sub-element of the objective element). For example, one could argue that, in the case study at hand, the subsidiary's POEM is located in the PaCo state because in the SubCo state, only one office exists and therefore the threshold with regard to the objective element of substance for the purposes of the POEM is not exceeded. Closely related to this problem is the question about which quality the assets owned by the subsidiary should have (qualitative sub-element of the objective element). For instance, are offices more important than financial assets?

Let us first begin dealing with the two questions as to the quantitative and the qualitative sub-element of the objective element (sections B.III.1. and B.III.2.) and then move on to the question regarding the relationship between the objective element, on the one hand, and the personal and functional elements, on the other, for the purposes of the POEM (section B.III.3.).

1 *Existence of a Quantitative Threshold: On the Quantitative Sub-element of the Objective Element*

If the determination of the POEM is dependent upon exceeding a quantitative threshold as regards the objective element of substance, then each time the subsidiary fails to exceed this threshold in the state it claims to have its POEM according to the personal and functional elements, it will not have the POEM in this state. The POEM will probably be considered the state of the parent because the threshold as regards the objective element is passed (e.g., there is a huge headquarters in that state). The question now arises whether the POEM raises such a threshold requirement with regard to the objective element of substance.

Commentators have proposed a novel definition of residence for the purposes of DTCs, which includes a threshold requirement in the form of the existence of 'a fixed place of business through which the business of an enterprise is wholly or partly carried on' in accordance with the PE definition in Article 5(1).[233] This would, of course, lead to an indirect application of such a threshold for the purposes of the POEM. That is, a residence-residence conflict would only arise if a subsidiary has a residence and therewith a fixed place of business in more than one state. The winner of the tiebreaker would, thus, in any case, be a subsidiary which has a fixed place of business in its POEM.

Still, this is a *de lege ferenda* proposal. Article 4(3) of the 2014 version of the OECD MTC itself as well as the accompanying Commentary do not stipulate such a threshold requirement. Systematically, this makes sense. If no such requirement exists with regard to the existence of business operations in the POEM state (section B.II.1.a.cc. of this chapter) as well as with regard to the quantity of decisions and decision-makers in the POEM state (sections B.II.3.a. and B.II.3.b. of this chapter), then

233. Gooijer (2019), pp. 249-250 and 254-256.

it would be unreasonable to require a subsidiary to possess empty chairs and unused computers in its POEM state.

2 *Qualities of the Assets Owned by the Subsidiary: On the Qualitative Sub-element of the Objective Element*

Although no quantitative threshold exists with regard to the assets owned by the subsidiary whose POEM is in question, it could be that the POEM requires a subsidiary to have assets with certain qualities. In fact, the Commentary on Article 4(3) of the 2014 version of the OECD MTC does not include any guidance in this respect. Courts and administrative practice on the domestic substance-oriented residence criteria, however, stress the importance of the existence of office premises in the state of residence.[234]

In a similar vein, other tangible assets, like telephones, computers, and other kinds of equipment, also seem to play a role in ascertaining residence for domestic tax law purposes.[235] It is no coincidence that the authorities cited specifically point to the significance of assets like telephones and computers and not, for example, machines. This is because the tangible assets must be related to and enable the relevant activities for the purposes of the POEM which are decision-making functions. One needs a computer and not a sledgehammer to make and communicate decisions. Finally, to the author's knowledge, no relevance has been accorded to the ownership of financial and/or intangible assets by the subsidiary.

Another issue relates to what happens when assets with the qualities described above (i.e., offices and other tangible assets related to the decision-making process) exist in more than one state. Then all states involved may justifiably make the residence claim and the issue now is how the POEM breaks the tie. In such a case, all other things being equal, the quantity of the assets should point to the tiebreaker. But what happens when other things are not equal?

In particular, there can exist cases where the personal and functional elements in the states claiming residence are not the same, that is, one state prevails in this respect. Take the modification of the case study presented in the introductory remarks to this section. It demonstrates that there can exist cases where the objective element points to one state as the POEM (in the case study this state is the SubCo state where the office premises exist) and the personal and functional elements point to another (in the case

234. *Australia:* High Court of Australia, *Bywater Investments Limited v. Commissioner of Taxation*, at para. 116.
Germany: Töben/Birk (2016), p. 524 and the case law cited there.
Italy: Pötgens et al. (2014a), p. 383.
Switzerland: Bundesgericht, 2C_1086/2012, 2C_1087/2012, at para. 2.4.
The Netherlands: Burgers (2007), p. 379.
United Kingdom: Cerioni/Eden (2018), p. 676 referring to the HMRC practice.

235. *Italy:* Pötgens et al. (2014a), p. 383.
Switzerland: Bundesgericht, 2C_1086/2012, 2C_1087/2012, at para. 2.4.
It can be surmised that the existence of other tangible assets is less relevant than the existence of office premises. This assertion is due to the less sources found pointing to their relevance.

study that is the PaCo state from which the relevant decisions are in substance made). The question in such cases revolves around the relationship between the substance elements for the purposes of the POEM. The next section delves into this issue.

3 *Relationship Between the Objective Element and the Personal and Functional Elements*

The previous section has shown that the objective element of substance may play a role in the purposes of the POEM. But how much importance can be ascribed to this element of substance? Can it trump the other two for the purposes of the POEM?

In the author's view, the wording of the Commentary on Article 4(3) of the 2014 version of the OECD MTC (not the provision itself but the Commentary!) does not allow such an interpretation. The Commentary explicitly relates the POEM to the place where decisions are made. If a subsidiary has assets and premises in State A but the strategic decisions are taken in State B, then State B, again according to the Commentary, should be declared as the POEM state.[236] The opposite solution (i.e., State A as the POEM state) would run completely counter to the wording of the Commentary on Article 4(3) of the 2014 version of the OECD MTC (again, not the wording of Article 4(3) of the 2014 version of the OECD MTC itself).

One could adopt the following, reconciling solution: if the other elements of substance already point to a state as the POEM state, then recourse to the objective element is not necessary. If the other elements, however, do not provide sufficient answers ('all other things being equal'), then the objective element can break the tie and point to the POEM. Such a solution has also been accepted in literature, although there it was not the objective element but the existence of business operations that broke the tie.[237]

As previously noted and criticized, the indifference of the POEM towards the existence of business operations in a state other than the one in which decisions are made that the application of the POEM can lead to unsatisfactory results (section B.II.1.a.cc. of this chapter). The same holds true with regard to the indifference of the POEM towards the existence of assets and premises in a state other than the one in which decisions are made. Imagine that a subsidiary may have hundreds of employees working on premises and using/exploiting assets in State A, whereas the legally appointed directors live and act from State B, where only an office exists where the

236. One can also interpret German case law in this sense. In particular, in a recently rendered judgment the *Finanzgericht* of Munich did not consider the argument of the taxpayer that it had office premises in Luxembourg (its POI state) and ruled that the POM and POEM were in Germany in the relevant assessment periods. *See* the argument of the taxpayer in Finanzgericht of Munich, 10 V 1479/20, at para. 40.

237. According to the proposal of Maisto et al. (2018), p. 33, the POEM rule could have the following wording: 'Where by reasons of the provisions of paragraph 1, a person other than an individual is a resident of both Contracting States, then it shall be deemed to be a resident only of the State in which the place of effective management is situated. *If the place of effective management cannot be determined,* the person shall be deemed to be a resident of the State in which the *business or such activity as it conducts is primarily carried on.*' (Emphasis added). *See* above n. 40 in this chapter.

latter meet every once in a while. The POEM is in State B, although it could be ascertained that the subsidiary is more economically connected to State A than State B. As already maintained in section B.II.1.a.cc. of this chapter, this shortcoming must be rectified in a second step when applying rules to limit DTC benefits, like the LOB, and when attributing profits by applying the ALP.

4 *Synthesis*

There is no quantitative threshold requirement with regard to the application of the objective element of substance to the POEM (section B.III.1.). As to the qualities of the assets required for the purposes of the POEM, one looks at office premises and decision-related tangible assets. If these assets exist in more than one state, the state in which a larger quantity of these assets exists should win the tiebreaker (section B.III.2.). Furthermore, the personal and functional elements take precedence over the objective element. This may be deficient in some cases, from a perspective of ascertaining the economic allegiance of a subsidiary to its residence state. This shortcoming can be, however, rectified in a second step by applying anti-abuse and transfer pricing rules (section B.III.3.).

C INTERIM CONCLUSIONS

In this chapter, the content of the substance requirement for the purposes of the POEM has been analysed. The core conclusions drawn are summarized as follows:

- The personal and functional elements of substance coincide since the POEM concentrates on decisions taken by persons pertaining to the subsidiary in question. Reference is made to decisions related to the whole business (holistic approach) of a single subsidiary (stand-alone perspective). However, the POEM is indifferent towards the existence of business operations in the residence state (section B.II.1.a.).
- The relevant decisions for the purposes of this work are the strategic ones (section B.II.1.b.) and the relevant decision-making stage can be both the decision-making stricto sensu and the monitoring stage (section B.II.1.c.).
- As regards the personal element stricto sensu, it is the board of directors that, as a rule, is relevant for the purposes of the POEM. However, economic reality shakes this assumption and it can be that the exception occurs and outsiders, especially the parent, usurp the subsidiary's management (sections B.II.2.a. and B.II.2.b.). One needs to draw a line between the mere influence of the management and usurpation. The following constitute rebuttable presumptions pointing to the usurpation of management from the legally appointed directors: a lack of information (section B.II.2.c.cc.), knowledge and expertise both in technical and an economic sense on the side of the legally appointed decision-makers (section B.II.2.c.dd.), violation of the subsidiary's interests by the managers (only if this is not dictated by other laws like corporate law;

section B.II.2.c.ee.), and limitations of authority where the supervisory board must approve all strategic decisions and it does so in a place other than the one in which the management board makes the respective decisions should the place of approval be the decisive one (section B.II.2.c.ff.). If these criteria are sufficiently present, constitute sufficient conditions for usurpation of management to occur (section B.II.2.c.ii.). By contrast, in the author's view, other limitations of authority (section B.II.2.c.ff.), appointment of managers of the parent also as managers of the subsidiary (section B.II.2.c.gg.), and outsourcing of decision-making with regard to strategic decisions, so long as the control over these decision remains in the hands of the board (section B.II.2.c.hh.), do not lead to usurpation of management by the parent.
- As to the quantitative sub-element, one must differentiate between the number of decisions and the number of decision-makers. In both cases, there is no absolute threshold requirement but there may exist a relative threshold, although the qualitative sub-element should first be consulted and take priority when pointing to different results from the one suggested by the quantitative sub-element (section B.II.3.).
- Finally, the POEM does not stipulate any quantitative threshold requirement as regards the objective element of substance. Here, reference is made to the office premises and other decision-related tangible assets of the subsidiary, while intangible and financial assets seem to play no role. The objective element is of less importance for the purposes of the POEM than the personal and functional element (section B.III.).

In the form of a 'checklist', one could sum up the conclusions so far as follows.

Figure 4 Substance Checklist in the POEM

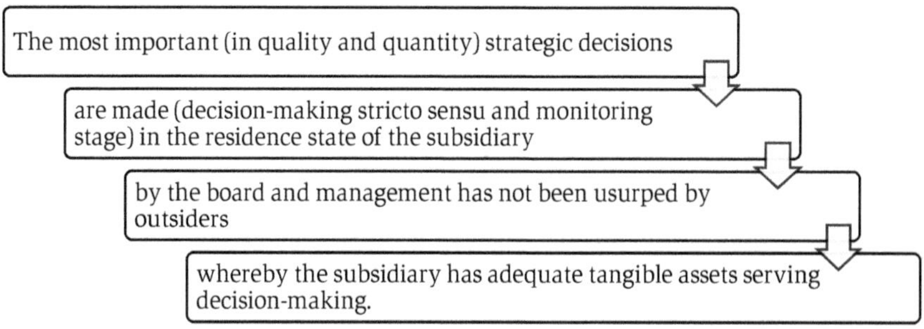

The last element of the substance checklist functions as a rebuttable presumption against the taxpayer where it is up to the latter to disprove the presumption, while the first three elements function as irrebuttable presumptions of lack of substance.[238] If, for

238. On substance requirements as rebuttable and irrebuttable presumptions, *see* above s. B.III.5. of the introduction.

example, the taxpayer is arguing that the POEM is in State A, although the tax authorities prove that the taxpayer does not possess adequate tangible assets supporting decision-making in State A, it is up to the taxpayer to bring forward arguments that support their classification of the facts of the case (rebuttable presumption). The taxpayer could then argue that the most qualitatively and quantitatively important strategic decisions are made in State A by the board and management has not been usurped. These facts may trump the presumption created by the lack of objective substance. By contrast, if the most qualitatively and quantitatively important strategic decisions are made in another state than the asserted POEM state or they are only formally made in the asserted POEM state because management has been usurped, the existence of objective substance in the latter state cannot help the taxpayer further (irrebuttable presumption).

CHAPTER 2
The Substance Requirement for the Purposes of Transfer Pricing Rules

A PRELIMINARY REMARKS

Before delving into the analysis of the content of the substance requirement for the purposes of transfer pricing rules, the reader must become acquainted with the functions (section A.I.1.) and mechanism (section A.I.2.) of transfer pricing rules. By doing so, the relevance of the investigation is revealed (section A.II.).

I Functions and Mechanism of the ALP

1 Functions of the ALP

Imagine your parents own a bicycle repair shop. You are the one running the shop arranging and conducting all the repairs, etc., whereas your parents only retain an oversight function. For running the shop, you only get some extra pocket money and, of course, no employment contract is concluded between you and your parents. Certainly, if your parents had to hire an employee to perform all these tasks, they would have to pay them a lot more than some extra pocket money. But you do not protest. At the end of the day, your parents' money is also your money; and the less labour costs the shop incurs, the more profit reaches your parents' pockets. If you rendered these services for another bicycle repair shop, however, you would certainly make a more profitable deal and demand that everything be contractually documented.

Now, apply this trivial example to the MNE context. The ultimate parent's money is also the subsidiaries' money. Thus, the subsidiaries, just like a kid helping its parents out, are prone to price their services to other members of the MNE group according to their parent's wishes (not only under- but also overprice them). After all, it's all about the parent's pockets.

The a priori tendency existing in the MNE to price services and goods according to the parent's best interest[1] interferes with the equal treatment between related and unrelated parties for tax law purposes.[2] And a cardinal principle of law, and of course tax law as well, is the principle of equality, under which similar situations should be treated similarly under the law.[3] In tax law, the principle of equality is expressed in the ability-to-pay principle.[4] Now, how can international tax law preserve taxation according to the ability-to-pay principle?[5]

International tax law uses a tool or, better formulated, a fiction for this purpose: the ALP.[6] The ALP 'follows the approach of treating the members of an MNE group as operating as separate entities rather than as inseparable parts of a single unified

1. ATO, TR 2014/6, para. 103: 'divergence of interests may not exist between associated entities, such that they may not feel the same need to conform to contractual terms and conditions, because of their association with the other party'. From the literature, *see, e.g.*, Schoueri/Galendi (Jr.) (2020), p. 154; Ponticelli/Tronci (2021), s. 1.
2. Take a manufacturing subsidiary located in a high-tax country. It manufactures goods and sales them to another group company entrusted with the distribution of these goods. In order to reduce the tax burden and thereby increase its parent's after-tax profits it underprices the goods sold to the distribution company, say EUR 5 per item. An independent company in the same jurisdiction prices the exact same goods with EUR 10. Accordingly, its taxable profits are double as high as the ones of the manufacturing subsidiary.
3. According to Gustav Radbruch: 'Where justice is not even pursued, where equality, which is the core of justice, is deliberately denied in the establishment of positive law, there the law is not only "flawed" law, but lacks the nature of law completely.' Radbruch (1946), p. 107 (author's unofficial translation).
4. The ability-to-pay principle has two prongs, or better formulated, results: On the one hand, the ability-to-pay principle refers to a principle underlying a tax system that is designed in a way 'that everyone should contribute to public expenditure "as nearly as possible, in proportion to their respective abilities; that is, in proportion to the revenue which they respectively enjoy under the protection of the state"'. *See* Englisch (2014), p. 440 quoting Adam Smith. On the other hand, '[a]bility to pay ... is of interest because, by general assumption, the fair treatment of taxpayers requires that burdens be equal. The greater one's ability to pay, the higher the fair tax, and perhaps the higher the fair rate of tax'. *See* Utz (2002), pp. 868-869. Under this prong, equal situations must be treated equally under tax laws, i.e., the ability to pay is the yardstick that tax law employs in order to preserve equality.
5. Under- and overpricing in the MNE context does not only interfere with the ability-to-pay principle. From an economic perspective, it creates competition distortions. A modification of the bicycle repair shop example may illustrate that. Assume, there is also a neighbouring bicycle shop in the area and the neighbouring bicycle shop's owners do not have a kid that works for them, but external workers. Thus, they have to incur the additional labour costs. Consequently, they either have to reduce their profit margin and go bankrupt or raise prices. By doing the latter, though, they have a huge competitive disadvantage vis-à-vis the bicycle repair shop using their kid's labour. This is why literature refers to neutrality as regards the choice of organizational form, i.e., 'make or buy question' (s. A. of the Introduction), as the normative basis for the ALP. *See* from the literature Schön (2010a), p. 233; Baistrocchi (2022), s. 1.1.2.; Schoueri/Galendi (Jr.) (2020), p. 156; Li (2002), p. 828 referring to this kind of neutrality as 'transactional neutrality'. However, it must be stated that contemporary authors deny a normative basis of neutralities in the international tax law system. *See* Peters (2014), s. 9.2.3.; Hongler (2019), pp. 422 et seq. And economists treat neutralities as 'a ritual' and argue 'that the real analysis [for international tax policy] lies elsewhere'. *See* Weisbach (2015), p. 645.
6. On the ALP as a means to measure the ability-to-pay *see* Schoueri (2015), pp. 695 et seq.; Schoueri/Galendi (Jr.) (2020), p. 156; Navarro (2018), p. 354; Navarro (2020), p. 101. *See also* Schön (2010a), pp. 237-238: 'transfer pricing adjustments are meant to promote the equal treatment of taxpayers, whether in an independent or dependent business framework'.

business'.[7] This corresponds to the stand-alone perspective espoused for the purposes of the POEM (section B.II.1.a.aa. of Chapter 1).

In order to implement the aforementioned fiction, the ALP would assume that:

(1) there is no MNE relationship between the related parties;
(2) a contract exists between them; and
(3) this contract includes terms and conditions[8] similar to those that independent parties would have agreed upon.[9]

The ALP is enshrined in the OECD MTC and has two functions.[10] In particular, Article 9(1) of the OECD MTC stipulates that:

> 1. Where
>
> a) an enterprise of a Contracting State participates directly or indirectly in the management, control or capital of an enterprise of the other Contracting State, or
> b) the same persons participate directly or indirectly in the management, control or capital of an enterprise of a Contracting State and an enterprise of the other Contracting State,
>
> and in either case conditions are made or imposed between the two enterprises in their commercial or financial relations which differ from those which would be made between independent enterprises, then any profits which would, but for those conditions, have accrued to one of the enterprises, but, by reason of those conditions, have not so accrued, may be included in the profits of that enterprise and taxed accordingly.

The wording of Article 9(1) of the OECD MTC manifests the first function of the ALP in the DTC framework, i.e., allocating profits to persons (and thereby indirectly to

7. OECD TPG, para. 1.6. Commentators call it 'the Orphan Approach' because '[f]or transfer pricing purposes, each subsidiary is treated as orphaned from the group'. *See* Li/Li (2017), p. 267. It must be said, though, that this is, at least in a legal sense, not so much of a fiction. A subsidiary, legally, is a separate taxpayer (*see* above s. B.I. of the introduction). One could argue, though, that economically the group is to be treated as a whole, thus treating each entity pertaining to the group separately is a fiction. *See* Quek (2011), p. 317.
8. Words are chosen carefully here. The ALP in the DTC context 'addresses [not only] "profit" distortions' between associated enterprises but also mispricing. That is, not only the price pertaining to a transaction between associated enterprises is subject to the ALP control but also other terms and conditions thereof if they lead to a profit allocation that would not occur between independent parties. *See* Wilkie (2012b), pp. 145-146.

   It must be clarified, though, that reference is made to price-sensitive conditions, namely the ones that, if changed, affect the price agreed upon between the parties and thereby can lead to profit distortions. For example, a loan with a payment duration of two years, all other things being equal, has another interest than a loan with a payment duration of 5 years. On the requirement of the price-sensitivity of the terms, *see* Wittendorff (2009), p. 116.
9. *See* Petruzzi (2016), p. 11.
10. The two functions of the ALP presented here are adopted relying on Kane (2014), p. 302 and Navarro (2017), pp. 80-83. *See*, however, Kraus (2019), p. 132, according to whom the limitation of the taxing rights of states is only an incidental effect of Article 9(1) of the OECD MTC.

territories). By applying the ALP in their domestic tax laws, states fulfil this function by doing the following:

(1) they determine the amount of profits attributable to each part of an MNE (*see* Article 9(1)(a) of the OECD MTC referring to 'control' that an entity, i.e., the parent, has over another entity, i.e., the subsidiary);
(2) they may[11] rectify the profit allocation agreed by the persons involved ('included'); and
(3) they may do so only if it does not correspond to what independent parties would have agreed upon ('conditions ... which differ from those which would be made between independent enterprises').

Simultaneously (and that is the second function of the ALP), the ALP sets limits to the authority of states when they determine the profits of a company.[12,13] That is, if the arm's length price for royalty payments, for example, is EUR 10, the residence state of the entity receiving the royalties cannot claim for itself profits exceeding EUR 10. By doing so, and in conjunction with Article 9(2),[14] stipulating the so-called corresponding

---

11. The modal verb 'may' signalize *entitlement* to conduct transfer pricing adjustments based on domestic tax law. It does not introduce an obligation for the states to create the appropriate legal framework and make transfer pricing adjustments. A comparison with the wording of Article 9(2) of the OECD MTC, using the modal verb 'shall', makes this finding even more apparent. *See* above n. 14 in this chapter.

    Furthermore, the states cannot rely on Article 9 to make an adjustment; it is their domestic law that offers them the legal basis to do so (i.e., Article 9 is not a self-executing rule). *See* Federal Court of Australia, 23 Oct. 2015, *Chevron Australia Holdings Pty Ltd. v. Australian Tax Office*, FCA (2015), p. 1092 (at para. 62). From the literature Collier/Andrus (2017), para. 2.16; Navarro (2017), p. 83. *Contra* Tavares et al. (2016), pp. 177-178; Baistrocchi (2022), s. 6.2.5.1. arguing that pricing according to the ALP is mandated by customary international law.
12. *See* Bundesfinanzhof, 11 Oct. 2012, I R 75/11, BStBl. II (2013), p. 1046 (at para. 9) also on the non-self-executing nature of Article 9 of the OECD MTC. More recent case law does not completely reverse the jurisprudence of the Bundesfinanzhof in this matter. *See* Bundesfinanzhof, 27 Feb. 2019, I R 73/16, BStBl. II (2019), p. 394 (at para. 27); confirmed by many subsequent judgments, e.g., Bundesfinanzhof, 14 Aug. 2019, I R 14/18 and 34/18, BFH/NV (2020), p. 754. These decisions only reject that Article 9 of the OECD MTC limits states to correct only the price of a transaction and not other terms and conditions thereof. They do not completely negate the function of Article 9 of the OECD MTC of setting boundaries to the power of the states when determining which profits are allocable to entities located in their territory. From the literature, on this function of the ALP, *see* Navarro (2021), p. 806 with further references.
13. Of course, this means a state that disregards the limits imposed by the ALP to its domestic law via a DTC (for instance, by applying a method that does not take into consideration third party behaviour at all) runs afoul of treaty obligations (treaty override).
14. '2. Where a Contracting State includes in the profits of an enterprise of that State – and taxes accordingly – profits on which an enterprise of the other Contracting State has been charged to tax in that other State and the profits so included are profits which would have accrued to the enterprise of the first-mentioned State if the conditions made between the two enterprises had been those which would have been made between independent enterprises, then that other State shall make an appropriate adjustment to the amount of the tax charged therein on those profits. In determining such adjustment, due regard shall be had to the other provisions of this Convention and the competent authorities of the Contracting States shall if necessary consult each other.'

adjustments,[15] the ALP in the DTC framework ensures that no economic double taxation arises.[16,17]

Summing up, the function of the ALP in the DTC framework is a twofold one: first, it is applied to determine the profits allocable to different parts of an MNE group (and thereby to different states) according to the ability-to-pay principle. For this purpose, the ALP makes recourse to the terms and conditions third parties would have agreed upon. Reliance on third party behaviour introduces a structural element into the international tax law system.[18] That is, the behaviour of the MNE 'family' is only accepted by tax authorities if it corresponds to the one of unrelated market players.[19] If it does not, then tax authorities may rectify the profits allocable to a part of an MNE. And this is where the second function of the ALP becomes important: it limits the authority of states when rectifying the profits of an MNE member to the arm's length profit (no more no less) and obliges (Article 9(2) of the OECD MTC: 'shall make an appropriate adjustment') the other state involved to conduct a corresponding adjustment.

The question now arises as to how the ALP performs these functions. In order to perform both functions, an arm's length profit must be determinable. But how can the arm's length profit be determined? In order to answer this question, the next section sheds light on the mechanism of the ALP.

Notice that the other State 'shall' make a corresponding adjustment; it is not entitled to do so, but *obliged*, in order for double taxation to be eliminated. *See also* above n. 11 in this chapter as to the difference in wording ('shall' versus 'may') between Article 9(1) and 9(2) of the OECD MTC. On the issue, *see* Striefler/Kostikidis (2022), p. 765.

15. So, in our example, the residence state of the company receiving the royalties, in accordance with Article 9(1) of the OECD MTC, will increase its profit by EUR 10. Conversely, the residence state of the paying company must reduce its profit by EUR 10 in accordance with Article 9(2) of the OECD MTC so that no economic double taxation will arise.
16. So, if the residence state of the company receiving the royalties would defy the arm's length price (EUR 10) and set the price for each royalty payment by EUR 15, economic double taxation would arise with respect to the EUR 5 that exceed the arm's length price (15–10 = 5) even if the foreign jurisdictions of the other subsidiaries carry out corresponding adjustments in accordance with the ALP, since these adjustments will only cover the arm's length compliant part of the royalty payments, i.e., EUR 10.
17. It is not the purpose of this work to take posture to the other purposes of the ALP that have been proposed in the literature. A concise summary thereof can be found in Prasanna/Sollund (2019), p. 14; Navarro (2020), pp. 100-101. Especially, it is important to underline that the ALP in the DTC context does not have an anti-abuse function, as it can have in the domestic context. *See* KPMG (2015), pp. 546-547; Pankiv (2016), p. 474; Navarro (2017), p. 50 with further references of the contrary viewpoint in n. 215; Screpante (2020), p. 864. According to Collier/Andrus (2017), para. 4.80 the transfer pricing regime 'establish[es] limits on the anti-avoidance jurisdiction of local transfer pricing rules'; the same can be said with regard to domestic anti-abuse rules. *See* Wittendorff (2009), p. 118.
18. This idea is borrowed by Lederman (2007), p. 699 who discusses this concept in another context, though (whether unreimbursed losses should be treated equally as reimbursed ones). *See also* Avi-Yonah/Benshalom (2011), p. 379 giving the ALP a more negative tone by calling it a 'structural limitation'.
19. *See* OECD TPG, para. 1.14 in fine; from the literature *see*, e.g., Brauner (2008), p. 104: 'The arm's length standard is basically an articulation of the traditional market approach to valuation.'

2 *Mechanism of the ALP*

a *What Is Subject to the ALP?*

With regard to the mechanism of the ALP, it must be remembered that the ALP gains its specific contours in the OECD TPG (section B.III.2. of the introduction). The latter are not legally binding, but their application by states constitutes an 'essential consensus'. Thus, when reference is made to 'transfer pricing rules', the OECD TPG are meant and not the domestic legal rules implementing the ALP, which, again,[20] are necessary for the ALP to be applied, since Article 9(1) of the OECD MTC is not a self-executing rule.

Now, the first issue to be clarified as to the mechanism of the ALP is what is subjected to the transfer pricing rules. Thus far, reference has been made to 'profits' of an MNE member. So, one could say that what matters is that, in the final analysis, the total profits of the particular MNE member are fairly allocated in comparison with other market players under similar circumstances. This is not the approach chosen by the OECD. In its TPG, the OECD clarifies that the '[a]pplication of the arm's length principle is based on a comparison of the conditions in a controlled transaction with the conditions that would have been made had the parties been independent and undertaking a comparable *transaction* under comparable circumstances'.[21] Thus, in contrast to the POEM, which as we have seen in section B.II.1.a.aa. evaluates the whole spectrum of the decisions taken referring to all transactions of a subsidiary (holistic approach), subject to the ALP control are single[22] transactions (transactional approach);[23] and in particular transactions between 'associated enterprises' which is what subsidiaries in relation to their parent (and other sub-subsidiaries) always are.[24]

In this respect, a first divergence as to the content of substance for the purposes of the POEM, on the one hand, and profit allocation, on the other, can be detected. While for the purposes of the POEM the business of the subsidiary *as a whole* (holistic approach) is relevant (section B.II.1.a.aa. of Chapter 1), that is, a subsidiary may have enough substance for its business in its totality or it may not have it, for the purposes of profit allocation the existence of substance is determined on a transactional basis.

20. *See* above n. 12 in this chapter.
21. OECD TPG, para. 1.33 (emphasis added).
22. Admittedly, more than one transaction may also be aggregated and treated together for the purposes of the ALP analysis if they are linked to each other. As to when such link exists, *see* Pichhadze (2016), pp. 188 et seq.
23. OECD TPG, para. 3.9. The term transactional approach is adopted by Collier/Andrus (2017), para. 3.13. *Contra* Li (2002), p. 838 rightly pointing out that 'the word "transaction" is not found in article 9'. For a definition of the term 'transactions', *see* Wilkie (2012a), p. 228.
24. Paragraph 1 first sentence of the Commentary (2017) on Article 9 referring to 'parent and subsidiary companies' as 'associated enterprises'. *See* already Fiscal Committee, *Report to the Council on the Fourth Session of the Committee,* C.399.M.204. 1933.II.A. (1933), p. 7[4247]. It is not the purpose of this work to deal with this undefined term. Therefore, the work proceeds on the basis of the assumption mentioned in the text, i.e., that subsidiaries in relation to their parent (and other sub-subsidiaries) are always associated enterprises. On the latter term, *see, e.g.,* Rotondaro (2000); Dwarkasing (2013);Ponticelli/Tronci (2021), s. 3.

That is, a subsidiary may have substance for one transaction, while it may be lacking for another.

From a practical perspective, this means that the spill over effect[25] that may occur when determining the existence of substance for the purposes of the POEM may not occur in the realm of profit allocation. This difference is justified considering the mechanism of each rule. While residence is determined for an entity as a whole, profit allocation is linked to individual transactions.

b *How Does the ALP Determine the Profit Pertaining to a Transaction?*

After it has been clarified *what* is subject to the ALP (i.e., transactions between associated enterprises; 'controlled transactions'), now it is time to assess *how* the ALP determines how much profit pertains to the controlled transaction. Recourse can be made, again, to the OECD TPG:

> There are two key aspects in such an analysis: the first aspect is to identify the commercial or financial relations between the associated enterprises and the conditions and economically relevant circumstances attaching to those relations in order that the controlled transaction is accurately delineated; the second aspect is to compare the conditions and the economically relevant circumstances of the controlled transaction as accurately delineated with the conditions and the economically relevant circumstances of comparable transactions between independent enterprises ['uncontrolled transaction'].[26]

Thus, the analysis determining the arm's length profit pertaining to a controlled transaction commences with an accurate delineation of the controlled transaction.

aa Accurate Delineation of the Controlled Transaction

So what is meant by accurately delineating the controlled transaction? Again, the OECD TPG provide clear guidance:

> The accurate delineation of the actual transaction or transactions between the associated enterprises requires analysis of the economically relevant characteristics of the transaction.'[27] 'The economically relevant characteristics or comparability factors that need to be identified in the commercial or financial relations between the associated enterprises in order to accurately delineate the actual transaction can be broadly categorized as follows:
>
> - The contractual terms of the transaction (D.1.1).
> - The functions performed by each of the parties to the transaction, taking into account assets used and risks assumed, including how those functions relate to

25. *See* below s. B.II.1.a.aa. of Ch. 2 where the spill over effect is explained: 'although a subsidiary [may] not have substance for an individual transaction (e.g., granting loans), it may have substance for another transaction (e.g., rendering administrative services) and, thus, still be considered to have enough substance for the purposes of the POEM'.
26. OECD TPG, para. 1.33.
27. *Ibid.*, para. 1.35.

the wider generation of value by the MNE group to which the parties belong, the circumstances surrounding the transaction, and industry practices (D.1.2) ['functional analysis'].
- The characteristics of property transferred or services provided (D.1.3).
- The economic circumstances of the parties and of the market in which the parties operate (D.1.4).
- The business strategies pursued by the parties (D.1.5).[28]

Therefore, the first stage in determining the arm's length profit allocable to a controlled transaction, i.e., the accurate delineation of the controlled transaction, consists of the five aforementioned sub-stages. From these, the first two are relevant to this work and are thus analysed.[29] First, the *contractual terms of the transaction* must be delineated. The importance of this sub-stage is explained in the following example.

Assume you want to build a house. You consider offers from two different construction companies, one from a very experienced construction company and one from a 'start-up' construction company. The experienced construction company agrees to a flat-rate remuneration of, for instance, EUR 200. It knows the complications that may arise, but it knows how to solve them in order to earn the profit it expects. This is not the case with the inexperienced start-up, which probably wants a remuneration according to the time spent on the project.

The different forms of remuneration contractually agreed reflects the parties' attitude towards the risks accompanying the project.[30] The flat-rate remuneration demonstrates that the experienced construction company carries, for example, the risk that the soil is less steady than expected and different material must be used, whereas, in the case of the inexperienced construction firm, it is you (i.e., the principal ordering the construction) who carry such risk (since you will have to continue to pay the construction firm during the delay of the project caused by this complication).[31]

Now, the example is modified a little bit. Suppose both construction firms are start-ups. Still, one of them is willing to make the flat-rate deal. But why would a start-up construction company with poor financial resources make the flat-rate deal, exposing it to risks, like the capacity utilization risk? The company is well aware that it does not have the financial capacity to 'survive' should such risk materialize. Therefore, the facts of the case (i.e., the construction firm lacking the financial capacity

28. *Ibid.*, para. 1.36.
29. The characteristics of property transferred or services provided have nothing to do with the substance of the controlled party but with the one of the product/service in question. The economic circumstances of the parties and the market in which the parties operate have also nothing to do with substance in the form of functions, persons, and assets but rather with factors like the competitive position of the controlled party. *See* OECD TPG, para. 1.130. Finally, the business strategies pursued by the parties also have nothing to do with the substance but rather deal with issues like market penetration schemes. *See* OECD TPG, paras 1.135 et seq.
30. Of course, the contract does not explicitly state which party bears which risks. It is by interpretation of the contract that the intentions of the parties to bear risks can be ascertained. On the role of contractual interpretation in this stage of the ALP analysis, *see* Wilkie (2012a), p. 236; Pichhadze (2015), pp. 131-132 and 143-144; Pichhadze (2016), pp. 182-184.
31. This is called the 'utilization risk'. *See,* based on another example, OECD TPG, para. 1.85.

to take on risks) do not correspond to the contractual agreement of a flat-rate remuneration.

Factually, it is you, the principal, who bear the capacity utilization risk because, should the risk materialize, the start-up will not survive it and liquidate, and you will have to find another construction company for your project. Such cases may arise in the case of controlled transactions where 'the fact of ... common control implies that those contracts will not be adversarially enforced and that they normally can be changed at the will of the parent company'.[32] For this reason, the OECD stipulates that the delineation of a controlled transaction does not stop with what the parties to the transaction in question have agreed upon, but must be accompanied by a *functional analysis* which 'focuses on what the parties actually do and the capabilities they provide'.[33]

bb Comparability Analysis

After having accurately delineated the controlled transaction in the way presented in the above section, one needs to find (a) comparable transaction(s) ('comparable(s)') between independent parties and set the price for the controlled transaction according to the price agreed in the comparable. For this purpose, the second stage of the ALP analysis is employed, i.e., the comparability analysis. 'Below is a description of a typical process that can be followed when performing a comparability analysis.'[34]

> Step 1: Determination of years to be covered.
> Step 2: Broad-based analysis of the taxpayer's circumstances.
> Step 3: Understanding the controlled transaction(s) under examination, based in particular on a functional analysis, in order to choose the tested party (where needed), the most appropriate transfer pricing method to the circumstances of the case, the financial indicator that will be tested (in the case of a transactional profit method), and to identify the significant comparability factors that should be taken into account.
> Step 4: Review of existing internal comparables, if any.
> Step 5: Determination of available sources of information on external comparables where such external comparables are needed taking into account their relative reliability.
> Step 6: Selection of the most appropriate transfer pricing method and, depending on the method, determination of the relevant financial indicator (e.g., determination of the relevant net profit indicator in case of a transactional net margin method (TNMM)).
> Step 7: Identification of potential comparables: determining the key characteristics to be met by any uncontrolled transaction in order to be regarded as

32. Li (2002), p. 833.
33. OECD TPG, para. 1.51.
34. *Ibid.*, para. 3.4.

potentially comparable, based on the relevant factors identified in Step 3 and in accordance with the comparability factors set forth in section D.1 of Chapter I.
Step 8: Determination of and making comparability adjustments where appropriate.
Step 9: Interpretation and use of data collected, determination of the arm's length remuneration.[35]

The first step from the above step-analysis is easy to comprehend, so the focus is placed on the ones that follow.

First of all, under steps two and three, one needs to '[analyse] the taxpayer's circumstances' and '[u]nderstand the controlled transaction(s) under examination, based in particular on a functional analysis'. This is in principle a reiteration of the accurate delineation of the transaction based on the five sub-stages described in the previous section.[36] This process intends to 'identify the significant comparability factors that should be taken into account'.[37] That is, by accurately delineating the controlled transaction, the characteristics are enlisted that an uncontrolled transaction must have in order for it to be comparable with the controlled transaction.

After setting out the comparability factors, one needs to search for comparables. The transactions can take place either between a company of the MNE group and an independent company ('internal comparables') or between two independent companies ('external comparables'). Steps 4 and 5 amount to the search for such comparables.

The comparability analysis culminates in steps 6-9. In these steps, one first needs to select 'the most appropriate transfer pricing method'. This work does not purport to delve deeply into these issues. Thus, it suffices to say that there exist five methods, divided into two categories: the traditional methods, referring to prices or gross margins, and the transactional profit methods, referring to profits. 'As a general introduction to traditional and transactional profit methods, it can be stated that, in order to test or establish the arm's length conditions relating to the controlled transactions, the CUP [comparable uncontrolled price] method compares prices, the RPM [resale price method] compares gross margins, the CPM [cost plus method] compares gross profit markups on costs, the TNMM [transactional net margin method] compares net margins and, lastly, the TPSM [transactional profit split method] compares the allocation of profits between the parties.'[38]

Now, that the mechanics of the ALP have been briefly explored, the question arises: what does substance have to do with all that? The next section provides an answer to that question.

35. *Ibid.*
36. *Ibid.*, para. 1.33 in fine.
37. *Ibid.*, para. 3.4.
38. Brown/Orlandi (2019), p. 92.

II Relevance of the Investigation

1 *Relevance for the Purposes of the Accurate Delineation of the Controlled Transaction*

Going back to the definition of substance for the purposes of this work in section D. of the introduction, it has been established that substance has an objective, a functional and a personal element. Now, looking at the mechanics of the ALP, we see how the aforementioned elements come into play for the purposes of the ALP analysis. When accurately delineating a transaction, the second step after establishing which the contractual terms of the controlled transaction are and what they stipulate, is to conduct a functional analysis where assets used and risks assumed are taken into account.

So functions and assets, constituting elements of substance, are taken into account when delineating the controlled transaction. And this makes sense. The more intensely one invests in an activity, the more profit one may claim out of the transaction in question.[39]

But that is not where the relevance of substance at the stage of delineating the controlled transaction stops. First, substance plays a significant role for the purposes of risk allocation according to the OECD TPG. Again, risk assumption is a relevant factor when delineating the controlled transaction; that is because the amount of risk-taking influences the expected profit.[40] In particular, profit 'can be viewed as comprised of three different elements or components: the real risk-free rate of return, the risk premium, and inframarginal return'.[41] The riskier an investment, the higher the second component of profit is, i.e., the risk premium.

According to the OECD TPG, contractually assuming risk is not a guarantee for the parties to the controlled transaction that the risk, and therewith the risk premium, is allocated to the party contractually assuming the risk, the latter party also having to 'perform control functions and risk mitigation functions'.[42] So according to the OECD, risk and profit from risk follow 'risk management functions', which in turn entail decision-making.[43] And by whom are decisions made? The reader should already know that: people. Thus, the personal element of substance influences the allocation of risk itself and thereby of the risk premium arising from risk assumption. And since risks are

39. *See* Luckhaupt et al. (2012), p. 100; Wright et al. (2016), p. 99.
40. OECD TPG, para. 1.56. Although this is not a panacea, *see* Collier/Dykes (2020), p. 708: 'for some businesses, profits are hugely influenced by the quality of ongoing decision-making concerning risk, whereas for others it may be their assets or long-term contractual arrangements that are more important in delivering their profits'.
41. Cunningham (1996), p. 23. The risk-free rate of return is the theoretical rate of return of an investment with zero risk (theoretical because every investment entails some degree of risk-taking). The risk-premium relates to the return for risk-taking, for example, the return relating to assuming the utilization risk. The inframarginal return is related to 'unique opportunities with returns greater than the market return'. *See* Weisbach (2004), p. 19. The OECD TPG refer only to the first two components of this profit definition, i.e., the risk-free return and the risk premium.
42. OECD TPG, para. 1.60.
43. *Ibid.*, para. 1.61.

borne in assets,[44] by allocating risk to the entity which assumes decision-making functions the OECD '"located" assets in the country where the risk with respect to the assets was managed, that is, where the personnel performing the significant people functions were'.[45,46]

Furthermore, substance plays a role in the attribution of returns from intangible assets. In particular, the OECD TPG dedicate a whole section of the pertinent chapter of the OECD TPG dealing with intangibles (section B.2.1. of Chapter VI of the OECD TPG) to the 'Performance and Control of Functions', whereby decision-making also plays a prominent role.[47] A quote from the OECD TPG may illustrate this:

> the legal owner of the intangible should also compensate the entity performing *control functions* related to the development, enhancement, maintenance, protection, and exploitation of intangibles on an arm's length basis. In assessing what member of the MNE group in fact controls the performance of the relevant functions, *principles apply analogous to those for determining control over risk* in Section D.1.2.1 of Chapter I.[48]

This means, in a nutshell, that according to the OECD, just like in the case of risk allocation, a corporation needs enough substance (in the form of decision-making persons, i.e., its personal substance) in order to attract intangible-related returns, even though it may legally be the owner of the intangible.

All in all, the conclusion can be drawn that substance as defined here is relevant when delineating the controlled transaction in two ways: profit follows functions, assets, and risks, on the one hand, and assets and risks follow decision-making functions, on the other.[49] The latter means that decision-making functions determine the allocation of risks, and thereby the allocation of the risk premium, and the allocation of intangible-related profits.[50]

---

44. Schön (2010a), p. 243; Vann (2010), p. 336: 'risk should not be treated as a separable issue and should be seen as residing in the property'.
45. Vann (2010), p. 328.
46. For this reason, reference is often made to 'profit from an asset', although the OECD guidance in s. D.1.2.1. of Ch. I relates to risk allocation and not asset allocation. Although it is the risk that is allocated and not the asset, the profit from the risk borne in the asset follows the risk. It can be surmised that that is why *Vann* put the word located in quotation marks.
47. OECD TPG, para. 6.56.
48. *Ibid.*, para. 6.53 (emphasis added).
49. *See* above s. D.II.2. of the Introduction and the text accompanying n. 88. *See also* the accurate comment by Nikolakakis (2021), p. 558: 'The problem with this approach is that it substitutes the trinity of functions, assets and risks, with a different trinity, being functions, functions and functions.'
50. It must be underlined that the OECD TPG respect the allocation of legal ownership of intangibles; it just does not respect its value creating capacity. So ultimately the OECD says: 'I accept and respect you as the owner of asset X, but that does not mean that you also get the profit out of it.' In this respect, *see* Screpante (2019), p. 460; Greinert et al. (2020), p. 526; Schuster et al. (2022), pp. 151-152 with further references. By contrast, the OECD approach on risk lies in reallocating risks when the decision-making functions are not performed by the party assuming the risk.

    From that it follows that the decision-making functions operate in two ways within the OECD TPG: (1) as a threshold for the purposes of risk allocation ('If you pass the threshold, you are allocated the risk in question.'), (2) return from intangibles follow the decision-making functions (in this respect, no threshold must be passed.). *See* Collier/Andrus (2017), para. 7.55, n. 33.

2 *Relevance for the Purposes of the Comparability Analysis*

It is exactly because of its relevance during the stage of accurately delineating the controlled transaction that substance, as defined here, is also relevant, at least indirectly, for the purposes of the comparability analysis.[51] First, the functional analysis, in which the substance of a subsidiary for the purposes of the controlled transaction plays a role, determines the outcome of the search for the appropriate comparables. This statement requires some further explanation.

It must be known by now that the accurate delineation stage shows us what is to be controlled according to the ALP. For example, using fruits for illustration purposes, say that the delineation of the transaction produces red apples. Accordingly, the search for comparables is exactly what the phrase reveals, i.e., a search for comparables. That is, non-comparable fruits are excluded. Now, comparable according to what criterion? If it is the form of the issue, it could be that a grocery store puts in front of oranges the label red apples. In this case, red apples and oranges are formally similar. But if it is the substance of the fruit that is the relevant comparability criterion, and thus one looks at the functions of red apples, then red apples could be similar only to green apples.

Now, applying this example to the ALP, the fact that substance, i.e., functions, assets, and risks and the decision-makers behind them, is relevant in the delineation of the transaction necessarily means that one does not search for formally similar comparables but for comparables that are similar in substance, as defined here, i.e., comparables where functions, assets, and risks and the decision-makers behind them are similar.[52]

Second, the factual analysis also determines which is the most appropriate method to use. In particular, the degree of functions performed, risks assumed, and assets employed make the use of some methods harder.[53] Take a sale from a manufacturer to an associated distributor. Normally, in such cases, the Resale Price Method (RPM) can be employed.[54] Again, the RPM compares gross margins, i.e., the turnover minus the cost of goods sold. Now, assume further that the associated distributor employs much substance for the purposes of this transaction. For example, it invests heavily in advertising and marketing the products it distributes. The costs arising from the latter functions are not classified as cost of goods sold but as operating expenses. Say that the gross margin of the associated distributor is 5%. Distributors with the exact same gross margin do not employ so much substance in their transactions; they simply buy and resale goods. Thus, because of the substance that the associated distributor has, the use of the RPM must be discarded, as the latter does not

51. Valta (2014), p. 443.
52. With respect to risk OECD TPG, para. 1.73: 'Where potential comparables are identified, it is relevant to determine whether they include the same level of risks and management of risks.' With respect to the decision-makers OECD TPG, para. 48 of Annex to Ch. VI: 'In determining the amount of compensation due Company S, the relative skill and efficiency of the Company S R&D personnel ... should be considered as comparability factors.'
53. Screpante (2019), p. 463; Screpante (2020), p. 873. On the influence of the allocation of risks on the selection of the appropriate method, *see* Grotherr (2021), p. 1103.
54. US Treas. Reg., §1.482-3(c)(1).

account for the differences in the functional profile between the associated distributor and the comparable.[55] The TNMM comparing operating margins, and thus accounting for operating expenses like the ones incurred by the associated party in the controlled transaction at hand (i.e., advertising and marketing expenses),[56] would be a better fit in this case.[57]

3 *Summary*

In sum, substance, as defined here, plays a role as a factor to be taken into account in the delineation of the controlled transaction, as it influences profit. Furthermore, according to the OECD, a corporation (and thus a subsidiary) claiming profit needs substance in the form of decision-making persons in order to have risks allocated to it, and therewith also the risk premium, and intangible-related profits. The fact that substance plays such a major role in the delineation stage permeates into the stage of the comparability analysis. First, comparables must be comparable to the controlled transaction in substance, as defined here. Second, the substance that an associated party brings into a transaction is determinative as to the choice of the most appropriate method.

III Scope of the Investigation

With regard to the scope of the investigation in this chapter, it is necessary to clarify which meaning the term 'substance' in the OECD TPG has and which meaning is relevant for the purposes of this work. As to the term substance, the definition developed in this work is based on the day-to-day usage of the term substance referring to the essential qualities of something. But it has already been ascertained that the term substance can also refer to the 'quality of being based on facts or the truth' (section D.I. of the introduction).

In fact, the word 'substance' in the OECD TPG is not only used in order to refer to the essential qualities that a taxpayer must have in order for profit to be allocated to them but also as a point of reference to the 'true' facts, or as commentators have called it the 'real deal',[58] as opposed to the false pretence that the parties may have created contractually. For example, the OECD TPG in paragraph 1.46 stipulate that:

> Where there are material differences between contractual terms and the conduct of the associated enterprises in their relations with one another, the functions they actually perform, the assets they actually use, and the risks they actually assume, considered in the context of the contractual terms, should ultimately determine the factual substance and accurately delineate the actual transaction.

---

55. *Ibid.*, §1.482-3(c)(3)(ii).
56. *Ibid.*, §1.482-3(c)(3)(ii)(C): 'differences in functions performed are often reflected in operating expenses'. *See also* para. (c)(3)(ii)(C)(3) listing advertising and marketing expenses within the operating expenses.
57. US Treas. Reg., §1.482-5(c)(2)(ii).
58. Collier/Andrus (2017), para. 6.11; Screpante (2019), p. 456.

According to this passage, one needs to differentiate between what the parties contractually agreed and what the parties are actually ('in substance') doing (i.e., the real deal), whereby profit allocation must be based on the latter pattern and not on the formal agreements. It becomes apparent that the OECD TPG make reference to substance in two ways: as a yardstick referring to the qualities that a taxpayer should have in order to attract profit, on the one hand, and as a word pointing to the real deal that should form the basis of profit allocation, on the other.

In this work, and thus henceforth, only the first meaning of the substance requirement in the OECD TPG is explored. That is, the question is asked regarding the qualities that a subsidiary is required to have in order for profits to be allocated to it (content of the substance requirement). Thus, the meaning of the term substance referring to the real deal is excluded from the scope of the work.

Finally, it has been stated that substance influences both the allocation of risk and intangible-related profits. Henceforth, reference is made only to the guidance on risk, as the guidance on intangibles also gives recourse to it.[59]

B THE CONTENT OF THE SUBSTANCE REQUIREMENT IN TRANSFER PRICING RULES

I Opening Remarks

1 Purpose of the Substance Orientation of the Transfer Pricing Rules

Before analysing substance, we need to first comprehend why transfer pricing should be substance-oriented. Why not stick to profit allocation based on the formal agreements of the parties and not the substance of the corporation claiming the profit, as commentators have argued?[60]

In fact, the OECD, by putting to the fore substance in the form of persons assuming decision-making functions for the purposes of transfer pricing rules, is trying to solve a fundamental problem: intangibles, as well as risks, of MNEs, may be held by subsidiaries located in low-tax jurisdictions and remain either low or non-taxed. This is because, in contrast to immovable factors like immovable property, both risks and intangibles can easily be 'shifted'[61] from the parent jurisdiction, or another high-tax

59. OECD TPG, para. 6.53: 'In assessing what member of the MNE group in fact controls the performance of the relevant functions, principles apply analogous to those for determining control over risk in Section D.1.2.1 of Chapter I.' *See also* Collier/Dykes (2020), p. 705, n. 35.
60. *See* Schön (2014), p. 290: 'We come to the conclusion that (unless we go for formulary apportionment) "ownership", "funding" and "contractual risk allocation" under private law remain the most relevant factors as they delineate the economic outcome of risky activities for the entities involved. The notions of "decision-making", "control" or "activity" are of secondary importance for the allocation of this residual profit.' *See also* Kane (2014), p. 311, n. 46 whose 'claim embodies a preference for paying heed to legal ownership rather than "economic ownership" in the associated enterprise context'.
61. As Musselli (2018), p. 6 has noted, the term 'shifted' is mostly inaccurate. This is because, normally, tax-planning with intangibles does not include the transfer of an extant intangible (either as an asset contribution or as a sale in return of a payment) or the licensing of rights on

jurisdiction, to entities resident in low-tax jurisdictions. And these entities normally do not have any, or in any case only very little, personnel, premises, and other movable or immovable assets, i.e., substance.

By requiring substance from a subsidiary in order for it to be attributed the profits pertaining to intangibles and risks, the OECD guarantees that very few profits are booked to subsidiaries resident in low-tax jurisdictions if the latter actually happens to lack the appropriate substance.[62] It must be stressed, though, that the OECD tries to solve the problem (shifting and accumulation of profits in low-tax jurisdictions) not by curing the cause (easy 'transferability' of risks and intangibles), but by fighting the symptoms (the lack of substance of the subsidiaries gaining the profits).

Be that as it may, it becomes apparent that with the substance orientation, the OECD has departed from the 'original' function of the ALP.[63] Again, the ALP is the standard for the allocation of profits gained in transactions between members of an MNE. In order to realize and preserve taxation according to the ability-to-pay principle, the ALP uses third-party conduct as a benchmark (section A.I.1. of this chapter). Now the ALP has gone beyond that function. It now functions as a mechanism in the hands of tax administrators in order to overbook profits to high-taxed, substance-rich entities just to prevent them from being low-taxed in the hands of substance-poor subsidiaries.

---

the latter to a low-taxed entity. In fact, the creation of a new intangible belonging to the low-taxed entity through a CCA takes place. *See* Pinkernell (2013), pp. 181-182. As far as risks is concerned, it has already been emphasized (s. A.II.1. of this chapter) that risks reside in assets. Thus, in order for risk-shifting to result in profit-shifting 'tangible or intangible assets [must be] transferred to other group members, thus disguising rents as risky income'. *See* Schön (2014), p. 288.

That is why the words 'shifted' and/or, later on, 'transferred' are put in quotation marks.

62. Verlinden et al. (2016), p. 113; Hoor (2018), p. 535; Verlinden et al. (2019), p. 1045.

63. There are many arguments against the OECD risk approach. In this note the author tries to categorize them. The first argument goes: 'there is the question whether the new approach to risk is even compliant with the arm's length principle. This is because third parties seem in some cases to assume or bear risks in respect of which they have little or no "control" in the OECD sense of that term, yet for the OECD having control of a risk is generally a precondition for bearing or managing that risk for tax purposes'. *See* Collier/Vella (2019), p. 178. On this argument *see also* Schön (2010a), p. 243; Helderman et al. (2013), p. 365; Schön (2014), p. 290; Hoor (2018), pp. 531-532 and 535-536; Grotherr (2021), pp. 1106-1107.

Another argument is that the new OECD approach on risk 'can effectively be translated into a formula for legal tax avoidance from a transfer pricing perspective' and it 'prompted a new normative *functional-formula-based* standard that will allocate profits based on functions and risks to where they are supposed to be but without necessarily considering what a third party does'. *See* Screpante (2020), p. 862. On this argument *see also* Musselli/Musselli (2009), p. 243; F. Arnold (2021), p. 45.

Another argument is that the new OECD approach on risk contradicts economic theory since 'it would be incorrect to state that mere legal ownership generates a limited – or any – return for the owner'. *See* Polonska (2018), p. 108. On this argument *see also* Wittendorff (2013), p. 1333; Musselli/Musselli (2017), p. 338; Hafkenscheid (2017), pp. 21-22.

Finally, against the new OECD approach on risk speaks also 'the vanishing possibility of pinpointing those personal decisions geographically within complex, integrated organizations'. *See* Schön (2007), p. 1067. On this argument *see also* Milewska (2017), p. 55; Navarro (2017), p. 234.

2 *Structure of the Analysis*

It has been stressed that pursuant to the OECD TPG profit follows functions, assets and risks, on the one hand, and assets and risks follow decision-making functions, on the other (section A.II.1. of this chapter). As regards the functional element of substance, one can notice a dichotomy in the OECD TPG between decision-making functions entitling one to profits arising from intangible assets and risks, on the one hand, and other functions only entitling one to risk-free remuneration on the other.

So, for example, a subsidiary entrusted with the process of developing a valuable intangible by its parent is not entitled to any intangible-related returns other than a remuneration for the services it renders, unless it performs the decision-making functions related to the development of the intangible. In a similar vein, if one reads example 3 in paragraph 1.85 of the OECD TPG, it becomes apparent that the same logic applies to tangible assets and the risks underlying them.[64] In this example, company A owing the tangible assets in question is only entitled to a risk-free return, while company B that is factually performing the decision-making functions as to the utilization of the assets in question is allocated the risk and the return pertaining thereto.[65] If company B were not to perform the decision-making functions but other functions (e.g., offer administrative services), it would not be entitled to anything other than a risk-free remuneration for these functions.

The bias in favour of decision-making functions and against other functions reminds one of the approach for the purposes of the POEM. In that instance, it has been found that this approach may be problematic in cases where business activities other than decision-making functions predominantly take place in a state other than the POEM state. But, as stated there (section B.II.1.a.cc. of Chapter 1), this shortcoming can be eliminated by taking business activities into account in a second step when applying transfer pricing rules. A preliminary conclusion could be that the OECD guidance rather follows for the purposes of profit allocation and also the POEM approach and biases against functions other than decision-making functions. By doing so, the OECD also treats the aforementioned cases where business activities take place predominantly in a state other than the POEM state insufficiently.

However flawed this approach is, though, these are the rules that this work has promised to analyse. So if decision-making functions are at the centre of the substance requirement for the purposes of profit allocation, the questions arise: what are these functions? And who performs them? The next sections answer these questions in this order: first, the functional element is dealt with (section B.II.), and then the personal element of substance is explored (section B.III.). A separate section (section B.IV.) ponders whether the objective element of substance, related to the utilization of assets, premises, etc., has any stand-alone relevance, i.e., separated from the functional and the personal elements.

64. It is reminded (*see* above s. A.II.1. of this chapter) that risks reside in assets. Thus, by allocating risks, and therewith the risk premium, the OECD indirectly also allocates assets and the profit pertaining thereto.
65. OECD TPG, para. 1.103.

II The Functional Element of the Substance Requirement in Transfer Pricing Rules

This work has already shown that the functional element of the substance requirement consists of a qualitative and a quantitative sub-element. The first refers to the qualities that the decisions being made must have, and the second to their number. Correspondingly, section B.II.1. deals with the first and section B.II.2. with the second sub-element respectively. Section B.II.3. sums up.

1 Qualitative Sub-element of the Functional Element of Substance: What Kind of Decision-Making Functions Are Required?

In this section dealing with the qualitative sub-element of the functional element of substance in transfer pricing rules, similar questions are raised as in the same section on the substance in the POEM (section B.II.1. of Chapter 1). What kind of decisions are relevant (section B.II.1.a.)? Which stage in the decision-making process is relevant (section B.II.1.c.)? And furthermore, which are the peculiarities of outsourcing (section B.II.1.b.)?

a What Kind of Decisions Are Relevant?

aa Strategic or Operational Decisions?

When determining the content of the substance requirement for the purposes of the POEM, two decision categories have been distinguished: strategic and operational decisions (section B.II.1.b.aa. of Chapter 1). The categorization depends on the degree of certainty and complexity of the decisions with regard to their realization, the degree of detail of the decisions, and the time range within which the decisions need to be implemented. Following this categorization also for the purposes of the substance requirement in transfer pricing rules, the question arises as to which category of decisions is relevant in order for profit to be allocated to a subsidiary. In other words, which decisions should persons take, which pertain to the staff of the taxpayer, in order for profit to be allocated to them?

Examining the literature and domestic guidance results in mixed findings. Some authors detect in the OECD TPG the need for strategic decisions to be taken by personnel of the taxpayer for it to be eligible as *residual claimant*.[66,67] Others consider

66. Helderman et al. (2013), p. 363: 'The Discussion Draft ... refers to "important functions" and provides a list of functions that can be considered sufficiently important for purposes of an entitlement to intangible-related returns. As mentioned, these functions include design and control of research and marketing programmes; management and control over budgets; and control over strategic decisions. Although it is not a straightforward determination, it seems that such activities would cover the "tactical level activities" and the "strategic level activities" rather than the strategic level activities only.' However, it must be said that tactical decision-making refers to decisions in-between the operational and the strategic ones. For the purposes of this work, the use of the decision category of 'tactical decisions' has been denied (s. B.II.1.b.aa. of

the operational decisions as relevant.[68] By contrast, for the purposes of the US Treasury, *Intercompany Transfer Pricing Regulations under Section 482* (1994) (US Treas. Reg.), which have influenced the OECD TPG as far as the risk guidance is concerned,[69] the making of either the strategic or the operational decisions, with regard to risk especially, suffices for a return on risk to be allocated to the taxpayer. In particular, §1.482-1(d)(3)(iii)(B)(3) of the US Treas. Reg. states that:

> In considering the economic substance of the transaction, the following facts are relevant ... The extent to which each controlled taxpayer exercises *managerial or operational control* over the business activities that directly influence the amount of income or loss realized. (Emphasis added).

According to this passage, the taxpayer must exercise 'managerial or operational control' in order for risk allocation and therewith allocation of the profit from risk and assets to have substance, so if one of the alternatives between managerial and operational control exists, risk allocation to the taxpayer has substance. But do the terms 'managerial or operational control' refer to the terms strategic and operational decisions used in this work?

Undoubtedly, operational control refers to operational decisions. As management literature informs us: 'For operational controlling, questions of tactical and operational planning are decisive. ... The focus here is on quantitative values. Via "hard" data, influence is exerted on the enterprise development.'[70] As has already been mentioned in section B.II.1.b.aa. of Chapter 1, only operational management is concerned with concrete 'numbers', or as the quoted passage calls them, 'hard' data.

Now the term 'managerial control' is more difficult to adapt to the terminology used here. It has been subject to different interpretations in literature.[71] In the author's

---

Ch. 1), so that what Helderman et al. call tactical decision-making can be both strategic and operational decisions. But since the relevance of operational decisions is rejected by these authors, it can be assumed that their reference to tactical decisions concerns decisions that can be only classified as strategic decisions in this work. The same conclusion can be reached regarding Florian Navisotschnigg's work, also putting emphasis on strategical and tactical decision-making. *See* Navisotschnigg (2022), p. 30.

67. As economic theory teaches us, the profits from an asset are attributable to the owner of the pertinent asset, commonly referred to as the 'residual claimant'. *See, e.g.*, Picot (2012), p. 355; Schwarz (2015). With regard to the 'asset' corporation, *see* Blair/Stout (1999), p. 262 who also give a nice definition of the term 'residual (profit)' used henceforth: 'the principal is understood to be the owner of the firm, as well as the residual claimant who receives all profits – that is, economic rents – left over after her contractual obligations to all the agents below her have been met'.
68. Peng/Lagarden (2019), p. 7: 'the important functions established by the OECD are the operational-level activities and the tactical-level activities, rather than the high-end activities at top management or board level'. Here the tactical decision-making refers to the operational decisions, since Peng/Lagarden deny the relevance of the strategic decisions, although it is surmised that they understand strategic decisions in a different way than the author, as they define strategic decisions as 'strategic (*policy*) level activities ... which have a major impact on the *whole organization*', Peng/Lagarden (2019), p. 7. (emphasis added).
69. *See* Wittendorff (2009), p. 123, according to whom the control over the risk factor 'also originated from the 1994 Sec. 482 regulations'.
70. Daum et al. (2016), pp. 198-199 (author's unofficial translation).
71. While according to Andreas Bullen 'an enterprise exercises "managerial ... control" over a business activity if it is authorized to and effectively does make decisions over how the activity

opinion, the term relates to control exerted by the management of the taxpayer. The control can refer to both the operational and the strategic management and the decisions pertaining to it. It can be concluded that the US Treas. Reg. have a wide ambit in this respect, whereby both strategic and operational decision-making suffice for their own right in order for return on risk to be allocated to the taxpayer.

The OECD TPG, by contrast, are more demanding than the US Treas. Reg. as to the category of decisions that the personnel of a subsidiary must take in order for profit from risk to be allocable to it:

> Risk management comprises three elements: '(i) the capability to make decisions to take on, lay off, or decline a risk-bearing opportunity, together with the actual performance of that decision-making function, (ii) the capability to make decisions on whether and how to respond to the risks associated with the opportunity, together with the actual performance of that decision-making function, and (iii) the capability to mitigate risk, that is the capability to take measures that affect risk outcomes, together with the actual performance of such risk mitigation.'[72] Further, '[i]t is not necessary for a party to perform the day-to-day mitigation, as described in (iii) in order to have control of the risks. Such day-to-day mitigation may be outsourced'.[73]

Like the US Treas. Reg., the OECD TPG do not use the terminology employed in this work. It is thus not straightforward to determine which types of decisions are meant to fall under this guidance. However, it can be argued that decisions on risk assumption pertain to strategic decisions, whereas decisions on how to mitigate the risk are more operational in nature. This is obvious if one looks at the time horizons to which risk assumption and risk mitigation refer.

Risk assumption entails long-term bonding and, thus, is of a strategic nature.[74] By contrast, risk mitigation is a short-term, or at the most a medium-term, issue and, thus, is of an operational nature. The classification of responding to risks is more challenging since risk mitigation can be considered synonymous with responding to risk.[75] Systematically, it makes sense that decisions responding to risk are considered strategic.

As the quoted passages above suggest, only risk-mitigating decisions can be outsourced, whereas risk assumption and risk responding cannot be. This shows that risk assumption and risk response are seen as equivalent. From that it follows that risk responding refers to strategic decisions on risk; here, the four criteria denoted in order to distinguish strategic from operational decisions (*see* above in this section) may help to distinguish operational risk mitigation from strategic risk responding.

---

is to be conducted', Jérôme Monsenego connects the term with the 'formal authority to make decisions'. *See* Bullen (2011), s. 18.5.2.1. and Monsenego (2014), p. 14, n. 41. Another commentator refers to the term as meaning 'whether the group entity that is contractually assigned the risk is in control of it' without further considerations. Torvik (2018), p. 214.

72. OECD TPG, para. 1.61.
73. *Ibid.*, para. 1.65.
74. Daum et al. (2016), p. 198.
75. This 'inclarity on the distinction between actions that respond to risk and those that mitigate risk' is criticized by Collier/Andrus (2017), para. 6.25, n. 37.

So, critical for the purposes of the qualitative sub-element of the functional element of substance in transfer pricing rules, like for the purposes of the POEM (section B.II.1.b.cc. of Chapter 1), are the strategic decisions,[76] while the operational decisions may be outsourced.

It must be underlined that this finding shows that there can be harmony among the various substance requirements. The POEM, the standard on the nexus for the taxation of corporations (i.e., residence), and transfer pricing, the standard on the attribution of profits to corporations, point to the strategic decisions and are thus aligned in this respect. By contrast, the Authorised OECD Approach (AOA), the standard on the profit attribution to PEs, points to the operational decisions. The same holds true with regard to the POM, the rule in Article 5(2)(a) of the OECD MTC giving rise to a nexus for source taxation (i.e., a PE). The AOA and the POM are thus also aligned in this respect.[77] So residence taxation as regards the nexus and the attribution of profits is connected to the place where strategic decisions are taken, whereas source (meaning PE) taxation is connected to the state where operational decisions take place.[78]

bb Outsourcing of the Operational Decisions

The question that now arises relates to the conditions under which the operational decisions may be outsourced in order for profit to still be allocated to the controlled taxpayer (minus an arm's length service fee payable to the related party performing the outsourced operational decision-making functions). The OECD TPG provide straightforward guidance in this respect:

> Where these day-to-day mitigation activities are outsourced, control of the risk would require capability to determine the objectives of the outsourced activities, to decide to hire the provider of the risk mitigation functions, to assess whether the objectives are being adequately met, and, where necessary, to decide to adapt or terminate the contract with that provider, together with the performance of such assessment and decision-making.[79]

76. One can argue whether this is a good policy. Collier/Dykes (2022), p. 28 negate that based on the following argument: 'where the relevant decision-making is "strategic" or irregular (i.e. where decisions are taken on a much less "active" basis), the use of the decision-making test is potentially much less effective in delivering its intended policy objective, as the irregular and/or infrequent decision-making is a much weaker constraining mechanism on mere booking arrangements'. Interesting is the analysis by Metzner (2016), pp. 128 et seq. who based on an economic analysis comes to the opposite conclusion, at least with regard to risk allocation, that the residual profit should be allocated to the strategic decision-makers as superior risk bearers.
77. On the operational decisions as the relevant ones for the purposes of the POM *see* above s. B.II.1.b.cc. of Ch. 1. On the operational decisions as the relevant ones for the purposes of the AOA, *see* Barreiros Rosalem (2010), p. 13: 'the PE Report attributes the risk to the part of the company with the functions of managing it on a day-to-day basis'; Navarro (2017), p. 224: '(AOA), which is based on significant people functions (SPF), a criterion mainly focused on day-to-day management.' It is reminded that the day-to-day management corresponds to what is referred to here as operational management, *see* above s. B.II.1.b.bb. of Ch. 1.
78. *See* above s. B.II.1.b.cc. of Ch. 1.
79. OECD TPG, para. 1.65.

This treatment corresponds to what has already been laid out for the purposes of the POEM, namely that delegation and control of the agents themselves constitute acts of management (section B.II.2.c.hh. of Chapter 1). By further demanding, though, that the outsourcing party is able to 'assess whether the objectives are being adequately met', the OECD TPG require the active involvement of the outsourcing party going beyond the mere decision to outsource an activity.

Merely outsourcing the operational decision-making does not suffice in and of itself in order for a return to be allocated to the controlled taxpayer. This requirement is further refined by examples in the OECD TPG. In particular, regular reporting to the outsourcing party,[80] the establishment of a reviewing and approval process[81] together with quality checks conducted by the outsourcing party[82] are some of the ways that the necessary assessment of the outsourcing may take place so that profit from risk and assets is allocable to the controlled taxpayer.

cc Distinguishing Strategic Decisions from Parent Policy-Making

Finally, strategic decision-making must be distinguished from parent policy-making. The OECD TPG stipulate that parent policy-making, just as for the purposes of the POEM (section B.II.1.b.aa. of Chapter 1), is not relevant when defining to which taxpayer a return should be allocated:

> in an MNE group other parties may not be involved in setting general policies that are relevant for the assumption and control of the specific risks identified in a transaction, without such policy-setting itself representing decision making.[83]

Commentators have complained about the difficulty of delineating parent policy-making from the notion of control, as defined up until this point.[84] Admittedly, the parent provides the capital and gives to a subsidiary its purpose. By doing so, the parent controls the subsidiary's operations. It can pull the plug at any time by firing managers, changing the overall strategy of the group, liquidating the subsidiary, etc.

But notice that none of the aforementioned decisions are related to one transaction but to the overall business of the group or the subsidiary. Only when these kinds of actions have direct reference to a certain transaction can the issue of decision-making by the parent be raised. And even if this is the case, one can also distinguish cases of parent policy-making by referring to corporate law, just like for the purposes of the POEM (section B.II.1.b.aa. of Chapter 1). The decisions reserved for the shareholder by corporate law should be regarded as policy-making even if they refer to a specific transaction (e.g., decisions regarding specific assets or transactions may be made only after the approval of the parent). Otherwise, the OECD TPG would require MNEs to run afoul of corporate law in order to achieve the desired transfer pricing

80. *Ibid.*, para. 1.83; OECD TPG, para. 51 of Annex to Ch. VI.
81. OECD TPG, paras 26 and 47 of Annex to Ch. VI.
82. *Ibid.*, para. 1.84; OECD TPG, para. 59 of Annex to Ch. VI.
83. OECD TPG, para. 1.76.
84. National Foreign Trade Council (2015), p. 606; Verlinden et al. (2016), p. 111.

results.[85] '[T]his would imply the existence not of a substance-over-form approach, but of a separate international tax [corporate] law.'[86]

dd Summary

In sum, profit from risk and assets follows strategic decision-making (section B.II.1.a.aa.). The latter cannot be outsourced and must be distinguished from parent policy-making when the latter is not transaction-related or, if it is, when the pertinent decisions are reserved for the parent by corporate law (section B.II.1.a.cc.). Operational decision-making may be outsourced, but on condition that the outsourcing party maintains oversight of the outsourced functions (section B.II.1.a.bb.). However, other Actions of the BEPS Project, as well as commentators, take a stricter stance on outsourcing. The next section expounds on this issue.

b Detailed Discussion of Outsourcing

As already implied, other Actions of the BEPS Project and commentators take a stricter approach to outsourcing. They distinguish between outsourcable and non-outsourcable activities based on the person to whom an activity is outsourced or the nature of the activity.

BEPS Action 5 relating to preferential regimes, *inter alia*, for IP-related income, takes the first approach, i.e., it differentiates between outsourcable and non-outsourcable activities based on the person to which an activity is outsourced. In particular, BEPS Action 5 introduces the nexus approach which 'allows a regime to provide for a preferential rate on IP-related income to the extent it was generated by qualifying expenditures'.[87] And for the purposes of the nexus approach 'expenditures for activities undertaken by related parties ... would not count as qualifying expenditures'.[88] By contrast, '[t]he nexus approach would allow all qualifying expenditures for activities undertaken by unrelated parties ... to qualify'.[89]

85. Another argument could be that shareholder transactions do not fall within the purview of the ALP in the first place. This argument is made by Eigelshoven/Retzer (2021), para. 167 on Ch. I of the OECD TPG; Grotherr (2021), p. 1106. However, the overwhelming consensus in the literature is that 'the notion of "commercial and financial" relations is frequently contrasted with the effects of pure shareholder relations (e.g., in-kind dividend distributions as well as increases and decreases in share capital). This, of course, does not mean that relations based on the shareholder relationship are excluded from Article 9(1) OECD and UN MC as it is exactly the function of this provision and the arm's length principle to identify the conditions that are made or imposed based on control. Hence, shareholder relations may certainly qualify as "financial relations", unless they serve to establish the relationship between the two enterprises'. *See* Kofler (2021), para. 70; *see also* Collier/Andrus (2017), para. 5.34. And with references to recent case law on this issue Collier/Dykes (2020), p. 717, n. 110.
86. The argument resembles and quotes that of Kostić (2019), p. 218.
87. *See* OECD, *Countering Harmful Tax Practices More Effectively, Taking into Account Transparency and Substance* – 2015 Final Report, para. 29 (hereinafter 'OECD Action 5').
88. *Ibid.*, at para. 49.
89. *Ibid.*

No exhaustive argumentation is necessary to illustrate the flaws that the adoption of such an approach would have for the purposes of profit allocation. Should the OECD TPG follow such an approach, it would simply distort parity between taxpayers, instead of ensuring it, which is the current rationale of the ALP,[90] as it would discriminate outsourcing to related parties.[91] But it could be that a distinction must not be made according to the person to which an activity is outsourced (which is the approach taken in Action 5) but according to the nature of the activity itself.

An interesting opinion in this respect has been expressed before the OECD TPG (2022) were introduced by Matthias Valta. He distinguished between services that may be outsourced and others that may not be outsourced on the basis of whether 'the provision of [the pertinent] services requires the knowledge of company and business secrets'.[92] He brings up the following example: 'a company like Coca-Cola may outsource the redilution of a cola concentrate and the filling of the cola. However, the preparation of the concentrate, which requires knowledge of the ingredients and the preparation process, is likely to be performed exclusively in-house'.[93]

Although this example is convincing, one needs to differentiate between theory and reality. On the one hand, economic theory supports Valta's example; more generalized capital and knowledge are more susceptible to outsourcing as specific capital.[94] On the other hand, reality teaches us that there may be cases where even strategic decisions are outsourced to third parties.

Take, for example, private equity transactions. Investors entrust their money to a private equity fund of their choice. They decide to invest, trust a specific private equity fund, and provide some information on the investment type they prefer, which corresponds to the policy-making referred to with respect to entities (section B.II.1.a.cc. of this chapter). The rest is up to the fund manager. And the rest consists of all strategic decisions. To invest in this or that firm, whereby both fit into the investment profile of the investor, is a strategic decision with great uncertainty and long-term consequences. Still, the decision is taken by the third party and not by the investor. The latter retains control by having the choice to withdraw their investment or cancel future investments in the private equity fund in question, just like the parent retains control via its policy-making (e.g., the decision to liquidate the subsidiary).

90. *See* above s. A.I.1. of this chapter.
91. On the lack of conformity of Action 5 with the ALP Nikolakakis (2021), pp. 554-555.
92. Valta (2014), pp. 462-463 (author's unofficial translation). In a similar vein, although with reference to substance for the purposes of the CFC rules, but with reference to the OECD TPG, Smit (2014), p. 265 arguing for the possibility of outsourcing 'activities ... of an ancillary or marginal nature' but not 'key entrepreneurial management activities'; Hoor et al. (2022), p. 235: 'The decision-making on significant functions is rarely outsourced and instead handled internally by the entity's directors (during board meetings that should be held in the entity's residence state).' *See also* OECD Action 5, para. 50: 'it is unlikely that a company will outsource the fundamental value-creating activities to an unrelated party'.
93. Valta (2014), pp. 462-463 (author's unofficial translation).
94. Klein et al. (1978), p. 321.

This example demonstrates that there is no black or white.[95] Third parties may even delegate strategic decision-making in its totality. Accordingly, if comparables exist, then outsourcing of strategic decisions must be accepted. The same applies with regard to the outsourcing of operational decision-making.

In sum, a total exclusion of outsourcing to related parties, as Action 5 suggests, would run afoul of the rationale of the ALP as a mechanism for putting related and unrelated taxpayers on an equal footing, and must therefore be rejected for the purposes of profit allocation. Distinguishing between outsourcable and non-outsourcable activities based on the nature of the activity in a black-or-white manner must also be rejected, as there may be comparables that indicate that a prima facie non-outsourcable activity is actually outsourced in unrelated transactions.[96]

c Which Stage in the Decision-Making Process Is Relevant?

When determining the content of the substance requirement for the purposes of the POEM, three decision-making stages have been discerned: the planning stage, the implementation stage, and the monitoring stage. Within the planning stage, there exist two sub-stages: the preparation sub-stage and the decision-making stricto sensu (section B.II.1.c.aa. of Chapter 1). The question arises as to which of these stages and/or sub-stages in the decision-making process is/are relevant for the purposes of substance in transfer pricing rules.

Section B.II.1.a. of this chapter has offered some useful insights in this regard. With respect to the operational decisions, the monitoring stage of the decision-making process is relevant, as the taxpayer must be able to at least have an oversight of the operational decision-making when the latter is outsourced. With respect to the strategic decisions, both the decision-making stricto sensu and the monitoring stage are required in order for risk to be allocated to a taxpayer.

The monitoring stage is relevant because it is also relevant for the purposes of the operational decisions. If it is relevant for these decisions, which play a less important role than the strategic decisions, then it should be all the more (a fortiori) relevant for the purposes of the strategic decisions. Moreover, the decision-making stricto sensu is

95. The author understands the following statement as an acceptance of a 'no black or white solution' too: 'Performance management is relatively easy for machine-paced or highly automated processes, but becomes more complicated and thus costly for tasks that are not programmable, but that require judgment and on-the-spot decisions, or for those that require employees to be dispersed over space. This may serve to explain why some activities are franchised while others are operated with employees of the MNE.' *See* Fris (2003), pp. 197-198.

96. One could ask: What if comparables do not exist? It is admitted that this is a fundamental problem of the ALP, especially with regard to intangibles since the latter 'may be difficult to define [and] may be unique to the MNE's business'. *See* Collier/Andrus (2017), para. 4.24. But this is the current legal framework under which this work written and which this work respects. Accordingly, even though a reference to comparables may be an inadequate solution, it is the only one we have under the current legal framework. This relates also to other instances in this work where it is explained/justified missing OECD guidance with the need to refer to comparable transaction in order to define substance.

also required because the OECD TPG refer to 'the capability to *make* decisions'.[97] A strict grammatical interpretation of the word 'make' leads to the conclusion that the decision-making stricto sensu is relevant except if the other canons of interpretation suggest another solution.[98] In fact, the OECD TPG also include an example pointing to the preparatory sub-stage.[99] So it could be that it is not the decision-making stricto sensu together with the monitoring stage that is relevant but (also? only?) the preparatory sub-stage. In the following, the argument is advanced that the preparatory sub-stage does not play a role for the purposes of profit allocation.

A systematic argument underpins this position. Remember that according to Article 5(4) of the OECD MTC preparatory activities do not give rise to a PE (section B.II.1.c.cc. of Chapter 1). Consequently, profit allocation to a PE for preparatory activities does not take place, at least if preparatory activities are the only activities carried on through the place of business in question.[100] If activities carried out in a state do not give that state the right to tax these activities (i.e., do not give rise to a PE), then allocating profit to that state would be a paradox, since the state cannot tax the profit allocated to it; the profit would remain untaxed.[101] And if preparatory activities do not play a role for the purposes of profit allocation to PEs, then they should not play a role for profit allocation to subsidiaries either. A change in the organizational form (either PE or subsidiary) should not induce a change as far as the treatment in tax laws, and in this case profit allocation, is concerned unless such a difference is justified.[102,103] In

97. OECD TPG, para. 1.61 (emphasis added).
98. *See also* the analysis with reference to the word 'make' for the purposes of the POEM s. B.II.1.c.bb. of Ch. 1.
99. OECD TPG, para. 9.123. *See* already Monsenego (2014), p. 14, although noting that 'the facts of the example are extreme, as no preparatory work is performed in the country where the decisions are made'.
100. It has been rightly pointed out that when a PE exists conducting both preparatory and other activities, whereby only the latter give rise to the PE in the first place, it should be allocated profit for both the preparatory and the other activities. *See* Castelon (2018), p. 204.
101. According to Brian Arnold, the opposite case, however, makes sense. Preparatory activities could give rise to a PE, although this PE would not be allocated any profit for these activities. *See* Arnold (2003), p. 479.
102. According to commentators aligning profit allocation between separate enterprises and PEs has been the main goal of the AOA on the attribution of profits to PEs. *See* Petruzzi/Holzinger (2017), p. 274. One of the authors of the last cited article, Raphael Holzinger, also wrote a whole book making exactly this argument. *See* Holzinger (2020).

    Irene Burgers has identified a justification for the different treatment of PEs from separate enterprises in 'legal requirements posed to subsidiaries that have nothing to do with people functions [and] should not be deemed to apply to permanent establishments'. However, this justification does not apply with regard to the functional element of substance: 'Due to these differences in legal requirements the determination of the tax base for permanent establishments differs from that of subsidiaries. The most important other legal difference, to wit the fact that a contract is not available for internal delivery of goods, services and assets, should not result in a different determination of the tax base as this difference concerns the performance of people functions. *The people functions performed, associated risks and capital required to perform these people functions are the same whether performed by a permanent establishment or by a subsidiary*' (emphasis added). *See* Burgers (2009), p. 73. *See also* Friese (2010), pp. 239-241.
103. One could say that there is a contradiction here to what has been in established in s. B.II.1.a.aa. of this chapter, namely that the AOA and the OECD TPG point to different kinds of decisions as the relevant ones for profit allocation to PEs (AOA) and corporations (OECD TPG). In

this case, such a justification does not exist. If preparatory activities are not considered value-creating for a PE, then why should they be for a subsidiary?

Now, it has been maintained that with regard to the strategic decisions *both* decision-making stricto sensu and monitoring are relevant. The question arises as to what happens when the decision-making stricto sensu and the monitoring stage are separated. For example, if the owner of an asset outsources the decision-making stricto sensu but retains control over the party to which the decision-making stricto sensu is outsourced. Remember that the same issue also arose for the purposes of the POEM where both decision-making stricto sensu and monitoring are relevant (section B.II.1.c.cc. of Chapter 1).

For the purposes of profit allocation, since the OECD guidance requires both the decision-making stricto sensu and the monitoring stage of the decision-making process to be exercised by the owner of the asset claiming to also be the residual claimant, the latter does not solely earn the residual if they do not fulfil the aforementioned requirement. It follows from this that in such a case the residual profit on the asset must be allocated between the owner of the asset and the party to which the decision-making stricto sensu has been outsourced. Commentators have already complained about the lack of guidance in OECD TPG as regards how such allocation should take place.[104] In the author's opinion, there is no need for further guidance here: the allocation of the residual must follow the one that is seen in comparable transactions.[105]

In total, with regard to the strategic decisions, both decision-making stricto sensu and monitoring are relevant. If decision-making stricto sensu and monitoring are separated, the allocation of the residual must be based on the one taking place in comparable transactions. With regard to the operational decisions, only the monitoring part is relevant according to the OECD TPG. The preparatory sub-stage is not relevant due to systematic reasons (alignment of profit allocation between PEs, on the one hand, and between corporations, on the other), irrespective of misleading OECD guidance.

2 Quantitative Sub-element of the Functional Element of Substance: How Many Decisions Are Necessary?

It has been shown that, for the purposes of the POEM, there exists no absolute threshold as regards the number of decisions made in one state in order for the POEM

particular, it has been found there that the AOA focuses on the operational decisions, while the OECD TPG on the strategic ones. There is no contradiction, however. In fact, the alignment between these two concepts is, as commentators inform us, somewhere else. *See* Gonnet (2016), p. 48: 'The two terms, SPF [significant people functions] (at an operational level) and important functions (at a more strategic level), are comparable as they both emphasize the distinction between performing certain activities versus the control issue.' Tracana (2017), p. 415: 'both the AOA and the TPG refer to active (performance of) decision-making functions'. So this is where the two concepts align: they both refer to active decision-making, what this work referred to as decision-making stricto sensu.

104. International Underwriting Association (2015), p. 490.

105. Here applies also the counterargument that comparables may not exist. As to the author's response to this argument *see* above n. 96 in this chapter.

to be located there (section B.II.3.a. of Chapter 1). One could ask the exact same question with respect to profit allocation. Assume, for example, that a subsidiary holds a software and makes only two risk-related decisions. Should it be allocated the residual on the software, although it only makes two decisions, or is there an *absolute* threshold that the residual claimant should reach in this respect (section B.II.2.a.)?

Further, when decision-making functions are outsourced to related or unrelated parties, it is questioned whether the outsourcing party should retain a specific number of decisions for itself in order for return to be allocated solely to it. In the aforementioned example, assume that ten risk-related decisions have to be made. The subsidiary only makes two out of ten. The other decisions are made by another group company to which certain functions with regard to the software have been outsourced.

The question arises whether the subsidiary may remain the sole residual claimant with regard to the software, although it only makes two out of ten of the relevant decisions. Does the number of decisions made influence the taxpayer's participation in the profit from risks and assets (section B.II.2.b.)? Would profit allocation be the same if the subsidiary took all ten decisions? In other words, is there a *relative* threshold in this respect? The following two sections deal with these questions.

a Is There an Absolute Quantitative Threshold?

The first question regarding the existence of an absolute threshold as regards the number of decisions has already been asked in literature as a plea for more guidance by the OECD.[106] These commentators are right to point towards the lack of guidance coming from the OECD. Indeed, the OECD, like in the case of the POEM (section B.II.3.a. of Chapter 1), does not stipulate a quantitative threshold requirement as regards the functional element of the substance requirement but only refers in the TPG to 'a number of relevant decisions' that should be made by the taxpayer in order for them to retain the return on risk.[107] In the author's opinion, the OECD TPG correctly do not provide for a threshold. A teleological, a practical, and a policy argument underpins this position.

From a teleological perspective, the existence of a threshold would contradict the purpose the ALP serves. Again, the ALP primarily allocates profits to persons in a way that depicts their ability to pay. For this purpose, comparable taxpayers and transactions are used as a structural element (section A.I.1 of this chapter). Against this background, applying a threshold, while comparable uncontrolled taxpayers in comparable transactions gain returns although they do not reach the given threshold, would treat related parties unequally when compared to unrelated parties. It follows from that that the focus should be on the return that taxpayers with a comparable number of decisions maintain.[108]

From a practical point of view, it would be impossible to set a specific or even an abstract threshold in this respect. The degree of heterogeneity of international business

106. Helderman et al. (2014), p. 5.
107. OECD TPG, paras 1.69 and 1.83.
108. Concurring, with regard to the number of decision-makers though, Monsenego (2014), p. 19.

is simply too high in order for concrete threshold numbers to be determined.[109] But even if this were possible, it would be flawed from a policy perspective. Like every kind of line-drawing in tax law,[110] it would create enormous pressure on taxpayers to cross the line in order for them to be the residual claimant of profits, without, in the final analysis, offering that much in respect of fighting the cause of the problem the OECD wants to eliminate (section B.I.1. of this chapter). Taxpayers would easily be able to manipulate a numeric threshold. What the OECD can do, though, is, at the most, offer criteria according to which the number of decisions taken by the taxpayer affects the amount of residual profits allocable to them. This leads us to the second question raised here, namely whether the number of decisions made influences the taxpayer's participation in the profit from risk and assets.

b Does the Number of Decisions Made Influence the Taxpayer's Participation in the Profit from Risk and Assets?: On the Existence of a Relative Quantitative Threshold

The issue of whether the number of decisions made influences the taxpayer's participation in the profit from risk and assets arises in situations where more than one party to the transaction exercises control over a specific risk. In such cases, it could be that the number of decisions made by the parties influence the risk allocation.

Paragraph 1.94 of the OECD TPG deal with cases where 'more than one party to the transaction [is] exercising control over a specific risk'. According to this paragraph, 'the fact that other associated enterprises also exercise control over the same risk does not affect the assumption of that risk by the first-mentioned enterprise'. This passage has two implications for this work.

First, the findings of this work up until this point must be interpreted in light of the quoted passage in order not to be considered contradictory. Remember that in section B.II.1.a.aa. of this chapter, the conclusion was drawn that strategic decision-making cannot be outsourced. Now, this passage does not support this conclusion in its totality. According to this passage, control over risk (i.e., what we call strategic decisions on risk, as opposed to risk mitigation constituting operational decision-making) may also be exercised by parties other than the controlled taxpayer. Therefore, the statement in the aforementioned section that strategic decision-making cannot be outsourced must be relativized, meaning that not *all* strategic decisions may be outsourced; or, put differently, strategic decision-making should not be outsourced in its totality, whereas all operational decisions may be outsourced.

Second, this passage implies that 'the employees of the entity must make some, but not necessarily all or even most, of the decisions of the group related to taking on, laying of, or mitigation of the risk'[111] in order for the entity to be allocated a risk and thereby constitute the sole owner of risk-related returns. In other words: there is no

109. In this regard, profit allocation should take the form of a standard and not a rule. Regarding this distinction *see* above s. B.II.3.c. of Ch. 1.
110. Schön (2009), pp. 87-88.
111. Collier/Andrus (2017), para. 7.13. *See also* Arnold (2021), p. 42.

relative threshold as regards the quantity of the decision-making functions rendered. So it could be argued that in our example the fact that the subsidiary makes two out of ten decisions does not exclude it as the sole residual claimant. Applying the OECD position to our example would mean that making either two out of ten or all ten decisions does not make any difference in respect of the controlled taxpayer's status as the sole residual claimant.[112]

This finding must be assessed as regards its conformity with paragraph 1.98 of the OECD TPG. According to this passage:

> If multiple associated enterprises are identified that both exercise control and have the financial capacity to assume the risk, then the risk should be allocated to the associated enterprise or group of associated enterprises exercising *the most* control. The other parties performing control activities should be remunerated appropriately (emphasis added).

One would assume, thus, that the findings so far may be rebutted by this passage, since it seems that the amount of control plays a role in risk allocation, i.e., that there is a relative threshold ('most'). The devil is in the detail, though. Notice that in order for risk, and therewith profit, allocation to go to the party exercising the most control, this party must *both* exercise control and have the financial capacity to assume the risk. Let us return to our example and simply assume further that the subsidiary making two out of ten risk-related decisions also has the financial capacity to assume the risks arising from these functions. By contrast, the other party to which these functions have been outsourced, which makes the other eight decisions, does not have the financial capacity to assume the risks. Since this party does not *both* exercise control and have the financial capacity to assume risks, the latter are allocated to the subsidiary although it has less substance (in the form of the quantity of the decisions on the software attributable to it) than the other party. The role of financial capacity constitutes a novelty compared to the POEM where it does not play any role.

For cases where a party exercises decision-making but does not assume the risk because it does not have the financial capacity to do so, paragraph 1.105 of the OECD TPG provides:

> In circumstances where a party contributes to the control of risk, but does not assume the risk, compensation which takes the form of a sharing in the potential upside and downside, commensurate with that contribution to control, may be appropriate.

112. Commentators have already taken issue with the fact that the OECD guidance 'defeat[s] the primary objective of the new rules on risk'. *See* Collier/Andrus (2017), para. 7.15; Collier/Dykes (2020), p. 711. Concurring Arnold (2021), p. 43. Remember the OECD's intention behind the introduction of the substance requirement into the OECD TPG has been to combat shifting and accumulation of profits in low-tax jurisdictions via the 'transfer' of intangibles and risks thereto (s. B.I.1. of this chapter). By allowing taxpayers to outsource a large part of the strategic decisions and all operational decisions, the OECD creates a lot of tax-planning potential. Taxpayers may fill subsidiaries with a little bit of personal substance so that a small part of the strategic decision-making can be documented to be made by its employees and business (meaning profit shifting) will go on as usual. *See* Collier/Andrus (2017), paras 7.14 and 7.18; Martín Jiménez (2017), pp. 40-42; Martín Jiménez (2018), p. 623; Arnold (2021), p. 46.

The question is now who has more 'substance' and should be allocated more profit. Is it the company making two out of ten decisions and having the financial capacity to assume risks or the other company making the rest eight decisions? The OECD TPG do not provide an answer in this respect.[113] Apparently, the weight falls on comparable transactions.[114]

c Summary

In sum, pursuant to the OECD TPG, there is no threshold as regards the number of decisions to be taken by the taxpayer for them to be residual claimants (section B.II.2.a.). Although the quantity of decisions plays a role in determining the allocable profit, there are cases where the party making fewer decisions is attributed profit because of its financial capacity. This is a difference compared to the POEM where financial assets do not play any role (section B.II.2.b.).

3 Synthesis

- For the purposes of profit allocation, both strategic and operational decision-making are relevant. The latter can be completely outsourced but only under the condition that the taxpayer retains oversight of the outsourced decision-making functions (section B.II.1.a.aa.). Strategic decision-making cannot be outsourced in its totality (sections B.II.1.a.aa. and B.II.2.b.). Strategic decision-making must be distinguished from parent policy-making, the latter being irrelevant when it is not transaction-related or, if it is when the pertinent decisions are reserved for the parent by corporate law (section B.II.1.a.cc.).
- A stricter approach to outsourcing must be rejected. Both a total exclusion of outsourcing to related parties, as Action 5 suggests, as well as a distinction between outsourcable and non-outsourcable activities in a black-or-white manner, as suggested in academic literature, must be rejected (section B.II.1.b.).
- The relevant stage in the decision-making process is different for the purposes of strategic decisions, on the one hand, and operational decisions, on the other. With regard to the strategic decisions, both decision-making stricto sensu and monitoring are relevant. If decision-making stricto sensu and monitoring are separated, the allocation of the residual must be based on the one taking place in comparable transactions. With regard to the operational decisions, only the monitoring part is relevant according to the OECD TPG.

113. Fabian Arnold has taken issue with that. *See* Arnold (2021), p. 43: 'these rules ultimately do not make it clear as to whether there is a difference in the level of remuneration between (i) a party that exercises the most control; and (ii) a party that has some (but not most) of the control over risk but should be compensated for this with participation in the upside and downside financial consequences'.

114. Here applies also the counterargument that comparables may not exist. As to the author's response to this argument *see* above n. 96 in this chapter.

The preparatory sub-stage is not relevant due to systematic reasons (section B.II.1.c.).

- The OECD TPG rightly do not include an absolute threshold as regards the number of decisions that the taxpayer has to make in order for them to be the residual claimant (section B.II.2.a.).
- The quantity of decisions made influences profit allocation. Still, there are cases where a party outsourcing decision-making functions is allocated profit because of its financial capacity (section B.II.2.b.).

A comparison of the findings on the functional element of substance for the purposes of profit allocation with the one in the POEM chapter can be made. It has been laid out that, for the purposes of the POEM, strategic decisions are the relevant ones (section B.II.1.b.cc. of Chapter 1), and that operational decisions can be unconditionally outsourced (these not being relevant for the purposes of determining the POEM), whereas the strategic decisions can be outsourced but only as long as the legally appointed directors retain control over the persons making the strategic decisions (section B.II.2.c.hh. of Chapter 1). By contrast, for the purposes of profit allocation the strategic decisions may not be outsourced, at least not in their totality, while the operational decisions may be outsourced, but only under the condition that the outsourcing party maintains oversight of the outsourced functions. We therefore notice a higher threshold for the purposes of profit allocation as far as outsourcing is concerned.

The usage of a higher threshold in this respect may be justifiable against the backdrop that the POEM establishes the nexus for taxation. The fact that a taxpayer has sufficient economic connections with a state so that they are taxable there does not inform one how much of their income is taxable there. In other words, one needs to differentiate nexus from profit allocation, whereby other thresholds may apply for the purposes of each.[115]

So it could be that profit allocation, in some respect, like, for example, outsourcing of strategic decisions, poses some additional requirements. Having residence is the first step; being allocated profit is the second, 'harder' or, less crudely formulated, more demanding step.

III The Personal Element of the Substance Requirement in Transfer Pricing Rules

The personal element of substance comprises the personal element stricto sensu, the quantitative, and the qualitative sub-element. The personal element stricto sensu consists of identifying the relevant persons, whereas the qualitative sub-element relates to the qualities that these persons should have and the quantitative sub-element to their number. The next three sections deal with each sub-element of the personal

115. Exactly this is the argument brought forward by Arnold (2003), p. 479 to justify that preparatory activities may create a sufficient nexus for the existence of a taxing right, although they may not be awarded any profit. *See* above n. 101 in this chapter.

element of substance for the purposes of profit allocation: section B.III.1. deals with the personal element stricto sensu, section B.III.2. with the qualitative sub-element, and section B.III.3. with the quantitative sub-element of the personal element of substance in transfer pricing rules. Section B.III.4. summarizes the findings of the previous sections.

1 Personal Element Stricto Sensu: Which Persons Carry Out the Necessary Decision-Making Functions?

a The Role of the Existence of an Enforceable Right and Managerial Liability

We have seen that, for the purposes of the POEM, the existence of an enforceable right does not play a role when determining who is managing the subsidiary in question. That is, even outsiders, e.g., the parent, may be deemed to exercise the management of the subsidiary, although they cannot legally (e.g., contractually or based on corporate law statutes) oblige the subsidiary to follow their instructions (section B.II.2.b.bb. of Chapter 1). Let us see how the OECD TPG deal with this issue with respect to profit allocation. Should the persons exercising the decision-making functions be legally authorized to do so or does a factual relationship suffice?

In this respect, the OECD TPG provide that 'control over risk should be understood as the capability and *authority* to decide to take on the risk, and to decide whether and how to respond to the risk'.[116] By referring to the decision-making authority, the OECD TPG arguably require that the decision-makers 'should be authorized by law, a statute of the company or any other internal document to make and implement the decisions'.[117] Furthermore, the decision-makers should also ('capability *and* authority') have the capability to make decisions on risk; authority in and of itself seemingly does not suffice.

Now, what if the managers are authorized but do not in substance make the relevant decisions because they are not capable of doing so? Suppose they merely formalize decisions that the competent persons have made for them. In such a case, the POEM would point to the persons who are able to and in fact, do exercise the decision-making functions. Does profit allocation function in this way as well?

This passage does not provide us with information in this respect; in fact, it requires both the authority and the competence to make the pertinent decisions. Monsenego has claimed that in such a case the formal authority is decisive for the purposes of profit allocation.[118] He offers an argument according to which, between independent parties, formal authority to make a decision that binds the corporation

116. OECD TPG, para. 1.67 (emphasis added).
117. Polonska (2018), p. 101; Werner (2019), p. 108.
118. Monsenego (2014), p. 15; *see also* Koomen (2015b), p. 238. *Contra* Metzner (2016), pp. 138-139.

always exists, whereas competence may not. If formal authority does not exist, then the decision does not bind the corporation, and transactions are null and void. Thus, the mechanism of the ALP referring to third-party behaviour as a yardstick for depicting the taxpayer's ability to pay requires formal decision-making to take precedence over competence.

This interpretation contradicts the OECD TPG:

> Neither a mere formalising of the outcome of decision-making in the form of, for example, meetings organised for formal approval of decisions that were made in other locations, minutes of a board meeting and signing of the documents relating to the decision, nor the setting of the policy environment relevant for the risk (*see* paragraph 1.76), qualifies as the exercise of a decision-making function sufficient to demonstrate control over a risk.[119]

According to this passage, the formal authority to make decisions does not suffice in and of itself for risk, and therewith profit, to be allocated to the taxpayer; rather, substantial decision-making is crucial.[120] Here, the OECD seems to endorse the approach taken for the purposes of the POEM. This is also the most favourable approach, since not concentrating on the formally authorized decision-makers better serves the purpose of the OECD TPG to tackle shifting and accumulation of profits in low-tax jurisdictions (section B.I.1. of this chapter). It is easier to shift formal decision-making than substantial decision-making to low-tax countries.[121] In order to eliminate this contradiction, the OECD may consider deleting the requirement of authorization to make decisions and require only the competence to make them.

Regarding the role of managerial liability, there is no guidance in the OECD TPG.[122] It has been seen for the purposes of the POEM (section B.II.3.c.bb. of Chapter 1) that this is a purely formal criterion. Taking into account the purpose of the OECD TPG to tackle shifting and accumulation of profits in low-tax jurisdictions, one should argue against trying to locate decision-making functions to the place where the 'accountable persons' are, since these are also easier to shift.

In sum, in principle, the decision-makers should be both capable and authorized to make decisions. If capabilities and authorization are split among different persons, concentrating on the formally authorized persons when determining who renders the important decision-making functions is not supported by the OECD. The author agrees with this finding. Similarly, locating decisions based on which persons are accountable for them is not a notion deduced from the OECD TPG and conforming with their purpose.

119. OECD TPG, para. 1.66 in fine. From the literature in favour of a substantive approach in this sense Greinert et al. (2020), p. 527.
120. With 'substantial' reference is made to the day-to-day term of substance meaning having the 'quality of being based on facts or the truth'. *See* above s. D.I. of the introduction.
121. This is not to say that this work endorses the substance orientation of the OECD TPG. For the critique thereon *see* above s. B.I.1. of this chapter.
122. Commentators propose putting the most weight on the 'accountable' persons. *See* Peng/Lagarden (2019), p. 8; Greinert et al. (2020), p. 529.

b The Relevant Persons from an Institutional Perspective

When dealing with substance for the purposes of the POEM, it has been laid down that management from an institutional perspective is divided into top-level management (normally consisting of the board of directors), middle-level management, and lower-level management (section B.II.1.b.aa. of Chapter 1). For the purposes of the POEM, it has been found that in principle the board of directors is the organ of the subsidiary whose decisions matter (section B.II.2.b.aa. of Chapter 1). The question now is which management level is relevant for the purposes of profit allocation from an institutional perspective.

Commentators have underlined the lack of guidance in the OECD TPG in this respect.[123] This has led to confusion in the literature. It is contemplated, on the one hand, that '[b]oth the need to be on the board or executive level and the possibility to be performed on a level below the executive level can be argued'.[124] On the other hand, other commentators detect a specific level of management as the relevant one:

> Both the AOA and the TPG refer to active (performance of) decision-making functions, focusing on the activities of mid-level management rather than senior management.[125]

Or, to quote another commentator:

> The discussion draft allocates returns from risk to those managing the risk. The managing of global risk is one of the principal functions of senior management and the Board of Directors.[126]

The fact that the OECD TPG do not include guidance as regards which are the relevant persons from an institutional perspective implies that the classification of management from an institutional perspective does not matter for the purposes of profit allocation. By contrast, for the purposes of the POEM, as already reiterated, the board of directors is identified as the relevant organ whose decisions matter. So in the OECD TPG, there is no 'default rule' in favour of a specific level of management, like in the case of the POEM. That this result is correct is confirmed by comparing the telos of the transfer pricing versus that of the POEM.

It has been shown that the POEM is the tiebreaker rule functioning as a preference criterion, meaning that it needs to follow an all-or-nothing approach and point to one state which wins the residence-residence conflict (section B.I.1. of Chapter 1). Having a default rule with regard to the personal element stricto sensu contributes to locating the POEM more easily. Only if doubts arise as to whether the board actually makes the relevant decisions is research conducted on whether some of the rebuttable presumptions laid down in section B.II.2.c. of Chapter 1 exist, and, thus, the POEM is not located with the board. On the contrary, there is no need for such a default rule for

123. De Baets (2018), p. 253.
124. Werner (2019), p. 108 following De Baets (2018), p. 253.
125. Tracana (2017), p. 415.
126. USCIB (2015), p. 845.

the purposes of profit allocation. Profit may be allocated to more than one state, in contrast to the POEM, which must be located in only one state.

But maybe the OECD TPG identify the relevant persons not by referring to their institutional status but indirectly by referring to the qualities that these persons must have. The next section deals with this issue.

2 *Qualitative Sub-element of the Personal Element of Substance*

a *The Role of Information*

It has been established that with regard to the POEM the possession of information and the knowledge/expertise are factors to be considered when determining whether the legally appointed directors, and not outsiders, are actually managing the subsidiary (sections B.II.2.c.cc. and B.II.2.c.dd. of Chapter 1). These personal qualities also play a role in profit allocation. For example, paragraph 1.66 of the OECD TPG provides that:

> Decision-makers should possess competence and experience in the area of the particular risk for which the decision is being made and possess an understanding of the impact of their decision on the business. They should also have access to the relevant information.

The relevance of information for the purposes of substance requirements concentrating on decision-making functions has already been underlined (section B.II.2.c.cc. of Chapter 1). Decision-making prerequisites possess information, thus the existence of the requirement that the decision-makers are informed for the purposes of both the POEM and profit allocation is justified. The question is now what type of and how much information.

As far as the type of information is concerned, paragraph 1.66 of the OECD TPG provides that:

> Decision-makers should possess competence and experience *in the area of the particular risk* for which the decision is being made ... They should also have access to the *relevant* information (emphasis added).

It is somehow intuitive, but in any case, a welcome clarification that there must be a connection between the subject matter to which a decision relates and the information required. We may notice a parallel to the POEM, which evaluates the business of a subsidiary in order to determine which decision-making functions are the relevant ones (section B.II.1.a. of Chapter 1). So it can be concluded that the content of the information that the decision-makers should possess for the purposes of the substance requirement in profit allocation is antecedent to the business of the entity to which they pertain and especially to the particular decision(s) in question, just like in the case of the substance requirement for the purposes of the POEM.

Regarding the second part of the question, i.e., the amount of information required, a commentator has made an important observation:

> [T]he question of whether the risk manager and the party bearing the risk should be characterized as having the same (relevant) information is of considerable importance. If they do, there may be no moral hazard issue and the statement that 'between unrelated parties it generally makes sense for parties to be allocated a greater share of those risks over which they have relatively more control' would not apply.[127]

If this reasoning is adopted as regards the quantity of information that the party controlling the risk, and therewith claiming the profit pertaining thereto, should possess, this party must always have more information than the other party in the transaction in question. But as the principal-agent theory teaches us, the party with the most information is almost always the party to which the principal outsources a task, i.e., the agent.[128] It is exactly because this party has more information that the principal outsources the task.

For example, you go to the doctor because they have substantially more information about your health problem than you do. Still, you are the sole risk-bearer in this case and also the 'residual owner'. If the doctor fails in their treatment, it is your health that will deteriorate, while the doctor will still get their payment. What is being said here is that there are cases where the principal possesses much less information than the agent, and the former is still the sole risk-bearer.

But imagine that you go to a doctor you have been visiting since you were a child and who knows that you are their most valuable patient. The doctor knows that if they fail, especially if they fail willingly, they will lose you. This new type of transactional relationship changes the risk-allocation fundamentally. The doctor is now also a risk-bearer; they bear the downside of the risk, i.e., losing you as a patient, and also the upside of the risk, i.e., continuing a thriving transactional relationship. Notice that the information allocation remains the same in both examples; still, the risk-bearing situation, and therewith the profit and loss allocation, changes dramatically depending on the transactional relationship. Thus, there is no black or white as regards the amount of information the residual claimant, or more accurately the decision-makers of the residual claimant, must possess. The solution lies in the search for comparables.[129]

The OECD TPG must be interpreted in that way. Since they do not provide for any references pointing to a certain amount of information but only plainly refer to the existence of the information, it is in line with the telos of the ALP not to require a certain amount of information in order for a party to be the residual claimant. Rather, the circumstances of each case change the risk allocation, and therewith the residual profit allocation, which supports the view that the focus should be on the search for comparables and not on strict information thresholds that must be passed. As long as the decision-makers possess a minimum of information sufficient for them to render

127. Miall (2015), p. 708.
128. Oehlrich (2016), p. 121. The following reasoning as well as the example are based on Oehlrich's work.
129. Here applies also the counterargument that comparables may not exist. As to the author's response to this argument *see* above n. 96 in this chapter.

their decision-making functions, the information requirement in the OECD TPG should be seen fulfilled.

Such an interpretation would create friction with the POEM, where the step approach is partly adopted by domestic courts in this respect. According to this approach (section B.II.2.c.cc. of Chapter 1), the decision-makers must have sufficient information and not only a minimum thereof in order for management to not be usurped. However, it has been argued that for the purposes of the POEM a minimum of information should also suffice. The alignment of the interpretation of substance in this respect can be added to the arguments presented there in favour of only requiring a minimum amount of information and against adopting the step approach.

In sum, the decision-makers must make informed decisions for the purposes of profit allocation. The type of decisions relates to the particular type of transaction, similar to the POEM, and the amount of information is not particularly prescribed. Along the lines of the information requirement for the purposes of the POEM, as long as a minimum amount of information exists, the information requirement in the OECD TPG should be seen fulfilled, and the focus should be placed on the search for comparables.

b *The Role of Knowledge/Expertise*

The OECD TPG emphasize the importance of knowledge/expertise that the decision-makers must possess: 'Decision-makers should possess competence and experience in the area of the particular risk for which the decision is being made.'[130] Even commentators criticizing the OECD approach on substance acknowledge that '[a]t the end of the day, common sense dictated that one needs the people with the expertise and authority to credibly oversee entrepreneurial risk in the "right location" when dealing with international tax planning'.[131]

Similarly, with the approach this work has taken with regard to the POEM, it is important to determine what type of knowledge is relevant when it comes to identifying the persons who possess this knowledge. For the purposes of the POEM, we found that the legally appointed directors must possess both technical and economic knowledge (section B.II.2.c.dd. of Chapter 1). Monsenego holds the same position with regard to profit allocation. Analysing the OECD guidance in particular with regard to intangibles, Monsenego found that:

> [I]t would make sense to include managerial skills in the expectations placed on the competence of employees ..., as any independent enterprise needs certain managerial skills to carry on its business activities, in addition to the technical or scientific skills that are necessary to its core business.[132]

Monsenego is right to state that economic knowledge, or as he calls it 'managerial skills', is a conditio sine qua non for all entrepreneurship and should be relevant.

130. OECD TPG, para. 1.66.
131. Verlinden et al. (2016), p. 114.
132. Monsenego (2014), p. 12.

Actually, the OECD TPG in paragraph 1.66 of Chapter I, which is the general chapter not only referring to intangibles, affirm Monsenego's position by stating that '[d]ecision-makers should possess ... an understanding of the impact of their decision on the business'. This kind of understanding prerequisites what this work calls economic knowledge. Therefore, the decision-makers are required to have economic knowledge, meaning that they are able to understand the impact of their decision on the business.

As regards technical knowledge, the OECD TPG demonstrate that the level of technical knowledge required may differ from case to case. For example, the OECD TPG provide in paragraph 6.64 that:

> The higher the development risk and the closer the financial risk is related to the development risk, the more the funder will need to have the capability to assess the progress of the development of the intangible.

This example shows that the operational status combined with the nature of the investment may influence the capabilities that the investing party must possess.

This approach corresponds with third-party behaviour. Again (section B.II.1.b. of this chapter), the private equity industry offers an appropriate example. 'There are two major types of investment in the private equity market: (i) venture capital (VC), which is aimed at new start-up companies, and (ii) buy-outs, which target more mature and developed businesses.'[133] In contrast to the case of buy-outs where the investor 'might not possess the experience and skills of the fund manager',[134] in the case of VC investments 'the investor in a VC financing scenario may take both risks – financial and operational. Usually, when the development is at an early stage and has no own funds available, the financing party is more involved in the operational activity. The reason for such an active involvement is that the investment risk is very high and depends primarily on the results of the operational activity. Therefore, the funder wants to be in control not only of investment risk but also of operational risk.'[135]

This example shows that different types and amounts of knowledge are required for different types of investments, although, as the OECD TPG correctly imply,[136] some amount of economic knowledge should be always required. Again, just like with regard to the proper amount of information dealt with in the previous section, we see that there is no all-or-nothing solution. Instead, there is a continuum of knowledge required, a fact that is also shown to be affirmed by referring to third-party behaviour. So again the focus should be on comparables. The type and volume of knowledge the decision-makers have in the controlled transaction influences the search for comparables.[137]

It can be concluded that the comparability analysis should be the key with regard to knowledge and, as has been laid down in the previous section, information that the decision-makers should possess.

---

133. Polonska (2018), p. 108.
134. *Ibid.*, at p. 109.
135. *Ibid.*, at pp. 111-112.
136. OECD TPG, para. 1.66: '[d]ecision-makers should possess ... an understanding of the impact of their decision on the business'.
137. Here applies also the counterargument that comparables may not exist. As to the author's response to this argument *see* above n. 96 in this chapter.

3 *Quantitative Sub-element of the Personal Element of Substance: How Many Decision-Makers Are Necessary?*

Not only the number of decisions but also the number of decision-makers may be relevant when determining whether a taxpayer has the appropriate substance in order to allocate the profit from risk and assets.[138] Monsenego acknowledges the fact that 'under the OECD Guidelines the number of employees is a practical matter that may be taken into consideration when determining the necessary substance to support a given intercompany transaction'.[139] But he then goes on to admit that 'the OECD Guidelines do not provide indications as to how many employees are needed to reach a sufficient level of substance, as this issue necessarily depends on the facts and circumstances at hand'.[140]

The author agrees with this finding. The OECD TPG do not contain any guidance with respect to the number of decision-makers that are required. It can thus also be maintained that, just like for the purposes of the POEM (section B.II.3.b. of Chapter 1), no absolute threshold exists as to the quantitative sub-element of the personal element of substance. But this is logical and laudable. It would be at least naïve to think that such an endeavour would be successful given the complexity and heterogeneity of the business world. And it is in conformity with the mechanism of the ALP to leave it up to the comparability analysis to determine the significance of the number of decision-makers employed case-by-case.[141]

4 *Relationship Between the Functional and Personal Elements: On the Nature of the Personal Element*

As to the degree of importance of the quantitative sub-element of the personal element, guidance is also lacking in the OECD TPG. Irrespective of this fact, it is submitted that quantity should be seen through the lens of quality, just like with regard to the quantitative sub-element of the functional element where, however, guidance in this

138. *See, e.g.*, OECD TPG, para. 9.122: 'The development, maintenance and execution of a worldwide marketing strategy are the main value drivers of the MNE, performed by *125 employees* at Company A's head office.' (Emphasis added); OECD TPG, para. 84 of Annex to Ch. VI: 'Company S has a *large research staff*, including management personnel responsible for technologies of the type acquired from Company T.' (Emphasis added).
139. Monsenego (2014), p. 19. *See also* Eigelshoven/Retzer (2021), para. 147 on Ch. I of the OECD TPG; Petruzzi/Myzithra (2020), p. 436 also presenting the other side of the story: 'In other terms, an entity with many employees will not necessarily be considered to have substance at arm's length, and, likewise, an entity with only one employee will not necessarily be considered as not having substance at arm's length.'
140. Monsenego (2014), p. 19. In this vein also, Polonska (2018), p. 101; Verlinden et al. (2019), p. 1046. *See also* KPMG (2015), p. 538: 'the OECD may want to consider if it is appropriate to define minimal levels of substance and decision making capability' and 'the OECD Guidance could set forth a level of decision making resources and capability that is needed in a principal company (e.g., that it have some senior employees that are capable of actively participating in the decision making of the relevant MNE business)'.
141. In this sense, Monsenego (2014), p. 19. Here applies also the counterargument that comparables may not exist. As to the author's response to this argument *see* above n. 96 in this chapter.

respect exists (section B.II.2.b. of this chapter). Accordingly, the quality of the functions performed matters more than the number of decision-makers. And it would also be sensible to add that it is also not the qualities (in terms of information and knowledge) of decision-makers that are mostly decisive, but the quality of the functions they perform, i.e., that the qualitative sub-element of the functional element takes also precedence over the qualitative sub-element of the personal element.

This reveals that the qualities and the quantity of the persons making the relevant decisions are only *presumptions* of substance. If specific persons make the relevant decisions, then the fact that they do not possess information and/or knowledge or that they may be less in number than in a comparable transaction can only function as a presumption that these persons do not really make the relevant decisions. It is not *required* that these persons have information/knowledge and reach a specific number; it is only required that they render the relevant decision-making functions.

Relying on presumptions for the purposes of the ALP is not the right policy, though. Taking into account the ALP's function, it can and should not work with presumptions, but with what the parties are bringing into a transaction and how comparable taxpayers value the respective contributions.

5 *Synthesis*

- The OECD TPG require that decision-makers should be both capable and authorized to make decisions. If capabilities and authorization are split among different persons, the solution lies in the search for comparables where a similar split takes place (section B.III.1.a.).
- The OECD TPG do not offer guidance as to who the relevant decision-makers from an institutional perspective are (section B.III.1.b.).
- Information and knowledge/expertise that the decision-makers possess are also relevant factors for the purposes of the substance requirement in profit allocation. As long as the decision-makers possess a minimum amount of information, the information requirement in the OECD TPG should be seen as fulfilled (section B.III.2.a.).
- With respect to the knowledge/expertise that the decision-makers need to possess, different types and amounts of knowledge are required for different types of investments, although some amount of economic knowledge should always be required. There is a continuum of knowledge required, a fact that is also shown to be affirmed by referring to third-party behaviour. The focus should be on comparables (section B.III.2.b.).
- The OECD TPG purportedly assign some relevance to the quantitative sub-element of the personal element of the substance requirement, although no further guidance is provided and no absolute threshold exists in this respect. This is not a shortcoming of the OECD TPG, but a natural consequence of its mechanism (section B.III.3.).

- No guidance exists either with regard to the degree of importance of the quantitative sub-element of the personal element. It has been concluded, though, that the qualitative and quantitative sub-element of the personal elements are of subordinate importance compared to the qualitative sub-element of the functional element, which means that only the rendering of functions on risk is required, while the qualities and quantities of the decision-makers only indicate extant or missing substance (section B.III.4.).

IV The Objective Element of Substance in Transfer Pricing Rules

1 The Objective Element of Substance Is Relevant for the Purposes of Transfer Pricing Rules

The objective element of substance is relevant for the purposes of profit allocation in two ways: first, the ownership and utilization of assets must be taken into consideration within the functional analysis; second, financial assets play a key role in the assumption of risk.

With regard to the role of the ownership and utilization of assets for the purposes of the functional analysis, paragraph 1.54 of the OECD TPG stipulates that:

> The functional analysis should consider the type of assets used, such as plant and equipment, the use of valuable intangibles, financial assets, etc., and the nature of the assets used, such as the age, market value, location, property right protections available, etc.

So assets, consisting of the objective element of the substance requirement, certainly play a role within the functional analysis. As to the type of assets that are relevant, financial assets are also of importance for the purposes of risk allocation. In particular, risk is allocated to a party not only under the condition that it has the functional and personal substance, as determined in sections B.II. and B.III.; the party claiming profit from risk should also have the 'financial capacity'[142] to bear the risk. One also has to remember that, particularly in scenarios where risk-related decision-making is for the most part outsourced to a party without the financial capacity to assume risks from a party that has this capacity, the latter seems to play a very important role. Although the outsourcing party does not have 'substance' in terms of decision-making functions, it has 'substance' in terms of money (section B.II.2.b. of this chapter). But what does financial capacity mean? Again, the OECD TPG underline the importance of the objective element of substance in this respect:

> Financial capacity to assume risk can be defined as access to funding to take on the risk or to lay off the risk, to pay for the risk mitigation functions and to bear the consequences of the risk if the risk materializes. Access to funding by the party

142. OECD TPG, para. 1.60.

> assuming the risk *takes into account the available assets* and the options realistically available to access additional liquidity, if needed, to cover the costs anticipated to arise should the risk materialize.[143]

This passage underlines the importance of financial assets and other types of assets that could support access to funding for the purposes of risk allocation. This is an intuitive notion. A subsidiary with 1 million cash in its bank accounts can certainly assume a risk that in case of materialization is worth the same value. But it may even assume a higher risk if access to funding is easy because it has many valuable assets to collateralize and borrow money.

2 *The Objective Element of Substance Is Subordinate to the Functional and Personal Elements: On the Relationship Between the Objective Element and the Personal and Functional Elements*

The two passages from the OECD TPG quoted in the previous section show that ownership of assets is a relevant factor for the purposes of the functional analysis and for the allocation of risk. Let us remember, though, that pursuant to the OECD TPG profit follows functions, assets and risks, on the one hand, and assets and risks follow decision-making functions, on the other (section A.II. of this chapter). In plain English, this means that the objective element of substance is *subordinate* to the functional and personal elements.[144] The ownership and utilization of assets, irrespective of their nature (tangible, *inter alia*, financial and intangible) are only of importance for the purposes of profit allocation if they are supported by substance in the form of personnel making decisions. Let us demonstrate this by bringing up three examples.

Example 1 (other tangible assets): Assume parent company P is selling its products in country A through subsidiary S. P is first selling its products to S which in turn sells the products to third-party customers. We have seen in section B.II.1.a.aa. of this chapter that the economist would say that in such a scenario S, as the owner of the products, is the residual claimant. That is, the net profit arising from the transaction with third parties is attributable to S. The OECD TPG practically negate this finding. If S does not take the relevant decisions (section B.II. of this chapter) and possesses the necessary personnel (section B.III. of this chapter), although it remains the owner of the tangible assets, is entitled only to risk-free returns. This practically deprives S of most of its profit and thereby negates its status as residual claimant.

So, assume further, if the group wants to shift profit to the jurisdiction where P is resident – because the latter is low-taxed – it only has to follow the following steps:

(1) let the personnel of S make the operational decisions regarding the asset-related risks (inventory and product-recall risk);

143. *Ibid.*, para. 1.64 (emphasis added). For a more 'generous' interpretation of this passage, according to which 'any company with functionality to control risks will have access to capital that will allow it to assume risks' *see* Hafkenscheid (2017), p. 20 and following this interpretation Navisotschnigg (2022), p. 35.

144. *Concurring* Navisotschnigg (2022), p. 35.

(2) establish some form of review process carried out by P with regard to these decisions;
(3) P does not outsource all the strategic decisions on the inventory and product-recall risks; and
(4) P possesses competent and informed managers.

By doing so, profit is by default shifted to the jurisdiction where P is resident. It does not matter that S owns the products. If it does not possess the functional and personal substance, as determined in sections B.II. and III. of this chapter, its profit from the third-party transaction will be attributed to P.

Example 2 (financial assets): Assume company S wants to develop a new intangible. It does so by financing another group company. Our economist friend would tell us that at the end of the research process, S is the winner or the loser of the whole project. That is, if research succeeds, S will yield the profits out of the new intangible, but if research fails, S will have to bear the loss. This is not the way things are according to the OECD TPG. If S does not have the functional and personal substance, as determined in sections B.II. and B.III. of this chapter, with regard to the *operational* risks of the project (i.e., the risks relating to the R&D), it will only be entitled to a risk-adjusted return on the funding.[145] And it is entitled to that only as long as it has the functional and personal substance, as determined in sections B.II. and B.III., with regard to the *financial* risks. Should this not be the case, S is then 'entitled to no more than a risk-free return for its funding activities'.[146]

So it does not matter whether S has loads of dollars in its bank account; it needs clever decision-makers in order for it to attract profit.

Example 3 (intangible assets): Assume company S is a distributing company. In conducting its activities, i.e., selling products to third parties, it utilizes, *inter alia,* a marketing intangible. A large part of the profit S makes from its business activity is attributable to the utilization of the aforementioned intangible. However, the functional analysis reveals that S does not have the functional and personal substance, as determined in sections B.II. and B.III. of this chapter, that is required in order for a return attributable to the utilization of the intangible to be allocated to its owner.

Assume that the functional analysis reveals that S's parent, P, possesses the necessary personnel that render the relevant decision-making functions on the intangible. P, without becoming the owner of the intangible, is entitled to returns arising from the utilization of the intangible; only a risk-free return may be allocated to S.

These three examples demonstrate that the ownership and utilization of assets, by default, do not guarantee that the return attributable to them is allocated to the party owing or utilizing them. A party owing and utilizing tangible assets may be entitled only to risk-free profits if it does not possess the personnel that renders the relevant decision-making functions regarding the asset. Furthermore, financial investment in an asset does not entitle one to any return on the asset, other than risk-free returns, unless the funding party has the necessary functional and personal substance with regard to

145. OECD TPG, para. 6.61.
146. *Ibid.*, para. 58 of Annex to Ch. VI.

the operational and financial risks. All in all, it can be concluded that the personal and functional elements take precedence over the objective elements for the purposes of profit allocation.

This is a policy choice by the OECD in order to fight profit shifting to entities with a high amount of cash and/or intangible assets but a low amount of personnel. It has already been argued that this approach runs counter to the function of the ALP as the standard for the allocation of profits gained in transactions between members of an MNE in order to realize and preserve taxation according to the ability-to-pay principle (section B.I.1. of this chapter). For *Leukefeld*, though, the OECD approach is justifiable because:

> personal substance is implicitly associated with physical [in the terminology of this work 'objective'] and functional substance. For the exercise of personnel functions in a company, an appropriate infrastructure in the form of buildings, premises, adequate equipment, etc. must always be available.[147]

The author has sympathy with this argument. But, as *Leukefeld* himself acknowledges, there is only an implicit connection between the existence of personnel rendering decision-making functions, on the one hand, and business activities and assets, on the other. Such a connection could be, at the most, rebuttably presumed. Take example 1. There, parent P intends to attract returns on asset-related risks. It can do so by letting the personnel of its subsidiary S do all the dirty work, while one manager of P retains control of the operations of S. In this case, who invests the most substance into the transaction, P or S?

One could certainly argue, as it is surmised that *Leukefeld* does, that the parent P, in general, that is irrespective of how much objective substance it invests into this specific transaction, has enough substance in terms of premises, etc. But for the purposes of the ALP, following the transactional approach, it is not relevant how much substance a corporation generally has, but how much it invests in a concrete transaction. It may be that P has premises, assets, etc.; but this is immaterial as long as it does not utilize them for the purposes of the transaction in question. The ALP can and should not work with presumptions (section B.III.4. of this chapter).

3 Comparison with the Substance Requirement for the Purposes of the POEM

The OECD approach with regard to the objective element of substance for the purposes of profit allocation is similar to that for the purposes of the POEM and therefore does not rectify the flaws detected there. In particular, it has been concluded that the personal and functional elements take precedence over the objective element for the purposes of the POEM (section B.III.3. of Chapter 1). This may lead to the problematic result that substance for the purposes of both the POEM and profit allocation cannot depict the economic allegiance of a taxpayer to a state, and therewith the ability to pay

147. Leukefeld (2018), p. 126 (author's unofficial translation).

created within the borders of that state. Let us remember the example used there in order to demonstrate this result for the purposes of the POEM:

> Imagine that a subsidiary may have hundreds of employees working in premises and using/exploiting assets in State A, whereas the legally appointed directors live and act from State B, where only an office exists where the latter meet every once in while. The POEM is in State B, although it could be ascertained that the subsidiary is more economically connected to State A than State B.

If we adapt the example for the purposes of profit allocation, it becomes apparent that the OECD TPG share the exact same problem. Assume subsidiary S has hundreds of employees working on premises and using/exploiting assets in State A. The strategic decisions relating to the risks underlying the utilization and exploitation of the assets are made by the managers of S's parent, P, resident in state B. The profit from the risks underlying the utilization and exploitation of the assets is, according to the OECD guidance, by default attributable to B, although it could be ascertained that the subsidiary is economically connected more to State A than State B. Of course, this result is exacerbated by the fact that, apart from reducing the importance of the objective element of substance, the OECD focuses too much on decision-making functions (section B.I.2. of this chapter).

It can be concluded that the transfer pricing rules included in the OECD TPG do not rectify the flaws of the substance requirement for the POEM. In fact, they espouse the same approach of giving priority to the personal and functional elements of substance, as concretely determined in sections B.II. and B.III. of this chapter, over the objective element of substance related to tangible, financial and intangible assets. By mechanically doing so, they fail to ensure that taxation is based on the principles of economic allegiance and ability to pay.

4 *Synthesis*

- The objective element of substance is relevant for the purposes of profit allocation in two ways: first, the ownership and utilization of assets must be taken into consideration within the functional analysis; second, financial assets play a key role in the assumption of risk (section B.IV.1.).
- The ownership and utilization of assets, by default, do not guarantee that the return attributable to them is allocated to the party owning or utilizing them. Owners of assets and funding parties are only entitled to risk-free returns if they do not possess the necessary functional and personal substance with regard to the operational and financial risks. Thus, the personal and functional elements take precedence over the objective element for the purposes of profit allocation (section B.IV.2.).
- By giving priority to the personal and functional elements of substance over the objective element of substance related to tangible, financial and intangible assets, the transfer pricing rules included in the OECD TPG do not rectify the flaws of the substance requirement for the POEM. They fail to ensure that

taxation is based on the principles of economic allegiance and ability to pay (section B.IV.3.).

C INTERIM CONCLUSIONS

It is easier to comprehend the content of the substance requirement for the purposes of profit allocation if one uses the conclusions already drawn with regard to substance for the purposes of the POEM as a benchmark. In the following, the similarities and differences between the substance requirements in the POEM and transfer pricing and the reasons accompanying the latter are summarized:

- On the one hand, both the ALP and the POEM adopt a stand-alone perspective, that is, the entity whose substance is in question is separated from the group (section A.I.1.). On the other hand, while substance for the purposes of the POEM uses a holistic approach, substance for the purposes of profit allocation uses a transactional approach. This divergence is justified considering the different mechanisms of these two rules (section A.I.2.a.).
- As to the functional element of the substance requirement, there are primarily similarities and only one difference between the two substance requirements. With regard to the similarities, first, both the POEM and transfer pricing concentrate on decision-making functions. This has been found to be acceptable for the purposes of the POEM (section B.II.1.a.cc. of Chapter 1), but not for the purposes of profit allocation (section B.I.2.). Second, both substance requirements point to the strategic decisions at the level of the subsidiary as the relevant decisions and delineate them from parent policy-making; for the purposes of the latter task, corporate law may be consulted to ascertain which decisions are reserved for the parent to make (sections B.II.1.a.aa. and B.II.1.a.cc.). Third, both the decision-making stricto sensu and the monitoring stage are relevant in the decision-making process in both substance requirements (section B.II.1.c.). Fourth, both substance requirements share the commonality that there is no absolute quantitative threshold regarding the decisions to be made (section B.II.2.a.). Finally, quality takes precedence over quantity and should be seen through the lens of it (section B.II.2.b.).
- Divergence exists with regard to outsourcing. On the one hand, the OECD TPG demand that not all strategic decisions are outsourced, while on the other, for the purposes of the POEM, this is possible. Furthermore, operational decisions can be completely outsourced but only under the condition that the taxpayer retains oversight of the outsourced decision-making functions; in the POEM no such condition exists (section B.II.1.b.).
- Profit allocation and the POEM both reject a formal approach concentrating on the authority of the decision-makers or their accountability as regards the relevant decisions (section B.III.1.a.).
- While the POEM points to the members of the board as the relevant persons from an institutional perspective, the OECD TPG remain neutral in this

respect. This divergence has also been justified based on the different approaches to the legal rules in question (section B.III.1.b.).

- As far as the qualities of the relevant persons are concerned, the two substance requirements only present similarities. In both cases, information and knowledge/expertise of the decision-makers play a role. In particular, for the purposes of both substance requirements, the content of the information that the decision-makers should possess is antecedent to the business of the entity to which they pertain. Furthermore, both the POEM and transfer pricing only require the decision-makers to possess a minimum amount of information (section B.III.2.a.). Finally, both substance requirements require the decision-makers to have both technical and economic knowledge (section B.III.2.b.).
- Neither of the substance requirements is subject to an absolute threshold requirement as regards the number of decision-makers required (section B.III.3.).
- In contrast to the POEM, financial assets play a role in the OECD TPG (section B.IV.1.).
- Both substance requirements give priority to the functional and personal elements of substance over the objective one (section B.IV.3.).

Just like for the purposes of the POEM, a substance checklist in transfer pricing is laid down. Elements that are 'new' compared to the checklist in the POEM are emphasized in italics.

Figure 5 Substance Checklist in Transfer Pricing

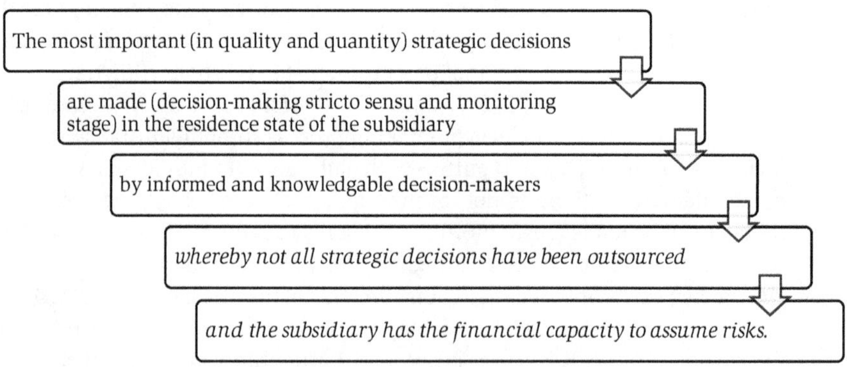

In this substance checklist, all but one element constitutes requirements and not mere presumptions of substance.[148] That is, they must exist in order for a subsidiary to

148. On substance requirements as rebuttable and irrebuttable presumptions, *see* above s. B.III.5. of the introduction.

attract risk-related profits. If one element does not exist, then the taxpayer cannot argue that they have substance based on the existence of another element. If, for example, all strategic decisions have been outsourced, then the taxpayer is only eligible for risk-free returns on an asset, although they may have the financial capacity to assume risks.

The one element that is a presumption of substance refers to the fact that decisions are made by informed and knowledgeable managers. As explained in section B.III.4., the quality of the decision-making functions takes precedence over the quality and quantity of the decision-makers. If the relevant decision-making functions are attributed to a subsidiary and the latter does not possess informed and knowledgeable managers, it still can be the one to which profit is allocated, according to comparable transactions. The fact that the decision-makers are not informed and knowledgeable can work as a presumption that the decision-makers are not the ones rendering the important decision-making functions, although it must be said that presumptions of substance cannot work in the ALP context where relevant is what actually happens in third party transactions and not what the OECD TPG presume.[149]

The following table summarizes the similarities and differences between the substance requirements in the POEM and transfer pricing.

Table 1 Similarities and Differences Between the Substance Requirements in the POEM and Transfer Pricing Rules

Areas of Comparison	*Similarities*	*Differences*
Scope		Holistic versus transactional approach
Functional Element	Decision-making functions are important - Strategic decisions are important (must be delineated from parent policy-making) - No quantitative threshold - Both decision-making stricto sensu and monitoring stage relevant - Quality takes precedence over quantity	Outsourcing decision-making stricter in transfer pricing
Personal Element	Content and amount of information - Type of knowledge - No quantitative threshold - Quality takes precedence over quantity	POEM points to board members while transfer pricing neutral

149. *See* above s. B.III.4 of this chapter.

Areas of Comparison	*Similarities*	*Differences*
Objective Element	Inferior role of the element in both substance requirements	Role of financial assets in transfer pricing

CHAPTER 3

The Substance Requirement for the Purposes of DTC Treaty Shopping Rules

A PRELIMINARY REMARKS

I Functions and Mechanism of DTC Treaty Shopping Rules

1 Functions of DTC Treaty Shopping Rules

It has already been explained that one of the functions of residence in DTCs is to delineate the personal scope of a DTC (section A.I. of Chapter 1). So, prima facie, a subsidiary with residence in state X, for instance, may draw benefits from its DTCs with other states. To illustrate how residence can be the key aspect when accessing treaty benefits, take again the example from the case study presented in section B.II. of the introduction. There, SubCo licenses a newly developed IP to SubSub, the latter residing in another state than the residence state of SubCo. SubSub pays royalties to SubCo for the licensed IP. The DTC between the SubCo and SubSub state provides that the SubSub state shall not impose withholding taxes on the outflowing royalty payments. SubCo is only eligible for this treaty benefit (i.e., to receive the royalties free from tax) because it is a resident of the SubCo state.

Now, imagine that the IP is licensed not by SubCo but by its parent, PaCo, and there is no DTC between the state of residence of PaCo, i.e., the PaCo state, and SubSub state. Now, the SubSub state is free to impose withholding taxes on the outflowing royalties, since there is no DTC that requires it to refrain from doing so. If the SubCo state has a DTC with both the SubSub and the PaCo state and both DTCs exempt outflowing royalty and dividend payments from withholding taxes, PaCo may be interested in not licensing the IP directly to SubSub. Instead, it can create a subsidiary in the SubCo state and park the IP there. Then, SubCo would license the IP to SubSub, receive the royalty payments free from withholding taxes, and transfer them to its parent in the form of dividends, also free from withholding taxes based on the DTC between the PaCo and the SubCo state.

It becomes apparent that taxpayers may create structures 'in which a person that is a resident of a particular state (the residence state) derives income from a second state (the source state) with which the person's home State does not have a tax treaty providing the desired benefit, and the person establishes a legal entity in a third state with which the source state has a tax treaty, but with which the person otherwise has no or little connection, in order to obtain the desired treaty benefits that would not be directly available to such person'.[1] These structures are called *treaty shopping*.

There are many arguments against treaty shopping, just as there are counterarguments defending it,[2] but it is not the task of this work to enter into the discourse in this regard. Rather, one thing is certain and relevant from a de lege lata perspective, which is also the perspective taken in this work (section E. of the introduction): the current DTC framework and Models include rules that tackle treaty shopping ('treaty shopping rules').[3] They do so by closing the door that the residence requirement opens. That is, without such rules, an entity must only have its residence in a DTC state in order to avail itself of treaty benefits.

DTC treaty shopping rules[4] impose conditions additional to the residence requirement in order for treaty benefits to be granted. Returning to the above example, it could be that SubCo is not entitled to the treaty benefit in question (the withholding tax exemption) because such a treaty shopping rule applies, even though it is resident of the SubCo state. In sum, treaty shopping rules function as a filter to the residence requirement in DTCs; they filter some eligible taxpayers out of the personal scope of the DTC.

Now that we know how these treaty shopping rules function, it is important to also detect which rules exist in this respect and shortly introduce their mechanisms (section A.I.2.). This work only addresses DTC treaty shopping rules. Again, unilateral measures against treaty shopping, although they may exist,[5] are not within the scope

1. Blessing (2020a), s. 2.1. On the definition of treaty shopping, *see also* Panayi (2007), pp. 37 et seq.; De Broe (2008), pp. 2008 et seq.; Rudolf (2012), pp. 10 et seq.; Schade (2013), p. 18.
2. For both sides of the coin, *see* Avi-Yonah/Panayi (2010), s. 2.2.; Wardzynski (2014), pp. 472-473; Karadkar (2017), s. 2.3.
3. Thus far, reference has been made to anti-abuse rules and not treaty shopping rules. The latter term is preferred because it is more precise. In particular, DTC abuse is divided into two categories: treaty shopping and rule shopping whereby the latter refers to 'arrangements undertaken by a person who as such is entitled to the benefits of a tax treaty pretending to benefit from a more favourable rule within the applicable treaty'. *See* Báez Moreno (2017), p. 438; *see also* Duff (2018a), pp. 671-672. So in order to signalize that this work deals only with rules against treaty shopping and not rule shopping the term treaty shopping rules is preferable to the more general term anti-abuse rules, the latter also including rules against rule shopping. The term anti-abuse rules has been thus far used because there has not been an introduction to the treaty shopping phenomenon and it would have been difficult for the reader to understand the term.
4. The acronym DTC in the term DTC treaty shopping rules is not redundant, as one could assume. In fact, it is used to specify that this work deals with treaty shopping rules contained in DTCs, and thereby to distinguish them from unilateral treaty shopping rules which are outside the scope of this work.
5. *See,* for example, the already cited works by Rudolf (2012), pp. 355 et seq. and Schade (2013), passim on the German treaty shopping rule (§50d(3) of the German Income Tax Act).

of this study, which comprises only rules in the DTC and EU tax law context (section C. of the introduction). After the rules against treaty shopping have been detected, the question is then posed and answered as to which of them are substance-oriented and thereby within the scope of this work (section A.II.).

2 *Mechanism of DTC Treaty Shopping Rules*

'Three main anti-treaty shopping provisions have rapidly made their way into many tax treaties. All of them have in common that they intend to raise the threshold to gain access to treaty benefits above the tax residence status on the basis that such a status is not enough to "deserve" the entitlement to treaty benefits thus requiring the taxpayer to comply with extra conditions.'[6]

Two of these rules must already be familiar to the reader. When analysing the unilateral and bilateral responses against the tax-minimizing interposition of subsidiaries, reference has been made to two DTC treaty shopping rules: the LOB clause and the PPT (section B.III.3. of the introduction). However, before the inclusion of these two rules in the OECD MTC,[7] another provision already existed. Reference is made to the BO clause, which has been included in the OECD MTC since 1977.

Now that we know which rules we are talking about, it is also important to understand how these rules exactly work. The analysis remains short and has only an introductory purpose:

(1) The BO clause provides that the recipient of passive income (i.e., dividends, interest, and royalties) must also be the beneficial owner thereof, that is, it is the person 'that has the right to receive income, profits, etc. from a property or investment that they own'.[8] It is questionable what the exact nature of the BO clause is, whether it is an anti-avoidance rule, a rule referring to the attributes of ownership over an item of income, a rule for the attribution of income, or a rule that asks whether the recipient of the income simply forwards it to another person.[9] For the purposes of this work, it suffices to say that if a subsidiary is not the beneficial owner of the passive income it receives, it is then denied the treaty benefits connected thereto (e.g., the reduction or elimination of withholding taxes at source).

(2) The LOB clause appears in a simplified and detailed version of the OECD MTC. The basic mechanism of the LOB clause remains the same in both versions, though. In particular, the LOB distinguishes between qualified and non-qualified persons by referring to many tests which a qualified person

6. Escribano (2019b), p. 939.
7. As already mentioned in s. B.III.3. of the introduction, the LOB clause and the PPT have been a product of Action 6 of the BEPS Project. Thus, these rules have only been first included in the 2017 OECD MTC.
8. BENEFICIAL OWNER definition | Cambridge English Dictionary.
9. On the approaches to the BO clause *see* Meindl-Ringler (2016), pp. 321-337; Navisotschnigg (2019), pp. 96-107.

must pass. For example, certain publicly traded companies and entities are considered qualified persons for the purposes of the LOB pursuant to Article 29(2) of the OECD MTC. If a person is a qualified person for the purposes of the LOB, they are then entitled to all treaty benefits regarding all items of income they receive in their residence state. If the taxpayer is not deemed a qualified person, then they may still enjoy treaty benefits but only regarding a specific item of income. For example, although a person may not be deemed a qualified person for the purposes of the LOB, they may enjoy treaty benefits regarding their income emanating from the active conduct of a business pursuant to Article 29(3) of the OECD MTC.

(3) The PPT is the newly introduced general anti-avoidance rule (GAAR) in DTCs. It tackles, *inter alia*,[10] treaty shopping structures by denying treaty benefits when it is reasonable to conclude that obtaining the treaty benefit was one of the principal purposes of the transaction or arrangement in question (in our case: the treaty shopping structure) (subjective prong of the test). This may happen, though, only under the condition that it cannot be established that granting that benefit in these circumstances would be in accordance with the object and purpose of the relevant provisions of the DTC (objective prong of the test).[11]

In total, the state of the art regarding DTC treaty shopping rules comprises three rules: the BO clause, the LOB clause, and the PPT. All these rules have the same function: they are used as a filter to the residence requirement in DTCs; a taxpayer falling under the purview of these rules is illegible for treaty benefits. It must have been made clear (irrespective of the very short way this has been introduced), though, that the three rules have different mechanisms. For instance, the BO clause covers only passive income, while the LOB and the PPT cover all types of income.

Since it is not the purpose of the study to talk generally about treaty shopping rules but rather to focus on the content of substance therein, the question arises whether substance is relevant in these three rules. The next section referring to the scope of the study deals with this issue.

II Scope of the Investigation

In section B.III.3. of the introduction, reference has only been made to the LOB and the PPT as substance-oriented DTC rules against treaty shopping. This already implies that

10. 'The PPT … applies to all distributive rules and to all forms of treaty abuse', *see* Danon (2020a), s. 15.3.2.; Báez Moreno (2021), p. 780. *See also* below ss B.IV.1. and B.IV.3. of this chapter.
11. For a different understanding of the PPT, *see* Schön (2022a), p. 6: '[The PPT] consists of the teleological element (prong 2), which looks at the material justification of a treaty benefit in the light of the provision's object and purpose, and of the protective threshold (prong 1), which allows the tax authorities or the judge to go beyond the literal meaning of the treaty provision in question only if obtaining a tax benefit is a principal purpose of an arrangement or transaction.'

the BO clause does not fall into the scope of this work, since it is not a substance-oriented rule.[12]

In fact, some countries have interpreted the term 'beneficial owner' in a substance-oriented fashion. For example, the Chinese tax administration provides that if the 'activities conducted by the recipient do not constitute substantial business activities (substantial business activities include substantial manufacture and sales and management activities, and substance must be determined by reference to functions performed and risks assumed)', this will 'have an adverse effect in determining BO status'.[13] In a similar vein, the Danish Tax Tribunal in the *HHU* case denied the beneficial ownership status of the intermediary companies because they had no business in their resident state supported by employees, an office or an administration.[14] Furthermore, in the Spanish case *Colgate,* the Spanish National Court 'concluded that the Swiss company [whose BO status was in question] did not perform any function or control any risk or asset regarding the intangibles (despite the fact that it had a licence from the US owner of the intangibles). Therefore, it could not be regarded as the BO of the royalty'.[15] Finally, on 13 February 2020, the Arbitration Court of Moscow denied the beneficial ownership status of a Dutch intermediary holding company because the latter 'was not performing genuine business activities'.[16]

By contrast, other countries do not follow the above-mentioned substance-oriented approach. For example, in the *Prévost* case, the Tax Court of Canada (TCC) ruled that '[t]here is no evidence that PHB.V. [the interposed company] was a conduit for Volvo and Henlys [its shareholders][,] [although] *[i]t is true that PHB.V. had no physical office or employees in the Netherlands or elsewhere*'.[17] So one can detect different approaches from country to country as to the role of substance for the purposes of the BO clause.

But this should actually not be the case. In fact, the OECD MTC and its Commentaries provide sufficient information to construe the meaning of the BO clause or at least to exclude the possibility that substance plays a role for the purposes of the BO clause.[18] What is being said here is that the 'beneficial owner' term must be

12. With 'substance-oriented' reference is made to substance as defined for the purposes of this work in s. D.I. of the introduction, i.e., referring to the essential qualities that a subsidiary corporation must have (in this case in order for a subsidiary to be able to draw treaty benefits). It has been shown in s. A.III. of Ch. 2 that there can be behind a substance analysis the search for the 'real deal'. Like there, here reference is made to substance only in the first sense and not the second one.
13. Martín Jiménez (2022a), s. 5.10., n. 211.
14. Bundgaard (2012), p. 68.
15. Martín Jiménez (2022a), s. 5.7.2.2.
16. Milogolov (2020).
17. Tax Court of Canada, 22 Apr. 2008, *Prévost Car Inc. v. Her Majesty the Queen*, TCC (2008), p. 231 (at para. 102) (emphasis added). *See* from the literature Martín Jiménez (2022a), s. 5.5.1.: 'the holding company was the owner of the dividends because it enjoys discretion to use the funds (*despite its minimal substance, there being no office or employees*' (emphasis added).
18. *See* especially para. 12.4 of the Commentary (2017) on Article 10: 'In these various examples (agent, nominee, conduit company acting as a fiduciary or administrator), the direct recipient of the dividend is not the "beneficial owner" because that recipient's right to use and enjoy the dividend is constrained by a contractual or legal obligation to pass on the payment received to another person. Such an obligation will normally derive from relevant legal documents but may

interpreted autonomously and uniformly for the purposes of the DTC and not based on any – quite often diverging – domestic interpretations. Indeed, the fact that an autonomous interpretation of the term 'beneficial owner' can lead to diverging interpretations like the one seen here referring to the role of substance for its purposes, urges commentators to argue for an autonomous meaning of the term 'beneficial owner', independent of any domestic notion.[19]

As to the autonomous meaning of the term 'beneficial owner', commentators have already underlined that 'when interpreting the notion of beneficial owner, the OECD does not have a broad approach, which considers facts and circumstances also beyond the existence of a contractual or legal obligation to pass on the payment received to another person'.[20] And although 'it is certainly helpful if the recipient of the item of income comingles the item of income received with other funds and has enough functionality[,] [u]nder the OECD analysis of the beneficial owner, and this is true particularly in respect of the functionality, the lack thereof should, in principle, not lead to denying its (legal) status of beneficial owner of the payment. It should only incite questions in respect of the correct (economic) transfer pricing allocation of the payment, and this only in the even of transactions between related parties'.[21]

So it can be submitted that an autonomous interpretation of the term beneficial owner suggests that substance should not play a role for the purposes of the BO clause in DTCs based on the OECD MTC. An interesting issue relates to whether this is also the case with regard to DTCs concluded by EU states.

In fact, commentators have prophesied that:

> If the EC [now EU] concept goes its own ... way, there is, in view of the lack of clarity of the term used in the OECD MC, a fair chance that Courts in EC Member

---

also be found to exist on the basis of facts and circumstances showing that, in substance, the recipient clearly does not have the right to use and enjoy the dividend unconstrained by a contractual or legal obligation to pass on the payment received to another person.' And Danon (2020a), s. 15.2.5.2.3. interpreting this passage: 'The reference to "facts and circumstances" and "in substance" used by the Commentaries in this passage could suggest that the OECD has, at least not completely, ruled out the possibility to assess beneficial ownership on the basis of a substance-over-form interpretation. Another possible interpretation, by contrast, would be to consider that the facts may here serve as a tool to prove the existence of an unwritten but nevertheless legal or contractual obligation. Under this analysis, beneficial ownership would be subject to a legal interpretation but also considering what could be described as "legal substance".'

19. Meindl-Ringler (2016), pp. 295-297 with abundant references in this respect; for the autonomous meaning of the BO clause from the latest literature *see* Navisotschnigg (2019), p. 95; Danon (2020a), s. 15.2.4. both with abundant references, *inter alia*, to the famous *Indofood* case. *See* UK Court of Appeal, 2 Mar. 2006, *Indofood International Finance Ltd v. JP Morgan Chase Bank NA, London Branch*, STC (2006), p. 1195 (at para. 42).
20. De Pietro (2020), p. 1078.
21. Janssen/Sada Garibay (2020), p. 1103. Categorically against any substance orientation of the BO clause: De Broe (2008), p. 714; De Broe/Gommers (2019), p. 295; Danon (2020a), s. 15.2.5.1. Apparently *contra* and thus in favour of the substance-orientation of the BO clause Monsenego (2014), p. 17; Wardzynski (2014), p. 476; Martín Jiménez (2020a), p. 211; Navisotschnigg (2022), pp. 132 et seq.

> States interpret the term 'beneficial owner' used in their bilateral tax treaties in the same way as they do for purposes of the Directives.[22]

Without going into detail, according to some commentators,[23] the CJEU in the so-called *Danish withholding tax* cases[24] gave the BO clause a substance orientation. In fact, the CJEU ruled in these cases that:

> The fact that a company acts as a conduit company may be established where its sole activity is the receipt of interest and its transmission to the beneficial owner or to other conduit companies. The absence of actual economic activity must, in the light of the specific features of the economic activity in question, be inferred from an analysis of all the relevant factors relating, in particular, to the management of the company, to its balance sheet, to the structure of its costs and to expenditure actually incurred, to the staff that it employs and to the premises and equipment that it has.[25]

So it could be that, if this quote is referring to the BO clause, the CJEU interprets the term 'beneficial owner' in a substance-oriented fashion for the purposes of the IRD. In this case, the question would arise whether EU Member States should follow the course allegedly set by the CJEU and interpret their DTCs introducing a substance requirement into the BO clause. This is not the case, however, since this CJEU quote, obviously containing a substance requirement,[26] does not refer to the BO clause but to the concept of wholly artificial arrangements.[27] And as commentators inform us, although both concepts are intertwined in the CJEU's analysis, they still remain separate concepts.[28] So the CJEU, by introducing a substance requirement into the concept of wholly artificial arrangements, has not also done so with regard to the BO clause.

---

22. De Broe (2008), p. 675; *see also* Tenore (2010), pp. 234-235; Avella (2012), pp. 118-121; Hernández González-Barreda (2019), p. 418; van Hulten/Korving (2019), p. 800; Danon (2020a), s. 15.2.1.; De Broe (2020), s. 16.2.1.-3.; Marres/de Groot (2021), p. 341.
23. De Pietro (2020), p.1080; Janssen/Sada Garibay (2020), p. 1103; Martín Jiménez (2022a), s. 5.9. *See* already before the CJEU's judgment and expressing his personal opinion by commenting on the Opinion of AG Kokott Lazarov (2018), p. 875.
24. CJEU, 26 Feb. 2019, C–116/16 and C–117/16, *Skatteministeriet v. T Danmark and Y Denmark*, ECLI:EU:C:2019:135; CJEU, C-115/16, C-118/16, C-119/16 and C-299/16, *N Luxembourg 1*.
25. CJEU, C–116/16 and C–117/16, *T Danmark*, at para. 104; CJEU, C-115/16, C-118/16, C-119/16 and C-299/16, *N Luxembourg 1*, at para. 131.
26. Baerentzen (2020), p. 48.
27. According to scholars commenting on the *Danish withholding tax cases* the substance requirement has been one of 'a set of indicia that national courts must take into account in assessing *whether a transaction is abusive*'. (Emphasis added). *See* CFE (2019), p. 499; Hernández González-Barreda (2019), p. 414; Danon et al. (2021), p. 509: 'both in the PSD and IRD cases, the Court was merely providing indicators here designed to detect a possible abuse of rights'. Weber (2022), p. 59. On the content of the wholly artificial arrangements doctrine in the context of this work, *see* below s. B.II. of Ch. 4.
28. *See* Haslehner/Kofler (2019): 'in applying the IRD, the Court appears to keep the two concepts more clearly separate in cases C-115/16 and others'. Barba de Alba/Arribas (2019); De Broe/ Gommers (2019), pp. 295-296; Hernández González-Barreda (2019), p. 414; Jochimsen/Gsödl (2021), p. 390; Marres/de Groot (2021), p. 333 concluding: 'The CJEU thus appears to regard "not being the beneficial owner" as relevant in the context of abuse but does not equate this with abuse.' Weber (2022), pp. 61-63.

Thus, even if the prophecy that the meaning of the BO clause in the EU context may permeate the DTC context becomes true, in the EU context the BO clause is also not substance-oriented even after the *Danish withholding tax* cases, contrary to the aforementioned scholarly opinion. In line with this finding, the scope of the work is reduced to the content of the substance requirement in the LOB clause and PPT.

As regards the LOB now, only two of its tests are substance-oriented and therefore relevant to this work. These are the active conduct of a business test stipulated in Article 29(3) of the OECD MTC and the headquarters company test and, in particular, the first of the six requirements this test provides for, namely the PPMC (Article 29(5)(a) of the OECD MTC). Both these rules require the taxpayer seeking treaty benefits to present some kind of substance in terms of the rendering of functions. The rest of the LOB tests are not relevant to this work and are thus not dealt with. They concentrate on factors other than the taxpayer's substance like ownership (e.g., Article 29(2)(e) of the OECD MTC). Finally, the PPT is also within the scope of this work, since, as already stated in section B.III.3. of the introduction, it is also 'substance-oriented' according to the literature.

III Relevance of the Investigation

If the LOB clause and the PPT are only rules in the Models and are not reflected in the current treaty framework or will not become part of it, then the enquiry as to their substance-oriented content is merely theoretical. In the following, it is argued that this is not the case.

Indeed, Action 6 of the BEPS Project has accelerated the relevance of treaty shopping rules for the current DTC framework, since the inclusion of treaty shopping rules in DTCs constitutes a 'minimum standard' of Action 6 of the BEPS Project, which itself also constitutes a minimum standard of the BEPS Project as a whole.[29] Action 6 offers three alternatives to the OECD Member States as to which treaty shopping rule they may choose. According to paragraph 22 of the Report on Action 6:

> Depending on their own circumstances, States may wish to adopt only the general anti-abuse rule of paragraph 9 of the Article [i.e., the PPT], may prefer instead to adopt the detailed version of paragraphs 1 to 7 that is described below [i.e., the detailed version of the LOB clause], which they would supplement by a mechanism that would address conduit arrangements not otherwise dealt with by the provisions of the Convention, or may prefer to include in their treaty the general anti-abuse rule of paragraph 9 together with any variation of paragraphs 1 to 7 described below [i.e., either the simplified or the detailed version of the LOB].[30]

So, there is a strong political commitment for OECD members to implement either all (i.e., both the LOB and the PPT) or some (either one or the other) of the substance-oriented rules against treaty shopping. But this statement already reveals

29. OECD, *BEPS Project Explanatory Statement* (2015), para. 11.
30. Paragraph 1 in fine of the Commentary (2017) on Article 29.

two weaknesses of the BEPS Project as a whole regarding its relevance for the current treaty framework. First, the commitment that OECD Member States have entered into is only a political one. That is, as already underlined,[31] the OECD documents as well as the BEPS Reports, induce soft law obligations at most. And it cannot be contested that they have materialized into 'hard' law.[32] Second, these recommendations are only directed to OECD Member States, although non-Member States were also involved in designing the BEPS Actions.[33] These two drawbacks of the BEPS Project in general, i.e., the lack of a hard law obligation and the very limited scope (only OECD Member States), are alleviated by other developments initiated by the OECD.

First, there is a way to convert OECD policies into 'hard' law. And this way is to adopt OECD policies in DTCs. The PPT and the LOB clause can thus be adopted by states in their DTCs. Second, the OECD policies may also be adopted by non-Member States if they wish to do so. As far as the conversion of OECD policies into hard law is concerned, there are basically two alternatives for states. They can either bilaterally agree to adopt an OECD policy or they may avail themselves of another tool put at their disposal by the OECD: the MLI.[34] And as far as the reach of OECD policies is concerned, it has already been mentioned (section C. of the introduction) that this has now been elevated to a global dimension through the establishment of the Inclusive Framework, again by the OECD.

The MLI and the Inclusive Framework have led to a wide acceptance of the OECD's policies and in particular of the minimum standard in Action 6. The OECD informs us that '[o]n 1 July 2020, over 350 bilateral agreements between members of the Inclusive Framework complied with the minimum standard'.[35] And as the MLI gains traction, the number of treaties including treaty shopping rules will rise. However, not all substance-oriented treaty shopping rules enjoy the same acceptance among countries of the Inclusive Framework.

As the OECD informs us, '[i]n all compliant agreements, the preamble statement and the PPT were implemented to meet the minimum standard. Thirty-one of those agreements supplemented the PPT with a limitation on benefits (LOB) provision'.[36]

From the above statement, it emerges that while all DTCs amended based on the MLI include the PPT, only about one-tenth of them have also included the LOB. So a predominance of the PPT over the LOB can be observed. This means also that the content of the substance requirement for the purposes of the PPT is more relevant than the one for the purposes of the LOB.

Furthermore, it has been said that two tests within the LOB are substance-oriented: the active conduct of a business test in Article 29(3) of the OECD MTC and the

31. Section B.I. of the introduction and especially n. 35.
32. Pistone (2016), s. 8.3.4.; Maisto (2017), s. 2.6.; Schön (2020a), p. 286, n. 1; Schön (2021), p. 380, n. 162 with reference to the opposing viewpoint expressed by Mosquera Valderrama (2020).
33. OECD, *BEPS Project Explanatory Statement* (2015), para. 4.
34. *See* above s. A.III. of Ch. 1.
35. OECD, *Prevention of Tax Treaty Abuse: Third Peer Review Report on Treaty Shopping* (2021), p. 16 (hereinafter: 'OECD, Peer Review Report on Treaty Shopping').
36. *Ibid.*, at para. 47.

PPMC in the headquarters company test (Article 29(5)(a) of the OECD MTC). However, out of these two tests, the application of the first one is more relevant than the one of the latter provision. This is because the headquarters company test is only part of the detailed version of the LOB. And that version of the LOB is not included in the MLI.[37] This provision has and will also continue to have some relevance, though, because it forms part of the US DTC policy. In particular, '[t]he United States expects to comply with the minimum standard through a detailed LOB which is not available through the MLI. Therefore, the United States did not sign the MLI and will implement the minimum standard bilaterally'.[38]

In total, substance-oriented treaty shopping rules are implemented at a different pace. The PPT is the most favoured option among the countries of the Inclusive Framework. The MLI has also accelerated the inclusion of the LOB into DTCs, but only in its simplified version, containing the active conduct of a business test. The other substance-oriented test within the LOB clause, the PPMC in the headquarters company test, is of relevance predominantly for DTCs signed with the United States. One thing is clear, though that all three provisions are out there. They form part of the current DTC framework, thus their content deserves to be investigated.

B THE CONTENT OF THE SUBSTANCE REQUIREMENT IN THE LOB AND PPT

I Opening Remarks

1 Purpose of the Substance Orientation in the LOB and the PPT

As this work proceeded for the purposes of the POEM, it first seeks the purpose of the rules in question in order to ascertain why these rules are substance-oriented (section B.I.1. of Chapter 1). Beginning with the LOB clause, this has two major purposes.[39]

First, it has already been stressed that, according to the principle of economic allegiance, the personal scope of DTCs is only open to taxpayers economically connected to their state of residence (section A.I. of Chapter 1). LOB clauses purport to

---

37. OECD, *Explanatory Statement to the Multilateral Convention to Implement Tax Treaty Related Measures to Prevent Base Erosion and Profit Shifting* (2017), para. 90.
38. OECD, *Prevention of Tax Treaty Abuse: Third Peer Review Report on Treaty Shopping* (2021), p. 290. Of course, the fact that the United States prefer the detailed version of the LOB does not mean that also the headquarters company test forms part of the finally negotiated DTC. So it can be that a DTC based on the detailed version of the LOB does not include the headquarters company test. In fact, this provision has had a turbulent history in US DTC practice but now seems to gain traction. As Fleming (2012), p. 249 informs us: 'This alternative was included in the 1992 Netherlands-US Treaty, the 1996 Austria-US Treaty, the 1996 Switzerland-US Treaty and the 2006 Belgium-US Treaty. But then it was omitted from the latest US Model promulgated in 2006. Now, however, it has reappeared in the 2010 treaties with Chile and Hungary.' Furthermore, the newest US Model (2016) includes the headquarters company test. Thus, it can be surmised that the provision will attract more attention in the future. Concurring Vega Borrego (2017), p. 185.
39. Jiang (2015), p. 140; Ramharter/Szudoczky (2019), p. 58; Blessing (2020b), s. 8.1.3.

exclude taxpayers or items of income that they derive which do not meet this fundamental requirement.

Second, LOB clauses preserve the reciprocity of DTCs. In particular, DTCs are, bluntly formulated, package deals where two states agree on a final treaty reciprocally, making concessions and achieving negotiation victories.[40] However, this reciprocity is not preserved when treaty shopping structures are entered into. Let us elucidate that based on the following example.

Assume the ultimate parent is resident in Germany and it interposes a subsidiary in the Netherlands which then receives dividends from a sub-subsidiary in Spain. The DTC between Spain and the Netherlands is applicable to the dividends, rather than the DTC between Germany and Spain. If the taxpayer can circumvent the application of the DTC between Germany and Spain, then it does not make any sense for these states to conclude a DTC. It becomes apparent that preserving the reciprocity of DTCs is a second major rationale for the introduction of LOBs in DTCs.

Now, from these two purposes that the LOB serves, the substance-oriented active conduct of a business test is attributable only to the first one. In particular, the rule acknowledges that there may be triangular situations like the one in the example above 'which are presumed to have bona fide status due to the nature of the income for which treaty benefits are sought, and its intrinsic relation to the business activity that earns such income'.[41] So the per se substance-oriented rule in the LOB, the active conduct of a business test, exists as a safety valve for taxpayers engaging in triangular structures where the interposed entity is set up for a real business purpose.[42] As the headquarters company test is based on the same notion,[43] the above analysis also applies to this test.

The PPT also fights nexus abuse through subsidiaries without substance. Recently, Schön has explained why. In particular, '[t]he principal purpose of double taxation conventions is to promote, by eliminating international double taxation, exchanges of goods and services, and the movement of capital and persons'.[44] 'In the context of a double tax convention the notion of economic substance can be linked to the afore-mentioned treaty purpose of supporting genuine economic transactions which contribute to an efficient allocation of persons, goods, services and capital. A cross-border arrangement, which does not lead to a reallocation of productions factors or to a similar outcome, does not deserve the protection under the treaty and can therefore be rejected without violating the object and purpose of the treaty.'[45]

40. *See* Kostikidis/Hintermayer (2022), p. 76.
41. Tavares (2016), p. 141; Gooijer (2019), p. 244. On this presumption, *see also* Lukjanenko (2016), p. 215.
42. Vega Borrego (2017), p. 164.
43. US Treasury, *Preamble to 2016 U.S. Model Income Tax Convention* (2016), p. 7: '[t]he new headquarters company test is analogous to the active-trade-or-business test'; Van Weeghel (2019), p. 39. *See also* Duff (2018a), p. 667: 'through these provisions [the active conduct of a business test and the headquarters company test] as well, the US LOB provisions extend specific treaty benefits to residents with a significant economic connection with a contracting state, even if they are not qualified persons'.
44. Paragraph 54 of the Commentary (2017) on Article 1.
45. Schön (2022a), pp. 11-12.

2 *Structure of the Analysis*

The active conduct of a business test, the PPMC, and the PPT are the substance-oriented rules that constitute the scope of this chapter and whose content is analysed. Sections B.II.-B.IV. deal with the content of the substance requirement in each test respectively.

II Content of the Substance Requirement in the Active Conduct of a Business Test

Substance contains three elements: the functional, the personal, and the objective element. Accordingly, the next three sections (B.II.1.-B.II.3.) deal with these three elements of the substance requirement in the active conduct of a business test. Section B.II.4. provides a conclusion.

1 *The Functional Element of the Substance Requirement in the Active Conduct of a Business Test*

Article 29(3) of the OECD MTC, stipulating the active conduct of a business test, has three paragraphs:

(1) According to Article 29(3)(a) of the OECD MTC, the interconnected subsidiary must actively carry on business activities in its residence state and the income derived from the source state must emanate from, or be incidental to, the aforementioned business activities. Accordingly, the functions that must be exercised in order for the test to be fulfilled must have these two qualities, which are respectively analysed in sections B.II.1.a.aa. and B.II.1.a.bb.

(2) Article 29(3)(b) of the OECD MTC provides that if the aforementioned income is derived from activities of the interposed subsidiary in the source state or persons connected to it therein, the income may pass the active conduct of a business test 'only if the business activity carried on by the resident in the first-mentioned State [i.e., the residence state] to which the item is related is substantial in relation to the same or complementary business activity carried on by the resident or such connected person in the other Contracting State [i.e., the source state]'. The term 'substantial' points to the quantitative content that these functions should have, which is analysed in section B.II.1.b.

(3) Finally, Article 29(3)(c) of the OECD MTC lays down rules on the conformity of income from outsourced activities with the active conduct of a business test. Outsourcing is dealt with in a separate section, section B.II.1.c., just like this work proceeded with regard to outsourcing in the POEM (section B.II.2.c.hh. of Chapter 1) and transfer pricing (section B.II.1.b. of Chapter 2).

a *Qualitative Sub-element of the Functional Element of Substance*

aa The Subsidiary Must Actively Carry on Business Activities in Its Residence State

The first requirement in order for a subsidiary's income to pass the active conduct of a business test is that it actively carries on business activities in its residence state.[46] The fact that the activities must be conducted in the residence state is a first similarity with the other two substance requirements dealt with so far. In particular, it has been demonstrated how diffuse decision-making may lead to questions as to which state the POEM is situated in (*see* the examples in sections B.II.1.c.bb. and B.II.3.a. of Chapter 1). So each state that comes into question asks how numerous and how important the decisions being taken within their territory are. Extraterritorial decisions are not taken into account; on the contrary, they may lead to a relocation of the POEM. In a similar vein, in transfer pricing, 'the suggestion arising from the interpretation by the OECD is that functionality can be achieved only if the actions of the company are performed by employees of the company in the country where the company resides'.[47]

Now the important question is what these actively conducted business activities are exactly. As already alluded to in the POEM chapter (section B.I.2. of Chapter 1), when defining terms in DTCs, their content may follow a domestically oriented interpretation or an autonomous one. So in order to define the term active conduct of a business, one needs first to lay down the standard upon which this term is to be defined.

There is a debate as to the interpretation of the term 'business' in the context of Article 7 of the OECD MTC whereby both an autonomous and a domestically oriented interpretation are suggested in literature.[48] However, as scholars have stressed, the term 'business' is not the same as 'active conduct of a business'.[49] In fact, there is also a debate in literature with regard to the interpretation of the latter term.[50]

46. It is only the subsidiary and not other group companies that needs to render the relevant functions. What is being said is that the active conduct of a business test, like the POEM (s. B.II.1.a.aa. of Ch. 1) and the ALP (s. A.I.1. of Ch. 2), adopts the stand-alone perspective. This can be deducted from the wording of the active conduct of a business referring to 'A resident [that] ... is engaged in the active conduct of a business.' Although, as will be discussed in s. B.II.1.c. of this chapter, Article 29(3)(c) of the OECD MTC allows outsourcing without any conditions and limitations so one could argue that for the purposes of the active conduct of a business test the stand-alone perspective is not 'genuine'; it is established, in a first step, only to be undermined in a second step through Article 29(3)(c) of the OECD MTC.
47. Hafkenscheid (2017), p. 20; *contra* Navarro (2023), p. 16: 'If decision-making functions are performed by personnel pertaining to the enterprise, the related returns will be attributed to it, regardless of whether such personnel are located in the jurisdiction of residence of the enterprise or not.' Against this notion of pinpointing decisions in the MNE context Schön (2007), p. 1067; Monsenego (2014), p. 14; KPMG (2015), p. 535; Breslin (2015), p. 633; Verlinden et al. (2016), p. 111; Werner (2019), p. 108.
48. Kostikidis (2022), pp. 146-147.
49. Kuźniacki (2018a), p. 126.
50. For an autonomous interpretation of the term: *Ibid.*; Lukjanenko (2016), p. 214; with regard to the term in the US DTC context Vega Borrego (2017), p. 168. Seemingly so also Gooijer (2019), p. 245 who, albeit acknowledging that the Commentary on this provision in para. 71 provides for

In the author's opinion, an intermediary solution is possible. The Commentary itself makes reference to the domestic law interpretation.[51] But at the same time, it makes some quite concrete statements, as shown below, with regard to the content of the term, which the interpreter should take into account. Thus, the term may be determined by domestic law but only insofar as it does not contradict the framework that Article 29(3) of the OECD MTC and the accompanying Commentary provide for.

Now, what is this framework? Article 29(3) of the OECD MTC and the accompanying Commentary include one positive and one negative pointer as to the content of the active conduct of a business test. First, it is not the business that must be active but the conduct of the business.[52] That is, also passive business actively conducted (e.g., management of shareholdings) falls under the term. Second, paragraph 71 of the Commentary (2017) on Article 29 of the OECD MTC provides that '[a]n entity generally will be considered to be engaged in the active conduct of a business only if persons through whom the entity is acting (such as officers or employees of a company) conduct substantial managerial and operational activities'. Commentators have complained about the lack of more precise guidance as to what these operational and managerial activities exactly are.[53]

That being said, this work may offer some insights as to the content of this passage by referring to the content of the other two substance requirements. In particular, one first conclusion is that, in contrast to the POEM concentrating on the decision-making functions (section B.II.1.a.bb. of Chapter 1) and the OECD TPG only attributing to operational activities a risk-free return (section B.I.2. of Chapter 2), for the purposes of the active conduct of a business test not only decisions to be made but also operations to be carried on are necessary in order for the test to be passed. The 'and' in the passage quoted above can be assumed to being used in a joint sense,[54] thus making it clear that the active conduct of a business test requires both decision-making and operations to take place in the residence state in order for the test to be passed.

---

a domestically based interpretation, draws conclusions from the guidance provided as to the content of the term in the Commentary; Ramharter/Szudoczky (2019), p. 66: 'The term "business" itself is not defined and has therefore been interpreted by reference to domestic law. What has to be considered as "engaged in the active conduct of a business" is defined by the OECD in the Commentary on Article 29 of the OECD Model (2017).' *Contra* Rudolf (2012), p. 308, although before BEPS Action 6 and the amendment of the Commentary containing guidance on the content of the term and with respect to the term in the USA-Germany DTC; Leukefeld (2018), p. 117; Weggenmann/Nehls (2021), para. 80.

51. Paragraph 71 of the Commentary (2017) on Article 29.
52. Weggenmann/Nehls (2021), para. 80.
53. Lukjanenko (2016), p. 215.
54. Conjunctions can create enormous ambiguity in legal drafting. This is the case '[w]ith reference to "and" [where] the question is whether it is to be (or has been) used in its "several" sense (A and B, jointly or severally) or in its "joint" sense (A and B, jointly but not severally)'. *See* Kirk (1970/1971), p. 238.

    It is admitted that the author's assumption that 'and' in this case is used in a joint sense is not supported by the text of the Commentary which gives no pointer whatsoever as to whether the 'and' is used in a several or a joint sense. For an argument relating to the other substance-oriented test in the LOB, namely the PPMC in the headquarters company test, *see* below n. 98.

So, decision-making functions suffice at the first stage for the purposes of the POEM, but at the second stage operational activities should be relevant when determining whether a subsidiary is eligible for DTC benefits. It becomes apparent that the way towards DTC benefits is harder, or, more subtly formulated, combined with more demanding substance requirements than simply falling into the personal scope of a DTC by being resident of a DTC state.

The question, however, still remains: what operational activities and decision-making functions are necessary to be conducted in order for the test to be fulfilled? As regards the latter, a systematic argument points to the exercise of strategic decision-making as key for the purposes of the test. In particular, it would be systematically erroneous to open the personal scope of a DTC to subsidiaries performing strategic decision-making functions based on the residence requirement and then exclude them because they do so, at a second stage based on the active conduct of a business test. Again, the 'plus' that this test adds relates to the existence of operational activities, while nothing changes with regard to the decision-making functions.

Now, as regards the operational activities, it is true that the Commentary offers no guidance at all. But remember: the term active conduct of a business is to be interpreted according to domestic law within the framework that Article 29(3) of the OECD MTC and the Commentary thereon provides for. Since the Commentary is silent in this respect, this means that the content of the term active conduct of a business, as regards the operational activities required, is defined according to domestic law. But this does not apply totally. In fact, Article 29(3)(a) of the OECD MTC itself contains a negative definition of the term, that is, it excludes a list of activities from its scope. These are:

(i) operating as a holding company;
(ii) providing overall supervision or administration of a group of companies;
(iii) providing group financing (including cash pooling); or
(iv) making or managing investments, unless these activities are carried on by a bank or [list financial institutions similar to banks that the Contracting States agree to treat as such], insurance enterprise or registered securities dealer in the ordinary course of its business as such.

So these 'passive' activities must be excluded from the content of the term 'active conduct of a business', irrespective of whether they are actively conducted. It follows that they also cannot constitute operational activities for the purposes of the application of Article 29 of the OECD MTC.[55] Here, one can observe again that the substance requirement in a treaty shopping rule, i.e., the LOB, is stricter than the one in the POEM. In particular, it has already been submitted that the nature of the activity plays no role in the purposes of the POEM (section B.II.1.a.bb. of Chapter 1). By contrast, in

55. However the Commentary (2017) on Article 29 in para. 73 acknowledges that '[s]ome States consider ... that some or all of the activities listed in subdivisions (i) through (iv) should be included in what constitutes the active conduct of a business' and allows 'these States ... to adopt a different formulation of subparagraph a)'.

the active conduct of a business test, it plays a role, since as we can see some activities are not 'worthy of' DTC benefits.

In sum, the term active conduct of a business refers to strategic decision-making and operational activities, whereby both must be performed in the residence state of the subsidiary claiming DTC benefits. The nature of the activity also plays a role, since a series of 'passive' activities is excluded as active conduct of a business. Thus, one may notice that the substance requirement in the active conduct of a business test is stricter than the one in the POEM.

bb The Income Must Emanate from, or Be Incidental to, Such Activities

The active conduct of a business test is also stricter than the POEM in another sense. In particular, for the purposes of the former, the income for which DTC benefits are invoked must emanate from, or be incidental to, the managerial and operational activities as defined in the above section rendered in the residence state of the entity claiming the DTC benefits. By contrast, there is no such requirement in DTC residence, as commentators have already pointed out, since 'the definition of resident is not the appropriate place to assure a justifiable treaty application with regard to a specific item of income. ... [In this sense it is preferable] to rely on other instruments'.[56] This can be justified when one considers the nature of the LOB as a treaty shopping rule. The functional relationship between the activities of the entity claiming DTC benefits in the residence state and the income which it receives 'serves as evidence of the non-abusive intention of the taxpayer and shows that the structure was not solely set up artificially, in order to redirect income to the residence state'.[57]

As to the content of the terms 'emanates from' and 'is incidental to', it suffices to say here that there is some guidance in the Commentary[58] boiling down to a requirement of down- or upstream integration.[59] Parallel integration, while originally included in Action 6 of the BEPS Project,[60] is now not mentioned as an eligible form of integration, which is in line with voices from the literature indicating the breadth of the terms in case of including parallel integration and the effect this would have on safeguarding the LOB's purpose as a treaty shopping rule.[61]

b Quantitative Sub-element of the Functional Element of Substance

As already noted above, Article 29(3)(b) of the OECD MTC contains a substantiality requirement 'in cases where the business generating the item of income in question is carried on either by the person deriving the income or by a connected person in the

56. Gooijer (2019), pp. 265-266.
57. Ramharter/Szudoczky (2019), p. 65; *see also* Jiang (2015), p. 146.
58. Paragraphs 74-76 of the Commentary (2017) on Article 29.
59. Paragraph 75 of the Commentary (2017) on Article 29.
60. OECD Action 6, p. 38.
61. Tavares (2016), p. 161; Lukjanenko (2016), pp. 221-222.

State of source'.[62] The term 'substantial' intuitively refers to the volume of the activities carried on in the residence state and thus to the quantitative sub-element of the substance requirement in the active conduct of a business test.[63] What can but should not be overlooked, however, is that another substantiality requirement also exists. So before analysing the substantiality requirement in Article 29(3)(b) of the OECD MTC, the other substantiality requirement in the active conduct of a business test is dealt with, namely the one in Article 29(3)(a) of the OECD MTC referring to the term active conduct of a business itself.

aa The Substantiality Requirement in Article 29(3)(a)

The substantiality requirement in Article 29(3)(a) exists in the wording of the provision itself:

> An entity generally will be considered to be engaged in the active conduct of a business only if persons through whom the entity is acting (such as officers or employees of a company) conduct *substantial* managerial and operational activities.[64]

So the managerial and operational activities conducted in the residence state of the entity claiming DTC benefits must be substantial. The word substantial speaks for the existence of an absolute quantitative threshold, in contrast to what we have seen so far for the purposes of the POEM (section B.III.1. of Chapter 1) and transfer pricing (section B.II.2.a. of Chapter 2) where no such threshold exists. The question is now what the word 'substantial' in the aforementioned passage means. Unfortunately, Article 29 of the OECD MTC and the Commentary thereon include no guidance in this respect.[65] The first question that arises is based on which benchmark the substantiality of an activity can be measured. Second, once it is clear what the benchmark is, one needs to define when the substantiality requirement is fulfilled. Both issues, as already stated, remain unaddressed in the Commentary.

bb The Substantiality Requirement in Article 29(3)(b)

Apart from the general requirement that the business conducted in the residence state of the entity claiming DTC benefits must be substantial, Article 29(3)(b) of the OECD MTC stipulates an additional substantiality requirement 'in cases where the business generating the item of income in question is carried on either by the person deriving the income or by a connected person in the State of source'.

Now, what is the content of the substantiality requirement in Article 29(3)(b) of the OECD MTC? First, with regard to the benchmark against which substantiality is measured, the Commentary informs us that 'the business carried on in the State of

62. Paragraph 77 of the Commentary (2017) on Article 29.
63. Rudolf (2012), pp. 309-310; Vega Borrego (2017), p. 171; Weggenmann/Nehls (2021), para. 83.
64. Paragraph 71 of the Commentary (2017) on Article 29 (emphasis added).
65. Lukjanenko (2016), p. 215; Kuźniacki (2018a), p. 125, n. 11; Gooijer (2019), p. 245.

residence, under these circumstances, must be substantial *in relation to the activity in the State of source*'.[66] So here we have our benchmark: the activity in the residence state and the one in the source state are compared in order to establish a substantiality relationship. The threshold is a *relative* one, just like in the POEM (section B.II.3.a. of Chapter 1).

Second, the substantiality of the activity in the residence state in comparison to the activity in the source state is measured 'based upon all the facts and circumstances, including the comparative sizes of the businesses in each Contracting State, the relative sizes of the economies and markets in the two States, the nature of the activities performed in each State, and the relative contributions made to that business in each State'.[67] Commentators have suggested including safe harbour rules in the Commentary, along the lines of the US DTC practice,[68] where '[r]eference could be made, for example, to quantitative facts and data, such as the relative value of assets, gross income, or payroll expenditure, along with the qualitative circumstances of the business activity in each Contracting State, such as operational risks managed through functions performed and relevance of activities'.[69]

Finally, it must be said that the quantitative sub-element in Article 29(3)(b) of the OECD MTC is relevant for all elements of substance. That is, not only the volume of the operational and decision-making functions is relevant but also the volume of the assets and the persons employed. Again, at least the US DTC practice and the commentators that use it as an inspiration in order to fill the term 'substantial' with content refer to the 'value of assets, gross income, or payroll expenditure'.[70] The gross income points to the volume of the operations and the value of assets and payroll expenditure to the quantity, or also indirectly the quality (more qualitative assets and staff imply more expenditure in this respect), of the assets (objective element) and staff (personal element).

cc Summary and Conclusion

In sum, Article 29(3) of the OECD MTC includes two threshold requirements. First, an absolute threshold requiring that the active conduct of a business in the residence state must be substantial. Second, in cases where the business generating the item of income in question is carried on either by the person deriving the income or by a connected person in the state of the source, Article 29(3)(b) of the OECD MTC imposes a relative quantitative threshold where the activity in the residence state and the one in the source state are compared in order to establish a substantiality relationship. This comparison is made by referring to the quantity of not only the operations of a subsidiary (functional element) but also that of its staff (personal element) and assets (objective element).

66. Paragraph 77 of the Commentary (2017) on Article 29 (emphasis added).
67. Paragraph 77 of the Commentary (2017) on Article 29.
68. *See* Vega Borrego, p. 174 and especially n. 162 on the DTCs that contain safe harbour rules.
69. Kuźniacki (2018a), p. 130 based on Tavares (2016), p. 157.
70. *See* above n. 69.

The existence of an absolute quantitative threshold contradicts what we have so far encountered for the purposes of the POEM and transfer pricing rules, where it has been found that no such threshold exists (on the POEM section B.II.3.a. of Chapter 1 and on transfer pricing section B.II.2.a. of Chapter 2). This difference between the substance requirements is easy to justify when considering the nature of the LOB as a treaty-shopping rule. Without the existence of substantiality requirements, it would be easy to interpose subsidiaries whose activities are conducted either in the source states or by other connected persons. In particular, in the context of Article 29(3)(b) of the OECD MTC, it has been argued that it aims at 'preclud[ing] a person from treaty shopping by using an entity with minimal business activities in the residence state to claim treaty benefits'.[71] So the nature of the LOB as a treaty shopping rule justifies the purpose of a rule concentrating on quantitative substance.

c *Outsourcing*

The previous sections have analysed the qualities and the quantity that the activities constituting active conduct of business should have. This section deals with the issue of whether the entity claiming DTC benefits should conduct the aforementioned activities itself or whether it suffices that other parties (related or unrelated to the entity), to which these activities have been outsourced, do so.

According to Article 29(3)(c) of the OECD MTC 'activities conducted by connected persons with respect to a resident of a Contracting State shall be deemed to be conducted by such resident'. It follows that an entity that does nothing on its own but outsources all its operational and management activities to connected persons may still invoke DTC benefits. The same should also hold true a fortiori for activities outsourced to unrelated persons.[72] Furthermore, it can be submitted that the outsourced activities must not be rendered in the residence state of the entity claiming the DTC benefits.[73]

This rule has been criticized in literature. As Adolfo Martín Jiménez points out:

> This [rule] leaves a considerable margin for the resident entity to outsource or fragment activities to related persons in a third state while still taking advantage of the tax treaties of the state in which the trade or business is carried on.[74]

The same author goes on to observe that:

> This fits perfectly with the new framework of Actions 8-10 BEPS, in which substantial economic activity is identified with factual control over risks, the capacity to bear them or significant people functions in connection with risks, which also admits outsourcing models where an entity oversees, manages or

71. Bates et al. (2013), p. 399.
72. Leukefeld (2018), p. 119.
73. Tavares (2016), p. 143; Lukjanenko (2016), p. 228. *Contra* Weggenmann/Nehls (2021), para. 84; with respect to the DTC between Germany and the USA and based on the telos of the provision Rudolf (2012), p. 310.
74. Martín Jiménez (2017), p. 51 citing Tavares (2016), p. 143. *See also* Kuźniacki (2018a), pp. 128-130; Weggenmann/Nehls (2021), para. 84.

> controls the activities of other controlled parties, as long as all of them are remunerated at arm's length.[75]

This observation is correct. There is a similarity as to how the OECD TPG and the active conduct of business go about outsourcing. However, it must be stressed that in the active conduct of a business test, we notice an even looser stance of the OECD with regard to outsourcing. In particular, it has been shown that for the purposes of both the POEM and the OECD TPG, the outsourcing party must retain control over the outsourced activities (on the POEM section B.II.2.c.hh. of Chapter 1 and on the OECD TPG section B.II.1.a.bb. of Chapter 2). Such a requirement is mentioned in neither Article 29(3)(c) of the OECD MTC nor the accompanying Commentary and can thus not be read into the provision. Furthermore, it has been found that for the purposes of risk allocation, not all strategic decisions relating to that risk can be outsourced (section B.II.2.b. of Chapter 2). Such a limitation does not exist in Article 29(3)(c) of the OECD MTC or the accompanying Commentary.

It becomes apparent that the OECD's approach with regard to outsourcing contradicts what we have seen so far (section B.II.1.a. of this chapter), namely that the requirements of the active conduct of a business test are stricter than the ones in the POEM. And it is not in conformity with the purpose of the rule, namely to provide access to treaty benefits to taxpayers economically connected with their state of residence since there will be no economic connection if all activities are outsourced by the resident entity to parties outside its residence state.

Błażej Kuźniacki has indicated the justification of this rule in EU law restraints:

> Freedom of establishment is particularly protected under EU law, including the CJEU case law, apart from wholly artificial arrangements. The absence of the attribution rule would therefore restrict a taxpayer's right of establishment too much ... Consequently, although the attribution rule seems to haze the understanding of the term 'active conduct of a business', its existence under the active business test is pretty much justified.[76]

In fact, EU law only demands, as we will *see* in detail below (section B.II.1.a.aa. of Chapter 4), that the taxpayer is given the opportunity to disprove the assumption of tax abuse based on sound economic reasons. So if Article 29(3)(c) were more restrictive towards outsourcing, it would not run afoul of EU law as long as the taxpayer was given the opportunity to prove that sound economic reasons support the outsourcing.

A de lege lata proposal would be to interpret the rule restrictively (*teleologische Reduktion*) so as to only include outsourced activities conducted in the residence state of the entity claiming DTC benefits.[77] A *de lege ferenda* proposal would be to 'require a certain level of presence in [the residence state] *versus* [the other state where the outsourced activities take place], or [to] grant proportionate benefits under the

75. *Ibid.*
76. Kuźniacki (2018a), pp. 126-127.
77. *See* above n. 73.

[residence-source state] treaty'.[78] Both options of course should be accompanied by the opportunity for the taxpayer to prove the existence of sound economic reasons supporting the outsourcing.

Overall, outsourcing is allowed without restrictions for the purposes of the active conduct of a business test, in contrast to the POEM and transfer pricing substance where limitations as to the volume (transfer pricing) and the method (control must be retained for the purposes of both the POEM and transfer pricing substance) exist. Either a *teleologische Reduktion* or *de lege ferenda* proportional granting of DTC benefits, both accompanied with the opportunity for the taxpayer to prove the existence of sound economic reasons supporting the outsourcing, could align the rule with the principle of economic allegiance.

2 The Personal Element of the Substance Requirement in the Active Conduct of a Business Test

'An entity will generally be considered to be engaged in the active conduct of a business only if *persons* through whom the entity is acting (*such as officers or employees* of a company) conduct substantial managerial and operational activities.'[79] This is the only pointer that the Commentary on the active conduct of a business test gives us as to the content of the personal element of the substance requirement in the active conduct of a business test. What can be maintained is that, since it has been found that both operational and managerial activities must take place in the residence state, it makes sense to require that all hierarchy levels are present in the residence state, that is, all three levels of management[80] as well as operational staff. So, at first sight, the substance requirement in the active conduct of a business test seems to be more demanding than the one in the POEM, the latter concentrating, at least in the first stage, on the board of directors, i.e., the top-level management (section B.II.2.b.aa. of Chapter 1).

This finding, however, does not stand up to closer scrutiny. In particular, a company does not even need its own employees in order to claim DTC benefits. This can be deduced from Article 29(3)(c) of the OECD MTC which, as already discussed in the previous section, allows the outsourcing of the relevant functions. And of course, outsourcing means the personnel of the company does not perform relevant activities, but the personnel of another entity. So Article 29(3)(c) of the OECD MTC allows entities without their own personnel in the residence state to claim DTC benefits. What has already been said with regard to either the *teleologische Reduktion* of this provision or its *de lege ferenda* amendment applies also here.

Finally, as to the qualifications that the relevant persons should have (e.g., information and knowledge), no mention is made in the Commentary; as regards the quantity, i.e., the number of these persons, it has already been submitted in section

78. Tavares (2016), p. 143.
79. Paragraph 71 of the Commentary (2017) on Article 29 (emphasis added).
80. Top-level management (normally consisting in the board of directors), middle-level management, and lower-level management. *See* above n. 41 in Ch. 1.

B.II.1.b.bb. that in the cases of Article 29(3)(b) of the OECD MTC the quantitative threshold of substantiality applies.

Overall, it can be concluded that the active conduct of a business test is, at first sight, more demanding than the POEM as regards the personal element of substance, requiring that all hierarchy levels are present in the residence state, that is, all three levels of management as well as operational staff. Nevertheless, Article 29(3)(c) of the OECD MTC allows entities without their own personnel in the residence state to claim DTC benefits.

3 *Content of the Objective Element of Substance in the Active Conduct of a Business Test*

According to Robert Leukefeld, the objective element of substance is not mentioned in Article 29 of the OECD MTC and the Commentary thereon, that is, no mention of the role and importance of assets, premises, etc., is made.[81] However, the same commentator reckons that 'the existence of physical presence can be implicitly assumed due to the performance of activities'.[82] Other commentators simply submit that 'the active conduct of a business implies economic substance in terms of premises, personnel and activities',[83] which seemingly implies that we are concerned with three elements that have equal importance. Finally, it has been also suggested that the employment of assets 'reinforce[s]' activities conducted through the personnel of the entity claiming treaty benefits,[84] which implies that the objective element has a reinforcing/auxiliary character compared to the functional and personal elements.

This plethora of different opinions as regards the role and importance of the objective element of substance is attributable to the missing guidance in Article 29(3) of the OECD MTC and the accompanying Commentary. In the opinion of the author, the objective element of substance, although not mentioned in either Article 29(3) or the accompanying Commentary, should play a role for the purposes of the active conduct of a business test. A fortiori argument supports this proposition.

If the objective element plays a role for the purposes of the POEM (section B.III. of Chapter 1), then it should, a fortiori, also play a role for the purposes of the active conduct of a business test, which again (section A.I.1. of this chapter), as a treaty shopping rule, closes the door that the residence requirement opens.

However, now that we have found that the objective element should matter, new questions arise. Just as has been investigated for the purposes of the POEM (section B.III. of Chapter 1), we need to expand on the necessary quantity and quality of the assets and the relationship of the objective element with the other elements of substance. Should they be considered equally or are the other substance elements more important, just like in the case of the POEM and transfer pricing?

81. Leukefeld (2018), p. 119.
82. *Ibid.* (Author's unofficial translation).
83. De Broe/Luts (2015), p. 130.
84. Tavares (2016), p. 154.

With regard to the last issue, it can be maintained that the objective element is in fact of secondary importance for the purposes of the active conduct of a business test. The main argument for this is that the objective element is not mentioned anywhere either in Article 29(3) of the OECD MTC or in the accompanying Commentary, as already stated above. The only thing that the interpreter can add to this complete disregard of the objective element is that a fortiori, the objective element in the active conduct of a business test at least should have the role that it has in the POEM, as already argued.

As to the qualities of the assets, although again guidance is completely lacking, one critical conclusion can be made. Since both managerial and operational activities must be rendered in the residence state, it makes sense to demand that the assets necessary for these activities are also located in the residence state. Here, we may notice a difference compared to the objective element in the POEM, where mainly assets related to the decision-making functions are relevant, like telephones, computers, etc. (section B.III.2. of Chapter 1). On the contrary, for the purposes of the active conduct of a business test, the assets related to both the managerial and operational activities must exist. Accordingly, there is a 'plus' that must exist, namely the assets serving the operational activities. Again (section B.II.1.a. of this chapter), we notice that the requirements of active conduct of a business are more difficult to fulfil than those of the POEM.

As to the quantity of the assets, guidance is lacking in the Commentary. In the author's opinion, one could at least require the same amount of assets that are required for the purposes of the existence of a PE. But why should one espouse this interpretation?

As a starting point, every assertion of taxing jurisdiction must be based on a substantial connection of the taxpayer or their income with the state intending to tax. So both source and residence taxation are prerequisites for this substantial connection. For the purposes of source taxation, an acceptable, and therewith substantial connection for the assertion of taxing rights by the source state is the existence of a PE. And a PE exists if business is carried out through physical facilities,[85] which remain fixed on a specific geographic point,[86] with a certain degree of permanency (over six months)[87] and the fixed place through which business is carried on must be at the enterprise's disposal.[88]

I suggest resorting to literature, guidance, and jurisprudence on the PE term, also to ascertain whether a connection exists justifying the assertion of taxing rights based on residence since literature, guidance, and jurisprudence are lacking in this context. Accordingly, an economic activity in the residence state is substantial if it would constitute business for the purposes of Article 7 of the OECD-MTC. This interpretation is in line with authors like Vann who argue for a 'cross-over'[89] between source and

85. Paragraph 10 of the Commentary (2017) on Article 5.
86. Paragraph 21 of the Commentary (2017) on Article 5.
87. Paragraph 28 of the Commentary (2017) on Article 5.
88. Paragraph 10 of the Commentary (2017) on Article 5.
89. Vann (2009), p. 233.

residence, that is, they are 'a priori interconnected concepts'[90] 'designed to produce a similar outcome for the taxation of foreign direct investment, whether in the form of a PE or as the subsidiary of a foreign enterprise'.[91,92]

In cases where the business generating the item of income in question is carried out either by the person deriving the income or by a connected person in the source state, it has already been set out in section B.II.1.b.bb. of this chapter that Article 29(3)(b) of the OECD MTC contains a relative quantitative threshold with respect to the assets employed, namely the substantiality requirement where the relative value of the assets in the residence when compared to the one in the source state plays a role.

In total, the objective element, although not mentioned in either Article 29(3) or the accompanying Commentary, plays the same role it plays for the purposes of the POEM. The assets must be capable of serving both the managerial and the operational activities carried on in the residence country and they must be enough to justify PE taxation; in cases where the business generating the item of income in question is carried out either by the person deriving the income or by a connected person in the state of source, the assets must pass the threshold of the substantiality requirement laid down in Article 29(3)(b).

4 *Synthesis*

- The active conduct of a business test requires, in a qualitative sense, that both strategic decision-making functions and operational activities are carried out in the residence state of the interposed subsidiary. The requirement of operational activities constitutes a 'plus' compared to the other two substance requirements (section B.II.1.a.aa.). Similarly, the fact that the income, in respect of which DTC benefits are being invoked, must emanate from, or be incidental to, the aforementioned activities also constitutes a 'plus' and demonstrates that the substance requirements in the active conduct of a business test are more demanding than the one in the POEM (section B.II.1.a.bb.).
- In a quantitative sense, the business in the residence state must be substantial, whereby guidance is lacking as to what 'substantial' means in this context (section B.II.1.b.aa.). In cases where the business generating the item of income in question is carried on either by the person deriving the income or by a connected person in the state of source, the business activities must be

90. Cui (2017), p. 247.
91. Baistrocchi (2022), s. 6.2.1. The whole quote reads 'The combined operation of the PE, the business profits and associated enterprises rules are designed to produce a similar outcome for the taxation of foreign direct investment, whether in the form of a PE or as the subsidiary of a foreign enterprise.'
92. *See also* Kostikidis (2024), p. 41: 'Residence and source are not mutually exclusive concepts but also not tautological. That is, there are forms of integration that could qualify both as residence and source and others that are either of these.'

substantial in relation to the ones conducted in the source state (section B.II.1.b.bb.).

- Contradicting the findings of section B.II.1.a. as to the relationship between the substance requirements in the active conduct of a business test and the POEM as well as the principle of economic allegiance, Article 29(3)(c) of the OECD MTC is very loose towards outsourcing, as it ultimately allows the interposed subsidiary to outsource all decision-making functions and activities to connected persons and/or third parties and still pass the active conduct of a business test. This can be rectified if one applies a *teleologische Reduktion* or follows the *de lege ferenda* proposal of granting proportional DTC benefits, both accompanied by the opportunity for the taxpayer to prove the existence of sound economic reasons supporting the outsourcing (section B.II.1.c.).
- Article 29(3)(c) of the OECD MTC also allows entities without their own personnel in the residence state to claim DTC benefits. So although the active conduct of a business test is more demanding than the POEM, as regards the personal element of substance, requiring that all hierarchy levels are present in the residence state, Article 29(3)(c) of the OECD MTC makes DTC access even easier than the POEM does (section B.II.2.).
- Although the objective element of substance is not mentioned in either the Commentary or Article 29(3) of the OECD MTC, it should at least have the role it has in the POEM (thus, a secondary role compared to the functional and personal elements). Compared to the objective element in the POEM, however, the objective element in the active conduct of a business test refers to both managerial and operational activities, which also influence the qualities that the assets should have. As to the quantity of the assets, their volume must be sufficient to justify PE taxation. Finally, the threshold in Article 29(3)(b) also applies thereto (section B.II.3.).

III Content of the Substance Requirement in the Headquarters Company Test

Headquarters companies are exempted from the ambit of the active conduct of a business test.[93] Although as already stated in section B.I.1. these two tests are based on the same notion, they are not the same. In fact, the OECD's reluctance to include this test in Action 6 of the BEPS Project has incited some reaction, since headquarters companies, these being excluded from the active conduct of a business test, would not pass the LOB and therefore be denied treaty benefits.[94] Thus, a special provision for headquarters companies has been introduced into the OECD MTC: the headquarters

93. OECD Action 6, p. 38: 'a headquarters company will not be considered to be engaged in the active conduct of a business for purposes of paragraph 3'. The same approach takes the forefather of the LOB provisions, the United States. *See* US Model Technical Explanation (2006), p. 69. For an additional argument, *see* below s. B.IV.2. of this chapter.
94. *See* only the initial comments on the Discussion Draft on Action 6 (14 Marc. 2014): Dutch Association of Tax Advisers (2014), p. 194; EY Global Services Limited (2014), p. 202;

company test. From the perspective of this work, the requirement that the headquarters company has its PPMC in its residence state is interesting. This requirement strongly resembles, at first glance, the POEM. Is the content of the PPMC the same as that of the POEM?

The following sections expand on the content of the PPMC using the exact same structure that was used in the section on the content of the active conduct of a business test: section B.III.1. analyses the functional element, section B.III.2. the personal element, and section B.III.3. the objective element of substance. Section B.III.4. provides a conclusion.

1 *The Functional Element of the Substance Requirement in the Headquarters Company Test*

The functional element of substance has two sub-elements: the qualitative and the quantitative sub-elements. The next two sections dissect the content of these two sub-elements for the purposes of the PPMC.

a *Qualitative Sub-element of the Functional Element of Substance*

When referring to the qualities of the functions that a subsidiary[95] must render in order for its PPMC to be found in its residence state, we need to first identify the relevant functions. For example, are both managerial and operational activities relevant like in the active conduct of a business test?

The fact that the test is called PPMC as well as the need that the OECD saw in clarifying that the PPMC must be distinguished from the POEM[96] imply that, similar to the latter, decision-making functions play the key role in this test.[97,98] Furthermore, just like for the purposes of the POEM, transfer pricing and the active conduct of a business only test activities in the residence state of the entity claiming DTC benefits are considered.[99] So now that we know that decision-making functions are the relevant

SwissHoldings (2014), p. 480; Valente Associati GEB Partners (2014), p. 540. *See also* Krasnobaeva (2021), p. 417 with further references.

95. It is only the subsidiary and not other group companies that needs to render the relevant functions. What is being said is that the PPMC, like the POEM (s. B.II.1.a.aa. of Ch. 1) and the ALP (s. A.I.1. of Ch. 2), adopts the stand-alone perspective. This can be deducted from para. 150 of the Commentary on Article 29 referring to the 'company's or entity's primary place of management and control'.
96. Paragraph 149 of the Commentary (2017) on Article 29.
97. This finding corresponds to '[t]he most traditional, and obvious, function of headquarters is that of a home for managerial talent and key decision-makers'. Desai (2009), p. 1277.
98. So operational activities play no role for the purposes of this test. And it has been stated that a headquarters company carrying on only managerial activities would not pass the active conduct of a business test (n. 94). This in turn implies that the active conduct of a business test requires the existence of not only managerial activities, otherwise headquarters companies would pass the test. This is an argument in favour of interpreting the 'and' in the term 'managerial and operational activities' as an 'and' in a joint and not several sense. *See* above n. 54 in this chapter.
99. *See* para. 150 of the Commentary (2017) on Article 29 underlying that the relevant activities must be conducted 'in that State', i.e., the residence state.

functions for the purposes of the PPMC, two further questions arise, namely the ones asked for both the purposes of the POEM and transfer pricing: what kind of decisions are relevant? And which stage in the decision-making process is relevant?

aa What Kind of Decisions Are Relevant?

In this respect, the Commentary on the PPMC in paragraph 150 paints a very blurry picture:

> [T]he executive officers and senior management employees exercise *day-to-day responsibility* for more of the strategic, financial and operational policy decision making for the company or entity and for its direct and indirect subsidiaries (emphasis added).

So we may observe that different decision categories like strategic decision-making, day-to-day management (referring to what this work calls operational management), and also policy decision-making are referred to as relevant for the purposes of the PPMC. Accordingly, the question arises whether these decision categories must all cumulatively take place in the residence state of the headquarters company, or whether the existence of one of them suffices. The answer is all of them should be relevant in ascertaining where the PPMC is. Both strategic and operational decision-making, as well as parent policy-making, must take place in the residence state. This interpretation is in line with the wording of the Commentary but also with the role of headquarters companies in MNEs.

Management literature informs us that:

> [T]here are four basic roles played by the corporate center in a multibusiness corporation. The first, and most important role ... are the value-creating or coordinative functions governing the development allocation, and deployment of valuable corporate resources within the hierarchy ... what [is being] refer[red] to as 'value-added parenting' ...
>
> The second role [that the headquarters plays is to] operate a control system that monitors and evaluates the performance of its constituent units in order to minimize the agency costs of delegating substantial decision-making authority ...
>
> Third, corporate headquarters ... must perform all the obligatory reporting and compliance functions, whether legal, financial, or regulatory, that are required to demonstrate due diligence on behalf of shareholders. ...
>
> The fourth role is providing shared services to the businesses where these are subject to scale economies.[100]

So we see that the corporate headquarters combines operational activities (e.g., services) and the decision-making pertaining to them and strategic management, as well as 'value-added parenting', or what this work refers to as parent policy-making. It thus seems logical that the law (i.e., the headquarters company test in Article 29(5) of the OECD MTC) tries to reflect reality by requiring a company to perform all the decision-making functions that a regular headquarters company does in order for the

100. Collis et al. (2007), pp. 387-388.

former to also be characterized as such. Still, it must be underlined that a test demanding that both strategic and operational decision-making, as well as parent policy-making, must take place in the residence state is quite strict and restricted in scope. Two insights, again from the management literature, support this proposition.

First, in the context of corporate headquarters, decisions regarding operational tasks along with the tasks themselves may be either 'outsourced or managed as separate profit centers'.[101] Accordingly, headquarters companies choosing this kind of organization, i.e., outsourcing operational tasks and management, will not be able to pass the headquarters company test. Second, one must distinguish between corporate headquarters and business unit headquarters. While the corporate headquarters relates to the whole group, the business unit headquarters is more restricted in scope, namely related to a specific business unit, itself related to a specific product, geographical area, etc. As to the role of the business unit headquarters:

> Business unit HQ [i.e., headquarters] is responsible for the formulation and implementation of competitive strategy – the positioning of the business within its industry, and the means by which it strives to achieve above average returns within that industry.[102]

So the business unit headquarters is entrusted with strategic and operational decision-making functions, the latter relating to the implementation of the strategic decisions (section B.II.1.c.cc. of Chapter 1), but not with parent policy-making.

This analysis shows that, on the one hand, corporate headquarters may not perform operational decision-making functions, while, on the other business unit headquarters are not entrusted with parent policy-making. Against this background, there are two possible interpretations of the PPMC. On the one hand, one can choose the interpretation that both strategic and operational decision-making, as well as parent policy-making, must take place in the residence state. On the other hand, one can also choose an interpretation more lenient towards headquarters companies and regard only strategic decision-making functions as relevant.[103] Only the performance of strategic decision-making functions in the residence state would be necessary because corporate headquarters may outsource operational decision-making functions and business unit headquarters are not entrusted with parent policy-making, this leading to the exclusion of those two decision categories as relevant.

In the author's opinion, only the first interpretation is in line with the purpose of the headquarters company test. Again (section B.I.1. of this chapter), the headquarters company test is based on the same notion and shares the same rationale as the active conduct of a business test. It purports to limit the personal scope of a DTC to only those taxpayers who have economic connections to the residence state. By referring to the strategic decisions, the headquarters company test would demand exactly what the POEM also demands and would thereby not function as a filter qualifying DTC

101. Birkinshaw et al. (2006), p. 683.
102. *Ibid.*, p. 683.
103. In this sense, Kaeser (2022), para. 184.

residence.[104] By contrast, by demanding that a headquarters company renders both strategic and operational decision-making, as well as parent policy-making in its residence state, the headquarters company test raises the bar and allows only deeply economically connected taxpayers to draw DTC benefits.

bb Which Stage in the Decision-Making Process Is Relevant?

With regard to the question of which stage in the decision-making process is relevant, this work has distinguished between the planning stage, the implementation stage, and the monitoring stage, while within the planning stage, there exist two sub-stages: the preparation sub-stage and the decision-making stricto sensu. The name of the test itself as the PPMC points to the relevance of the decision-making stricto sensu and the monitoring stage, just like in the case of the POEM (section B.II.1.c.cc. of Chapter 1). However, the Commentary on the PPMC also refers to 'the staff that support such management [i.e., management making operational, strategic decisions, and parent policy-making] in preparing for and making those decisions' as relevant for the purposes of the PPMC.

The relevance of the staff entrusted with preparatory tasks also entails a relevance of the preparatory phase in the decision-making process, something that constitutes a novum, as the relevance of the preparatory sub-stage has been rejected in both the POEM (section B.II.1.c.cc. of Chapter 1) and transfer pricing (section B.II.1.c. of Chapter 2).[105] We can also observe here a case where the substance requirement in the headquarters company test is stricter than the one in the POEM, the preparatory stage in the decision-making process being the 'plus' that the LOB requires for access to DTC benefits.

cc Summary

All in all, the PPMC is far more demanding than the POEM in a qualitative sense, as far as the decision-making functions required are concerned. Not only strategic decisions but also a bundle consisting of both strategic and operational decision-making, as well as parent policy-making, must be rendered in the residence state. Not only the decision-making stricto sensu and monitoring stage but also the preparatory stage in the decision-making process are relevant.

b Quantitative Sub-element of the Functional Element of Substance

The active conduct of a business test introduces a quantitative threshold as regards the functions that must be rendered in the residence state of the subsidiary claiming DTC

104. Remember that according to para. 149 of the Commentary (2017) on Article 29 the PPMC must be distinguished from the POEM. They are not the same so they also should not pose the same requirements.
105. *See also* Kaeser (2022), para. 184.

benefits (section B.II.1.b. of this chapter). In a similar vein, the Commentary on Article 29 of the OECD MTC in paragraph 150 refers to 'day-to-day responsibility for *more* of the strategic, financial and operational policy decision making' and requires that 'the staff that support such management in preparing for and making those decisions conduct *more* of their necessary day-to-day activities, *in that State than in the other State or any third State*', while underlining that 'it will be a necessary, but not a sufficient, condition that the chief executive officer and other top executives *normally* are in the Contracting State of which the company is a resident'. (Emphasis added).

These passages show that in the PPMC, like in the case of the POEM (section B.II.3.a. of this chapter) and the substantiality test in the active conduct of a business test, a relative threshold exits (section B.II.1.b.bb. of this chapter).[106] Thus, the approach used to measure the relative quantitative importance of the functions used for the purposes of the substantiality test in Article 29(3)(b) of the OECD MTC can also be applied for the purposes of the PPMC.

Finally, here the relevant substantiality of the functions rendered in the residence state is not only measured in comparison to the source state (like in the case of the substantiality test in the active conduct of a business test), but functions performed in third states are also considered. This makes it all the more clear that the purpose of the test, as argued in section B.I.1. of the OECD MTC, is not to preserve the reciprocity of the DTC in question, otherwise, the substantiality relationship would only concern the residence and the source state, and would not include third states. Depicting deep economic connections with the residence state is the purpose of the test. And this can only be possible if the whole picture is considered, that is, all activities of the entity claiming to be a headquarters company are measured in order to ascertain whether the connections with the residence state are the deepest ones.

2 *The Personal Element of the Substance Requirement in the Headquarters Company Test*

The personal element of substance like the functional element has a qualitative and a quantitative sub-element, but it also has a personal element stricto sensu, aiming to identify which persons are the significant ones for the respective substance requirement. Let us begin the analysis as regards the personal element of substance with the personal element stricto sensu and then deal with the qualitative and the quantitative sub-elements like this work did in the chapter on substance in transfer pricing (section B.III. of Chapter 2).

a *Personal Element Stricto Sensu*

As regards the personal element stricto sensu, two questions arise. First, which role does the existence of an enforceable right play and what is the importance of

106. *See also ibid.*, para. 185.

managerial liability (section B.III.2.a.aa.)? Second, who are the relevant persons from an institutional perspective (section B.III.2.a.bb.)?

aa The Role of the Existence of an Enforceable Right and Managerial Liability

The Commentary contains no guidance regarding the role of the existence of an enforceable right and managerial liability. The fact that the Commentary does not mention these two factors supports the conclusion that the existence of an enforceable right and managerial liability does not play a role when determining where the PPMC is. This can be confirmed by taking into account the telos of the PPMC which, as shown in section B.III.1.b. of this chapter, is to depict deep economic connections with the residence state of the subsidiary claiming to be a headquarters company. Concentrating on formal factors like the existence of an enforceable right and managerial liability would not suffice in this respect.

bb The Relevant Persons from an Institutional Perspective

Article 29 of the OECD MTC in paragraph 150 requires that:

> [T]he executive officers and senior management employees exercise day-to-day responsibility for more of the strategic, financial and operational policy decision-making for the company and its direct and indirect subsidiaries, and the staff that support such management in making those decisions conduct more of their necessary day-to-day activities, than the officers or employees of any other company or entity.

So, with regard to who the relevant persons are from an institutional perspective the Commentary on the PPMC concentrates, first, on 'executive officers and senior management employees'. These persons may be members of the board of directors, which is the relevant organ from an institutional perspective for the purposes of the POEM, but this is not necessary. Thus, it is submitted here that the PPMC in the quoted passage refers to both the top- (consisting of the members of the board) and the middle-level management, as opposed to the POEM referring only to the top-level management. However, not only the top- and middle-level management are relevant but the Commentary also refers to 'the staff that support such management'. This passage refers to persons not entrusted with decision-making functions per se, but with operational tasks as regards the preparation of the decisions.

The fact that top- and middle-level management as well as persons entrusted with the preparation of decision-making are the relevant persons from an institutional perspective is in line with the findings in section B.III.1.a. of this chapter on the qualitative sub-element of the functional element. There it has namely been submitted that a headquarters company must render both strategic decision-making and operational activities, as well as parent policy-making in its residence state (section B.III.1.a.aa.). Accordingly, one needs both the policy-and strategy-makers, i.e., the board members, as well as the operational decision-makers pertaining to the middle-level management. Furthermore, the fact that preparatory activities are also relevant for the purposes of the PPMC (section B.III.1.a.bb.) translated into the terms of the personal decision-making stricto sensu, means that the persons entrusted with preparing these decisions are also relevant persons from an institutional perspective.

It can be noted that relying on both the top- and the middle-level management does not fully concur with the US approach. In particular, according to the US Model Technical Explanation (2006):

> To apply the test, it will be necessary to determine which persons are to be considered 'executive officers and senior management employees'. In most cases, it will not be necessary to look beyond the executives who are members of the Board of Directors.[107]

So we see that the US Model Technical Explanation (2006) does not demand the existence of both the top- and the middle-level management in the residence state but recognizes that '[i]n most cases' the board suffices. This divergence between the OECD Model and the US Model, again the latter constituting the origin of the LOB provision,[108] can be explained. In fact, the US Model and the US DTC policy never made use of the POEM as the tiebreaker rule; instead, the POI was used.[109] Thus, the board members did not appear as relevant persons for DTC entitlement, while the OECD MTC already had the POEM and thus demanded the existence of the board decision-makers in the residence state. So, it can be submitted that the US Model with the headquarters company test compensates for the non-existence of a substantive criterion for treaty access, like the POEM, whereby the substantive criterion focuses on the board members of a company.

In total, both top- and middle-level management as well as persons entrusted with the preparation of decision-making are the relevant persons from an institutional perspective for the purposes of the headquarters company test.

b Qualitative Sub-element of the Personal Element of Substance

No guidance is given in the Commentary regarding the qualities that the relevant persons should have. However, practical experience shows that a headquarters company possesses high volumes of information and the necessary knowledge and expertise in order to use this information.[110] Furthermore, guidance regarding the

107. US Model Technical Explanation (2006), p. 67.
108. *See* above s. B.III.3. of the Introduction.
109. Article 4(4) of the US Model (2006) referred to the state under the laws of which a corporation is created or organized as the state that wins the tiebreaker. The current Model takes another course: it does not even solve the tie; it treats dual-resident corporations as non-residents (Article 4(4) of the US Model (2016)).
110. Foss (2019), p. 6: 'usually much more information flows to CHQ [corporate headquarters] than mere accounting statements containing profit/loss figures. Such information need to be understood, digested, assimilated, and synthesized – which requires the right knowledge and skill set in the CHQ'. *See also* Collis et al. (2007), pp. 388 and 390-391: 'The obligatory public company functions of a corporate headquarters primarily involve the aggregation and reporting of financial, tax, and legal data. Since all corporations seek to perform these tasks as efficiently

application of the PPT refers, as is shown in section B.IV.2. of this chapter, to the headquarters company test and places emphasis on the 'board of directors of [the company claiming DTC benefits which] is composed of a majority of State R [the company's residence state] resident directors *with expertise* in investment management'.[111]

From this, it follows that the relevant decision-makers must have some expertise and information. Lacking further guidance, one can make recourse to the requirements in this sense of the POEM and argue that at least they should apply, just like this work did with regard to the objective element of the active conduct of a business test where guidance is also lacking (section B.II.3. of this chapter).

c Quantitative Sub-element of the Personal Element of Substance: How Many Decision-Makers Are Necessary?

The quantitative threshold already addressed in section B.III.1.b. of this chapter with regard to the functions that the headquarters company must perform in its residence state does not exist with respect to the number of decision-makers. So here we can notice a difference compared to the POEM (section B.II.3.b. of Chapter 1) and the active conduct of a business test, where a relative quantitative threshold in this respect exists (section B.II.1.b.bb. of this chapter).

One can only speculate as to why there is no relative quantitative threshold in the headquarters company test, while there is one in the active conduct of a business test, especially against the background that there is a quantitative threshold in the functional element of the PPMC. In the POEM and in transfer pricing, there is no quantitative threshold both in the functional (section B.II.3.a. of Chapter 1 for the POEM and section B.II.2.a. of Chapter 2 for transfer pricing) and in the personal element (section B.II.3.b. of Chapter 1 for the POEM and section B.III.3. of Chapter 2 for transfer pricing). By contrast, in the active conduct of a business test, there is a quantitative threshold both in the functional and in the personal elements (section B.II.1.b. of this chapter). So we notice that the quantitative sub-element concurs in its functional and personal forms: if a threshold is required in the one, it is also required in the other, and vice versa. Why is this concurrence not abided by in the case of the PPMC?

This inconsistency could be solved by interpreting the PPMC as demanding a relative quantitative threshold regarding the number of decision-makers in the residence state of the headquarters company. Such an interpretation is possible since the Commentary provides that 'it will be a necessary, but not a sufficient, condition that the chief executive officer and other top executives *normally* are in the Contracting

as possible, information processing ... is the appropriate theoretical lens' and '[b]ehavioral control requires executives to have sufficient understanding of the businesses' key success factors to evaluate operational decisions'.

111. Paragraph 182 of the Commentary (2017) on Article 29 (emphasis added) and subsequently in s. B.IV.2. of this chapter.

State of which the company is a resident'.[112] One could interpret the word 'normally' as including a quantitative threshold similar to the one existing in the functional element (section B.III.1.b. of this chapter). This interpretation would be in line with the purpose of the test to depict economic allegiance with the residence state and should thus be preferred, also by taking into account that solving inconsistencies in the law is better than preserving them.[113]

In sum, it is argued that the PPMC includes a relative quantitative threshold with respect to the number of decision-makers in the residence state of the headquarters company.

3 *Content of the Objective Element of Substance in the Headquarters Company Test*

Just like in the active conduct of a business test, no mention is made regarding the importance of assets for the purposes of the PPMC either in the Commentary or in the headquarters company test itself. Thus, the analysis conducted with respect to the role of the objective element of substance for the purposes of the active conduct of a business test also applies here (section B.II.3. of this chapter).

That is, the objective element, although not mentioned, plays a role for the purposes of the PPMC. It plays at least the exact same role that it does in the POEM, but only a secondary one compared to the functional and personal elements of the substance requirement. As regards the qualities of the assets, since the PPMC concentrates, like the POEM, on decision-making functions, one could apply the findings reached there. That is, the assets must serve the decision-making functions, and thus the existence of tangible assets like premises, telephones, computers, etc., is decisive.

4 *Synthesis*

- The PPMC, like the POEM, demands decision-making functions be carried on in the residence state. Nevertheless, the PPMC is more demanding than the POEM, requiring that both strategic decision-making and operational activities, as well as parent policy-making, must take place in the residence state. As far as the relevant stage in the decision-making process is concerned, similar principles with the POEM apply with the 'plus' that the preparatory sub-stage must also take place in the residence state (section B.III.1.a.).
- The PPMC contains a relative threshold as regards the decision-making functions that need to be conducted in the residence state. The threshold is

112. Paragraph 150 of the Commentary (2017) on Article 29 (emphasis added).
113. *See* the argument, although with regard to the PPT especially, mounted by Landsiedel (2021), p. 109. In this sense also Kaeser (2022), para. 186 where Christian Kaeser also makes the argument that outsourcing activities to persons pertaining to entities residing in the same state as the one in which the subsidiary claiming DTC benefits resides should be less harmful than outsourcing to persons pertaining to entities residing in other states.

related to the decision-making functions performed in the source state and third states (section B.III.1.b.).

- From an institutional perspective, both the top- and middle-level management as well as persons entrusted with operational tasks as regards the preparation of the decisions are relevant and must be present in the residence state of the headquarters company in order to meet the requirements of the PPMC (section B.III.2.a.).
- Although no guidance exists as regards the qualities that the relevant decision-makers should possess, practical experience and guidance on the PPT, referring to the headquarters company test underline the importance of information and expertise in headquarters companies. In this sense, reference can be made to the information and knowledge requirements for the purposes of the POEM (section B.III.2.b.).
- A relative quantitative threshold, similar to the one contained in the functional element, also exists with regard to the number of decision-makers (section B.III.2.c.).
- The objective element, although not mentioned, plays a role for the purposes of the PPMC. It plays at least the exact same role that it does in the POEM, thus only a secondary one compared to the functional and personal elements of the substance requirement. As regards the qualities of the assets, the latter must serve the decision-making functions, and, thus, the existence of tangible assets like premises, telephones, computers, etc., is decisive (section B.III.3.).

IV Content of the Substance Requirement in the PPT

1 *Relevance for the Purposes of the PPT*

The existence of a substance requirement in this rule is not straightforward at all when only examining the provision itself. As shown in the next section, only after one reads the Commentary on Article 29(9) of the OECD MTC, containing the PPT, does it become clear that the existence of substance plays a role for the purposes of this rule.[114] But what role does it play? Does the existence of substance, for example, completely eliminate the possibility of applying the PPT?

In order to provide an answer to this question, one needs to understand the mechanism of the PPT. The PPT is the DTC GAAR. That is, as opposed to the LOB, which only targets specific abusive structures, i.e., treaty shopping, the PPT covers all kinds of DTC abuse, not only treaty shopping.[115] It does so by denying treaty benefits when it is reasonable to conclude that obtaining the treaty benefit was one of the

114. *See* the next section as well as the analysis of the substance-oriented examples in the Commentary in Martín Jiménez (2017), pp. 53-54; Danon (2018a), p. 48; Kuźniacki (2018b), p. 267; Chand (2018), pp. 33-35; Duff (2018b), pp. 993 et seq.; van Weeghel (2019), pp. 34-35; Martín Jiménez (2020a), p. 209; Mithe (2020), pp. 151-152; Danon (2020b), p. 257.
115. *See* above n. 10 in this chapter.

principal purposes of the transaction or arrangement in question (subjective prong of the test). This may only happen, though, on condition that it cannot be established that granting that benefit in these circumstances would be in accordance with the object and purpose of the relevant provisions of the DTC (objective prong of the test).

Now, for which of these two PPT prongs is the existence of substance relevant? The question seems to be not an academic one at all because the burden of proof in these two prongs differs. In particular, the Commentary on Article 29(9) of the OECD MTC places the burden of proof as regards the subjective prong of the PPT on the tax authority, while it is for the taxpayer to disprove the objective prong of the PPT:

> The provisions of paragraph 9 have the effect of denying a benefit under a tax convention where one of the principal purposes of an arrangement or transaction that has been entered into is to obtain a benefit under the convention. Where this is the case, however, the last part of the paragraph allows the person to whom the benefit would otherwise be denied the possibility of establishing that obtaining the benefit in these circumstances would be in accordance with the object and purpose of the relevant provisions of this Convention.[116]

So, at first glance, if the substance excludes the fulfilment of the subjective prong of the PPT, it is for the tax authority to investigate this, while if it excludes the fulfilment of the objective prong, it is the taxpayer who may bring the substance argument forward. Against this background, it seems important to know for which PPT prong the existence of substance is relevant and therewith by whom the latter must be proven. In this respect, Robert Danon informs us that a 'controversial point is whether the level of nexus or "substance" that the taxpayer has with the State of residence matters in the PPT analysis. For some commentators, this element is relevant to both the subjective and objective component of the PPT, while other scholars tend to connect it to the latter'.[117] Others connect substance to the subjective prong of the PPT.[118] Schön connects commercial reasons and economic substance to the objective prong of the PPT, which is why it needs to be proven by the taxpayer.[119]

In the author's opinion, the existence or non-existence of substance needs to be considered by both parties involved in a dispute, namely both by the tax authority and the taxpayer, and accordingly, it does not play a role in whether it excludes the fulfilment of the subjective or the objective prong of the PPT. As regards the tax

116. Paragraph 170 of the Commentary (2017) on Article 29.
117. Danon (2020b), p. 257. On this debate, *see* more recently Schön (2022a), p. 3.
118. Danon (2018a), p. 48; Danon (2020b), p. 257; Mithe (2020), p. 151; Danon et al. (2021), p. 495; Navisotschnigg (2022), p. 137. In this sense Navarro (2021), p. 811, n. 75 when he submits that 'as the PPT incorporates a subjective test ("obtaining the said benefits was one of the principal purposes of any arrangement or transaction that resulted directly or indirectly in that benefit"), transfer pricing concepts such as the "functions, assets, and risks" triad may be useful to measure substance'.
119. Schön (2022a), p. 16: 'It is therefore possible (and this is decisive when we have to apply Art.29(9) OECD MTC in practice), that there exists a principal tax motive under the first prong (which opens the gate to the GAAR) but that there also exist valid commercial reasons, which under the second prong secure the compatibility of the tax benefit with the object and purpose of the treaty provision.' Following Schön, Martín Jiménez (2022b), p. 458.

authority, this should consider the existence of substance because, in the final analysis, the tax authority needs to consider both prongs of the PPT:

> It is ... highly unlikely that the tax authorities will try to deny treaty benefits by concluding that the requirement for doing so is met under the first element [subjective prong] while being assured that the second element [objective prong] allows taxpayers to neutralize this denial. Indeed, the tax authorities will take into account the second element of the PPT at the concluding stage of their first element consideration, even though the wording of the PPT does not require them to do so.[120]

Accordingly, the tax authority needs to check the existence of substance of the interposed subsidiary either when proving the fulfilment of the subjective prong, or when considering the fulfilment of the objective prong.

The taxpayer, needing to prove the PPT's objective prong, may certainly need to take into account the existence of substance if this excludes the fulfilment of the objective prong. But what if the existence of substance excludes the fulfilment of the subjective and not the objective prong? In this case, the tax authority has to prove the missing substance and the taxpayer can respond to the tax authority's claim by proving the existence of substance.

It can be concluded that it does not matter for which PPT prong the existence of substance is relevant. In fact, both tax authority applying the PPT and the taxpayer proving that the PPT does not apply should consider it. But have we come to the conclusion that the substance of the interposed subsidiary is relevant for the purposes of the PPT in the first place? The next section affirms this assertion.

2 *Content Pursuant to the Commentary*

The Commentary on Article 29(9) of the OECD MTC, containing the PPT, includes in its paragraph 182 a series of examples that illustrate the application of the paragraph. Here, the author concentrates only on the two examples in particular making use of a quite substance-oriented language; an extensive analysis of the PPT and the Commentary thereon is not intended. In particular, in example G the interposed subsidiary is considered to pass the PPT because:

> Assuming that the intra-group services to be provided by RCO [the interposed subsidiary], including the making of decisions necessary for the conduct of its business, constitute a real business through which RCO *exercises substantive economic functions, using real assets and assuming real risks, and that business is carried on by RCO through its own personnel* located in State R [RCO's residence

120. Kuźniacki (2018b), p. 249. In favour of this 'unitary interpretation' Landsiedel (2021), pp. 101-103. For another argument *see* Lavez (2022), s. 3.1.3.: 'as long as the tax authorities base the denial of the treaty benefit on the GAAR, the burden to demonstrate that both elements of the legal hypothesis of the rule are fully satisfied lies with the tax authorities. ... [a]n opposite conclusion would entail a disproportional restriction to the principle of the observance of the rights of defence, as construed by the Court of Justice of the European Union'.

> state], it would not be reasonable to deny the benefits of the treaties concluded between State R and the five States where the subsidiaries [to which RCO offers services and accordingly receives remuneration] operate (emphasis added).

The passage in italics reminds one of the active conduct of a business test, according to which '[a]n entity generally will be considered to be engaged in the active conduct of a business only if *persons* through whom the entity is acting (such as officers or employees of a company) conduct *substantial managerial and operational activities*'. (Emphasis added).[121]

Similar language is used in example K:

> RCO [the interposed subsidiary] employs an experienced local management team to review investment recommendations from Fund [the parent] and performs various other functions which, depending on the case, may include approving and monitoring investments, carrying on treasury functions, maintaining RCO's books and records, and ensuring compliance with regulatory requirements in States where it invests. The board of directors of RCO is appointed by Fund and is composed of a majority of State R [RCO's residence state] resident directors with expertise in investment management, as well as members of Fund's global management team. ... In this example, in the absence of other facts or circumstances showing that RCO's investment is part of an arrangement or relates to another transaction undertaken for a principal purpose of obtaining the benefit of the Convention, it would not be reasonable to deny the benefit of the State R-State S [the state in which RCO is considering to invest in by buying shares in a local company, SCO] tax convention to RCO.

Example K in particular implies that investment management companies may pass the PPT. However, as already shown in section B.II.1.a.aa. of this chapter, such companies do not pass the active conduct of a business test. It can be surmised that an additional reason for the inclusion of the headquarters company test in the LOB has been to cover such companies and thus to align the PPT with the LOB, so that headquarters companies managing investments may pass both the PPT and the LOB.[122] This hypothesis also offers an additional argument for the case that headquarters companies do not fulfil the active conduct of a business test and that the two tests contain different substance requirements (section B.III. of this chapter). If headquarters companies were to pass the active conduct of a business test, the PPT and the LOB would be in line and the headquarters company test would not be necessary in the first place.

In sum, these examples certainly bring to the fore that the existence of substance of the interposed subsidiary is enough to allow for DTC benefits. However, no specific contours are given as to which content the substance requirement should have for the purposes of the PPT.[123] So the next section attempts to come up with a tenable interpretation of the PPT and showcase the content of the substance requirement.

121. In this sense, van Weeghel (2019), p. 34.
122. Keidanren (2015), p. 259.
123. Blessing (2020a), s. 2.2.2.2.4.; Buriak (2019), p. 37; Mithe (2020), p. 152.

3 *Proposed Interpretational Approach*

This work proposes to interpret substance for the purposes of the PPT just like it is interpreted for the purposes of the LOB. This means that a subsidiary having substance for the purposes of the LOB also has substance for the purposes of the PPT. This proposition is supported by the relationship between the PPT and the LOB.

As already indicated (section B.IV.1. of this chapter), the PPT covers all kinds of abuse. Commentators have divided its ambit into two parts:

> One part relates ... to the legal nature, ownership and general activities of the residents of a contracting state. This part effectively addresses the reality of the connection of the taxpayer with the state of its residence for the purposes of the tax treaty. One could see this part as a backstop against improper use of the convention when article 4 fails to secure a sufficiently relevant connection with the state of residence to justify the granting of treaty benefits. This connection is often referred to as the 'nexus' with the state of residence. ... However, a sufficient nexus of the taxpayer with its state of residence is not enough for it to be entitled to tax treaty benefits. If that resident would enter into an arrangement or transaction that would effectively result in the availability of tax treaty benefits to persons for whom those benefits were not intended – including the taxpayer itself in the case of 'rule shopping' – treaty benefits should, nevertheless, not be available. This latter part of article 29 can be referred to as the 'abusive transactions' part or test.[124]

So the PPT covers nexus abuse and abusive transactions. The substance-oriented LOB, as already laid down in section B.I.1. of this chapter, purports to depict the taxpayer's economic connection with their state of residence. In the case of nexus abuse no such economic connection exists and the LOB is activated; DTC benefits are denied to the taxpayer. So the LOB covers nexus abuse.[125]

And since the LOB covers nexus abuse, 'if a tax treaty contains an LOB clause, the nexus part of the PPT is effectively covered by the LOB clause and the PPT's range of operation is limited to the abusive transactions part'.[126] If a DTC does not contain the LOB but only the PPT, then the interpretation of substance for the purposes of the LOB will also constitute the content of substance for the purposes of the PPT.[127] This proposition is supported by the Commentary on Article 29(9) of the OECD MTC,

---

124. Van Weeghel (2019), p. 28.
125. Danon (2020b), p. 260.
126. Van Weeghel (2019), p. 28. In a similar vein, Duff (2018b), pp. 962-963. Only with reference to the active conduct of a business test and not the LOB as a whole, Martín Jiménez (2017), p. 53: 'From the new commentary on the PPT clause in Action 6 BEPS, there is no reason to conclude that it will be interpreted very differently than the active-conduct-of-business clause in the LOB provisions.'
    This argument applies irrespective of the wording of the PPT itself stating that it applies '[n]otwithstanding the other provisions of this Convention'. In order to keep the work in manageable proportions, please refer to another scholar offering arguments for this proposition. *See* Báez Moreno (2017), p. 441; Báez Moreno (2021), pp. 783 et seq.
127. Van Weeghel (2019), p. 29.

containing the PPT, according to which '[p]aragraph 9 must be read in the context of paragraphs 1 to 7 and of the rest of the Convention'.[128]

Thus, in both cases one needs to examine the LOB in order to ascertain whether nexus abuse exists. Either one applies the LOB directly, if the LOB exists in the treaty, or recourse is made to its interpretation in order to fill the PPT with content and apply it in cases of nexus abuse if the treaty in question does not include an LOB.[129] From this it follows that the LOB's substance requirements, intending to depict economic connections to the residence state and therewith disprove nexus abuse (section B.I.1. of this chapter), are also the only ones: either they are directly applicable when the LOB exists in the treaty or the PPT refers to them when the treaty in question does not include a LOB.

In fact, the two examples in the Commentary on the PPT that use substance-oriented language, examples G and K, seem to refer to the LOB's two substance-oriented tests. Example G refers to the performance of 'substantive economic functions', and therewith seems to refer to the active conduct of a business test, and example K refers to the headquarters company test (section B.IV.2. of this chapter). *De lege ferenda*, it would be preferable to include in these two examples an explicit reference to the respective test in the LOB as to their content.

Overall, substance for the purposes of the PPT should have the content that it has for the purposes of the LOB, that is, the one in the active conduct of a business test and the headquarters company test. This means that a subsidiary passing one of these two tests is entitled to treaty benefits either because the LOB applies if it exists in the DTC, or because the PPT does not apply if no LOB exists in the treaty. No nexus abuse exists, although another kind of abuse may still exist. Accordingly, treaty benefits may still be denied to a subsidiary even if there is no nexus abuse because another abusive transaction may have been put in place.[130]

C INTERIM CONCLUSIONS

I Similarities and Differences in the Substance Requirements in the POEM, Transfer Pricing Rules, and DTC Treaty Shopping Rules

Just like this work did in Chapter 2, the conclusions drawn in Chapter 3 are presented by comparing the content of the substance requirement in DTC treaty shopping rules

128. Paragraph 173 of the Commentary (2017) on Article 29.

129. A counterargument would be 'that the absence of this rule in the context of a particular CTA [agreement covered by the MLI] evidences an intention on the part of the contracting jurisdictions to grant treaty benefits resulting from transactions or arrangements that would otherwise be subject to the rule'. Duff (2018b), p. 965 has successfully denied this argument: 'the fact that the minimum standard on treaty abuse may be satisfied by the PPT alone or by a combination of the PPT and LOB provisions suggests that the PPT could apply to benefits that might otherwise be denied under specific LOB provisions that do not modify and are not otherwise included in a particular CTA'.

130. Van Weeghel (2019), p. 28.

with the one in the POEM and transfer pricing rules. Since, as section B.IV. has shown, the content of substance for the purposes of the PPT is the same as the one in the LOB, only the content of the substance requirements in the LOB is recalled.

As far as the substance requirement in the active conduct of a business is concerned (section B.II.):

- Both in the active conduct of a business test and in the POEM, transfer pricing activities must be conducted in the residence state in order for them to play a role in the existence of substance (section B.II.1.a.aa.). Although Article 29(3)(b) allows for activities in the source state to constitute active conduct of business, this is accompanied by a relative threshold, i.e., that the activities in the residence state are substantial compared to the ones in the source state. So, here also the activities in the residence state are the relevant ones. Finally, the PPMC also only considers activities in the residence state of the headquarters company (section B.III.1.a.). Furthermore, the active conduct of a business follows the stand-alone perspective, like the POEM and the ALP (section B.II.1.a.aa). The same holds true with regard to the PPMC (section B.III.1.a.). However, the tests differ as regards the scope of the activities that need to be carried on in the residence state. While the POEM and transfer pricing only require decision-making functions, the active conduct of a business test also requires operational activities. Furthermore, in contrast to the POEM, the nature of the activities carried on plays a role for the purposes of the active conduct of business test, since 'passive' activities are excluded from the ambit of the active conduct of a business test (section B.II.1.a.aa.).
  Finally, in the active conduct of a business test there must be a connection between the income and the activity in the residence state. Such requirement does not exist in the POEM (section B.II.1.a.bb.).
- The active conduct of a business test includes two quantitative thresholds, an absolute one in Article 29(3)(a) of the OECD MTC and a relative one applicable in cases where the business generating the item of income in question is carried on either by the person deriving the income or by a connected person in the state of source (Article 29(3)(b) of the OECD MTC). The quantitative threshold in Article 29(3)(b) of the OECD MTC also applies with regard to the personal and objective element. The absolute threshold does not exist both in the POEM and in transfer pricing for the purposes of both the functional and the personal elements (section B.II.1.b.).
- The active conduct of a business test takes a more liberal stance compared to the POEM and transfer pricing with regard to outsourcing, since both include limitations as to the activities that can be outsourced and the conditions under which outsourcing may take place. The active conduct of a business test in Article 29(3)(c) of the OECD MTC lays down neither a limitation nor specific conditions that the outsourcing party must fulfil (section B.II.1.c.).
- At first sight, the active conduct of a business test is more demanding than the POEM as regards the personal element of substance, requiring that all hierarchy levels are present in the residence state, that is, all three levels of

management as well as operational staff. Nevertheless, Article 29(3)(c) of the OECD MTC allows entities without their own personnel in the residence state to claim DTC benefits (section B.II.2.).

- The objective element should at least have its current role in the POEM (thus, a secondary role compared to the functional and personal elements). The qualities of the assets has been found to differ between the POEM and the active conduct of a business test. In the POEM, the focus is on assets related to the decision-making functions, while for the purposes of the active conduct of a business test, assets related to both the managerial and operational activities must exist (section B.II.3.).

These findings are summed up in the form of a substance checklist, emphasizing the differences with the substance checklist in the POEM.

Figure 6 Substance Checklist in the Active Conduct of a Business Test

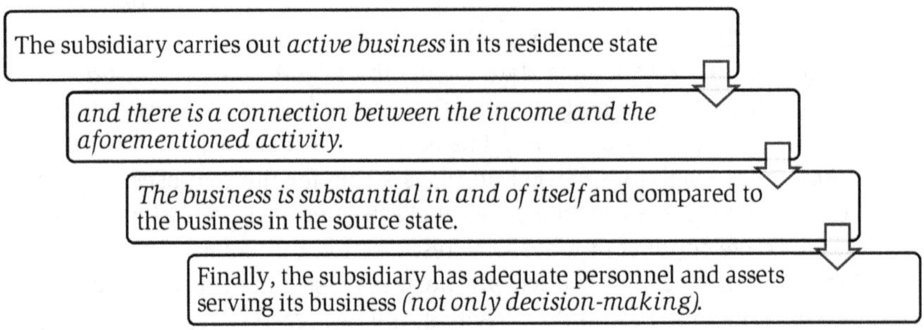

Some of the elements in the checklist are rebuttable presumptions, while others are irrebuttable presumptions of missing substance.[131] The first three elements, namely the active character of the business (i.e., passive activities are excluded), the connection between the income and the activity, and its substantiality are irrebuttable presumptions. That is, if they are not fulfilled, a subsidiary is deemed not to have substance for the purposes of the active conduct of a business test. On the contrary, the existence of personnel and assets is only an indicator that substance exists. That is, if personnel and assets are not deemed to be adequate, the taxpayer can still prove that they conduct active business in their residence state and thus have substance for the purposes of the test.

The following table summarizes the similarities and differences between the POEM, transfer pricing, and the active conduct of a business test.

131. On substance requirements as rebuttable and irrebuttable presumptions, *see* above s. B.III.5. of the Introduction.

Table 2 Similarities and Differences Between the Substance Requirements in the POEM, Transfer Pricing Rules, and the Active Conduct of a Business Test

Areas of Comparison	*Similarities*	*Differences*
Scope	- Only activities in the residence state considered (with the exception of Article 29(3)(b)) - Stand-alone perspective	
Functional Element	The POEM and the active conduct of a business test include a relative quantitative threshold (not required in transfer pricing)	- The active conduct of a business test also requires operational activities - 'Passive' activities are excluded from the ambit of the active conduct of a business test - Existence of a connection between the income and the activity in the residence state for the purposes of the active conduct of a business test - The active conduct of a business test lays down neither a limitation nor specific conditions for outsourcing
Personal Element	The POEM and the active conduct of a business test requirements include a relative quantitative threshold (not required in transfer pricing)	Article 29(3)(c) allows entities without their own personnel in the residence state to claim DTC benefits
Objective Element		In the active conduct of a business test, assets related to both the managerial and operational activities must exist

As far as the substance requirement in the headquarters company test, the PPMC, is concerned (section B.III.):

- The PPMC, like the POEM and transfer pricing, and unlike the active conduct of a business test, concentrates on decision-making functions. However, unlike the POEM and transfer pricing, which focus on strategic decision-making, the PPMC demands that a headquarters company renders both strategic and operational decision-making, as well as parent policy-making in its residence state (section B.III.1.a.aa.). Another difference between the substance requirement in the PPMC and the ones in the POEM and transfer pricing is the relevance of the preparatory sub-stage in the decision-making process in the former (section B.III.1.a.bb.).
- For the purposes of the PPMC, similar to the POEM and the active conduct of a business test, the decision-making functions in the residence state must be more than the ones performed in the source and any other third state, that is, there is a relevant threshold with regard to the quantity of the functions performed (section B.III.1.b.).
- For the purposes of the PPMC, both the top- (consisting of the members of the board) and the middle-level management as well as persons entrusted with operational activities consisting in preparing decision-making are relevant, while the POEM concentrates on the top-level management in the form of the board of directors. The headquarters company test is therefore more demanding than the POEM regarding the personal element of substance (section B.III.2.a.).
- The information and knowledge required for the purposes of the PPMC are arguably the same as for the purposes of the POEM (section B.III.2.b.).
- This work prefers an interpretation according to which the PPMC includes a relative threshold regarding the quantity of the persons rendering the relevant decision-making functions (section B.III.2.c.).
- As far as the objective element is concerned, reference can be made to what has already been said with regard to the objective element for the purposes of the active conduct of a business test. However, since the PPMC concentrates, like the POEM, only on decision-making functions and not on both decision-making functions and operational activities, the assets must serve the decision-making functions, and thus the existence of tangible assets like premises, telephones, computers, etc., is decisive, which is also the case in the POEM (section B.III.3.).

The substance checklist in the PPMC is as follows (again the differences when compared to the POEM are emphasized in italics).

Figure 7 Substance Checklist in the PPMC

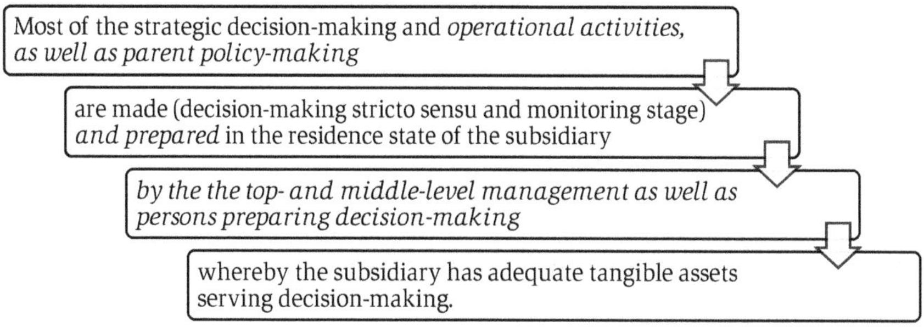

Regarding the nature of the substance checklist elements as rebuttable and/or irrebuttable presumptions, what we have already seen for the purposes of the POEM (section C. of Chapter 1) applies again. The first three elements constitute irrebuttable presumptions of substance, while the fourth element, referring to objective substance, only constitutes, like in the POEM, a rebuttable presumption which can be disproven by the taxpayer.

The following table summarizes the similarities and differences between the POEM, transfer pricing, and the PPMC.

Table 3 Similarities and Differences Between the Substance Requirements in the POEM, Transfer Pricing Rules, and the PPMC

Areas of Comparison	*Similarities*	*Differences*
Scope	- Only activities in the residence state considered - Stand-alone perspective	
Functional Element	- The POEM and the PPMC include a relative quantitative threshold (not required in transfer pricing)	- The PPMC requires that a headquarters company renders both strategic and operational decision-making, as well as parent policy-making in its residence state - The preparatory substage in the decision-making process is also relevant for the purposes of the PPMC

Areas of Comparison	*Similarities*	*Differences*
Personal Element	- Information and knowledge required for the purposes of the PPMC follows the POEM - The POEM and the PPMC include a relative quantitative threshold (not required in transfer pricing)	In the PPMC both the top- and the middle-level management as well as persons entrusted with preparing decision-making are relevant
Objective Element	In the PPMC, emphasis is placed on tangible assets like premises, telephones, computers, etc., like in the POEM	

II Stufenverhältnis Between the Substance Requirements in the DTC Context

In Chapter 2, this work has shown that in some cases the substance requirements in transfer pricing are stricter than the ones in the POEM. For example, this is the case with regard to outsourcing (section B.II.3. of Chapter 2). Similarly, this chapter has often referred to substance requirements in the LOB as a 'plus', compared to the ones in the POEM and transfer pricing. For example, the PPMC requires that both the top- and the middle-level management as well as persons entrusted with preparing decision-making are in the residence state, while the POEM focuses on members of the board of directors. This shows that there is a continuum of substance requirements beginning with the looser ones in the POEM and becoming more strict in treaty shopping rules. This work uses the German word *Stufenverhältnis* to refer to the relationship between the three substance requirements in the DTC context. This word literally means 'step relationship' referring to each substance requirement as one step followed by the other one, higher in the hierarchy and harder to reach.

The Stufenverhältnis between the substance requirements is justified by examining the systematic relationship between the POEM, transfer pricing, and the treaty shopping rules. Let us use an analogy to comprehend the relationship between these rules. The analogy relates to video games.

Almost every video game has levels. The POEM would be the first level, transfer pricing the second, and DTC treaty shopping the last level. There is an incremental rise in intensity as regards the actions that you need to take in order for you to pass each level. The first level is the easiest one, so you do not need to spend much time on it. The second level is harder so you may need to invest some more time in it. Finally, in order to pass the last level where you have to beat the ultimate 'bad guy', you may need to spend a whole night playing.

This incremental rise in the effort required to play a video game to the end can be analogously applied to the substance-oriented rules in international tax law. In order to establish nexus with a state, you need substance-oriented residence therein (or a nexus leading to source taxation). And in order to access profits allocated to you need some substance; the more substance the more profits. Finally, in order to access DTC benefits, you need the most substance.

This example shows that each step you take towards your ultimate goal is harder. This also holds true with regard to the substance requirements. The first step, namely treaty access via residence, is easier, less demanding. But the closer one gets to the ultimate goal, namely the invocation of treaty benefits, the stricter the requirements, in our case the substance requirements.

The only provision that interferes with this theory is Article 29(3)(c). It has been shown that this provision enables entities without functions and persons in their residence state to access DTC benefits. This runs afoul of the LOB's purpose (section B.I.1. of this chapter) and the Stufenverhältnis between the substance requirements in the four sets of legal rules dealt with in this work. This work has already suggested ways to alleviate this problem (section B.II.1.c.).

CHAPTER 4

The Substance Requirement in the EU Tax Law Context

A PRELIMINARY REMARKS

I Relevance of the Investigation

The following section introduces the reader to the mechanics of EU tax law. It is written in a highly generic fashion and is addressed only to readers without prior knowledge of EU tax law. Accordingly, this section does not delve more deeply into the nuances of certain disputes in tax theory and is concerned only with those issues that become relevant in the course of the chapter. It is suggested that readers with prior knowledge of EU tax law begin by reading the next section.

1 A Small Introduction to the Mechanics of EU Tax Law

EU law consists of primary and secondary sources of law. As primary EU law, we understand the provisions in the Treaty on European Union (TEU), Treaty on the Functioning of the European Union (TFEU), the Charter of Fundamental Rights of the European Union (Article 6 TEU), and the general principles of EU law (Article 6(3)). Secondary EU law includes regulations, directives, decisions, recommendations, and opinions (Article 288 TFEU). In order for the EU to enact secondary EU law, there must be a legal basis in the treaties pursuant to Article 5(2) TEU (principle of conferral).

With regard to direct taxes, EU legislative action is based on Article 115 TFEU, which enables the enactment of directives. On the basis of this provision, the following directives exist: the PSD, the IRD, the Merger Directive (MD),[1] the Directive on

1. Council Directive 2011/16/EU of 15 Feb. 2011 on Administrative Cooperation in the Field of Taxation and Repealing Directive 77/799/EEC, OJ L 64 (2011).

administrative cooperation in the field of direct taxation,[2] and the already mentioned ATAD and Shell Entities Directive (section B.III.4. of the introduction).

As far as primary EU law is concerned, the mechanism of the fundamental freedoms is relevant for this work. Now, what are the fundamental freedoms?

The Union's cardinal aim is to establish an internal market (Article 3(3) TEU). This internal market pursuant to Article 26(2) TFEU, 'shall comprise an area without internal frontiers in which the free movement of goods, persons, services and capital is ensured in accordance with the provisions of the Treaties'. In this passage, the TFEU lays down the foundation of the fundamental freedoms as a prerequisite for the establishment of the internal market. The fundamental freedoms, i.e., the free movement of goods (Article 34 TFEU), the free movement of people (Article 45 TFEU), the freedom of establishment (Article 49 TFEU), the freedom of services (Article 56 TFEU), and the freedom of movement of capital (Article 63 TFEU) can be invoked directly by their bearer, primarily an EU national,[3] when they are interfered with.

And they are interfered with when Member States or EU institutions introduce discriminatory measures against the person invoking the freedom in question. Discrimination exists when EU citizens of other Member States receive different treatment than citizens of a given Member State. Such discriminations can also be covert, that is, based on criteria other than nationality, for example, residence, which is relevant for tax law since it constitutes the reference point for unlimited tax liability.[4] However, any interference with the fundamental freedoms can be justified by the interfering Member State invoking written (Articles 36, 45(3), 52(1), and 65 TFEU) or, for tax law most importantly, unwritten justification grounds.[5]

Let us see how this provisionally explained mechanism works in practice by referring to a case decided by the CJEU where substance requirements made their appearance in EU tax law for the first time.

2 *Relevance of the Substance Requirement in EU Primary Law*

The seminal case ruled by the CJEU referring to substance requirements established in EU law is the *Cadbury Schweppes* judgment. The facts of the case are very straightforward.[6] A UK parent (Cadbury Schweppes plc) indirectly owned two subsidiaries in Ireland. Because subsidiary corporations are separate taxpayers, their profits are only taxable with the parent upon distribution thereto (*see* above section B.I. of the introduction). However, the parent jurisdiction can, as already seen in section B.III.4. of the introduction, tax undistributed profits by applying CFC rules. And these rules were applied by the UK tax administration (Commissioners of the Inland Revenue) in this case with regard to the profits of one of the Irish subsidiaries (since the other

2. *Ibid.*
3. The free movement of goods and capital can be also invoked by non-EU nationals.
4. Establishing covert discrimination based on residence, CJEU, 28 Jan. 1986, Case 270/83, *European Commission v. French Republic (Avoir Fiscal)*, ECLI:EU:C:1986:37, para. 11.
5. Establishing the so-called rule of reason doctrine, CJEU, 20 Feb. 1979, C-120/78, *Rewe-Zentral AG v. Bundesmonopolverwaltung für Branntwein (Cassis de Dijon)*, ECLI:EU:C:1979:42, para. 8.
6. CJEU, C-196/04, *Cadbury Schweppes*, at paras 13 et seq.

incurred a loss in the financial year in question). Cadbury Schweppes plc raised an appeal with the Special Commissioners of Income Tax against the Commissioners' tax notice. The court referred the matter to the CJEU in order to clarify whether the UK CFC rules were in conformity with the fundamental freedoms.

The freedom of establishment was applicable.[7] In particular, the CFC rules interfered with the freedom of a UK company to establish subsidiaries in other Member States. Although, as the CJEU acknowledges, in the final analysis, the UK company would not have to pay more tax on the profits of the Irish subsidiary, for the CJEU it was sufficient that the CFC rules only applied to cross-border and not merely national cases in order to accept a discrimination.[8]

The substance requirement became a part of the CJEU's analysis in two senses.[9] On the one hand, in order to invoke the freedom of establishment in the first place 'the actual pursuit of an economic activity through a fixed establishment in that State for an indefinite period'[10] is required. Accordingly, it seems that the CJEU considers substance, in the form of functions ('economic activity') and objects and personnel ('fixed establishment'), as a prerequisite for invoking the freedom of establishment. Companies without substance are carved out from the scope of application of the freedom of establishment.

On the other hand, the CJEU traces the relevance of substance at the level of justifying discrimination. Accordingly, Member States are justified in discriminating against cross-border transactions when they to do so in order to combat abusive practices. The CJEU has given life to the term 'abusive practices' by referring to them as 'wholly artificial arrangements'.[11] And such arrangements do not exist when

7. *Ibid.*, at paras 29-33. *See also* Article 49 TFEU, pursuant to which the freedom of establishment applies also 'to restrictions on the setting-up of agencies, branches or subsidiaries by nationals of any Member State established in the territory of any Member State'.
8. *Ibid.*, at paras 44-46. *See* already before the *Cadbury Schweppes* judgment Schön (2001), p. 254; Lang (2002), p. 375; for a restriction of the fundamental freedoms Schönfeld (2004), p. 447.

   There are also other issues that the CJEU did not identify, though. First, 'the earlier payment of corporation tax in the resident state of the ultimate parent company (the United Kingdom), [is] accompanied by *liquidity issues*'. *See* Meussen (2007), pp. 15-16 (emphasis added). Second, other scholars underline the additional compliance costs connected with the application of the CFC regime as such as a factor leading to discrimination of the cross-border case. *See* Fontana (2006), p. 323 (although accepting a restriction and not a discrimination).
9. Based on the analysis by Schön (2020a), p. 290; Schön (2020b), pp. 641-642. Commentators have identified these two dimensions already before the *Cadbury Schweppes* judgment. *See* Schön (2001), p. 252; Lang (2002), p. 375. *See also* the critique mounted by Englisch (2009b), pp. 7 and 17-18; Englisch (2020a), para. 7.251.
10. CJEU, C-196/04, *Cadbury Schweppes*, at para. 54.
11. *Ibid.*, at para. 55. *See* already before *Cadbury Schweppes*, CJEU, 16 Jul. 1998, C-264/96, *Imperial Chemical Industries plc (ICI) v. Kenneth Hall Colmer (Her Majesty's Inspector of Taxes)*, ECLI:EU:C:1998:370, para. 26; CJEU, 12 Dec. 2002, C-324/00, *Lankhorst-Hohorst GmbH v. Finanzamt Steinfurt*, ECLI: EU:C:2002:749, para. 37; CJEU, 13 Dec. 2005, C-446/03, *Marks & Spencer plc v. Halsey (Her Majesty's Inspector of Taxes)*, ECLI:EU:C:2005:763, para. 57. Referring to 'purely artificial arrangements', CJEU, 21 Nov. 2002, C-436/00, *X & Y v. Riksskatteverket*, ECLI:EU:C:2002:704, para. 61; CJEU, 1 Mar. 2004, C-9/02, *Hughes de Lasteyrie du Saillant v. Ministère de l'Économie, des Finances et de l'Industrie*, ECLI:EU:C:2004:138, para. 50. From the literature, Schön (2001), p. 257 predicting the course of the CJEU jurisprudence with regard to CFC rules; Lang/Heidenbauer (2008), pp. 598-599.

'objective factors [exist] which are ascertainable by third parties with regard, in particular, to the extent to which the CFC physically exists in terms of premises, staff and equipment'.[12] According to this reasoning, substance plays a role when justifying measures interfering with the freedom of establishment, based on the justification grounds of combating abusive practices. Here, Member States are allowed to carve out companies without substance from the scope of application of the freedom of establishment.

In both senses, companies without substance are considered abusive practices (wholly artificial arrangements) which cannot invoke the freedom of establishment. But substance does not only play a role for the purposes of the invocation of the freedom of establishment. Recently, in its *X-GmbH* judgment the CJEU applied the same doctrine to the freedom of movement of capital.[13] Furthermore, on 26 February 2019, the same day that the CJEU ruled on the *X-GmbH* case, the *Danish withholding tax* cases were issued. There, the CJEU reminded us of the relevance of substance within the notion of the wholly artificial arrangements[14] and ascended the latter to a principle of EU law.[15]

It is important to distinguish this line of judgments from that existing in corporate law. In this regard, the seminal case is *Centros*.[16] Centros Ltd (Centros) was a corporation formed under UK law which had conducted economic activity only in Denmark, where its shareholders and director also resided.[17] The Danish Department of Trade refused to register a branch of Centros in Denmark 'on the grounds, *inter alia*, that Centros, which does not trade in the United Kingdom, was in fact seeking to establish in Denmark, not a branch, but a principal establishment, by circumventing the national rules concerning, in particular, the paying-up of minimum capital [prescribed in Danish law]'.[18]

The CJEU found the refusal of the Danish authorities to contradict the freedom of establishment. Especially the fact that Centros did not have any substance in its residence state was 'not sufficient to prove the existence of abuse or fraudulent conduct which would entitle the latter Member State to deny that company the benefit of the provisions of Community law relating to the right of establishment'.[19]

12. CJEU, C-196/04, *Cadbury Schweppes*, at para. 67.
13. CJEU, 26 Feb. 2019, C-135/17, *X-GmbH v. Finanzamt Stuttgart – Körperschaften*, ECLI:EU:C:2019:136, para. 73.
14. CJEU, C–116/16 and C–117/16, *T Danmark*, at para. 104; CJEU, C-115/16, C-118/16, C-119/16 and C-299/16, *N Luxembourg 1*, at para. 131.
15. CJEU, C–116/16 and C–117/16, *T Danmark*, at para. 70; CJEU, C-115/16, C-118/16, C-119/16 and C-299/16, *N Luxembourg 1*, at para. 96.
16. *See* CJEU, 9 Mar. 1999, C-212/97, *Centros Ltd v. Erhvervs- og Selskabsstyrelsen*, ECLI:EU:C:1999:126; CJEU, 30 Sep. 2003, C-167/01, *Kamer van Koophandel en Fabrieken voor Amsterdam v. Inspire Art Ltd*, ECLI:EU:C:2003:512; CJEU, 25 Oct. 2017, C-106/16, *Polbud – Wykonawstwo*, ECLI:EU:C:2017:804. On these decisions *see* Kindler (1999); Kindler (2003); Kindler (2018).
17. CJEU, C-212/97, *Centros*, at paras 2 et seq.
18. *Ibid.*, at para. 7.
19. *Ibid.*, at para. 29; CJEU, C-167/01, *Inspire Art*, at para. 139.

This passage seems to be at odds with the *Cadbury Schweppes* case law.[20] Nevertheless, a reconciling interpretation of the two judgments is possible.[21] *Centros* concerned the existence of a company. In this respect, Article 54 TFEU provides the Member States with the right to determine the requirements that a corporation must have in order for it to have legal personality.[22] Thus, a Member State is allowed to link legal personality only to the domestic incorporation. Now, another story is whether this corporation makes use of the right of establishment in another Member State. This transaction is subject to the substance requirements laid down in the *Cadbury Schweppes* case law.

Overall, companies without substance may be classified as wholly artificial arrangements abusively invoking the freedom of establishment and the freedom of movement of capital. The *Centros* case law changes nothing to this finding.

3 *Relevance of the Substance Requirement in EU Secondary Law*

The newly enacted ATAD includes in Article 7 a CFC rule. The CFC rule in the ATAD provides for two alternatives, whereby both alternatives include a substance requirement, as already discussed in section B.III.4. of the introduction. Article 7(2)(a), on the one hand, refers to 'a substantive economic activity supported by staff, equipment, assets and premises'. Article 7(2)(b), on the other hand, refers to 'non-genuine arrangements' where 'the entity or permanent establishment would not own the assets or would not have undertaken the risks which generate all, or part of, its income if it were not controlled by a company where the significant people functions, which are relevant to those assets and risks, are carried out and are instrumental in generating the controlled company's income'.

The other corporate tax directives also include substance requirements. The PSD includes a GAAR in Article 1(2) referring to arrangements which are 'not genuine'. Commentators have already analysed why this term must be translated in a sense that

20. de la Feria (2008), pp. 428-429; Kindler (2010); Martín Jiménez (2012), p. 272 noting 'that *Cadbury Schweppes* added important nuances to the *Centros* line of case law'.
21. This argument is based on Schön (2013b), pp. 350 et seq. Another explanation is given by Cerioni (2010), p. 13: 'it is possible to reconcile *Centros* and *Inspire Art* on the one hand with *Cadbury Schweppes* and *Lammers* on the other hand, by noting that the CJEU has simply been expressing the distinction between mere circumvention and abuse with a different approach. On the one hand, in *Centros* and *Inspire Art*, it has done so with a "positive" language, by indicating, in essence, *when* a circumvention *is allowed* and by specifying that it is allowed *when* it does not cause a prejudice to third parties' protection. On the other hand, in *Cadbury Schweppes* and *Lammers*, it has done so with a "negative" language by indicating, ultimately, when a circumvention - "wholly artificial arrangement" - is not allowed and by clarifying that it is not allowed when it *only* causes *a prejudice* to the financial interests (tax revenues) of the Member State of origin, which is the case in the absence of a genuine economic activity in the host State'.
22. CJEU, C-106/16, *Polbud*, at para. 43: 'as EU law currently stands, each Member State has the power to define the connecting factor required of a company if that company is to be regarded as incorporated in accordance with its national legislation'.

it refers to the doctrine of 'wholly artificial arrangements' developed by the CJEU,[23] which as already shown in the previous section since *Cadbury Schweppes* has a substance-oriented content. The GAARs in the IRD and MD do not refer to non-genuine arrangements (Article 5(2) of the IRD and Article 15(1) of the MD). However, national measures implementing the directives' GAARs have been tested by the CJEU as to their conformity with EU law based on the concept of 'wholly artificial arrangements'.[24] Finally, the Shell Entities Directive includes a substance test. Although the Shell Entities Directive has not been finally passed, it can be submitted that it substantiates the CJEU doctrine on wholly artificial arrangements.[25]

From this, it follows that secondary EU law, and especially the CFC rule in the ATAD and the Shell Entities Directive, include substance requirements.

II Scope of the Investigation

Now, these substance requirements as well as the ones in primary EU law do not have the same content. In fact, it can be said that the content of the notion of a 'wholly artificial arrangement' and therewith of the substance requirements in EU tax law are dependent on which rule is being abused. If, for example, the IRD is being abused, one needs to focus on whether the loan or licensing transaction falling under the scope of the IRD is artificial, and thus should not be eligible for the IRD's benefits. And in order to ascertain whether the loan or licensing transaction in question is artificial, one must concentrate on the substance that is needed for the transaction in question, for example, if the company providing the loan has personnel with the appropriate know-how for this transaction.[26]

What is being said here is that there is no one-size-fits-all concept of wholly artificial arrangements. In fact, the content and scope of the test should be dependent

23. Weber (2016), pp. 113 et seq. Other commentators argue that the term 'non-genuine' refers to substance requirements. *See* Tavares/Bogenschneider (2015), p. 486; Debelva/Luts (2015), p. 227; Leukefeld (2018), pp. 170-171.
24. Regarding the IRD, CJEU, C-115/16, C-118/16, C-119/16 and C-299/16, *N Luxembourg 1*, para. 109; regarding the MD, CJEU, 5 Jul. 2007, C-321/05, *Hans Markus Kofoed v. Skatteministeriet*, ECLI:EU:C:2007:408, para. 38; CJEU, 20 May 2010, C-352/08, *Modehuis A. Zwijnenburg BV v. Staatssecretaris van Financiën*, ECLI:EU:C:2010:282, para. 43; CJEU, 10 Nov. 2011, C-126/10, *Foggia – Sociedade Gestora de Participações Sociais SA v. Secretário de Estado dos Assuntos Fiscais*, ECLI:EU:C:2011:718, paras 33 and 50; CJEU, 8 Mar. 2017, C-14/16, *Euro Park Service v. Ministre des Finances et des Comptes publics*, ECLI: EU:C:2017:177, para. 53. Although these cases do not refer to 'wholly artificial arrangements' but to 'normal' or 'valid commercial reasons' it is submitted that the latter terms also refer to a wholly artificial arrangement. *See* Martín Jiménez (2012), p. 281: 'reference to "normal" in *Kofoed* could be read to mean that tax driven transactions where there are no "artificial" elements, where form is aligned with the substance, should be protected either in the context of the anti-abuse clause of the Directive or from the perspective of the fundamental freedoms. *Zwijnenburg* and *Foggia* permit the further development of this reasoning'. *See also* Pötgens/Straathof (2016), p. 617.
25. *See* von Brocke (2022), p. 198 also raising the question whether the Shell Entities Directive is immunized against primary EU law.
26. On this example, *see* Marres/de Groot (2021), p. 335.

on the rule that is being abused.[27] Thus, there are varying substance requirements in EU tax law. Nevertheless, only the ones in the CFC rule in the ATAD are dealt with. This is because CFC rules particularly target subsidiaries, which constitute the scope of the work. However, one should not forget that a Member State implementing secondary EU law, as the ATAD is, must respect primary EU law. And as already shown in section A.I.2. of this chapter, the CJEU has already formulated substance requirements that a subsidiary must fulfil in order for it to genuinely have access to the fundamental freedoms, and therewith a national measure denying them that access to be classified as unjustified. So if the Member States when implementing the ATAD apply stricter rules than the ones allowed by the CJEU based on its jurisprudence, then they are in breach of primary EU law. In other words, primary EU law forms the framework within which national measures – also the ones implementing secondary EU law – can develop. It is thus important to know what the framework is.

A caveat may apply, though. In particular, it can be argued that, as long as the ATAD includes minimum standards,[28] it may imply an exhaustive harmonization of CFC rules in the EU.[29,30] And the CJEU has ruled that in cases of exhaustive harmonization, the Member States' implementing measures can only be assessed as to

27. In this vein, De Broe/Gommers (2019), p. 284: 'as the objectives of the PSD or IRD are not the same as those underlying the TFEU freedom of establishment for which economic substance in the State of secondary establishment is required, the fact that the interposed company carries on a considerable economic activity and has commercial substance does by no means shield it off from a claim that it abuses the IRD if e.g., a back-to-back loan is routed through that company. The same goes a fortiori where a company is interposed on a large scale in such financial conduit arrangements and uses staff, premises and equipment for that activity'. *See also* Drüen (2020), p. 103; Marres/de Groot (2021), p. 335; Danon et al. (2021), p. 495. *See also* already before the *Danish withholding tax* cases Rudolf (2012), p. 168; Poulsen (2013), p. 239: 'In order to understand the reference made to "premises, staff and equipment" in Cadbury Schweppes and the relationship with the notion of "wholly artificial arrangements", it is therefore probably relevant to focus on what is really at stake in Cadbury Schweppes and similar cases concerning Controlled Foreign Company (CFC) legislation.' Lenaerts (2015), p. 350.

    It must be underlined, though, that the CJEU has forwarded another reasoning in the *Danish withholding tax* cases: 'any finding that there is an abusive or fraudulent arrangement, justifying the inapplicability of Directive 2003/49 [IRD], would also result in the fundamental freedoms guaranteed by the FEU Treaty being inapplicable'. CJEU, C-115/16, C-118/16, C-119/16 and C-299/16, *N Luxembourg 1*, at para. 177.

28. Pursuant to Article 3 of the ATAD: 'This Directive shall not preclude the application of domestic or agreement-based provisions aimed at safeguarding a higher level of protection for domestic corporate tax bases.'

29. *See* Smit (2019), s. 12.3.: 'given the express *de minimis* nature of the ATAD (see Article 3 ATAD) and the fact that it leaves Member States ample room to make diverging choices when implementing its provisions, the ATAD does not represent exhaustive harmonization, just as little as the anti-avoidance reservation of competence in the Merger Directive at issue in *Euro Park Service* represented exhaustive harmonization. It is clear, however, that the *minimum* standard is (meant to be) *common* and therefore does not leave any room for national lenience. Therefore, national implementation law conforming to that minimum will in principle only be assessed by the Court in the light of that minimum'. In a similar vein, Richter et al. (2020), p. 701; Fehling (2023), p. 596.

30. Another argument for the 'immunization' of secondary law against primary law, has been raised by Englisch (2020b), p. 531, although admittedly not referring to the ATAD. Joachim Englisch, in his commentary of the *Danish withholding tax cases*, argues that the interpretation of special abuse clauses in directives, for example, the MD in *Kofoed*, 'is questionable ... because it ignores the legislature's express preference for more or less strict standards to combat abusive practices'.

their conformity with EU law against the secondary EU law they are implementing.[31] In other words, measures implementing secondary EU law including exhaustive harmonization are thus being 'immunized' against primary EU law.

But even if the CFC rule in the ATAD implies an exhaustive harmonization of the CFC rules in the EU, the content of substance requirements in primary EU law is important for three reasons. First, it is not clear at all whether such an exhaustive harmonization has taken place; many authors deny this.[32] Second, even if this is the case, the Member States going beyond the minimum standards established in the ATAD are obliged to respect primary EU law, and thus the measures going beyond the minimum standards are not immunized.[33] Third, and most importantly, primary EU law constitutes the basis on which secondary EU law, and thus the ATAD, must be interpreted.

It can be concluded that this work deals with substance in the EU tax law context as construed by the CJEU for the purposes of the freedom of establishment and movement of capital and as laid down in the CFC rule in the ATAD. In the analysis, the latest development in the EU tax law context, i.e., the Shell Entities Directive, has also been included, as it can be submitted that it substantiates the CJEU doctrine on wholly artificial arrangements. But before delving into the analysis, it is important to know how CFC rules function. The mechanics of the Shell Entities Directive have already been analysed in section B.III.4. of the introduction and its function is easy to comprehend (similar to DTC treaty shopping rules, it denies benefits claimed by conduit companies), so that no further analysis is necessary.

III Function and Mechanism of CFC Rules in the EU Tax Law Context

1 *Function of CFC Rules*

In order to explain the function of CFC rules, let us revert to the case study laid down in section B.II. of the introduction. There, PaCo sets up a subsidiary in a low tax state, SubCo, which holds an IP developed by the two entities (SubCo only provides funding) and licenses it to other highly taxed subsidiaries who need it for their manufacturing activities. SubCo receives royalties and 'parks' the income corresponding to them in the

---

This opinion overlooks the hierarchy of legal norms. In the domestic context, for example, would a special legal rule be immune against constitutional law because of 'the legislature's express preference'?.

31. CJEU, 5 Oct. 1977, Case 5/77, *Tedeschi v. Denkavit*, ECLI:EU:C:1977:144, para. 35. In tax cases, *see* CJEU, C-14/16, *Euro Park Service*, at para. 19; CJEU, 7 Sep. 2017, C-6/16, *Eqiom SAS, formerly Holcim France SAS, Enka SA v. Ministre des Finances et des comptes publics*, ECLI:EU:C:2017:641, para. 15; CJEU, 20 Dec. 2017, C-504/16 and C-613/16, *Deister and Juhler Holding v. Bundeszentralamt für Steuern*, ECLI:EU:C:2017:1009, para. 45.
32. Hey (2017), p. 250; Gutmann et al. (2017), p. 19 arguing that '[t]he ATAD does not aim to harmonize all the anti-avoidance rules of the Member States'. Geringer (2020), pp. 449-450; Nyström (2021), p. 224; Haslehner/Pantazatou (2022), p. 14. Only in relation to the freedom of capital Danon (2018b), s. 17.5.2.1.; Danon (2018c), s. 10.3.1.; Schönfeld (2019), p. 400; Heckerodt (2019), p. 691.
33. *See* Hey (2017), p. 253; Schönfeld/Ellenrieder (2019), p. 259; Smit (2019), s. 12.3.; Govind/Zolles (2020), para. 647; Haslehner/Pantazatou (2022), p. 14.

low-tax jurisdiction (SubCo state). The residence state of PaCo (PaCo state) cannot tax SubCo's income because SubCo is a corporation and thus a separate taxpayer (section B.I. of the introduction). The PaCo state can only tax SubCo's income upon repatriation in the form of dividends if it applies a credit system. If, however, the PaCo state employs an exemption system, the dividend payment from SubCo to PaCo is exempted from PaCo state's tax base; the PaCo state may never get to tax the royalty income.

It becomes apparent that by setting up SubCo, PaCo either defers taxation in the PaCo state if the latter employs a credit system with advantages that we have already seen,[34] or it avoids taxation in the PaCo state completely if the PaCo state employs an exemption system (or switches from a credit system to an exemption system while the royalty income is parked in the SubCo state). Accordingly, depending on which system for dividend taxation is applied, CFC rules combat either the abuse of deferral (if a credit system is employed) or the abuse of exemption (if an exemption system is applied).[35]

2 Mechanism of CFC Rules in the EU Tax Law Context

The previous section explained that CFC rules are employed as a means to tackle deferral or exemption abuse. It has already been analysed in section B.III.2. how these rules work and no further explanation is necessary. However, it is important to understand what role substance requirements play in the CFC rule in the ATAD. In particular, according to Article 7(2)(a) of the ATAD the CFC rule and its legal consequence, i.e., the inclusion of the undistributed passive income of the subsidiary in the parent's tax base, does not apply 'where the controlled foreign company carries on a substantive economic activity supported by staff, equipment, assets and premises, as evidenced by relevant facts and circumstances'. So the existence of 'staff, equipment, assets and premises', i.e., substance elements, rules out the application of Article 7(2)(a) of the ATAD.

The same holds true for the second version of the CFC rule in the ATAD, Article 7(2)(b). This offers Member States an alternative option to Article 7(2)(a). In order for Article 7(2)(b) to apply 'the non-distributed income of the entity or permanent establishment [must] aris[e] from non-genuine arrangements' and 'an arrangement or a series thereof shall be regarded as non-genuine to the extent that the entity or permanent establishment would not own the assets or would not have undertaken the risks which generate all, or part of, its income if it were not controlled by a company where the significant people functions, which are relevant to those assets and risks, are carried out and are instrumental in generating the controlled company's income'. So again, we see that a company which has significant people functions (SPF) commensurate with the assets it owns and the risks it undertakes is considered a genuine

34. *See* above s. B.I. of the introduction and n. 30 there.
35. *See* Arnold (2012), pp. 475 et seq.; Dourado (2015), p. 352; Canè (2017), p. 525; Blum (2018), p. 302; Arnold (2019), p. 633.

arrangement and thus its income is not subject to the CFC rule in Article 7(2)(b) of the ATAD.

In sum, both versions of the ATAD are exempt from their scope subsidiaries fulfilling substance requirements.

B THE CONTENT OF THE SUBSTANCE REQUIREMENT IN THE EU TAX LAW CONTEXT

I Opening Remarks

1 Purpose of the Substance Orientation in the EU Tax Law Context

A subsidiary having substance is, on the one hand, considered by the CJEU as having been set up for legitimate and non-abusive purposes, therefore it is an eligible bearer of the fundamental freedoms and discriminating national measures are not justifiable. On the other hand, a subsidiary having substance is also carved out from the ambit of the CFC rule in the ATAD by the EU legislatures, thus implying that such a company cannot have been established for deferral or exemption abuse purposes. So both the CJEU and the EU legislature reckon that a subsidiary with substance cannot have been set up for abusive purposes.

Just like in the case of substance requirements for the purposes of DTC treaty shopping rules (section B.IV.3. of Chapter 3), substance in the EU tax law context is used as a proxy to exclude nexus abuse. A subsidiary with substance is assumed to be a legitimate bearer of the fundamental freedom of establishment by the CJEU and a legitimate bearer of the benefits of deferral or exemption by the EU legislatures; it is, e contrario, assumed not to have been set up by abusing residence rules in the state of establishment in order to enjoy the benefits of being a bearer of the fundamental freedom of establishment and eligible for deferral or exemption.[36] So there is a parallel purpose of the substance orientation in DTC treaty shopping rules and in the EU tax law context.

This also is unambiguous if we consider that DTC treaty shopping rules and CFC rules target the same situation. Christiana HJI Panayi puts it on the spot:

> In the treaty-shopping context, what is effectively at issue is the economic substance of the intermediary company and whether it performs a certain role other than just being a pass-through. In other words, the salient question is whether the intermediary company ... is a mere shadow of the ultimate recipient company ... that controls the intermediary. In the CFC scenario, what is at issue is whether the controlled foreign entity is a shadow of another company in a high-tax jurisdiction. In other words, the salient question is whether the high-tax company

36. That CFC rules combat nexus abuse can be confirmed if we consider a thought experiment: imagine corporate tax residence is coordinated around the world. Would there be a reason to resort to CFC rules? *See* Maisto (2014), s. 1: 'Realizing worldwide coordination in respect of corporate tax residence would, in principle, reduce the scope for the tax arbitrage that makes controlled foreign company (CFC) rules necessary.'

> controls the entity to such an extent so as to render it a mere shelter of the profits that in substance belong to the high-tax company. Therefore, the only distinguishing factor is the entity for whose benefit the allegedly 'sham' company exists.[37]

Intuitively, one may ask whether substance requirements in these two contexts are or should be the same. Surprisingly, the same question arises with regard to corporate residence. In particular, authors have already observed the parallels in the control that domestic courts perform in order to ascertain the substance-oriented residence of a corporation with the control that the CJEU performs in order to affirm the existence of substance and thereby deny the abuse of the fundamental freedom of establishment.[38]

In sum, the substance requirements in the EU tax law context referring to subsidiaries function as an assumption that nexus abuse does not exist. Since substance requirements in the DTC treaty shopping context have the same function, it is interesting to see whether their content matches. The same holds true with regard to substance requirements in the POEM.

2 *Structure of the Analysis*

The next sections dissect the content of substance in the fundamental freedoms and the CFC rule in the ATAD. The relevant freedoms are the freedom of establishment and the freedom of movement of capital, whereby a separate section is devoted to each freedom (section B.II. on the freedom of establishment and section B.III. on the freedom of movement of capital). Section B.IV. deals with substance in the CFC rule in the ATAD. This order of the analysis is justified if one takes into account the mechanics of EU law: secondary law must be interpreted in conformity with primary law, i.e., the fundamental freedoms (section A.II. of this chapter).

Still, the analysis of substance requirements in the Shell Entities Directive is integrated into the analysis of the substance requirement in the context of the freedom of establishment because, as already stated in section A.I.3. of this chapter, it substantiates the CJEU doctrine as wholly artificial arrangements and therefore can be consulted when interpreting its content. Another reason for not dealing with the Shell Entities Directive in a separate section, as done with respect to the ATAD, is that the former has not been yet finally passed.

---

37. Panayi (2007), p. 191. *See also* Martín Jiménez (2002), p. 625. This author also notes the parallel between treaty shopping and CFC rules.
38. Schön (2013a), pp. 11-12 citing Thiele (2011), pp. 203-204; Smit (2014), p. 262 noticing a parallel to the CMC and POM.

    It must be noted that all authors cited do not notice a parallel between substance orientation in the CFC rules and the POEM but one between CFC rules and *domestic* substance-oriented residence criteria. Although relevant for this work is the POEM and not the domestic substance-oriented residence criteria, the commonalities between DTC and domestic substance-oriented residence criteria (s. B.I.2. of Ch. 2) justify the assertion that the same parallel exists with regard to CFC rules and the POEM.

II Content of the Substance Requirement in the Context of the Freedom of Establishment

If a parent genuinely sets up a subsidiary in another Member State, it then does not abuse the freedom of establishment. In other words, if the freedom of establishment is genuinely invoked, the establishment (i.e., the subsidiary set up) is not wholly artificial. This finding is closely related to the CJEU's understanding of substance. As we saw in section A.I.2. of this chapter, the CJEU in *Cadbury Schweppes* requires substance for both the genuine invocation of the freedom of establishment (i.e., whether an establishment falls under the *scope* of the freedom of establishment) and in order to exclude an establishment as being a wholly artificial arrangement (and thus reject the *justification* of domestic measures targeting it). So if one knows when a subsidiary has substance and thus the establishment falls within the scope of the freedom of establishment, one can e contrario also detect which cases are wholly artificial and thus national measures targeting them are justified.

As to when the freedom of establishment is genuinely invoked, the CJEU in *Factortame*[39] and following this ruling in *Cadbury Schweppes*[40] has developed a formula (often referred to as the 'Cadbury formula') providing guidance in this respect:

> [T]he concept of establishment within the meaning of the Treaty provisions on freedom of establishment involves the actual pursuit of an economic activity through a fixed establishment in that State for an indefinite period.[41]

From that definition, one can deduct two requirements of the freedom of establishment:

(1) the actual pursuit of an economic activity; and
(2) the existence of a fixed establishment through which this activity is being pursued.

The first requirement corresponds to the functional element of substance, according to the definition of substance used in this work, while the second corresponds to the personal and objective elements. Accordingly, in section B.II.1, the content of the requirement of an 'actual pursuit of an economic activity' for the purposes of the freedom of establishment is analysed, and thus the content of the functional element of substance. In section B.II.2. the content of the term 'fixed establishment' is interpreted, and thus the content of the personal and objective elements is dissected.

---

39. CJEU, 25 Jul. 1991, C-221/89, *The Queen v. Secretary of State for Transport, ex parte Factortame Ltd and others*, ECLI:EU:C:1991:320.
40. CJEU, C-196/04, *Cadbury Schweppes*.
41. *Ibid.*, at para. 54 with reference to CJEU, C-221/89, *Factortame*, at para. 20.

1 *The Functional Element of the Substance Requirement in the Context of the Freedom of Establishment*

a *Qualitative Sub-element of the Functional Element of Substance*

aa 'The Actual Pursuit of an Economic Activity'

Which activities are considered an 'actual pursuit of an economic activity' for the purposes of the freedom of establishment? For example, do the activities of an SPV, i.e., only those relating to the acquisition of another company, qualify as such? Or do intra-group transactions constitute the actual pursuit of an economic activity? And can a loss-making subsidiary also actually pursue an economic activity?

These are questions the answers to which, although not directly provided by the CJEU, can be deducted from its judgments. But before answering these questions, a preliminary issue has to be clarified. Whose activities are we discussing? Just like we did with regard to the substance requirements in the POEM (section B.II.1.a.aa. of Chapter 1), we may at this point also ask whether the CJEU takes a stand-alone or a group perspective. In other words, are the subsidiary's activities the only relevant ones, or can the activities of other group companies also be considered? A similar although distinct issue is whether the activities are considered a whole, that is, in their totality, or whether the artificiality relates to individual transactions/business divisions.

Whose Economic Activities Matter?

Take the following example. Parent A sets up subsidiary B. B's activity is restricted to holding shares in active sub-subsidiaries which carry on substantial economic activities. When establishing whether A has genuinely set up B, do the activities carried on by the sub-subsidiaries play a role (that would be the group perspective) or is it only the activity of B (holding the shares in the sub-subsidiaries) that is considered (that would be the stand-alone perspective)?

There are conflicting opinions in the literature on this issue. Luc De Broe has espoused the group perspective:

> [U]nder the current and settled status of the CJEU's case law, a passive investment company, letter box company and the like can legitimately exercise their right of secondary establishment by setting up branches or subsidiaries in another Member State which conduct economic activities there.[42]

Daniël Smit has taken the opposite view:

> [I]t is submitted that the 'substance' test should, in any case, be performed at the level of the controlled foreign entity only, and that the activities carried out at the lower level of the group companies held by that foreign entity should not be taken into account.[43]

42. De Broe (2008), p. 859.
43. Smit (2014), p. 263. Following Smit, Pötgens/Straathof (2016), p. 616; Leukefeld (2018), pp. 166-167.

So where does the CJEU stand? In *Deister and Juhler Holding*,[44] confirmed by its subsequent decision in *GS*,[45] the CJEU stated that:

> [T]he finding of such an arrangement [referring to a wholly artificial arrangement] requires that, on a case-by-case basis, an overall assessment of the relevant situation be conducted, based on factors including the organisational, economic or other substantial features of the group of companies to which the parent company in question belongs and the structures and strategies of the group.[46]

Some authors have interpreted this passage as an endorsement by the CJEU of the group perspective.[47] Other commentators *see Deister and Juhler Holding* as a confirmation that the activities of other group companies in the host state (henceforth reference is made to the host state and not the subsidiary's residence state) can be also considered.[48] The *Danish withholding tax cases*, though, and in particular 'T Danmark fully lets go of that group idea – a novelty by the way – since the CJEU assesses purely at individual level whether the party receiving the dividend can be regarded as a conduit company, irrespective of its function in the group as such.'[49]

It is submitted that the latter view is the one that is mostly in line with the purpose of the CJEU doctrine of wholly artificial arrangements. This is to counter nexus abuse in the EU (section B.I.1. of this chapter). By endorsing the group perspective, the CJEU would create leeway for the exact arrangements that it purports to counter. Imagine parent company A, resident in a Member State, say Germany, sets up subsidiary B, also resident in a Member State, say the Netherlands. It does so in order to channel profits to another subsidiary C, resident in a tax haven outside the European Union, with which the Netherlands but not Germany has a DTC. Parent A knows that it has nothing to do other than merely transfer to B the shares in active subsidiaries within the European Union in order for B to be considered a genuine arrangement. B remains a letterbox company, which is what the CJEU imperatively has put up a fight against.[50]

This example makes apparent that the purpose of the wholly artificial arrangements doctrine calls for a stand-alone perspective. Admittedly, a parallel with the substance requirements in international tax law, also following a stand-alone perspective, can be made here.[51]

A caveat applies, though: cases where a subsidiary without any economic activities resides in the same Member State as an operational company of the same group may not be abusive. This, however, is not because the activities of the group

44. CJEU, C-504/16 and C-613/16, *Deister and Juhler Holding*.
45. CJEU, 14 Jun. 2018, C-440/17, *GS v. Bundeszentralamt für Steuern*, ECLI:EU:C:2018:437.
46. CJEU, C-504/16 and C-613/16, *Deister and Juhler Holding*, at para. 74; CJEU, C–440/17, *GS*, at para. 57.
47. Kraft (2019), p. 634; Hoor (2019), pp. 599-600; Benz/Böhmer (2022), p. 1036.
48. Beutel/Oppel (2018), p. 1472; Heinsen et al. (2020), p. 733. Hoor et al. (2022), p. 236 stating that there is 'CJEU case law that an entity may legitimately rely on the resources and infrastructure of another group entity that is resident in the same jurisdiction.' *See* already before *Deister and Juhler Holding* Scheipers/Linn (2011), p. 605.
49. Van Hulten/Korving (2019), p. 797.
50. CJEU, C-196/04, *Cadbury Schweppes*, at para. 68.
51. The POEM (s. B.II.1.a.aa. of Ch. 1), the ALP (s. A.I.1. of Ch. 2), the active conduct of a business (s. B.II.1.a.aa. of Ch. 3), and the PPMC (s. B.III.1.a. of Ch. 3) adopt the stand-alone perspective.

companies are taken as a whole, but because the abusive intention may be negated:[52] if the intention were to save taxes, then this could have happened without the interposition of the subsidiary since the tax-saving could happen through the operational company. The Shell Entities Directive supports this finding since it excludes from the reporting obligation, the first step of the substance test,[53] 'undertakings that have the main activity of holding shares in operational businesses in the same Member State while their beneficial owners are also resident for tax purposes in the same Member State' (Article 6(2)(c) of the Shell Entities Directive). It must be admitted, though, that the requirements are stricter because not only the holding subsidiary and the operational sub-subsidiaries but also the parent must be resident in the same Member State.[54]

Activities Taken as a Whole or Transactional Appraisal?

Imagine parent A, resident in a Member State, say Germany, has a subsidiary B in another Member State, say the Netherlands. B has two functions: on the one hand, it distributes goods manufactured by A around the European Union. On the other hand, it holds shares in a third state sub-subsidiary, C, resident in the Cayman Islands, with which only the Netherlands and not Germany have a DTC. So B has two functions: the distribution function and the 'conduit' function. It is obvious that B's distribution function is an actual economic activity deserving protection under the freedom of establishment. Does this suffice to also regard the more 'suspicious' activity, the holding of shares in the sub-subsidiary, as genuine? In other words, are the subsidiary's activities taken as a whole (holistic approach) or is every activity/division/sector/transaction considered in and of itself (transactional approach) for the purposes of the wholly artificial arrangements test? We have seen, for instance, that for the purposes of the POEM, a holistic approach is applied, thus leading to a spillover effect (section B.II.1.a.aa. of Chapter 1).

---

52. So German case law. *See* Finanzgericht of Köln, 23 Jan. 2019, 2 K 1315/13, EFG (2019), p. 1764 (at para. 25) with reference to case law of the Bundesfinanzhof the so-called *Hilversum II* decision. *See* Bundesfinanzhof, 31 May 2005, I R 74, 88/04, BStBl. II (2006), p. 118. The decision of the *Finanzgericht* of Köln has been reversed by the Bundesfinanzhof, which, however, adhered to the *Hilversum II* doctrine but pointed that the *Finanzgericht* of Köln wrongfully accepted that its requirements have been fulfilled in the case at hand because it did not conduct a comprehensive examination of the relevant group relationships. *See* Bundesfinanzhof, 10 Oct. 2021, I R 27/19, Deutsches Steuerrecht 21 (2022), p. 1038 (at para. 29). *See also* the recent decision Finanzgericht of Köln, 22 Sep. 2022, 6 K 2661/18, EFG (2023), p. 89 (at para. 31).

    See also the Ter Haar Expert Committee of the Dutch Ministry of Finance, although with the additional condition that 'a relationship exists between the activities of the active company in the Netherlands and the income received by the holding company'. *See* Offermanns (2022), s. 7.

    In the context of the PPT, van den Hurk (2021), p. 291 argues that such cases are in accordance with the object and purpose of a DTC, i.e., exclude the fulfilment of the objective element.

53. On the mechanics of the Shell Entities Directive *see* above s. B.III.4. of the Introduction.
54. This strictness is criticized by Benz/Böhmer (2022), p. 1036, n. 39. By contrast, Pistone et al. (2022), s. 4.3.3. take issue with Article 6(2)(c) of the Shell Entities Directive, as 'is based on a flawed assumption: that, internally, there are no advantages in setting up a shell entity'.

This issue has been extensively discussed in literature with proponents of both the holistic[55] and the transactional approach.[56] The CJEU in the *Danish withholding tax* cases seems to have ruled in favour of the transactional approach.[57]

In the author's opinion, one needs to differentiate the levels upon which the enquiry is made. Take the example from above to elucidate this. In the example, there are two arrangements that need to be evaluated based on the wholly artificial arrangements doctrine: on the one hand, the establishment of a subsidiary which is intended to render legitimate activities and, on the other, the transfer to it of the shares in another subsidiary so that profits can be channelled into it. The wholly artificial arrangements doctrine must be applied separately to each arrangement. So at the level of the parent, the wholly artificial arrangement test follows the transactional approach: it applies to the establishment of a subsidiary separately just like it applies to the transfer of shares separately.

But when we control whether the subsidiary constitutes a wholly artificial arrangement, it must be submitted that a subsidiary is either artificial or not.[58] It cannot be partly artificial, in contrast to 'an arrangement such as a distribution of profits [which] "may comprise more than one step or part" and, therefore, could be only partly genuine'.[59] This is a similar line of thinking as the one applied when arguing in favour of the holistic approach in the POEM (section B.II.1.a.aa. of Chapter 1). Now, if the subsidiary has some artificial transactions of its own, like in our example B's conduit function, and one wants to tackle them, this may happen in the following way: the transfer of the shares to B can be regarded as abusive by applying a unilateral anti-abuse rule which then in its turn could be controlled regarding its conformity with the wholly artificial arrangements doctrine. Alternatively, if no unilateral anti-abuse rule exists, according to the CJEU doctrine established in the *Danish withholding tax* cases, the Member State in question must directly apply the wholly artificial arrangements doctrine on the transaction to judge whether the latter is abusive.[60]

This differentiated approach means for the purposes of this work that the wholly artificial arrangements doctrine in the context of the freedom of establishment employs a transactional approach at the level of the parent and a holistic approach at the level

55. Kuźniacki (2016), p. 158; Richter et al. (2020), pp. 698-699; Kanduth-Kristen et al. (2021), p. 544.
56. Most prominently the ex-presiding judge of the first senate of the Bundesfinanzhof Wacker (2018), p. 888 commenting on the seminal 'Cyprus-case' Bundesfinanzhof, 13 Jun. 2018, I R 94/15, BStBl. II (2020), p. 755. *See also* Richter (2019), p. 339.
57. CJEU, C–116/16 and C–117/16, *T Danmark*, at para. 104; CJEU, C-115/16, C-118/16, C-119/16 and C-299/16, *N Luxembourg 1*, at para. 131: 'The absence of actual economic activity must, *in the light of the specific features of the economic activity in question*' (emphasis added). Also understanding this statement by the CJEU as an acceptance of a transactional approach, Englisch (2020a), para. 7.252; Englisch (2020b), p. 529; Anzinger (2020), p. 102.
58. Ekinci (2023), p. 196.
59. Kokolia/Chatziioakeimidou (2015), p. 154.
60. CJEU, C–116/16 and C–117/16, *T Danmark*, at para. 92; CJEU, C-115/16, C-118/16, C-119/16 and C-299/16, *N Luxembourg 1*, at para. 120: 'the Member States must, therefore, refuse to grant the advantage resulting from Directive 2003/49, in accordance with the general principle that abusive practices are prohibited, under which EU law cannot cover abusive practices of economic operators'. *See* the critique on this doctrine mounted by Schön (2019).

of the subsidiary. In our example, subsidiary B would qualify as rendering an actual economic activity, irrespective of the more suspicious conduit function. It becomes apparent that this approach would create leeway for tax arbitrage: MNEs could avoid the application of the wholly artificial arrangements doctrine by transferring 'suspicious' functions to active subsidiaries. This is the reason why this work rejected some pages back the group perspective for the purposes of the wholly artificial arrangements doctrine in the context of the freedom of establishment. However, if these suspicious activities are abusive, they may be tackled by applying the wholly artificial arrangements doctrine solely in relation to them, as described in the previous paragraph.

This analysis does not contradict the CJEU judgment in the *Danish withholding tax cases*, which, as already stated, seems to favour the transactional approach. This is because, in the *Danish withholding tax* cases, the CJEU referred in general to what constitutes abuse of rights.[61] In its analysis, it admittedly underlined that '[t]he absence of actual economic activity [pointing to a wholly artificial arrangement] must, [be ascertained] in the light of the specific features of the economic activity in question'. But with this passage, the CJEU did not endorse the transactional approach. It just simply clarified that, as a general matter, each arrangement must be tested in and of itself as to its conformity with EU law. If it is the freedom of establishment that is being abused, then the arrangement in question is the establishment of a subsidiary. The artificiality of this arrangement must be ascertained 'in the light of the specific features' of this activity. If it is the IRD that is being abused, the loan agreement is under control, again considering the specific features of this economic activity.

Overall, the wholly artificial arrangements test in relation to the freedom of establishment employs a holistic approach at the level of the subsidiary, whereby all activities of a subsidiary are considered. This is in line with CJEU case law, since the CJEU in the *Danish withholding tax* cases did not endorse, as literature supports, the transactional approach, but merely clarified that every arrangement must be assessed as to its conformity with the wholly artificial arrangements doctrine separately and considering its specific features.

What Kind of Economic Activities Are Relevant?

Does it matter that the subsidiary 'only', for example, administers property, e.g., shares in other group companies, and does not carry out a more 'hands on' activity, like manufacturing goods? Or do preparatory/auxiliary activities constitute the pursuit of an actual economic activity? These questions point to the overarching question raised above: what kind of economic activities are relevant for the purposes of the wholly artificial arrangements test?

61. The CJEU reformulates the questions referred by the Danish court. It answers the question as to the constituent elements of *any* abuse of rights, and thus lays down general criteria of the abuse of rights doctrine and specific ones, for example, in relation to a specific freedom. *See* CJEU, C-116/16 and C-117/16, *T Danmark*, at para. 67; CJEU, C-115/16, C-118/16, C-119/16 and C-299/16, *N Luxembourg 1*, at para. 82: 'the second topic addressed by the questions concerns the constituent elements of *any* abuse of rights and the conditions for proving it'. (Emphasis added).

According to the prevailing opinion in German-speaking literature, there should not be any qualitative threshold as regards the functions that the subsidiary performs, since the CJEU has not made any reference thereto.[62] Other commentators have supported this position with the additional argument that cross-border establishment of subsidiaries should be treated in the same way as domestic ones.[63] The argument then goes along the following lines: 'why should the German subsidiary of a French parent perform a specific kind of activity, while the German subsidiary of a German parent can be free to do whatever it wants, even be a letterbox without any activity?'

The lack of a qualitative threshold contradicts the substance requirements in the DTC treaty shopping rules, which also intends to prevent nexus abuse (section B.I.1. of Chapter 3). There (section B.II.1.a.aa. of Chapter 3), we saw that certain activities are considered per se abusive. These are:

(i) operating as a holding company;
(ii) providing overall supervision or administration of a group of companies;
(iii) providing group financing (including cash pooling); or
(iv) making or managing investments, unless these activities are carried on by a bank or (list financial institutions similar to banks that the Contracting States agree to treat as such), insurance enterprise or registered securities dealer in the ordinary course of its business as such.

If we accept the above-mentioned position of the literature that no qualitative threshold exists for the activities carried on by the subsidiary, then an exclusion along the lines of substance requirements in the DTC treaty shopping rules could not be accepted. Commentators have argued against[64] the notion that companies only performing passive activities, like the ones enlisted above irrefutably regarded as abusive for the purposes of the substance requirements in DTC treaty shopping rules, constitute fictitious establishments. CJEU[65] and Bundesfinanzhof in the *Cyprus* case[66] case law have also been interpreted in this vein.[67] De Broe[68] also accepts that companies engaged in passive activities can avail themselves of the freedom of establishment and

62. Köhler/Eicker (2006), p. 1872; Köhler/Eicker (2007), p. 333; Hey (2008), p. 179; Rudolf (2012), pp. 172-173; Haase (2016), p. 769; Leukefeld (2018), p. 142; Ekinci (2023), p. 163.
63. Gosch (2008), p. 608; Lang/Heidenbauer (2008), p. 608; Thiele (2011), pp. 129-130; Schlücke (2019), p. 43. *Contra* Schönfeld/Wassermeyer (2017), para. 468.
64. Köhler/Eicker (2006), p. 1872; Köhler/Haun (2008), p. 79; Gosch (2008), p. 612; Robert/Tof (2011), p. 438; Thiele (2011), p. 130, n. 600; Haase (2016), p. 768; Lehfeldt (2016), para. 182.22; Leukefeld (2018), p. 142; Moreno González (2021), p. 1007.
65. CJEU, C-504/16 and C-613/16, *Deister and Juhler Holding*, at para. 73; CJEU, C–440/17, *GS*, at para. 54.
66. Bundesfinanzhof, I R 94/15 (*Cyprus* case).
67. Kortendick et al. (2018), p. 3035; Ditz et al. (2019), p. 366. Cloer/Hagemann (2019), p. 1234 restrict this finding only with regard to the Bundesfinanzhof case law, underlying that the CJEU decides not based on the facts of the case but based on the legal rules contested in the case in question.
68. De Broe (2008), p. 847 and pp. 851 et seq. In the same vein, Pötgens/Straathof (2016), p. 611. In the same vein, although without citing *De Broe* but Smit (2014), p. 261 and Thömmes/Nakhai (2005), p. 79, Kuźniacki (2017), s. 4.1.2.

are not to be considered wholly artificial arrangements. However, he has differentiated between companies actively pursuing a passive activity (like finance, shareholding, asset management, etc.) and those doing so passively. Where does the CJEU stand?

To begin with, one thing is sure: 'Irrefutable presumptions intended to negate the pursuit of an "economic activity" or its "genuine nature" with regard to some business activities, for example, financial and insurance services or holding companies, must be held to be contrary to EC law.'[69] So if there is a bias against companies performing passive activities, this bias may lead at the most to a rebuttable presumption against such companies.

The CJEU's case law does not permit such a presumption, though. The CJEU in *Cadbury Schweppes* talked about an '*actual*' economic activity;[70] similarly, Advocate General (AG) *Léger* in his Opinion on the case made recourse to the '*genuine nature* of the services provided by the subsidiary'.[71] So what characterizes the quality of the economic activity is that it is 'actual', the word 'actual' is 'used to emphasize something that is real or exists in fact'.[72] Recent CJEU case law uses the same wording. In particular, in *X-GmbH*, a judgment rendered by the Grand Chamber of the CJEU just like the *Danish withholding tax cases* and also on the same day,[73] the CJEU referred to 'a fictitious establishment [that] does not carry out any genuine economic activity in the territory of the host Member State'.[74] Again, the emphasis is on the genuine nature of the activity and nothing else. In the *Danish withholding tax* cases, the CJEU also referred to an '*actual* economic activity'.[75] Finally, the passive holding of assets falls under the freedom of movement of capital.[76] Characterizing subsidiaries that conduct an economic activity consisting of the passive holding of assets and thus making use of the freedom of movement of capital would imply an infringement of the latter freedom.

It is thus submitted that, apart from an actuality control, the substance requirement for the purposes of the abuse of the freedom of establishment does not include stricter requirements, for example, excluding some activities, like the substance requirements in DTC treaty shopping rules (section B.II.1.a.aa. of Chapter 3) or requiring specific functions, like strategic decision-making, which is the case in the POEM and transfer pricing rules (section B.II.1. of Chapter 1 and section B.I.2. of

69. Maisto/Pistone (2008), p. 506. Referring to CJEU, C-196/04, *Cadbury Schweppes*, at para. 70. More recently *see* CJEU, C-504/16 and C-613/16, *Deister and Juhler Holding*, at para. 62.
70. CJEU, C-196/04, *Cadbury Schweppes*, at para. 54.
71. Opinion of Advocate General Léger, 2 May 2006, C-196/04, *Cadbury Schweppes plc and Cadbury Schweppes Overseas Ltd v. Commissioners of Inland Revenue*, ECLI:EU:C:2006:278, para. 113 (emphasis added).
72. https://www.oxfordlearnersdictionaries.com/definition/english/actual. Also understanding the CJEU in *Cadbury Schweppes* in this sense Bärsch/Schneider (2022), p. 84.
73. This is clarified in order to show that the *Danish withholding tax* cases do not change anything to this finding. Although without the same composition, the CJEU ruled on these cases on the same day, under the same presidency, and with the same Rapporteur.
74. CJEU, C-135/17, *X-GmbH*, at para. 82.
75. CJEU, C–116/16 and C–117/16, *T Danmark*, at para. 104; CJEU, C-115/16, C-118/16, C-119/16 and C-299/16, *N Luxembourg 1*, at para. 131 (emphasis added).
76. Schön (2013a), p. 16.

Chapter 2).[77] The intensity of the activity also does not play any role.[78] The Bundesfinanzhof also accepts this view. In the recent *Cyprus* case, the Court did not bother to classify the subsidiary as a genuine establishment, although the subsidiary whose substance was in question only conducted marginal administrative tasks.[79]

Finally, with regard to preparatory activities, it has been disputed whether they constitute in and of themselves an economic activity enabling sufficient integration in the host state and thereby opening access to the freedom of establishment. De Broe states that 'it would be wrong to deny an economic operator access to the right of establishment for the mere reason that the activity conducted in the other state is auxiliary, preparatory or supportive to the core activity conducted elsewhere in the Community'.[80] By contrast, Smit posits that '[a] CFC that carries on activities that do not go beyond straightforward asset management probably does not qualify. The same may be true where a CFC holds a fixed place for preparatory or auxiliary activities only'.[81]

There is state practice that points to the latter interpretation. In particular, in the Netherlands in order for the substance requirements to be fulfilled '[t]he work to be performed by the staff may not be purely ancillary or subordinate', as commentators inform us.[82] If one accepts the interpretation preferred here, concentrating on the actuality of the economic activity and not its specific qualities (decision-making, active or passive, preparatory or core activity), then preparatory activities should qualify as economic activities in the sense of the Cadbury formula.

Do Intra-Group Transactions Constitute the Actual Pursuit of an Economic Activity?

The German Bundesfinanzhof and the German tax administration have cast doubts as to whether intra-group services constitute economic activities for the purposes of the application of the German CFC rule.[83] This opinion, however, has been rejected by the German legislature.[84] As Schön correctly points out, 'the Court [meaning the CJEU] does not accept a general suspicion against intra-group transactions'.[85]

Can a Loss-Making Subsidiary Also Actually Pursue an Economic Activity?

AG Léger regarded as a criterion for evaluating whether a subsidiary actually pursues an economic activity 'the economic value of that activity with regard to the parent company and the entire group'.[86] The question has been posed whether a loss-making subsidiary can actually pursue an economic activity in order to provocatively show that

77. Explicitly so Schön (2013a), p. 15.
78. Pistone et al. (2021), p. 18.
79. *See* Bundesfinanzhof, I R 94/15 (*Cyprus* case); Kortendick et al. (2018), p. 3035.
80. De Broe (2008), p. 845. *See* from the German-speaking literature: Haun et al. (2007), p. 186; Thiele (2011), p. 195; Leukefeld (2018), p. 142.
81. Smit (2019), s. 12.4.3.4.
82. Korving/Wisman (2021), p. 924.
83. Schönfeld/Wassermeyer (2017), para. 474.
84. Lehfeldt (2016), para. 182.23.
85. Schön (2013a), p. 14 (author's unofficial translation) citing CJEU, 13 Mar. 2007, C-524/04, *Test Claimants in the Thin Cap Group Litigation*, ECLI:EU:C:2007:161.
86. Opinion of Advocate General Léger, C-196/04, *Cadbury Schweppes*, at para. 111.

the criterion endorsed by AG Léger can have far-reaching consequences, for example, excluding loss-making subsidiaries from the scope of the freedom of establishment.[87] Since they make losses, they do not add economic value to the group or the parent; on the contrary, the parent's share sinks when the subsidiary's share also sinks. In any case, in neither *Cadbury Schweppes* nor in subsequent case law has the CJEU referred to this criterion in order to evaluate the artificiality of a subsidiary.

bb 'In That State'

The Cadbury formula requires that the actual pursuit of an economic activity take place in the host state.[88] The EU legislature seems to have taken a similar position. Article 9 of the Shell Entities Directive lays down grounds leading to a rebuttal of the presumption established in the third step of the substance test,[89] i.e., that an undertaking is a shell entity. One such ground exists if there is 'concrete evidence that decision-making concerning the activity generating the relevant income is taking place in the Member State of the undertaking' (Article 9(2)(c) of the Shell Entities Directive).

This passage could qualify the Cadbury formula in the sense that the activity undertaken in the host state must be decision-making in particular. E contrario, operational activities must not be located in the host state. The fact that the existence of operational activities in the host state is not necessarily confirmed by the prevailing opinion in literature, which argues that integration in the local economic life can take place if the subsidiary participates therein as 'a customer',[90] that is if the subsidiary buys or rents an office, uses resources or services, employs personnel, etc., in the host state. The Bundesfinanzhof in the *Cyprus* case also adopted this view, since the fact that the subsidiary was only active as a customer in its host state did not bother the Bundesfinazhof to classify it as a genuine establishment.[91]

But what if the decision-making does not take place in the host state? Then, it is submitted that operational activities need to take place there, pursuant to the Cadbury formula.[92] The Commission simply finds the fact that decision-making takes place in the host state enough to rebut the presumption that a company is a shell entity. It does

87. One could also argue based on the usage of the adjective 'economic' that the activity must make sense from an economic point of view, i.e., be profitable. *See* Leukefeld (2018), p. 242, of course denying such a possibility as loss-making companies still fall under the scope of the freedom of establishment.
88. CJEU, C-196/04, *Cadbury Schweppes*, at para. 54.
89. On the mechanics of the Shell Entities Directive *see* the short introduction in s. B.III.4. of the Introduction.
90. Köhler/Eicker (2006), p. 1873; Schön (2008), pp. 90-91; Thiele (2011), pp. 131-132; Lehfeldt (2016), para. 182.20; Schönfeld/Wassermeyer (2017), paras 471-472; Leukefeld (2018), p. 142; Richter et al. (2020), p. 699.
91. *See* Kortendick et al. (2018), p. 3035.
92. Lang/Heidenbauer (2008), p. 604 argue in this sense also. They interpret *Eurofood* in the following way: '"[t]he mere fact that its economic choices are or can be controlled by a parent company in another Member State" is not enough to ignore the legal existence of this company as a resident of the other Member State. Thus, whenever the facts establish that the legal entity concerned carries out whatever type of business in the other Member State, its activities cannot be considered a "wholly artificial arrangement."' So even if the POEM of a subsidiary is with the

not say that a company whose decision-making does not take place in the host state is a shell entity. But there must be some kind of activity in the host state, either decision-making or operational. Otherwise, the office spaces and the personnel required to exist in the host state, as seen later in section B.II.2. of this chapter, are merely false pretences: what should empty chairs and board directors or employees serve other than tax abuse purposes?

In conclusion, either decision-making or operational activities need to take place in the host state, but not necessarily both. Operational activities in particular may be scattered all around the Union except for the host state, as long as decision-making takes place in the host state.

cc Should the Subsidiary's Income Emanate from, or Be Incidental to, Its Activities?

For the purposes of the substance requirement in the active conduct of a business test, it has been shown that commensurateness ('the income must emanate from, or be incidental to, the active conduct of business') between the income of the subsidiary and its activity in the residence state is required (section B.II.1.a.bb. of Chapter 3). Since, as already explained (section B.I.1. of this chapter), the substance requirements in the LOB aim to combat nexus abuse just like the substance requirements in the freedom of establishment combat nexus abuse in the EU context, it could be that the commensurateness requirement also applies in the latter. In fact, the German tax administration in a – meanwhile repealed – ruling analysing the application of the substance test for the purposes of the German CFC rule considered the commensurateness requirement as a factor for evaluating the subsidiary's artificiality.[93]

This view is erroneous. By applying the wholly artificial arrangements test, the CJEU intends to ascertain whether the establishment of a subsidiary in another Member State has taken place only in order to abuse the freedom of establishment. For this purpose, one looks at whether the entity has been sufficiently integrated into the host state's local economic life. This enquiry has nothing to do with commensurateness control.[94] What is being said here is that the establishment of the subsidiary can be genuine without necessarily all its income being commensurate with its activities. This finding actually corresponds with what has been shown with regard to the POEM, where there is also no commensurateness requirement (section B.II.1.a.bb. of Chapter 3).

b *Quantitative Sub-element of the Functional Element of Substance*

The previous section dealt with questions of the quality of the economic activities that a subsidiary should render in order to have substance for the purposes of the freedom

parent ('its economic choices are or can be controlled by a parent company') the fact that it carries out activities in the host state suffices for it to be 'established' there.

93. Bundesfinanzministerium, 8 Jan. 2007, IV B 4 – S 1351 – 1/07, BStBl. I (2007), p. 99.
94. *See* Vanistendael (2020), para. 1.27; Ballancin/Cannas (2021), p. 73 following him.

of establishment and therewith pass the wholly artificial arrangements test. Now, let us focus on the quantity that these activities must have.

German literature has already dealt with this question and finds no indications in the CJEU case law according to which there is a quantitative threshold that a subsidiary must pass in order to be considered a genuine arrangement.[95] The length of establishment in the host state is more important. In particular, the CJEU in *Cadbury Schweppes* pointed out that a subsidiary must via its activities penetrate the economic life of the host state 'on a stable and continuing basis'.[96] This contradicts the substance requirements in the rules against nexus abuse in the DTC context, i.e., DTC treaty shopping rules. It has been found that the two substance-oriented tests of the LOB, the active conduct of a business test and the PPMC, both include a quantitative threshold regarding the functions that the subsidiary claiming DTC benefits must render (section B.II.1.b. of Chapter 3 for the active conduct of a business test and section B.III.1.b. of Chapter 3 for the PPMC). It also contradicts the POEM, where there is also a relative quantitative threshold as regards the decision-making functions performed (section B.II.3.a. of Chapter 1).

In fact, one can notice a parallel treatment of the qualitative sub-element and the quantitative sub-element regarding holding companies in both the LOB and the wholly artificial arrangements doctrine. In particular, the LOB in the active conduct of a business test excludes economic activities carried out by holding companies as eligible for DTC benefits (section B.II.1.a.aa. of Chapter 3). It also excludes companies carrying out activities that are not 'substantial' in their host state (section B.II.1.b.aa. of Chapter 3). This could be, *inter alia*, the case with holding companies whose activities are often so insubstantial that they cannot reach a degree that would justify accepting that they conduct 'business' within the meaning of Article 7(1) of the OECD MTC.[97]

By contrast, holding companies may pass the wholly artificial arrangements test both in a qualitative and a quantitative sense, at least as far as their functions are concerned. In section B.II.1.a.aa. of this chapter we saw that no exclusion of holding company activities, similar to the one existing in Article 29(3)(a) of the OECD MTC, can be deduced from the CJEU wholly artificial arrangements doctrine. And in this section, we also saw that no quantitative threshold like the substantiality requirement in the active conduct of a business test can be accepted for the purposes of the wholly artificial arrangements doctrine.

So one can conclude that although DTC treaty shopping rules and the wholly artificial arrangements doctrine both tackle nexus abuse, the former is more 'skeptical' towards holding companies than the latter. The CJEU does not per se condemn

95. Köhler/Haun (2008), p. 79; Thiele (2011), p. 195; Schön (2013a), p. 15; Haase (2016), p. 768; Köhler (2016), p. 122; Schmidtmann (2019), p. 65. *Contra* the German tax administration, Bundesfinanzministerium, 17 Mar. 2021, IV B 5 – S 1351/19/10002, Deutsches Steuerrecht 12 (2021), p. 732 (at p. 733).
96. CJEU, C-196/04, *Cadbury Schweppes*, at para. 53. From the literature *see* Köhler/Haun (2008), p. 79; Robert/Tof (2011), p. 444; Haase (2016), p. 768; Watrin/Leukefeld (2018), p. 2287; Richter et al. (2020), p. 699.
97. As to the matter of the degree necessary in order for passive activities to fall under Article 7 of the OECD MTC, *see* Kostikidis (2022), p. 147.

companies conducting passive activities or having insubstantial activities; they may also be genuine establishments; and they may not. It is a case-by-case analysis issue.

According to Englisch, though, the *Danish withholding tax* cases have changed the landscape:

> It is no longer sufficient that there is some kind of minimum substance. Instead, the Court now acknowledges that it constitutes an indication of artificiality if the material and financial resources, the size of staff or the expenditure for outsourcing it, the transaction volumes, or the management activities, do not come close to what is usually required to carry out an economic activity in the respective field of business independently.[98]

So it could be that there is a quantitative threshold as regards the functions that a subsidiary must perform; the subsidiary must perform the functions that 'are usually required to carry out an economic activity in the respective field of business independently'. Such a 'test' would resemble the mechanics of the ALP and would mean the application of a relative quantitative threshold for the purposes of the wholly artificial arrangements doctrine: the functions of the subsidiary in question would be compared to the ones that other companies in the respective field of business render.

Englisch derives this interpretation of the *Danish withholding tax* cases from the following passage in the decisions:

> The absence of actual economic activity must, in the light of the specific features of the economic activity in question, be inferred from an analysis of all the relevant factors relating, in particular, to the management of the company, to its balance sheet, to the structure of its costs and to expenditure actually incurred, to the staff that it employs and to the premises and equipment that it has.[99]

It is obvious that the CJEU does not make any reference to which functions, assets, etc., other companies in the respective field of business employ. It just refers to evidence that must be consulted when determining whether a company constitutes a fictitious establishment.[100] Thus, it is submitted that nothing has changed with regard to the functional element of substance in the wholly artificial arrangements doctrine in the context of the freedom of establishment. There is still no quantitative threshold, either absolute or relative, in the functional element.

c *Outsourcing*

Just like this work did regarding the other substance requirements, let us proceed by exploring the role of outsourcing of activities. Does the outsourcing of activities render a subsidiary an abusive arrangement? And if yes, which activities are these? Is the

98. Englisch (2020b), pp. 528-529.
99. CJEU, C-116/16 and C-117/16, *T Danmark*, at para. 104; CJEU, C-115/16, C-118/16, C-119/16 and C-299/16, *N Luxembourg 1*, at para. 131.
100. *See also* Article 7(2) of the Shell Entities Directive where indicators like the 'amount of gross revenue and type thereof' and the 'amount of business expenses and type thereof' are listed as information that documentary evidence, to be submitted by undertakings controlled under the substance test, should include.

subsidiary allowed to outsource any activity or should specific activities be performed only through it?

There are different opinions in the literature in this respect, which are categorized as follows:

- According to one opinion, a subsidiary may outsource activities without being regarded as a fictitious establishment. This reflects business reality and the CJEU case law.[101]
- Another opinion refers to the situation in the substance-oriented residence criteria and concludes that outsourcing is not harmful as long as the subsidiary maintains control over the outsourced activities.[102]
- According to a third opinion, one needs to differentiate between outsourcable and non-outsourcable activities, a notion we have already encountered and rejected for the purposes of substance in transfer pricing (section B.II.1.b. of Chapter 2).[103]
- Finally, a combination of the latter two opinions has also been proposed.[104]

No answer can be derived from the CJEU case law on this matter. The only CJEU ruling which could provide at least a hint is *X-GmbH* where the CJEU referred to 'a company that does not pursue any economic activities *of its own*'.[105] However, this statement of the CJEU cannot be qualified as referring to outsourcing. The CJEU would have rather referred to 'a company that does not pursue any economic activities *on its own*'.

Contrary to the CJEU, the EU legislature seems to have taken a position on the matter. In particular, in the Shell Entities Directive, one of the criteria whose fulfilment leads to a reporting obligation is found in Article 6(1)(c) of the Shell Entities Directive, which reads:

> [I]n the preceding two tax years, the undertaking outsourced the administration of day-to-day operations and the decision-making on significant functions.[106]

This passage seems to accord with the third opinion stated above, that is, that the outsourcing of certain activities ('the administration of day-to-day operations and the decision-making on significant functions') renders the subsidiary suspicious.

101. Haase (2016), p. 768; Heinsen et al. (2020), p. 734; Richter et al. (2020), p. 700; Köhler (2021), p. 206; Kanduth-Kristen et al. (2021), p. 544; Ekinci (2023), pp. 192-194.
102. Schön (2013a), p. 16; Lehfeldt (2016), para. 182.21; Watrin/Leukefeld (2018), p. 2287; Leukefeld (2018), pp. 248-249.
103. Smit (2014), p. 265; Schönfeld/Wassermeyer (2017), para. 476; Kuźniacki (2017), s. 4.1.2. Apparently so also the German tax administration. *See* Bundesfinanzministerium, 17 Mar. 2021, IV B 5 – S 1351/19/10002, Deutsches Steuerrecht 12 (2021), p. 732 (at p. 733).
104. Köhler (2018), p. 457 where the following questions are raised: 'Which rights and obligations does the Managing Director have? Does the Managing Director manage and control the "actual activities" or does he only administer it? Which function(s) of the company in question would be outsourced also to third party and which not?' (Author's unofficial translation).
105. CJEU, C-135/17, *X-GmbH*, at para. 84 (emphasis added).
106. On the difficulties in interpreting this clause Benz/Böhmer (2022), p. 1030; Pistone et al. (2022), s. 4.2.3.; Martín Jiménez (2022b), p. 478, n. 79.

This approach goes further than anything that we have seen so far. Even the LOB, also combatting nexus abuse in the DTC context, allows outsourcing in Article 29(3)(c) of the OECD MTC (section B.II.1.c. of Chapter 3). However, the loose stance of the OECD towards outsourcing has already been criticized. By outsourcing activities, a subsidiary may remain 'an empty shell' which cannot exhibit any integration into the economic life of the host state. It is submitted, though, that the third opinion, to which the Shell Entities Directive ascribes, namely the division of activities into outsourcable and non-outsourcable ones, is not the right approach to deal with the problem. Rather, the second approach, which as stated resembles the one in the POEM, is preferable.

This approach is preferable because, in contrast to the third approach, it does not limit the freedom of taxpayers to conduct business as they wish. This postulate, of course, does not derive from the fundamental freedoms, but from the economic foundations upon which the EU is based, namely efficiency.[107] It may be more efficient for a subsidiary, for example, to outsource certain decisions, even if they are strategical in nature.

Consider the following example: a subsidiary resident in Spain wants to sell goods online in Greece. The Spanish directors, having no knowledge of the Greek market, have to rely on people with the respective knowledge and outsource strategic decisions regarding the product. Requiring them to take decisions on their own, would result in them having to bring into the Greek market a product that will probably fail. This is anything but efficient.

In sum, the CJEU has not expressed itself with regard to whether outsourcing of activities, and if so to which extent, renders a subsidiary a fictitious establishment. The literature has taken different positions and the Commission in its proposal for a Shell Entities Directive divided activities into outsourcable and non-outsourcable. This work submits, on the one hand, that an approach like the one in the active conduct of a business in the LOB, where outsourcing is completely allowed without any limitations, is not the right way to go forward. On the other hand, the European Commission's approach to the Shell Entities Directive is also not the right one. Rather, the approach used for the purposes of the POEM is favoured, in which activities may be outsourced as long as the subsidiary retains control over them.

2 *The Personal and the Objective Element of the Substance Requirement in the Context of the Freedom of Establishment*

a *Relationship Between the Business of the Subsidiary and the Content of the Personal and the Objective Element*

In the literature, there exists the postulate that the amount and qualities of assets and persons that are required in order for a subsidiary to pass the wholly artificial

107. Schönfeld (2005), pp. 16 et seq.; Friese (2010), p. 60 with further references.

arrangements test depends on the nature and scale of its business activities.[108] A holding company, for example, can and should not have the same amount of personnel as a distribution subsidiary; and their capabilities must be different.

One could only derive such a finding indirectly from the CJEU case law. In particular, the fact that the CJEU has not mentioned absolute thresholds in either a qualitative or quantitative sense anywhere (e.g., something along the lines of at least one director with a Master's degree is needed) indicates that the assessment takes place on a case-by-case basis where all circumstances are taken into account. If the business of the company in question is not taken into account, then what else is?

b Whose Staff and Assets?

There is a discussion in the literature as to whether the assets and personnel that are used by a subsidiary in conducting its activities should be its own or whether it can 'use' assets and staff pertaining to other group companies.[109]

The Shell Entities Directive demands that 'the undertaking has *own* premises in the Member State, or premises for its *exclusive use*' (Article 7(1)(a) of the Shell Entities Directive (emphasis added)) in order for a subsidiary to have minimum substance. It also excludes from the reporting obligation 'undertakings with at least five *own* full-time equivalent employees or members of staff *exclusively* carrying out the activities generating the relevant income' (Article 6(2)(e) of the Shell Entities Directive emphasis added). The Shell Entities Directive thus requires either ownership (with regard to the assets)[110] and employment relationship (with regard to the staff),[111] or exclusive use of assets and personnel.

But what does the CJEU tell us? In *Deister and Juhler Holding*, the CJEU was not concerned that Juhler Holding had no substance of its own but 'use[d] the premises, as

108. De Broe (2008), p. 853; Lang/Heidenbauer (2008), pp. 603-604; Robert/Tof (2011), p. 443; Thiele (2011), pp. 129-130; Rudolf (2012), p. 171; Haase (2016), p. 770; Lehfeldt (2016), pp. 182.20; Watrin/Leukefeld (2018), p. 2286; Hoor (2019), p. 599; Anzinger (2020), p. 103; Heinsen et al. (2020), p. 732; Hoor et al. (2022), p. 239. In this direction, Pötgens/Straathof (2016), p. 615: 'The performance of passive activities, such as certain holding company activities or ways of managing funding (finance loans) within a group, may require only an office and a director to carry out the required activities. This does not mean, however, that such activities, and thus the arrangements, are automatically classified as artificial.' Another opinion by Leclercq (2007), p. 243 according to whom: 'In the author's opinion, this substance should be measured both in absolute terms (e.g., are the resources sufficient for the existence of a real establishment?) and in relative terms (e.g., are the resources in proportion to the level of the establishment's business and profits in light of what is generally observable on the market?).'
109. Schmidtmann (2019), p. 67; Ekinci (2023), p. 189.
110. In this vein Pistone et al. (2022), s. 5.2.1. *Contra* Hoor et al. (2022), p. 236: 'the availability of premises requires neither ownership nor exclusive use. Rather, depending on the requirements of the specific case, an entity may rent premises for its exclusive use, on an ad hoc basis (such as when office spaces or meeting rooms are needed), or use the premises of other group companies resident in the same jurisdiction'.
111. *Contra* Pistone et al. (2022), s. 4.3.4. based on the argument that '[t] he proposal distinguishes between "employees" and "members of staff", indicating that non-employed individuals qualify'.

well as the other facilities and staff, of other companies within the group'.[112] However, one should not take this fact at face value. Remember that '[t]he CJEU does not rule on the concrete facts of the case, but on the abstract legal situation. It must therefore not be assumed across the board that the CJEU recognized the facts on which its decisions are based as sufficient simply because it considered the abstract regulatory situation to be contrary to Union law'.[113]

In fact, from the *Danish withholding tax* cases where the CJEU refers to 'the staff that [the subsidiary in question] *employs* and to the premises and equipment that it *has*',[114] one could derive a stricter approach, at least with regard to the assets. In particular, a subsidiary *has* assets if it owns or possesses them.[115] The verb 'employ', by contrast, referring to the staff, can be used in order to express that something is used for a particular purpose.[116] There is no prerequisite that what is being used is also owned or is constantly at someone's disposal. So it is submitted that because of these contradictory interpretations of CJEU case law, one cannot derive safe conclusions as to whether the assets and personnel that are used by a subsidiary in conducting its activities should be its own or whether it can 'use' assets and staff pertaining to other group companies.

In total, the Shell Entities Directive requires either ownership (with regard to the assets) and an employment relationship (with regard to the staff), or exclusive use of assets and personnel, whereas the CJEU is not clear on this matter. It remains to be seen whether the requirements of the Shell Entities Directive are in conformity with the CJEU's case law. This could also give the CJEU the chance to express itself explicitly on the matter.

c *Personal Element*

aa Personal Element Stricto Sensu

The personal element stricto sensu deals with the issue of the identity of the persons who are relevant for the purposes of the wholly artificial arrangements test in the context of the freedom of establishment. In particular, two questions may be raised: who are these persons from an institutional perspective? Does the subsidiary need to have, for example, both a board and employees? Or does the existence of an active decision-making board suffice? And which powers should these persons have?

The fact that the subsidiary must possess a decision-making organ is a conditio sine qua non for the existence of a corporation (section A. of the introduction). It must therefore exist in order for the subsidiary to have substance. It is submitted, though, that this organ must not only be authorized on paper to make decisions but it must also

112. CJEU, C-504/16 and C-613/16, *Deister and Juhler Holding*, at para. 22. In this vein also German case law. *See* Finanzgericht of Köln, 22 Sep. 2022, 6 K 2661/18, EFG (2023), p. 89 (at para. 31).
113. Cloer/Hagemann (2019), p. 1234 (author's unofficial translation).
114. CJEU, C–116/16 and C–117/16, *T Danmark*, at para. 104; CJEU, C-115/16, C-118/16, C-119/16 and C-299/16, *N Luxembourg 1*, at para. 131 (emphasis added).
115. https://www.oxfordlearnersdictionaries.com/definition/english/have_1.
116. https://www.oxfordlearnersdictionaries.com/definition/american_english/employ_1.

do so in substance. One can derive this postulate from AG *Kokott*'s Opinion in *Eqiom*. There AG Kokott stated:

> [A]n artificial arrangement can be assumed if the company is only a fictitious establishment in the form of a 'letterbox' company. But even where there is a physical presence, one might conclude, in light of the financial and staffing set-up, that the arrangement is artificial. In this regard, what appears to be relevant is, for instance, the actual authority of the company organs to take decisions.[117]

By 'the actual authority', AG Kokott means that the decision-making organ must actually exercise the authority that it has by law or contract. That is, a merely formal exercise will not do the work. In establishing in which cases this has taken place, one can refer to the criteria developed for the purposes of the POEM, also not referring to formal but substantial decision-making, in order to ascertain whether management has been usurped by outsiders (section B.II.2.c. of Chapter 1). If a subsidiary's management has been usurped and the persons who actually manage the subsidiary are doing so from another Member State, then the subsidiary has not been sufficiently integrated into the economic life of its host state and is thus a fictitious establishment.

An exception can be made, though. In cases where not the decision-making organ but other employees carry out the subsidiary's activities in the host state, it can be accepted that the subsidiary has been sufficiently integrated into the economic life of its host state, and thus can legitimately invoke the freedom of establishment. This position holds for the following reasons.

First, the CJEU does not differentiate between decision-making personnel and other personnel. It merely refers to 'staff'.[118] Second, freedom of establishment encompasses not only the setting-up of subsidiaries but also that of agencies and branches (Article 49 TFEU).[119] Agencies and branches are not obliged by law to have a decision-making organ and still their establishment in another Member State is legitimate pursuant to Article 49 TFEU. Accordingly, if a subsidiary does not have a decision-making organ in its host state, it can legitimately invoke the freedom of establishment by being an agency or branch.

Third, this finding is in line with the conclusion drawn in section B.II.1.a.bb. of this chapter that either decision-making or operational activities need to take place in the host state. Accordingly, either decision-makers or other staff must exist in the host state, depending on what activity is carried out there. Finally, the Shell Entities Directive demands as minimum substance that 'at least one director resident close to

117. Opinion of Advocate General Kokott, 19 Jan. 2017, C-6/16, *Eqiom SAS, formerly Holcim France SAS, Enka SA v. Ministre des Finances et des comptes publics*, ECLI:EU:C:2017:34, para. 57. The fact that the authorization to make decisions plays a role can also be derived from Article 7(1)(c) of the Shell Entities Directive, stipulating the substance test, pursuant to which it is an indicator of substance if a subsidiary has one or more directors who 'are qualified and authorised to take decisions in relation to the activities that generate relevant income for the undertaking or in relation to the undertaking's assets'.

118. CJEU, C-196/04, *Cadbury Schweppes*, at para. 67; CJEU, C–116/16 and C–117/16, *T Danmark*, at para. 104; CJEU, C-115/16, C-118/16, C-119/16 and C-299/16, *N Luxembourg 1*, at para. 131.

119. CJEU, 15 May 2008, C–414/06, *Lidl Belgium GmbH & Co. KG v. Finanzamt Heilbronn*, ECLI:EU:C:2008:278, para. 20.

the undertaking and dedicated to its activities or, *alternatively*, a sufficient number of the undertaking's employees that are engaged with its core income generating activities being resident close to the undertaking'.[120]

This 'alternatively' signalizes that the existence of either decision-making people or other employees in the host state of the subsidiary suffices for it to have been integrated into the economic life of its host state, and thus legitimately invoke the freedom of establishment. It also makes clear that both are not required to exist in the host state. This is also relevant, as the German tax administration demanded in a – meanwhile repealed – ruling 'that the company [must be able to prove that it] permanently employs both managerial and other staff there for the performance of its activities'.[121] This opinion can be rejected for the reasons stated above. Decision-making and other staff in the host state are alternatives: the existence of either in the host state suffices.[122]

This contradicts what we have seen so far in other substance requirements: the POEM, transfer pricing, and the PPMC concentrate on decision-makers (section B.II.2.b. of Chapter 1 for the POEM; section B.I.2. of Chapter 2 for transfer pricing; section B.III.2.a. of Chapter 3 for the PPMC), while the active conduct of a business test requires the existence of both decision-making and other staff in the residence state (section B.II.2. of Chapter 3). It becomes apparent that the wholly artificial arrangements doctrine in the context of the freedom of establishment is less demanding in this respect.

One last issue: why should either decision-making or other staff exist in the host state? Doesn't it suffice that the board of a Spanish corporation, for example, makes decisions in Portugal, where the parent company resides? Or, similarly, that the personnel carry out its activities in Portugal and not in Spain? In fact, it has been shown that the operational activities of a company must not necessarily be exercised in its host state for it to have been sufficiently integrated into the economic life of its host state, and thus legitimately invoke the freedom of establishment (section B.II.1.a.bb. of this chapter).

Accordingly, it is only logical that if a subsidiary is allowed to carry out economic activities in Member States other than its host state, it is also allowed to employ the necessary staff *there* and not in its host state. This does not contradict the findings so far. If a subsidiary is resident in Spain and its activities are carried out in other Member States, then it suffices that its decision-makers exercise their duties in Spain; the other staff are allowed to exercise their activities in the other Member States. Conversely, if a subsidiary is resident in Spain, but its management is being usurped by its parent in

---

120. Shell Entities Directive, *Explanatory Memorandum*, p. 9 (emphasis added). *See also* Article 7(1)(c) where there are two indicators of the existence of minimum substance the first one (i) referring to 'one or more directors of the undertaking' and the second one (ii) to 'the majority of the full-time equivalent employees of the undertaking'.
In this sense also, Graßl/Kemmer (2022), p. 230; comparing this with the stricter Luxembourgian substance rules, Offermanns (2022), ss 4.2. and 6.2.
121. Bundesfinanzministerium, 8 Jan. 2007, IV B 4 – S 1351 – 1/07, BStBl. I (2007), p. 99 (author's unofficial translation).
122. Also rejecting the opinion of the German tax administration Thiele (2011), p. 196; Leukefeld (2018), pp. 237-238; Schmidtmann (2019), p. 66.

Portugal, then the existence of other staff exercising activities in Spain can 'save the day'.

In sum, for a subsidiary to not be regarded as a fictitious establishment, it must employ either decision-making persons who actually exercise their authority, or other staff in its host state.[123]

bb Qualitative Sub-element of the Personal Element of Substance

Now, what qualities does the subsidiary's staff need to possess in order for it not to be regarded as a fictitious establishment? In the literature, it is partly accepted that staff competence plays a role.[124] German scholarship, by contrast, is more sceptical and points to the fact that the CJEU has not made any statements as to the competence/experience/capabilities that the staff members of a subsidiary should have in order for it to be a genuine establishment.[125]

The Shell Entities Directive considers the fact that one or more of its directors 'are qualified and authorised to take decisions in relation to the activities that generate relevant income for the undertaking or in relation to the undertaking's assets' (Article 7(1)(c)(i)(2) of the Shell Entities Directive) to be an indicator that a subsidiary possesses minimum substance. Admittedly, the fact that a subsidiary with qualified personnel is deemed to have enough substance does not mean that one without qualified staff is a fictitious establishment.

In the previous section, it has been argued that when the management of a subsidiary is usurped by persons located in a Member State other than the host state, this means that the subsidiary is a fictitious establishment if it also does not have other staff in its host state. One of the indicators when determining whether a subsidiary's management has been usurped is the expertise of its legally appointed decision-makers (section B.II.2.c.dd. of Chapter 1). Accordingly, this indicator should play a role when determining whether a subsidiary is a fictitious establishment. A parallel can be drawn with other substance requirements that look at the qualification of the decision-makers: transfer pricing (B.III.2. of Chapter 2) and the PPMC (section B.III.2.b. of Chapter 3).

The other staff must also possess competence, capabilities and experience, in particular the ones necessary for it to carry out the activities they have taken over.[126] The requirement that the rest of the staff must also be qualified to render the activities it has been entrusted with is included also in Article 7(1)(c)(ii) of the Shell Entities

123. According to Ravelli/Strik (2023) 'Focussing only on intra-territorial substance constitutes a breach of the EU freedoms.'
124. De Broe (2008), p. 853; Robert/Tof (2011), p. 437; Weber (2013), p. 259; Pötgens/Straathof (2016), p. 615; Leukefeld (2018), p. 238. Apparently so also the German tax administration. *See* the repealed ruling Bundesfinanzministerium, 8 Jan. 2007, IV B 4 – S 1351 – 1/07, BStBl. I (2007), p. 99 and currently Bundesfinanzministerium, 17 Mar. 2021, IV B 5 – S 1351/19/10002, Deutsches Steuerrecht 12 (2021), p. 732 (at p. 733).
125. Köhler/Eicker (2007), p. 333; Thiele (2011), pp. 196-197; Köhler (2021), p. 205. According to Haun et al. (2007), p. 186 facts like the qualification of the staff should only be relevant for transfer pricing purposes.
126. Schönfeld/Wassermeyer (2017), para. 490.

Directive. From an everyday perspective, the fact that the staff is not competent enough to carry out the activities entrusted to it is a strong indicator that the staff is engaged not for business but for abusive purposes. Imagine that lawyers are engaged as car manufacturers or brokers. This shows that they are not engaged to carry out the activities they are able to; it can be – at least rebuttably – presumed that no genuine purposes drive such an employment relationship.

Overall, although the CJEU has not openly required that the staff of an entity be qualified in order for it to be a genuine establishment, the Shell Entities Directive does so and the author agrees with such a notion. It is remarkable that all substance requirements are aligned in this respect.

cc Quantitative Sub-element of the Personal Element of Substance

Now how many employees should there be in the host state in order for a subsidiary to constitute a genuine establishment? It has been shown in section B.II.2.a. of this chapter that this is a question that needs to be answered by taking into account the business of the subsidiary. But is there also a threshold in this sense? Does the subsidiary need to have a specific number of employees (absolute threshold) or more employees than other subsidiaries (relative threshold)?

As commentators argue, the CJEU's case law provides no hints in this respect.[127] One can derive some guidance from the Shell Entities Directive, though:

(1) First, according to Article 6(2)(e) of the Shell Entities Directive, subsidiaries with 'at least five own full-time equivalent employees' are not obliged to report and are thus presumed to have enough substance. That does not mean that subsidiaries with fewer employees are fictitious establishments; it simply means that those with at least five are for sure not. So everything between one and five employees is the 'grey area' where a subsidiary can both have and not have substance. If we are in this grey area, then, according to Article 7(1)(c)(ii) of the Shell Entities Directive, 'the majority of the full-time equivalent employees of the undertaking [must be] resident for tax purposes in the Member State of the undertaking, or at no greater distance from that Member States insofar as such distance is compatible with the proper performance of their duties'. What is derived from the combination of these rules is the following:

> A subsidiary with five employees, irrespective of where they are located, has substance. A subsidiary with fewer than five employees has substance if the majority of its employees are located in the host state.

(2) Second, Article 7(1)(c)(i)(1) stipulates that if a subsidiary has at least one director who is resident in the host state 'or at no greater distance from that

127. Köhler/Eicker (2007), p. 333; Haase (2016), p. 768; Leukefeld (2018), p. 238; Schmidtmann (2019), p. 62.

> Member State insofar as such distance is compatible with the proper performance of their duties', the subsidiary has minimum substance. This tells us that one director will do the work.

So what one can derive from the Shell Entities Directive is that a subsidiary:

(1) having one director who is resident in the host state 'or at no greater distance from that Member State insofar as such distance is compatible with the proper performance of their duties'; or
(2) either five employees, irrespective of where they are located, or fewer than five employees if the majority of its employees are located in the host state

has substance. These are not minimum thresholds, but safe harbour rules.[128] We can notice here two differences compared to substance requirements in the DTC context. First, there are neither relative nor absolute quantitative thresholds referring to the number of staff members in the context of the wholly artificial arrangements doctrine.[129] Second, the Shell Entities Directive introduces safe harbour rules referring to the number of staff members; such rules do not exist in the DTC context.

Safe harbour rules serve legal certainty and therefore must be endorsed. Unfortunately, safe harbour rules only exist in the EU and not in the DTC context. The OECD could also adopt the same approach and establish safe harbour rules along these lines with regard to treaty entitlement so either in the LOB or, for countries having adopted only the PPT, in the PPT. The same rule can be included in the POEM.[130]

d *Objective Element*

Which qualities should the subsidiary's assets have in order for it to be a genuine establishment? Should Windows 11 be installed? Should the curtains be blue? And how many computers are necessary? The objective element consists of a qualitative and a quantitative sub-element. In the following, the requirements for these two sub-elements for the purposes of the wholly artificial arrangements doctrine in the context of the freedom of establishment are analysed.

aa Qualitative Sub-element of the Objective Element of Substance

As regards the qualitative sub-element, at the outset, it can be said that the qualities of the assets are dependent on the business of the company in question and cannot be

128. On the rules of the Shell Entities Directive as safe harbour rules, *see* Pistone et al. (2022), ss 2.3. and 6.1.
129. We have seen that the POEM (s. B.II.3.b. of Ch. 1), the active conduct of a business test (s. B.II.1.b.bb. of Ch. 3), and the PPMC (s. B.II.2.c. of Ch. 3) require the passing of a relative quantitative threshold in a personal sense.
130. Along these lines, Schön (2022b), p. 190; Graßl/Kemmer (2022), p. 234.

defined in absolute terms. However, the CJEU and the Shell Entities Directive require specific kinds of assets. The CJEU generally refers to 'premises and equipment'.[131] The EU legislature in the Shell Entities Directive also regards as an indicator of substance that 'the undertaking has own premises in the Member State, or premises for its exclusive use' (Article 7(1)(a) of the Shell Entities Directive). Some commentators also mention the importance of capital, although the CJEU does not include it among the indicators of substance.[132] The Shell Entities Directive in Article 7(1)(b) of the Shell Entities Directive even considers the existence of a bank account as an indicator of substance.

The reason why the Shell Entities Directive considers the existence of a bank account an indicator of substance is that stakeholder consultations have shown that '[a]s regards the features common in shell entities that present a risk for being misused for tax purposes, there is broad agreement that absence of an own bank account is one of them and is indicative'.[133] Irrespective of whether this is a fact, the author believes this to be a very low threshold, tackling only the very obvious cases of abuse. As far as the importance of capital endowment is concerned, due to the mobility of capital it is not difficult to capitalize companies that do not participate in the economic life of the host state, but have only been set up to incur tax advantages. Thus, capital endowment may be a signal that the company has enough substance but not the most decisive one; weight should be placed on the existence of 'premises and equipment'.

As to which kind of premises and which kind of equipment, this should depend on the activities that a company is carrying on and the persons that it employs to do so. As already concluded in section B.II.1.a.bb. of this section, either decision-making or operational activities need to take place in the host state. If, on the one hand, a company has its management in its host state and performs other activities in other Member States, then the premises and equipment located in the former state that relate to decision-making just like in the POEM (section B.III.2. of Chapter 1) should be decisive. On the other hand, if a company performs its operational activities in a Member State and has its management in another Member State, then it needs to have the premises and equipment relating to these operational activities in the former state in order for it to be genuinely established there. It must be clarified that, in contrast to the active conduct of a business test where the assets related to *both* the managerial and operational activities must exist (section B.II.3. of Chapter 3), for the purposes of the wholly artificial arrangements test in the context of the freedom of establishment, the assets related to *either* the managerial *or* the operational activities suffice.

131. CJEU, C-196/04, *Cadbury Schweppes*, at para. 67; CJEU, C–116/16 and C–117/16, *T Danmark*, at para. 104; CJEU, C-115/16, C-118/16, C-119/16 and C-299/16, *N Luxembourg 1*, at para. 131.
132. Schönfeld/Wassermeyer (2017), para. 492; Smit (2019), s. 12.4.3.4.: 'A business may not be considered to be independent where, for example, the (financial) situation of a company, as a whole, "makes inevitable the conclusion that it will very probably not be able to survive by its own means.".'
133. Shell Entities Directive, *Explanatory Memorandum*, p. 4.

bb Quantitative Sub-element of the Objective Element of Substance

As regards the quantity of the assets required, the CJEU does not specify how much objective substance is necessary. Just like in the POEM (section B.III.1. of Chapter 1), there is no quantitative threshold as regards the assets a company should employ. The key question should be: is this company with this quantity of assets capable of rendering the functions it is supposed to render? Or is this all a 'show'; just some substance meant to blur the tax authorities?

On the one hand, if a company has its management in a Member State and performs other activities in other Member States, then reference can be made to the POEM as a yardstick. If the quantity of the assets suffices in order for the company to have its POEM in the former state, then it should be regarded as a genuine establishment. On the other hand, if a company performs its operational activities in a Member State and has its management in another Member State, then reference can be made to the PE threshold as a yardstick when determining whether the company has been genuinely established in the former state. This is the approach this work also follows with regard to the quantity of the assets required in the active conduct of a business test. There the PE threshold signalizes a substantial connection with a state, granting it the right to tax income generated within its territory (section B.II.3. of Chapter 3). The existence of a PE thus tells us that an entity participates in the economic life of a state, which is what the CJEU requires a company to do in order for it to be genuinely established in a Member State. And remember (section B.II.2.c.aa. of this chapter), freedom of establishment encompasses not only the setting-up of subsidiaries but also that of agencies and branches, the latter terms referring to undertakings which, like the PE, are not separate taxpayers. Accordingly, the existence of PE can serve as a proxy for the existence of a branch or agency and therefore a genuine establishment.[134]

All in all, if a company has enough assets in a Member State in order to accept that it has its POEM or a PE in this state, it must be considered a genuine establishment.

3 *Relationship Between the Functional Element and the Personal and Objective Elements of the Substance Requirement in the Context of the Freedom of Establishment*

We have seen for the purposes of the other substance requirements that not all elements of substance have the same relevance. In the POEM, the personal and functional elements take precedence over the objective element (section B.III.3. of Chapter 1). The same holds true in the transfer pricing (section B.IV.2. of Chapter 2) and the DTC treaty shopping context (sections B.II.3. and B.III.3. of Chapter 3). So what is the relationship between the substance elements in the context of the wholly artificial arrangements test in the freedom of establishment?

134. The term 'branch' refers to PEs for tax purposes. *See* Zanotti (2004), p. 496.

Authors have argued that the functional element takes priority over the other two.[135] This position cannot be accepted.

A first characteristic of the nature of the relationship between the substance elements in the context of the wholly artificial arrangements test in the freedom of establishment is that they mutually influence each other. The quality and quantity of functions influence the quality and quantity of assets, as has already been concluded in section B.II.2.a. of this chapter. However, the author does not believe that the persons and assets are merely subordinate to the functions that a company carries out as the above-cited authors sustain. On the contrary, all three elements are of equal importance, as the CJEU does not prioritize any element in its Cadbury formula. The opinions of De Broe and Lang/Heidenbauer must be rejected. Especially the latter draw their conclusion that the functional element takes precedence over the objective and personal elements from the following passage in *Eurofood*:

> [W]here a company carries on its business in the territory of the Member State where its registered office is situated, the mere fact that its economic choices are or can be controlled by a parent company in another Member State is not enough to rebut the presumption laid down by the Regulation.[136]

In this passage, the CJEU only clarifies that, as we have also seen for the purposes of the POEM (section B.II.1.b.bb. of Chapter 1), parent policy-making is not detrimental when it comes to defining the centre of a company's main interests. This passage actually does not mention anything with regard to the relationship between the substance elements in the context of the wholly artificial arrangements test in the freedom of establishment.

Newer developments from the EU legislature show how important the existence of personnel and assets in the EU tax law context is. Remember how often reference has been made thus far to the Shell Entities Directive in section B.II.2. of this chapter, analysing the content of the objective and personal element, which demands the presence of qualified staff and the existence of premises and equipment in the host state.

In total, the substance elements in the context of the wholly artificial arrangements test in the freedom of establishment are of equal importance and mutually influence each other. This constitutes a difference compared to the substance requirements in the DTC context, which concentrate on functions and persons while assets play a secondary role.[137]

The approach adopted in the DTC context has already been criticized (sections B.IV.2. and B.IV.3. of Chapter 2). The elements of substance should be of equal importance, at least in the first step. In a second step, both the tax administration and

---

135. Lang/Heidenbauer (2008), p. 604; Thiele (2011), p. 132; Rudolf (2012), p. 171. One could, for example, interpret *De Broe* in that way when he submits that 'a "letter box" company is not a company that uses limited office space and/or has a small or no staff, but it is a company that carries on no activity'. *See* De Broe (2008), p. 852.
136. CJEU, 2 May 2006, C-341/04, *Eurofood IFSC*, ECLI:EU:C:2006:281, para. 36.
137. For the POEM *see* above s. B.III.3. of Ch. 1, for transfer pricing *see* above s. B.IV.2. of Ch. 2, for DTC treaty shopping rules *see* above s. B.II.3. of Ch. 3 for the active conduct of a business test and s. B.III.3. of Ch. 3 for the PPMC.

the taxpayer can argue that, although one element is not fulfilled, another is fulfilled to such a degree that this suffices for the subsidiary to have substance. For example, if the majority of important decisions are taken in a state other than the state claimed to be the POEM, this speaks for the POEM to be in the former state. But if there are overwhelming assets in the latter state, then the POEM may also be in the latter. It is for the judge to decide. One thing is certain: the enquiry should not always be prejudiced in favour of specific elements (the functional and the objective elements) and against the objective element.

4 *Synthesis*

- Like the POEM, the wholly artificial arrangements doctrine in the context of the freedom of establishment adopts a stand-alone perspective and a holistic approach (section B.II.1.a.aa.).
- Apart from an actuality control, the substance requirement for the purposes of the wholly artificial arrangements doctrine in the context of the freedom of establishment does not include stricter requirements, for example, excluding some activities, like the substance requirements in DTC treaty shopping rules or requiring specific functions, like strategic decision-making, which is the case in the POEM and transfer pricing rules. Preparatory and/or auxiliary activities in the host state also suffice (section B.II.1.a.aa.).
- Either decision-making or operational activities need to take place in the host state. Not necessarily both (section B.II.1.a.bb.).
- In contrast to the LOB and in conformity with the POEM, the wholly artificial arrangements test in the context of the freedom of establishment does not control whether the income of a company emanates from, or is incidental to, its activities (section B.II.1.a.cc.).
- There is no quantitative threshold in the functional element, either absolute or relative. This contradicts the approach taken in the POEM and the LOB (section B.II.1.b.).
- As in the POEM, outsourcing is not harmful as long as the subsidiary performs monitoring over the outsourced activities (section B.II.1.c.).
- The amount and qualities of assets and persons that are required in order for a subsidiary to pass the wholly artificial arrangements test depends on the nature and scale of its business activities (section B.II.2.a.).
- It is not clear whether the subsidiary must have ownership of the assets it employs and an employment relationship with its staff members or exclusive use of the assets and personnel, or whether the use of assets and personnel pertaining to other group companies suffices (section B.II.2.b.).
- In order not to be regarded as a fictitious establishment, a subsidiary must employ either decision-making persons who actually exercise their authority, or other staff in its host state. The wholly artificial arrangements doctrine in the context of the freedom of establishment is less demanding than the other substance requirements analysed so far in this respect (section B.II.2.c.aa.).

- Like all other substance requirements so far, the wholly artificial arrangements doctrine in the context of the freedom of establishment demands that the personnel of an entity invoking the freedom of establishment is qualified to perform the activities entrusted to it (section B.II.2.c.bb.).
- In contrast to the substance requirements in the DTC context, the wholly artificial arrangements doctrine does not impose any threshold, either absolute or relative, with regard to the quantity of the staff members employed. In this respect, only the Shell Entities Directive includes safe harbour rules referring to the quantity of personnel necessary for an entity to have substance (section B.II.2.c.cc.).
- Premises and equipment are the decisive assets that a subsidiary should have in order for it to have substance. As to which premises and equipment, this depends on the functions performed in the host state. In contrast to the active conduct of a business test where the assets related to both the managerial and operational activities must exist, for the purposes of the wholly artificial arrangements test in the context of the freedom of establishment, the assets related to either the managerial or the operational activities suffice (section B.II.2.d.aa.).
- As to the quantity of the assets required for the purposes of the wholly artificial arrangements test in the context of the freedom of establishment, if a company has enough assets in a Member State in order to accept that it has its POEM or a PE in this state, it must be considered a genuine establishment (section B.II.2.d.bb.).
- The substance elements in the context of the wholly artificial arrangements test in the freedom of establishment are of equal importance and mutually influence each other. This constitutes a difference compared to the substance requirements in the DTC context which concentrate on functions and persons, whereas assets play a secondary role (section B.II.3.).

In section B.I.1. of this chapter, the question has been raised whether the content of the substance requirement in the wholly artificial arrangements doctrine in the context of the freedom of establishment matches the content of the substance requirement in the DTC treaty shopping context or the POEM. It must have been made clear that there are similarities between the substance requirements in the wholly artificial arrangements doctrine and the ones in the POEM. There are, however, some differences as well.

First, the POEM contains a relative quantitative threshold with regard to the number of the decisions made in the residence state and the number of the decision-makers there. By contrast, the wholly artificial arrangements doctrine does not require the passing of such a threshold. If, for example, a subsidiary is managed from two Member States, the POEM can be only in the state where the most important decisions are made; this does not mean that the establishment in the other Member States (i.e., the ones losing the tiebreaker) is fictitious. The fact that the POEM includes relative quantitative thresholds has to do with its function as a preference criterion. If six out of ten decisions are made in Member State A and the other four in Member State B, then all things being equal the POEM is in Member State A. Nevertheless, this logic cannot apply in the context of the freedom of establishment and it should not do so. As long as there has been integration in the economic life of Member State B, the establishment there is genuine. The same holds when the POEM state is a third state and the state losing the tiebreaker is a Member State if and as long as there has been integration in the economic life there.[138]

Second, preparatory activities qualify in and of themselves as an economic activity in the sense of the Cadbury formula (section B.II.1.a.aa. of this chapter). This contradicts the finding that substance in the context of the freedom of establishment matches the POEM.

Apart from these two differences, one could argue that the substance requirement in the wholly artificial arrangements doctrine in the context of the freedom of establishment matches the content of the substance requirement in the POEM. This is in line with the literature, which has already observed this parallel (section B.I.1. of this chapter). So if a subsidiary has its POEM in its host state, it then does not constitute a fictitious establishment. If the subsidiary does not have its POEM in its host state, it may still be a genuine establishment, though. Thus, the match between the substance requirement in the wholly artificial arrangements doctrine in the context of the freedom of establishment and the POEM is only a partial one.

The same conclusion holds if the requirements for the existence of a PE are fulfilled in the host state. We have seen that an entity must *alternatively* carry out decision-making or operational activities in its host state; it must *alternatively* have decision-making or other staff in its host state; it must have enough personnel and assets in its host state to *either* have its POEM *or* a PE there. So a PE in a Member State constitutes a genuine establishment. Nevertheless, less integrated establishments are also considered genuine. The fact that preparatory activities also give rise to a genuine establishment confirms that since, as already explained in section B.II.1.c.cc. of Chapter 1, preparatory activities in and of themselves do not give rise to a PE.

From the analysis above it can be concluded that two normative requirements of international tax law, namely the POEM and the PE, can be used as a proxy for the purposes of EU tax law to depict substantial integration in the host state, and thus a genuine invocation of the freedom of establishment. However, since this work deals with substance requirements relating to *subsidiaries* and not PEs, we can maintain that if a subsidiary has its POEM in the host state, it is a genuine establishment.

However, not only a POEM and a PE in the host state give rise to a genuine establishment but there is also a continuum of integration whereby the POEM and the PE represent the outer edge of this continuum in the economic life of a Member State in the context of the freedom of establishment. Also 'less worthy', i.e., with less substance, establishments are considered genuine.

Accordingly, it must be observed that, although substance in both the wholly artificial arrangements doctrine in the context of the freedom of establishment and the DTC treaty shopping context tackles nexus abuse, the requirements in the former

138. *See* Kollruss (2015), s. 3.

context are looser than in the latter. In fact, the requirements in the wholly artificial arrangements doctrine in the context of the freedom of establishment partially correspond to the ones in the POEM, and there exists no Stufenverhältnis between them and that in the POEM context, as is the case between the substance requirements in the POEM and that in the DTC treaty shopping context.

That there is neither an exact match nor another kind of relationship, like a Stufenverhältnis, between the substance requirements in international tax law and that in the context of the freedom of establishment can be explained by taking into account the legal context within which the substance requirements exist. *Schön* makes this point clearly:

> there is a major difference between EU law and treaty law. The 'free flow' under treaty law is limited to the contracting states and their respective residents. Tax treaties are bilateral by nature and they are built on the principle of reciprocity. They are clearly not designed to unilaterally extend benefits to residents of third countries. Therefore, the interpretation of treaty law is much different from EU law, which aims at the establishment of a coherent 'Internal Market' covering the whole territory of the European Union.[139]

Finally, DTCs now aim at avoiding double-non taxation,[140] while the CJEU has accepted conferring double tax advantages in the EU.[141]

III Content of the Substance Requirement in the Freedom of Movement of Capital

1 Relevance of the Investigation

Remember this works deals with substance requirements as applied to subsidiaries. And with subsidiaries, this work refers to wholly-owned subsidiaries. E contrario, smaller shareholdings are not of interest. It could be, thus, that the freedom of capital is not relevant for the purposes of this work. This relates to the way the CJEU has delineated the scope of the freedom of establishment and the freedom of movement of capital.

The freedom of capital applies not only in cases of capital movements between citizens of EU Member States but also in relation to third countries.[142] A parent resident in Germany setting up a subsidiary in China can invoke the freedom of movement of

139. Schön (2022a), pp. 15-16. More generally, *see* Maduro (2008), p. 140: 'Teleological interpretation in EU law does not, therefore, refer exclusively to a purpose driven interpretation of the relevant legal rules. It refers to a particular systemic understanding of the EU legal order that permeates the interpretation of all its rules. In other words, the Court was not simply been concerned with ascertaining the aim of a particular legal provision. It also interpreted that rule in the light of the broader context provided by the EC (now EU) legal order and its "constitutional telos".'
140. *See* the Preamble to the OECD MTC: 'Intending to conclude a Convention for the elimination of double taxation with respect to taxes on income and on capital without creating opportunities for non-taxation or reduced taxation through tax evasion or avoidance.'
141. CJEU, 12 Dec. 2013, C-303/12, *Imfeld and Garcet*, ECLI:EU:C:2013:822, para. 78.
142. *See* above n. 3 in this chapter.

capital if the German legislation interferes with the aforementioned freedom. However, not every interference falls under the scope of the freedom of movement of capital.

In particular, 'national legislation intended to apply only to those shareholdings which enable the holder to exert a definite influence on a company's decisions and to determine its activities falls within the provisions of the Treaty on freedom of establishment ... On the other hand, national provisions which apply to shareholdings acquired solely with the intention of making a financial investment without any intention to influence the management and control of the undertaking must be examined exclusively in light of the free movement of capital'.[143]

From this passage one can derive that if the national measure under scrutiny targets only subsidiaries, where it is a fact that there is a dominant shareholder, then only the freedom of establishment is applicable. The freedom of movement of capital is applicable only in case the national measure under scrutiny targets smaller shareholdings. Since this work deals only with subsidiaries and not smaller shareholdings, it could be that the content of the substance requirement in the freedom of movement of capital is irrelevant.[144] This is not the case, though.

If the national measure under scrutiny targets subsidiaries *and* smaller shareholdings, it may fall under the freedom of movement of capital. In such cases one needs to differentiate whether the investment has been made into a Member State or a third state. In a Member State scenario, the CJEU takes account of the facts of the case. That is, if the investment relates to a shareholding safeguarding definite influence, the national measure interfering with it will be scrutinized under the freedom of establishment, while if the investment relates to a small shareholding, the national measure in question will be controlled under the freedom of capital.[145] So in the Member State scenario the content of the substance requirement in the context of the freedom of movement of capital is also irrelevant, as in the case of subsidiaries the freedom of establishment will always be applicable.

By contrast, in a third state scenario only the objective of the rule in question is relevant and not the facts of the case (i.e., whether in fact there is a dominant shareholder exerting such influence).[146] So if the rule in question targets both subsidiaries and smaller shareholdings, an investment in a third state by means of setting up a subsidiary is protected under the freedom of movement of capital. So in third country scenarios and when the national legislation does not only concern shareholdings which enable the holder to exert a definite influence on a company's decisions but the

143. CJEU, 10 Feb. 2011, C-436/08 and C-437/08, *Haribo Lakritzen Hans Riegel BetriebsgmbH and Österreichische Salinen AG v. Finanzamt Linz*, ECLI:EU:C:2011:61, para. 35. *See also* CJEU, 13 Nov. 2012, C-35/11, *Test Claimants in the FII Group Litigation v. Commissioners of Inland Revenue, Commissioners for her Majesty's Revenue & Customs*, ECLI:EU:C:2012:707, paras 91-92.

144. Of course, the freedom of movement of capital applies also in cases where the subsidiary itself makes capital investments, e.g., a portfolio investment in another corporation (s. B.II.1.a.aa. of this chapter).

145. CJEU, C-35/11, *Test Claimants in the FII Group Litigation*, at paras 93-94; Bundesfinanzhof, I R 94/15, at paras 32-33 (*Cyprus-case*).

146. *See* very clear Schön (2013a), p. 19; Schön (2016), p. 254.

freedom of movement of capital also applies and thus the content of the substance requirement becomes relevant.

2 Interpretation of the CJEU Ruling in X-GmbH

The CJEU had to deal with the interpretation of the wholly artificial arrangements doctrine in the context of the freedom of movement of capital in *X-GmbH*. There, the CJEU, as already stated in section A.I.2. of this chapter, clarified that the wholly artificial arrangements doctrine is also applicable in the context of the freedom of movement of capital.[147] As to the content of the wholly artificial arrangements doctrine, the CJEU ruled:

> That said, with respect to the question, expressly raised by the referring court, of what qualitative and quantitative requirements the shareholding held by a resident taxpayer in a company established in a third country must satisfy in order for it not to be regarded as 'wholly artificial', it should be borne in mind that the free movement of capital between Member States and third countries is intended not to frame the conditions under which companies can establish themselves within the internal market.[148]
>
> Therefore, in the context of the free movement of capital, the concept of 'wholly artificial arrangement' cannot necessarily be limited to merely the indications ... that the establishment of a company does not reflect economic reality, since the artificial creation of the conditions required in order to escape taxation in a Member State improperly or enjoy a tax advantage in that Member State improperly can take several forms as regards cross-border movements of capital. Indeed, those indications may also amount to evidence of the existence of a wholly artificial arrangement for the purpose of applying the rules on the free movement of capital, in particular when it proves necessary to assess the commercial justification of acquiring shares in a company that does not pursue any economic activities of its own. However, that concept is also capable of covering, in the context of the free movement of capital, any scheme which has as its primary objective or one of its primary objectives the artificial transfer of the profits made by way of activities carried out in the territory of a Member State to third countries with a low tax rate.[149]

What the CJEU says is not that the substance requirements regarding subsidiaries are different in the context of the freedom of establishment and in the freedom of movement of capital. It merely says that in the context of the freedom of movement of capital, the fact that a subsidiary has substance does not, in and of itself, ensure that the transaction in question, i.e., the capital contribution in exchange for shares, is a genuine arrangement. It is possible that the subsidiary has substance and the abovementioned transaction is still wholly artificial. It may also be that the subsidiary does not have substance but other commercial reasons justify the capital movement. So the Cadbury criteria are mere indications of abuse in the context of the freedom of

147. *Ibid.*, at para. 80.
148. *Ibid.*, at para. 83.
149. *Ibid.*, at para. 84.

movement of capital.[150,151]

As far as the requirements on substance is concerned, it is submitted that the same standards should apply to both freedoms. That is, if a subsidiary has enough substance for the purposes of the freedom of establishment, it also has enough substance for the purposes of the freedom of movement of capital. Accordingly, the analysis in section B.II. also applies here.[152]

Schön has explained why substance requirements in the freedom of establishment and the freedom of movement of capital should be uniform, even before the whole topic became 'hot' in view of the *X-GmbH* ruling:

> The dividing line between the scope of application of the freedom of establishment and the scope of application of the free movement of capital ... in the case law of the Court of Justice does not depend on the type of company activity, but on the level of participation of the shareholder. The question of whether the formation of a company as such constitutes an 'artificial construction' must, however, be assessed uniformly for both the majority shareholder and the minority shareholder.[153]

So the CJEU does not delineate the scope of the two freedoms based on the substance of the subsidiary. Take the following case: company A, resident in Germany, invests in Company C, resident in the Netherlands, by buying 99% of its shares. Company B, also resident in Germany, invests in Company C by buying the remaining 1%. Company A may invoke the freedom of establishment, while Company B the freedom of movement of capital. The differentiating factor is the size of shareholding. The size of the shareholding does not justify different substance requirements, though.

150. *See* Köhler (2019), p. 446; Heckerodt/van Lück (2020), p. 862; Weber/Zöller (2020), p. 292; Kuźniacki (2021), p. 10. Schönfeld (2019), p. 399 seems to suggest that the existence of substance suffices, that is, that the existence of substance in and of itself excludes the possibility of abuse: 'The taxpayer must have the possibility to prove that either there are economic reasons for his participation in the foreign company or that this company (as under the Cadbury doctrine) is engaged in a genuine economic activity. In this respect, the possibility of proof is merely extended by a further aspect relating to the motivation for the participation in the company.' (Author's unofficial translation). In this sense also Kahlenberg (2019), p. 1593; De Broe (2022), p. 439.
151. According to Nyström (2021), p. 233 the *Danish withholding tax cases* have the same effect in relation to the freedom of establishment. This means that 'a physically existent CFC may amount to abuse of the fundamental freedoms if the investment into the CFC appears not to make sense commercially. It might also be contended that the corollary should now hold true: a physically non-existent company may be considered genuine if it can be demonstrated that no physical presence is necessary to carry out its economic activity'. Nyström (2021), at p. 231. In this sense also de Groot (2019), p. 780.
152. In this sense, citing Schön (2013a), p. 11, Cloer/Hagemann (2019), p. 1235. *Contra* Kuźniacki (2021), p. 9: 'The exercise of the freedom of establishment clearly requires a certain degree of economic substance to exist while the free movement of capital either does not require it at all, or it is enough to have a marginal economic substance that suffices to carry out portfolio investments.' Anzinger (2020), p. 103: 'In the X-GmbH case, the CJEU established the need for a sector-specific concept of a wholly artificial arrangement for the free movement of capital with reference to the lack of internal market finality of this fundamental freedom in relation to third countries and thus created room for special substance requirements.' (Author's unofficial translation). *See* already before the *X-GmbH* ruling in favour of different substance requirements in the two freedoms Thiele (2011), p. 133; Rudolf (2012), p. 176.
153. Schön (2013a), p. 11 (author's unofficial translation).

If a company is a letterbox for the purposes of the freedom of establishment, it is also a letterbox for the purposes of the freedom of movement of capital. The 'chairs are empty' for both the 99% shareholder and the 1% shareholder. The fact that Company B only has a 1% shareholding does not change the fact that Company C's chairs are empty. Accordingly, there is no lower threshold in the context of the freedom of movement of capital, as Kuźniacki has argued.[154]

IV Content of the Substance Requirement in the CFC Rule in the ATAD

The CFC rule in the ATAD provides for two alternatives, whereby both alternatives include a substance requirement, as already discussed in section B.III.4. of the introduction. Article 7(2)(a), on the one hand, refers to 'a substantive economic activity supported by staff, equipment, assets and premises'. Article 7(2)(b), on the other hand, refers to 'non-genuine arrangements' where 'the entity or permanent establishment would not own the assets or would not have undertaken the risks which generate all, or part of, its income if it were not controlled by a company where the significant people functions, which are relevant to those assets and risks, are carried out and are instrumental in generating the controlled company's income'. In the next two sections, both alternatives are interpreted respectively.

1 Article 7(2)(a) of the ATAD

The CJEU in *Cadbury Schweppes* and the *Danish withholding tax cases* refers to an '*actual* economic activity' (emphasis added), while Article 7(2)(a) of the ATAD to 'a *substantive* economic activity' (emphasis added). According to one opinion, the same standards apply in both substance requirements.[155] Other authors, however, point to the fact that '[t]here is … a certain difference between existence and substance since something can be "genuine" without being "substantive"'.[156] Watrin/Leukefeld interpret the changed wording as a focus on the relevance of the activity.[157] Köhler sees behind the new wording the introduction of higher thresholds in a quantitative and a qualitative sense.[158]

Since the adjective 'substantive' refers to the economic activity, it can be argued that Article 7(2)(a) of the ATAD may only include a higher threshold with regard to the functional element of substance and not the objective and personal element. Nevertheless, we have seen in section B.II.3. of this chapter that the elements of substance in the context of the wholly artificial arrangements test in the freedom of establishment mutually influence each other. Accordingly, if the threshold for the functional element of substance is higher, then the threshold for the other two elements should also be

154. Kuźniacki (2021), p. 9.
155. Schlücke (2019), p. 44.
156. Schönfeld (2017), p. 150. In a similar vein, Müller (2021), p. 286, n. 68; Ekinci (2023), 185.
157. Watrin/Leukefeld (2018), p. 2286. *See also* Richter et al. (2020), p. 697; Bärsch/Schneider (2022), p. 84.
158. Köhler (2018), p. 459. In this sense also Bärsch/Schneider (2022), p. 84.

higher. The more a subsidiary 'does', the more it 'needs'. Output follows input and the other way round.

So overall, one could argue that Article 7(2)(a) of the ATAD demands 'more' substance than the CJEU does. But what does 'more' mean in this context? And is the EU legislature allowed to deviate from the standards established by the CJEU? This brings us to the issue whether Article 7(2)(a) of the ATAD is 'immunized' against EU primary law. We have seen in section A.II. of this chapter that the literature denies this. If this is the case, Article 7(2)(a) of the ATAD should be interpreted in conformity with the CJEU case law analysed in section B.II. of this chapter.[159]

This could take place if someone interprets the word 'substantive' as a synonym to the word 'actual', used so far by the CJEU since the enunciation of the Cadbury formula.[160] In particular, it has been laid down in section D.I. of the introduction that the word substance may refer to two things: first, 'quality of being based on facts or the truth' and, second, '[t]he essence of something; the essential quality of something as opposed to its mere form'. The adjective 'substantive' refers to something 'dealing with real, important or serious matters'.[161] Let us now rephrase Article 7(2)(a) of the ATAD based on this definition of the word substantive: 'a *real* economic activity', or 'an *important* economic activity' or 'a *serious* economic activity'.

The first phrase conforms to the Cadbury formula referring to an 'actual economic activity', whereby the word 'actual' is used as a synonym for the word 'real'. Accordingly, the wording of Article 7(2)(a) of the ATAD allows an interpretation in conformity with the CJEU's case law; and this interpretation should take precedence as secondary EU law - including the CFC rule in the ATAD, this not being immunized against EU primary law - should comply with and be interpreted in accordance with EU primary law (section A.II. of this chapter).[162] Hence, the substance requirement of Article 7(2)(a) of the ATAD is uniform with the substance requirement of the fundamental freedoms analysis.

2 Article 7(2)(b) of the ATAD

Panayi has raised the question of whether the threshold in the wholly artificial arrangements doctrine in the freedom of establishment is the same as the one in Article 7(2)(b) of the ATAD referring to 'non-genuine arrangements'.[163] She suggests that the thresholds are not the same and that not only wholly artificial arrangements fall under

159. Hey (2017), p. 253; Schönfeld (2017), p. 150; Bärsch/Schneider (2022), p. 84; de Groot/Larking (2019), p. 269; Nyström (2021), pp. 229-230.
160. The same argument has already been expressed by Nyström (2021), pp. 229-230.
161. https://www.oxfordlearnersdictionaries.com/definition/american_english/substantive_1.
162. The way some Member States implemented Article 7(2)(a) of the ATAD raises questions with regard to its conformity with the CJEU's case law. For example, de Groot/Larking (2019), p. 269 note correctly: 'The Austrian rules are also noteworthy in that they provide for a list of activities that are deemed not to satisfy the substance carve-out. This includes acting as a mere holding company or as a conduit company. In light of recent CJEU decisions, the tenability of these conditions may be questioned.'
163. Panayi (2018), p. 375.

Article 7(2)(b) of the ATAD.[164] As Navarro et al. maintain, the definition of the term 'non-genuine arrangements' by reference to 'significant people functions' could amount to an adoption of the AOA for the purposes of the substance analysis in Article 7(2)(b) of the ATAD.[165]

Two issues arise here. First, the AOA deals with profit allocation between the head office and PE. It does not deal with profit allocation between related companies; for this purpose the OECD TPG exist. Since the CFC rule in the ATAD applies not only to PEs but also to subsidiaries, the question can be raised whether the reference to the profit allocation in the PE context can also apply in the subsidiary context. The second question would be then what the content of the substance requirement is.

As to the first question, scholars have identified the issue and denied the possibility of the applicability of the AOA in the subsidiary context.[166] Arne Friese, on the contrary, has mounted an extensive argument in favour of legal form neutrality for the purposes of profit allocation in the European Union.[167] Furthermore, as we have seen,[168] Holzinger has argued that the AOA has aligned profit allocation between head office and PE with the one between related companies.[169] So as regards the first question, it is submitted that the reference to the AOA in the subsidiary context is not problematic.

In fact, the reference to the AOA can be interpreted as a more general reference to transfer pricing principles.[170] This may be attributable to the fact that transfer pricing legislation based on Article 9 of the OECD MTC has been found to conform with the fundamental freedoms. So it could be that Article 7(2)(b) of the ATAD refers to a line of CJEU rulings, namely the one beginning with the *SGI* judgment, where the CJEU found transfer pricing legislation to be in line with the freedom of establishment based on the justification grounds of preventing abusive behaviour and balanced allocation of taxing rights, taken together.[171] This resembles the case of Article 7(2)(a) of the ATAD where it has been found in the previous section that reference is being made to the wholly artificial arrangements doctrine of the CJEU and the substance requirements established therein.

This reference can be understood if one considers Recital 12 to the ATAD, according to which the substance carve-out is provided in order to comply with the fundamental freedoms. The EU legislature, by referring to the abovementioned CJEU jurisprudence, ensures that Article 7(2)(b) of the ATAD withstands the control against

164. *Ibid.*
165. Navarro et al. (2016), p. 126. *See also* Nyström (2021), p. 233; Pantazatou (2022), pp. 61-62; Haslehner/Pantazatou (2022), p. 24.
166. Navarro et al. (2016), p. 126.
167. Friese (2010), pp. 221 et seq.
168. *See* above n. 102 in s. B.II.1.c. of Ch. 2.
169. Holzinger (2020), pp. 280-281.
170. *See* Nyström (2021), p. 233; Pantazatou (2022), pp. 61-62 and Haslehner/Pantazatou (2022), p. 24 all referring generally to transfer pricing.
171. CJEU, 21 Jan. 2010, C-311/08, *Société de Gestion Industrielle SA (SGI) v. Belgian State*, ECLI:EU:C:2010:26, para. 69; CJEU, 31 May 2018, C-382/16, *Hornbach-Baumarkt-AG v. Finanzamt Landau*, ECLI:EU:C:2018:366, para. 49; and more recently in the PE context CJEU, 8 Oct. 2020, C-558/19, *Impresa Pizzarotti (Avantage anormal consenti à une société non-résidente)*, ECLI:EU:C:2020:806, paras 30 et seq.

the fundamental freedoms. It can be surmised that the reference to the AOA is influenced by the Action 3 of the BEPS Project, which suggests '[d]esigning CFC rules to explicitly ensure a balanced allocation of taxing power' and refers to the CJEU jurisprudence cited above.[172]

According to this interpretation, the term 'non-genuine arrangements' may refer to transfer pricing substance because transfer pricing legislation has been found to conform with the fundamental freedoms based on a combination of the justification grounds of preventing abuse and the balanced allocation of taxing rights.[173] This finding answers the second question raised above. The term 'non-genuine arrangements' refers to companies that do not have transfer pricing substance. So, as to the content of substance in Article 7(2)(b) of the ATAD, reference can be made to the findings in section B. of Chapter 2 analysing the substance requirement in the transfer pricing context.

3 *Application of the ATAD in Cases Where the Freedom of Movement of Capital Applies*

It is important to note that these findings apply also in third country scenarios where the freedom of movement of capital applies (section B.III.1. of this chapter).[174] At first sight, the CFC rule in the ATAD only applies to shareholdings enabling definite influence, since according to Article 7(1)(a) a 50% shareholding is required, which would speak for the application only of the freedom of establishment. Nevertheless, one can interpret the CFC rule in the ATAD in a way allowing also the freedom of movement of capital to apply.

In particular, Danon argues that 'the free movement of capital could already come into play on the basis of the minimum standard of article 7(1)(a) [referring to the ATAD], since, under this provision, the CFC rule would apply not only where a parent company "holds a direct or indirect participation of more than 50 percent of the voting rights, or owns directly or indirectly more than 50 percent of capital" but also where the parent is merely "entitled to receive more than 50 percent of the profits of that entity"'.[175] And one should also not forget that '[s]ince article 3 of the Directive [referring to the ATAD] states that a higher level of protection of domestic corporate tax bases should not be precluded by the Directive, a reduction in the requirement of

172. OECD Action 3, p. 18. According to Kuźniacki (2016), pp. 150-154 the substance test in Article 7(2)(b) of the ATAD is based on the Action 3 of the BEPS Project which is based on the UK's CFC rules which were amended introducing the use of the AOA in order to be immunized, as the HMRC views, against CJEU control.
173. *See*, however, Schön (2020a), p. 298: 'One can doubt whether the changes made under BEPS Actions 8–10 pass this test as they purport to create a new standard, which goes beyond the traditional discipline applied to non-arm's length arrangements.'
174. Although it must be said that the ATAD in Article 7(2)(a) gives to Member States the option not to apply the exception of companies with 'substantive economic activities' in the case of subsidiaries established in third states.
175. Danon (2018b), s. 17.5.2.1. *See also* Schönfeld (2017), p. 150; de Groot/Larking (2019), p. 269; de Groot (2019), p. 779; Heckerodt/van Lück (2020), p. 864; Kahlenberg/Quilitzsch (2021), p. 137; Nyström (2021), p. 229. This is overseen by Panayi (2018), p. 376.

control would still be an option, although it does not reflect political consensus. If Member States decide to decrease the threshold to 10% or even less, article 63 of the TFEU could come into play'.[176]

So either if one interprets Article 7(1)(a) of the ATAD as Danon does or in cases where Member States apply their CFC rules on shareholdings that do not ensure definite influence,[177] CFC rules in the European Union will continue[178] to be scrutinized as to their conformity with the freedom of capital.

4 *Synthesis*

Section B.IV. dealt with the substance requirements in the CFC rule in the ATAD. It has been shown that Article 7(2)(a) of the ATAD refers to the wholly artificial arrangements doctrine in the context of the freedom of establishment as developed by the CJEU since the *Cadbury Schweppes* judgment. The analysis of this CJEU line of jurisprudence has revealed that substance for the purposes of the wholly artificial arrangements doctrine in the context of the freedom of establishment partially corresponds with substance for the purposes of the POEM, as analysed in section B. of Chapter 1. This applies also in third country scenarios (freedom of movement of capital).

Article 7(2)(b) of the ATAD refers to another line of jurisprudence beginning with the *SGI* judgment, according to which the balanced allocation of taxing rights in combination with the prevention of abuse justify transfer pricing legislation. Thus, it could be that in this way the EU legislature refers to transfer pricing substance, as analysed in section B.II. of Chapter 2.

Interpreting the CFC rule of the ATAD in this sense leads to the conclusion that the substance in the ATAD is derived from the substance in the international tax law context, and in particular from the POEM and transfer pricing.

C INTERIM CONCLUSIONS

- The substance requirement in the wholly artificial arrangements doctrine in the context of the freedom of establishment partially matches the content of the substance requirement in the POEM. If a subsidiary has its POEM in its host state, it then does not constitute a fictitious establishment. The substance requirement in the wholly artificial arrangements doctrine in the context of the freedom of establishment is less demanding than the substance-oriented rules in the DTC context since companies with less substance are also considered genuine establishments (section B.II.).

176. Nielsen (2018), p. 575. *See also* Smit (2019), s. 12.4.3.4.
177. It is not clear which shareholdings ensure definite influence. '[T]he practice, most notably in the field of tax, queries whether in the area between 10 and 25% the rule in Art. 49 TFEU can find application.' Schön (2016), pp. 242-243.
178. *See* already CJEU, C-135/17, *X-GmbH*.

- The same substance requirements apply to both the freedom of establishment and the freedom of movement of capital (section B.III.).
- Substance in the CFC rule in the ATAD is derivative from substance requirements in international tax law. In particular, Article 7(2)(a) of the ATAD refers to the wholly artificial arrangements doctrine in the context of the freedom of establishment which introduces substance requirements corresponding with the ones required for the purposes of the POEM. Article 7(2)(b) of the ATAD refers to transfer pricing substance (section B.IV.).

Conclusions

- This work has provided a definition of the term 'substance' for the purposes of DTC and EU tax law. The definition can and should be adopted in the Models and used by the CJEU when interpreting substance-oriented rules in the EU tax law context (section D. of the introduction).
- Based on this definition, in Chapters 1-4 the content of the POEM, transfer pricing rules, DTC treaty shopping rules (the active conduct of a business test, the PPMC, and the PPT), and substance-oriented rules in the EU tax law context (the wholly artificial arrangements test in the context of the freedom of establishment and freedom of capital, the Shell Entities Directive, and the CFC rule in the ATAD) have been dissected, thereby answering the first research question raised in this work. As to the conclusions in this respect, the reader is referred to section C. of Chapters 1-4.
- As an overarching conclusion from this analysis, it is submitted that the content of these rules is nowhere near the same. It is literally a minefield-act for taxpayers to pass all substance-oriented rules. There are some similarities, though:
  - All rules require the engagement of knowledgeable and well-informed personnel.[1]
  - All rules in the DTC context prioritize the functional and personal elements of substance, while the objective element (i.e., the existence of assets) is of secondary importance.[2] In the EU tax law context this is not the case, since all elements have equal importance (section B.II.3. of Chapter 4).

1. *See* above ss B.II.2.c.cc. and B.II.2.c.dd. of Ch. 1 on the POEM, s. B.III.2. of Ch. 2 on transfer pricing, s. B.III.2.b. of Ch. 3 on the PPMC, and s. B.II.2.c.bb. of Ch. 4 on the wholly artificial arrangements test in the context of the freedom of establishment.
2. *See* above s. B.III.3. of Ch. 1 on the POEM, s. B.IV.2. of Ch. 2 on transfer pricing, s. B.II.3. of Ch. 3 on the active conduct of a business test, and s. B.III.3. of Ch. 3 on the PPMC.

  - All rules adopt a stand-alone perspective, that is, substance of other group companies is not considered, with the exception of Article 29(3)(c) of the OECD MTC.[3]
  - All rules only consider activities, persons, and assets in the residence state of the subsidiary. Only the active conduct of a business test allows activities in the source state to be taken into account in Article 29(3)(b) of the OECD MTC, although here also the activities in the residence state are the relevant ones. This is because Article 29(3)(b) is accompanied by a relative threshold, i.e., that the activities in the residence state are substantial compared to the ones in the source state.[4] This conclusion does not apply if legitimate outsourcing has taken place;[5] then activities carried out by other companies employing persons and using assets in a state other than the residence state are not considered harmful for the purposes of the respective substance requirement.
  - With the exception of the substantiality requirement in Article 29(3)(a) of the OECD MTC (section B.II.1.b.aa. of Chapter 3), there are no absolute quantitative thresholds and, with the exception of the Shell Entities Directive (section B.II.2.c.cc. of Chapter 4), there are no safe harbour rules. It has been found that the lack of safe harbour rules is a drawback. It would be desirable that the substance-oriented rules in the DTC context follow the example given by the Shell Entities Directive.
  - The fact that no absolute thresholds apply, implies that substance requirements are contingent on the business of the entity. Other substance requirements apply to an SPV and others to a manufacturing subsidiary, for example.
- The second research question concerns the relationship between the substance requirements in the four sets of legal rules dealt with in this work and asks whether there are differences between them and whether such differences are justified:
  - It has already been found that there is a Stufenverhältnis between the substance-oriented rules in the DTC context (section C.II. of Chapter 3). That is, there is a continuum of substance requirements beginning with the looser ones in the POEM and becoming stricter in treaty shopping rules. This relationship between the substance requirements in the DTC context can be justified if one takes into account their purpose. In

3. *See* above s. B.II.1.a.aa. of Ch. 1 on the POEM, s. A.I.1. of Ch. 2 on transfer pricing, s. B.II.1.a.aa. of Ch. 3 on the active conduct of a business, s. B.III.1.a. of Ch. 3 on the PPMC, and s. B.II.1.a.aa. of Ch. 4 on the wholly artificial arrangements test in the context of the freedom of establishment.
4. *See* above s. B.II.1.a.aa. of Ch. 3 on the active conduct of a business test and the POEM and transfer pricing and s. B.II.1.a.bb. of Ch. 4 on the wholly artificial arrangements test in the context of the freedom of establishment.
5. As to when outsourcing is legitimate *see* above s. B.II.2.c.hh. of Ch. 1 on the POEM, s. B.II.1.a.bb. of Ch. 2 on transfer pricing, s. B.II.1.c. of Ch. 3 on the active conduct of a business test, s. B.III.1.a.aa. of Ch. 3 on the PPMC, and s. B.II.1.c. of Ch. 4 on the wholly artificial arrangements test in the context of the freedom of establishment.

particular, the substance requirement in transfer pricing and DTC treaty shopping rules intends to close the loopholes that treaty residence creates. A company can easily be regarded as resident in a low-tax jurisdiction to which profit is shifted.[6] Substance-oriented transfer pricing intends to tackle the overbooking of profits to entities resident in low-tax jurisdictions. In a similar vein, DTC treaty shopping rules fight against nexus abuse, i.e., the abuse of the residence nexus via subsidiaries (section B.I.1. of Chapter 3). Both transfer pricing and DTC treaty shopping filter the unworthy resident subsidiaries and cut them out from profit distribution and DTC benefits respectively. Accordingly, they just cannot be the same as residence. If they were the same, a company having enough substance for the purposes of DTC residence would also have enough substance for the purposes of transfer pricing and DTC treaty shopping rules which would contradict their 'filtering' purpose.

- In the EU tax law context, the relationship to the substance-oriented rules in the DTC context is a derivative one, that is, Article 7(2)(a) of the ATAD refers to the wholly artificial arrangements doctrine, which has been found to partially match the requirements of the POEM (not only; but also a PE in the host state constitutes a genuine establishment), and Article 7(2)(b) of the ATAD refers to transfer pricing substance (section C. of Chapter 4). Especially with regard to substance for the purposes of the wholly artificial arrangements doctrine it is important to note that the match with the requirements of the POEM is only a partial one and that the requirements in the former have been found to be looser than the ones in the latter (section B.II.4. of Chapter 4) This has been also found to be justified taking into account the legal context within which the respective substance requirements exist. The EU legal order has as its constitutional telos the establishment of an internal market. Accordingly, an integration-friendly interpretation of its rules, and thus of the fundamental freedoms, is necessary. DTCs have a more limited scope and purpose, namely to further the economic relations between only two states and to avoid double non-taxation, whereby especially this last purpose is not pursued in the EU, at least according to CJEU case law.

Now the author would like to proceed to some conclusions that do not answer the two research questions, but do however contribute to a better understanding of the nature of substance requirements, in general, and to creating a systematic order between them.

6. Regarding the substance-oriented transfer pricing rules as complementing the residence principle, *see* Monsenego (2014), p. 19: 'That the substance requirement applies to the physical location of key employees is, in the author's opinion, in line with other general principles of international tax law relying on some form of substance requirement, such as EU law,[referring to the substance requirement in CFC rules] the determination of the place of effective management of a dual resident company or the existence of a permanent establishment as a consequence of having a fixed place of business or a dependent agent.'

- As to the nature of substance in general, substance is merely a legal word pointing to a set of facts that leads to a set of legal consequences, thereby systematically connecting them. If you have enough decision-making functions carried out in your residence state (facts), you have substance for the purposes of the POEM and thus the POEM is in the claimed residence state.
- What is problematic is that the legal rules dealt with so far do not make this connection clear. For example, the LOB does not contain any reference to substance arising, for example, when a subsidiary actively conducts a business. This inference has been made by the literature.[7] It would be preferable that the rules directly refer to substance, connect to it a legal consequence, and explain which facts give rise to substance. A – admittedly simplified legislative technique for this purpose would be:
  (1) If a company has substance (connecting word), it should gain access to DTC and EU law benefits. (Legal consequence).
  (2) A company has substance when ... (facts).[8]
  By doing so, the OECD, at the DTC level, and the EU legislature, at the EU level, would 'conceptualize the legal rules in such a way that they are reduced to systematic order and by this means to give an account of the law in force which is as plain and convenient as possible.'[9] So although there is no system, it is possible to create one.
- In this way, and in combination with the inclusion of the substance definition brought forward in this work, the application of the law would become almost a scientific exercise. For example, for the purposes of a tax audit in state B, the taxpayer claims that they have DTC residence in state A. The tax administration of state B, and maybe later on the judge(s), would first acknowledge the legal fact: in order for you to have residence in state A you need to have substance there (again, the substance-oriented legal rule would explicitly refer to 'substance' and connect the legal consequence thereto, in our case DTC residence). Then they would see that the content of substance is for the purposes of DTC residence (again, the rule would also explain which facts give rise to substance for the purposes of DTC residence), based on the definition of substance included in the DTC, as the author proposed, and compare it with the facts at hand. They would sketch a summary along the lines of the following checklist.

7. *See* above s. B.III. of the introduction where the substance-oriented rules are introduced. You may notice there that literature is cited interpreting, for example, the active conduct of a business test as a rule demanding from an intermediate company to have substance. The rule itself nowhere uses the word substance.
8. Whereby with 'facts' reference is made to the substance requirements as analysed and summarized above in s. C. of Chs 1-4.
9. Ross (1957), p. 819.

Table 4 Application of the Author's Classification

Definition of Substance	*Content in the Substance-Oriented Rule in Question*	*Facts*
Qualitative sub-element of the functional element	Strategic/operational decisions, etc.	Yes/no
Quantitative sub-element of the functional element	Absolute/relative threshold, safe harbour rule	Yes/no
Personal element stricto sensu	Institutional position, managerial liability, etc.	Yes/no
Qualitative sub-element of the personal element	Information, knowledge, etc.	Yes/no
Quantitative sub-element of the personal element	Absolute/relative threshold, safe harbour rule	Yes/no
Qualitative sub-element of the objective element	Tangible assets, financial assets, etc.	Yes/no
Quantitative sub-element of the objective element	Absolute/relative threshold, safe harbour rule	Yes/no

Bibliography

Alchian, A.A./Demsetz, H., *The Property Right Paradigm*, 33 The Journal of Economic History 1 (1973), pp. 16-27.

Alexy, R./Peczenik, A., *Coherence and Discursive Rationality*, 3 Ratio Juris 1 (1990), pp. 130-147.

Altshuler, R./Grubert, H., *Repatriation Taxes, Repatriation Strategies and Multinational Financial Policy*, 87 Journal of Public Economics 1 (2002), pp. 73-107.

Anzinger, H., *Folgerungen für die Substanzerfordernisse des § 50d abs. 3 EStG aus dem Europäischen Missbrauchsbegriff*, Recht der Finanzinstrumente 2 (2020), pp. 97-104.

Armour, J./et al., *What Is Corporate Law?*, in: Kraakman, R./Armour, J. eds, *The Anatomy of Corporate Law* (3rd edn Oxford University Press 2017), pp. 1-28.

Arnold, B.J., *Threshold Requirements for Taxing Business Profits under Tax Treaties*, 57 Bulletin for International Taxation 10 (2003), pp. 476-492.

Arnold, B.J., *A Comparative Perspective on the U.S. Controlled Foreign Corporation Rules*, 65 Tax Law Review 3 (2012), pp. 473-504.

Arnold, B.J., *The Evolution of Controlled Foreign Corporation Rules and Beyond*, 73 Bulletin for International Taxation 12 (2019), pp. 631-648.

Arnold, F., *In-Depth Analysis of the Concept of Control over Risk*, 28 International Transfer Pricing Journal 1 (2021), pp. 36-48.

Auer, M., *Methodenkritik und Interessenjurisprudenz: Philipp Heck zum 150. Geburtstag*, Zeitschrift für Europäisches Privatrecht 3 (2008), pp. 517-533.

Avella, F., *Using EU Law to Interpret Undefined Tax Treaty Terms: Article 31(3)(c) of the Vienna Convention on the Law of Treaties and Article 3(2) of the OECD Model Convention*, 4 World Tax Journal 2 (2012), pp. 95-124.

Avery Jones, J.F., *Place of Effective Management as a Residence Tiebreaker*, 59 Bulletin for International Taxation 1 (2005), pp. 20-24.

Avery Jones, J.F., *Revenue and Customs Commissioners v. Development Securities Plc: Seeing the Wood (v Holden) for the Trees*, British Tax Review 1 (2021), pp. 51-55.

Avery Jones, J.F./et al., *The Origins of Concepts and Expressions Used in the OECD Model and Their Adoption by States,* 60 Bulletin for International Taxation 6 (2006), pp. 220-254.

Avi-Yonah, R.S., *The Rise and Fall of Arm's Length: A Study in the Evolution of U.S. International Taxation*, 15 Virginia Tax Review 1 (1995), pp. 89-160.

Avi-Yonah, R.S., *International Taxation of Electronic Commerce*, 52 Tax Law Review 3 (1997), pp. 507-556.

Avi-Yonah, R.S., *International Tax as International Law,* 57 Tax Law Review 4 (2004), pp. 483-502.

Avi-Yonah, R.S., *International Tax as International Law* (Cambridge University Press 2007).

Avi-Yonah, R.S./Panayi, C.H., *Rethinking Treaty Shopping: Lessons for the European Union*, in: Lang, M./et al. eds, *Tax Treaties: Building Bridges Between Law and Economics* (IBFD 2010).

Avi-Yonah, R.S./Benshalom, I., *Formulary Apportionment: Myths and Prospects*, 3 World Tax Journal 3 (2011), pp. 371-398.

Baerentzen, S., *Danish Cases on the Use of Holding Companies for Cross-Border Dividends and Interest: A New Test to Disentangle Abuse from Real Economic Activity?*, 12 World Tax Journal 1 (2020), pp. 3-52.

Báez Moreno, A., *GAARs and Treaties: From the Guiding Principle to the Principal Purpose Test. What Have We Gained from BEPS Action 6?*, 45 Intertax 6/7 (2017), pp. 432-446.

Báez Moreno, A., *Unnecessary and Yet Harmful: Some Critical Remarks to the OECD Note on the Impact of the COVID-19 Crisis on Tax Treaties*, 48 Intertax 8/9 (2020), pp. 814-830.

Báez Moreno, A., *How Do 'The Old' and 'The New' Live Together? The Principal Purpose Test and Other Anti-avoidance Instruments in Tax Treaties*, 49 Intertax 10 (2021), pp. 771-785.

Bainbridge, S.M., *The Board of Directors,* in: Gordon, J.N./Ringe, W.-G. eds, *The Oxford Handbook of Corporate Law and Governance* (Oxford University Press 2018), pp. 275-333.

Baistrocchi, E., The Use and Interpretation of Tax Treaties in the Emerging World: Theory and Implications, 2008 British Tax Review 4 (2008), pp. 352-391.

Baistrocchi, E., Article 9, in: Global Tax Treaty Commentaries (IBFD April 2022).

Ballancin, A./Cannas, F., *The Development of the Doctrine of Abuse of Law and the Danish Cases: Time to Shift the Focus from Non-genuine Arrangements to Single (Abusive) Transactions?*, 31 EC Tax Review 2 (2021), pp. 70-80.

Barba de Alba, A./Arribas, D., *The Interplay Between Beneficial Ownership and Abuse in the Danish Cases on Dividends*, Kluwer Tax Blog (March 2019). Available at http://kluwertaxblog.com/2019/03/27/the-interplay-between-beneficial-ownership-and-abuse-in-the-danish-cases-on-dividends/.

Barreiros Rosalem, F., *The Agent Permanent Establishment Reconsidered: Application of Arts. 5, 7 and 9 of the OECD Model Convention*, 17 International Transfer Pricing Journal 1 (2010), pp. 12-33.

Bärsch, S.-E./Schneider, H., *Der neue Substanztest zur Vermeidung der Hinzurechnungsbesteuerung in EU-/EWR-Fällen*, Der Betrieb 2 (2022), pp. 81-86.

Bartlett, C.A./Ghoshal, S., *Tap Your Subsidiaries for Global Reach*, 64 Harvard Business Review 6 (1986), pp. 87-94.

Bates, J./et al., *Limitation on Benefits Articles in Income Tax Treaties: The Current State of Play*, 41 Intertax 6/7 (2013), pp. 395-404.

Beer, S./de Mooij, R./Liu, L., *International Corporate Tax Avoidance: A Review of the Channels, Magnitudes, and Blind Spots*, Working Paper 18/168 (IMF 2018). Available at International Corporate Tax Avoidance: A Review of the Channels, Magnitudes, and Blind Spots (imf.org).

Benshalom, I., *Rethinking the Source of the Arm's-Length Transfer Pricing Problem*, 32 Virginia Tax Review 3 (2013), pp. 425-460.

Benz, S./Böhmer, J., *Der Entwurf der sog. 'Unshell'-Richtlinie als Teil der EU-Initiative 'Eine Unternehmensbesteuerung für das 21. Jahrhundert'*, Der Betrieb 17 (2022), pp. 1028-1037.

Beretta, G., *The Notions of 'Beneficial Ownership' and 'Place of Effective Management' in Respect of a Passive Holding Company*, 57 European Taxation 6 (2017), pp. 253-257.

Berle, A.A./Means, G.C., *The Modern Corporation and Private Property* (Macmillan 1932).

Beutel, D./Oppel, F., Mehr Fragen als Antworten nach dem neuen BMF-Schreiben zu § 50d Abs. 3 EStG, Deutsches Steuerrecht 28 (2018), pp. 1469-1475.

Birkinshaw, J./et al., *Consequences of Perception Gaps in the Headquarters–Subsidiary Relationship*, 9 International Business Review 3 (2000), pp. 321-344.

Birkinshaw, J./ et al., *Why Do Some Multinational Corporations Relocate Their Headquarters Overseas?*, 27 Strategic Management Journal 7 (2006), pp. 681-700.

Blair, M.M./Stout, L.A., *A Team Production Theory of Corporate Law*, 85 Virginia Law Review 2 (1999), pp. 247-328.

Blessing, P.H., *Article 29*, in: *Global Tax Treaty Commentaries* (IBFD July 2020a).

Blessing, P.H., *Limitations on Treaty Access by or Through Commercial Entities*, in: Maisto, G. ed., *Current Tax Treaty Issues: 50th Anniversary of the International Tax Group* (IBFD 2020b).

Blum, D.W., *Controlled Foreign Companies: Selected Policy Issues – Or the Missing Elements of BEPS Action 3 and the Anti-Tax Avoidance Directive*, 46 Intertax 4 (2018), pp. 296-312.

Braumann, C., *Taxes and Custom: Tax Treaties as Evidence for Customary International Law*, 23 Journal of International Economic Law 3 (2020), pp. 747-769.

Bräumann, P., *Dual Residence for Non-individuals*, in: Lang, M./et al. eds, *Tax Treaty Entitlement* (IBFD 2019), pp. 169-193.

Brauner, Y., *Value in the Eye of the Beholder: The Valuation of Intangibles for Transfer Pricing Purposes*, 28 Virginia Tax Review 1 (2008), pp. 79-164.

Brauner, Y., *What the BEPS?*, 16 Florida Tax Review 2 (2014), pp. 55-116.

Brauner, Y., *Transfer Pricing in BEPS: First Round – Business Interests Win (But, Not in Knock-Out)*, 43 Intertax 1 (2015), pp. 72-84.

Breslin, P., *BEPS Action 8, 9 and 10: Discussion Draft on Revisions to Chapter 1 of the Transfer Pricing Guidelines – Comments by Pat Breslin of NERA Economic Consulting*, in: OECD ed., *BEPS Actions 8, 9 and 10: Revisions to Chapter I of the Transfer Pricing Guidelines (Including Risk, Recharacterisation, and Special Measures)* (OECD 2015), pp. 625-633.

Breuninger, G./Krüger, A., *Die abnehmende Lokalisierung von Unternehmen als Rechtsproblem im internationalen Steuer- und Gesellschaftsrecht*, in: Breuninger, G. ed., *Steuerrecht und europäische Integration* (C.H. Beck 1999), pp. 79-111.

Brown, M./Orlandi, M., *Transfer Pricing Methods (Part I): Transactional Profit Methods*, in: Lang, M./et al. eds, *Fundamentals of Transfer Pricing* (Wolters Kluwer 2019), pp. 91-124.

Bühler, O., *Prinzipien des internationalen Steuerrechts* (Internationales Steuerdokumentationsbüro 1964).

Bullen, A., *Arm's Length Transaction Structures* (IBFD 2011).

Bundgaard, J., *Danish Case Law Developments on Beneficial Ownership*, Tax Notes International (1 October 2012), pp. 63-74.

Burgers, I.J.J., *Some Thoughts on the Further Refinement of the Concept of the Place of Effective Management for Tax Treaty Purposes*, 35 Intertax 6/7 (2007), pp. 378-386.

Burgers, I.J.J., *The New OECD Approach on Profit Allocation: A Step Forward Towards Neutral Treatment of Permanent Establishments and Subsidiaries*, 10 Florida Tax Review, 1 (2009), pp. 51-76.

Burgstaller, E./Haslinger, K., *Place of Effective Management as a Tiebreaker-Rule: Concept, Developments and Prospects*, 32 Intertax 8/9 (2004), pp. 376-387.

Buriak, S., *The Application of the Principal Purpose Test under Tax Treaties*, in: Lang, M./et al. eds, *Tax Treaty Entitlement* (IBFD 2019), pp. 23-53.

Calderón, J., *The OECD Transfer Pricing Guidelines as a Source of Tax Law: Is Globalization Reaching the Tax Law?*, 35 Intertax 1 (2007), pp. 4-29.

Canaris, C.-W., *Die Feststellung von Lücken im Gesetz* (1st edn Duncker & Humblot 1964).

Canè, D., *Controlled Foreign Corporations as Fiscally Transparent Entities. The Application of CFC Rules in Tax Treaties*, 9 World Tax Journal 4 (2017), pp. 521-563.

Castelon, M., *International Taxation of Income from Services under Double Taxation Conventions* (Wolters Kluwer 2018).

Cerioni, L., *The 'Abuse of Right' in EU Company Law and EU Tax Law: A Re-reading of the CJEU Case-Law and the Quest for a Unitary Notion* (2010). Available at https://bura.brunel.ac.uk/bitstream/2438/4141/3/Law.pdf.

Cerioni, L./Eden, S., *The United Kingdom*, in: Traversa, E. ed., *Corporate Tax Residence and Mobility* (IBFD 2018), pp. 667-695.

CFE, *Opinion Statement CJEU-TF 2/2019 on the CJEU Decisions of 26 February 2019 in N Luxembourg I et al. (Joined Cases C-115/16, C-118/16, C-119/16 and C-299/16) and T Danmark et al. (Joined Cases C-116/16 and C-117/17), Concerning the 'Beneficial Ownership' Requirement and the Anti-Abuse Principle in the Company Tax Directives*, 59 European Taxation 10 (2019), pp. 487-502.

Chand, V., *The Principal Purpose Test in the Multilateral Convention: An In-depth Analysis*, 46 Intertax 1 (2018), pp. 18-44.

Chand, V./Malek, B., *The Relevant Economic Activity Test and Its Impact on the International Corporate Tax Policy Framework*, British Tax Review 3 (2019), pp. 394-424.

Cloer, A./Hagemann, T., *Grenzen der Hinzurechnungsbesteuerung: Auswirkungen der jüngeren Rechtsprechung von EuGH und BFH*, Der Betrieb 22 (2019), pp. 1228-1236.

Coase, R., *The Nature of the Firm*, 4 Economica 16 (1937), pp. 386-405.

Collier, R.S./Andrus, J.L., *Transfer Pricing and the Arm's Length Principle after BEPS* (Oxford University Press 2017).

Collier, R.S./Dykes, I.F., *The Virus in the ALP*, 74 Bulletin for International Taxation 12 (2020), pp. 702-720.

Collier, R.S./Dykes, I.F., *On the Apparent Widespread Misapplication of the OECD Transfer Pricing Guidelines*, 76 Bulletin for International Taxation 1 (2022), pp. 20-43.

Collier, R.S./Vella, J., *Five Core Problems in the Attribution of Profits to Permanent Establishments*, 11 World Tax Journal 2 (2019), pp. 159-187.

Collis, D./Young, D./Goold, M., *The Size, Structure, and Performance of Corporate Headquarters*, 28 Strategic Management Journal 4 (2007), pp. 383-405.

Cools, A., *Article 16 of the OECD Model: A Plea to Extend the Scope of the Ratione Personae*, 70 Bulletin for International Taxation 10 (2016), pp. 558-575.

Cordewener, A., *Article 16*, in: Reimer, E. ed., *Klaus Vogel on Double Taxation Conventions* (5th edn Kluwer Law International 2021).

Couzin, R., *Corporate Residence and International Taxation* (IBFD 2002).

Cui, W., *Minimalism about Residence and Source*, 38 Michigan Journal of International Law 2 (2017), pp. 245-270.

Cunningham, N.B., *The Taxation of Capital Income and the Choice of Tax Base*, 52 Tax Law Review 1 (1996), pp. 17-44.

Dagan, T., *The Tax Treaties Myth*, 32 New York University Journal of International Law and Politcs 4 (2000), pp. 939-996.

Dahlberg, M./Wiman, B., *General Report*, in: International Fiscal Association ed., *Cahiers de droit fiscal international*, Vol. 98a (IBFD 2013), pp. 17-56.

Daniel, A., *Perception Gaps Between Headquarters and Subsidiary Managers* (Gabler 2010).

Danon, R.J., *Treaty Abuse in the Post-BEPS World: Analysis of the Policy Shift and Impact of the Principal Purpose Test for MNE Groups*, 72 Bulletin for International Taxation 1 (2018a), pp. 31-55.

Danon, R.J., *Some Observations on the Carve-Out Clause of Article 7(2) (a) of the ATAD with Regard to Third Countries*, in: Pistone, P./Weber, D. eds, *The Implementation of Anti-BEPS Rules in the EU: A Comprehensive Study* (IBFD 2018b).

Danon, R.J., *EU Fiscal Protectionism Versus Free Movement of Capital: The Case of the ATAD CFC Categorical Model*, in Pistone, P. ed., *European Tax Integration: Law, Policy and Politics* (IBFD 2018c).

Danon, R.J., *The Beneficial Ownership Limitation in Articles 10, 11 and 12 OECD Model and Conduit Companies in Pre- and Post-BEPS Tax Treaty Policy: Do We (Still) Need It?*, in: Maisto, G. ed., *Current Tax Treaty Issues: 50th Anniversary of the International Tax Group* (IBFD 2020a).

Danon, R.J., *The PPT in Post-BEPS Tax Treaty Law: It Is a GAAR but Just a GAAR!*, 74 Bulletin for International Taxation 5 (2020b), pp. 242-263.

Danon, R.J./et al., *The Prohibition of Abuse of Rights after the CJEU Danish Cases*, 49 Intertax 6/7 (2021), pp. 482-516.

Danon, R.J./Malek, B., *Swiss Supreme Court Refers to the CJEU 'Danish Cases' in Outbound Dividend Case Involving the Swiss-EU Savings Agreement*, Kluwer Tax Blog (July 2020). Available at http://kluwertaxblog.com/2020/07/23/swiss-supreme-court-refers-to-the-cjeu-danish-cases-in-outbound-dividend-case-involving-the-swiss-eu-savings-agreement/#_ednref9.

Daum, A./Petzold, J./Pletke, M., *BWL für Juristen* (3rd edn Springer Gabler 2016).

De Baets, S., *Risk Assumption under the Authorised OECD Approach and the 2017 OECD Transfer Pricing Guidelines*, 2 Transfer Pricing International 5 (2018), pp. 243-254.

Debelva, F./Luts, J., *The General Anti-abuse Rule of the Parent-Subsidiary Directive*, 55 European Taxation 6 (2015), pp. 223-234.

De Broe, L., *International Tax Planning and Prevention of Abuse* (IBFD 2008).

De Broe, L., *Should Courts in EU Member States Take Account of the CJEU's Judgment in the Danish Beneficial Ownership Cases When Interpreting the Beneficial Ownership Requirement in Tax Treaties?*, in: Maisto, G. ed., *Current Tax Treaty Issues: 50th Anniversary of the International Tax Group* (IBFD 2020).

De Broe, L., *Tax Abuse in the European Union: The Current State of Affairs*, 14 World Tax Journal 3 (2022), pp. 435-440.

De Broe, L./Luts, J., *BEPS Action 6: Tax Treaty Abuse*, 43 Intertax 2 (2015), pp. 122-146.

De Broe, L./Gommers, S., *Danish Dynamite: The 26 February 2019 CJEU Judgments in the Danish Beneficial Ownership Cases*, 28 EC Tax Review 6 (2019), pp. 270-299.

de Groot, I., *Implementation of the Controlled Foreign Company Rules in the Netherlands*, 47 Intertax 8/9 (2019), pp. 770-783.

de Groot, I./Larking, B., *Implementation of Controlled Foreign Company Rules under the EU Anti-Tax Avoidance Directive (2016/1164)*, 59 European Taxation 6 (2019), pp. 261-272.

de la Feria, R., *Prohibition of Abuse of (Community) Law: The Creation of a New General Principle of EC Law Through Tax*, 45 Common Market Law Review 2 (2008), pp. 395-441.

Demsetz, H., *The Theory of the Firm Revisited*, 4 Journal of Law, Economics, & Organization 1 (1988), pp. 141-161.

De Pietro, C., *Beneficial Ownership, Tax Abuse and Legal Pluralism: An Analysis in Light of the CJEU's Judgment Concerning the Danish Cases on Interest*, 48 Intertax 12 (2020), pp. 1075-1086.

Desai, M.A., *The Decentering of the Global Firm*, 32 The World Economy 9 (2009), pp. 1271-1290.

Desai, M.A./Foley, C.F./Hines J.R. Jr., *Repatriation Taxes and Dividend Distortions*, 54 National Tax Journal 4 (2001), pp. 829-851.

Devereux, M.P./et al., *Taxing Profit in a Global Economy* (Oxford University Press 2021).

Dharmapala, D., *Base Erosion and Profit Shifting: A Simple Conceptual Framework*, 12 CESifo DICE Report 4 (2014), pp. 8-14. Available at https://www.ifo.de/DocDL/dicereport414-forum2.pdf.

Dharmapala, D., *The Economics of Corporate and Business Tax Reform*, Coase-Sandor Working Paper Series in Law and Economics, No. 757 (2016), pp. 1-34. Available at https://chicagounbound.uchicago.edu/cgi/viewcontent.cgi?article=2478&context=law_and_economics.

Dirkis, M., *Australia's Residency Rules for Companies and Partnerships*, 57 Bulletin for International Taxation 8 (2003), pp. 405-411.

Dischinger, M., *Profit Shifting by Multinationals: Evidence from European Micro Panel Data*, Working Paper (University of Munich 2010), pp. 1-18. Available at https://www.ecpol.econ.uni-muenchen.de/downloads/publis/dischinger_publis/dischinger_ps_new1.pdf.

Dischinger, M./Riedel, N., *Corporate Taxes and the Location of Intangible Assets Within Multinational Firms*, 95 Journal of Public Economics 7/8 (2011), pp. 691-707.

Ditz, X./Engelen, C./Quilitzsch, C., *Hinzurechnungsbesteuerung auf dem Prüfstand*, Deutsches Steuerrecht 8 (2019), pp. 361-367.

Dourado, A.P., *The Role of CFC Rules in the BEPS Initiative and in the EU*, 2015 British Tax Review 3 (2015), pp. 340-363.

Drüen, K.-D., *Ein neuer Missbrauchsbegriff im deutschen Internationalen Steuerrecht?*, Internationale Rundschau 3 (2020), pp. 98-108.

Duff, D.G., *Tax Treaty Abuse and the Principal Purpose Test: Part 1*, 66 Canadian Tax Journal 3 (2018a), pp. 619-678.

Duff, D.G., *Tax Treaty Abuse and the Principal Purpose Test: Part 2*, 66 Canadian Tax Journal 4 (2018b), pp. 947-1012.

Dutch Association of Tax Advisers, *Reaction NOB to OECD Discussion Draft 'Treaty Abuse'*, in: OECD ed., *BEPS Action 6: Preventing the Granting of Treaty Benefits in Inappropriate Circumstances* (2014), pp. 191-198.

Dwarkasing, R., *The Concept of Associated Enterprises*, 41 Intertax 8/9 (2013), pp. 412-429.

Dziurdź, K., *Attribution of Functions and Profits to a Dependent Agent PE: Different Arm's Length Principles under Articles 7(2) and 9?*, 6 World Tax Journal 2 (2014), pp. 135-167.

Egger, P./Eggert, W./Winner, H., *Saving Taxes Through Foreign Plant Ownership*, 81 Journal of International Economics 1 (2010), pp. 99-108.

Egger, P./et al., *Consequences of the New UK Tax Exemption System: Evidence from Micro-Level Data*, 125 The Economic Journal 589 (2015), pp. 1764-1789.

Eigelshoven, A./Retzer, D., *Der Fremdvergleichsgrundsatz*, in: Kroppen, H.-K./Rasch, S., *Handbuch Internationale Verrechnungspreise* (Otto Schmidt October 2021).

Ekinci, O., *Der Substanztest bei ausländischen Kapitalgesellschaften nach der Reform der Hinzurechnungsbesteuerung* (Nomos 2023).

Elkins, D., *A Scalar Conception of Tax Residence*, 41 Virginia Tax Review 2 (2022), pp. 149-202.

Englisch, J., *Germany*, in: Maisto, G. ed., *Residence of Companies under Tax Treaties and EC Law* (IBFD 2009a), pp. 461-518.

Englisch, J., *Verbot des Rechtsmissbrauchs: ein allgemeiner Rechtsgrundsatz des Gemeinschaftsrechts?*, Steuer und Wirtschaft 1 (2009b), pp. 3-22.

Englisch, J., *Ability to Pay*, in: Brokelind, C. ed., *Principles of Law: Function, Status and Impact in EU Tax Law* (IBFD 2014), pp. 439-464.

Englisch, J., *Rechtfertigungsmöglichkeiten*, in: Schaumburg, H./Englisch, J. eds, *Europäisches Steuerrecht* (2nd edn Otto Schmidt 2020a).

Englisch, J., *The Danish Tax Avoidance Cases: New Milestones in the Court's Anti-abuse Doctrine*, 57 Common Market Law Review 2 (2020b), pp. 503-538.

Escribano, E., *Jurisdiction to Tax Corporate Income Pursuant to the Presumptive Benefit Principle* (Wolters Kluwer 2019a).

Escribano, E., *Alternative Approaches to Address the (Yet to Be Defined) Treaty Shopping Phenomenon*, 47 Intertax 11 (2019b), pp. 938-949.

EY Global Services Limited, *Comments on OECD Discussion Draft on Preventing the Granting of Treaty Benefits in Inappropriate Circumstances*, in: OECD ed., *BEPS Action 6: Preventing the Granting of Treaty Benefits in Inappropriate Circumstances* (2014), pp. 201-206.

Fama, E.F., *Agency Problems and the Theory of the Firm*, 88 Journal of Political Economy 2 (1980), pp. 288-307.

Fama, E.F./Jensen, M.C., *Agency Problems and Residual Claims*, 26 Journal of Law and Economics 2 (1983), pp. 327-350.

Fehling, D., *Die Harmonisierung der direkten Steuern in der EU: Grundlagen, Grenzen, Ziele (Teil 1)*, Internationales Steuerrecht 17 (2023), pp. 589-600.

Felix, G., *Der Ort der Geschäftsleitung im Steuerrecht*, Deutsches Steuerrecht 18 (1962/63), pp. 421-423.

Fett, E., *Triangular Cases* (IBFD 2014).

Fleckner, A.M., *Antike Kapitalvereinigungen* (Böhlau 2010).

Fleming, C.J. Jr., *Searching for the Uncertain Rationale Underlying the US Treasury's Anti-treaty Shopping Policy*, 40 Intertax 4 (2012), pp. 245-253.

Fleming, C.J. Jr./Peroni, R.E./Shay, S.E., *Worse than Exemption*, 59 Emory Law Journal 1 (2009), pp. 79-150.

Fontana, R., *The Uncertain Future of CFC Regimes in the Member States of the European Union: Part 2*, 46 European Taxation 7 (2006), pp. 317-334.

Foss, N.J, *The Corporate Headquarters in Organization Design Theory: An Organizational Economics Perspective*, 8 Journal of Organization Design 8 (2019), pp. 1-9.

Friedman, M., *The Social Responsibility of Business Is to Increase Its Profits*, The New York Times Magazine (13 September 1970). Available at http://umich.edu/~thecore/doc/Friedman.pdf.

Friese, A., Rechtsformwahlfreiheit im Europäischen Steuerrecht (Otto Schmidt 2010).

Fris, P., *Dealing with Arm's Length and Comparability in the Years 2000*, 10 International Transfer Pricing Journal 6 (2003), pp. 194-203.

Garner, B.A./Black, H.C., *Black's Law Dictionary* (10th edn Thomson Reuters 2014).

Geringer, S., *Criteria for the Application of Anti-abuse Provisions to Holding Companies under CJEU Case Law: Their Significance in Interpreting and Applying ATAD Provisions*, 60 European Taxation 10 (2020), pp. 443-450.

Gerlach, C./Niemeyer, N., *The New Tiebreaker Rule for Companies According to BEPS Action Point 6: A (Too) Radical Change?*, 46 Intertax 10 (2018), pp. 753-765.

Gonnet, S., *Risks Redifined in Transfer Pricing Post-BEPS*, in: Lang, M./Storck, M./Petruzzi, R. eds, *Transfer Pricing in a Post-BEPS World* (Wolters Kluwer 2016), pp. 33-59.

Gooijer, J., *Tax Treaty Residence of Entities* (Wolters Kluwer 2019).

Gosch, D., *Die Zwischengesellschaft nach 'Hilversum I und II', 'Cadbury Schweppes' und den Jahressteuergesetzen 2007 und 2008*, in: Kirchhof, P. ed., *Festschrift für Wolfram Reiß zum 65. Geburtstag* (Otto Schmidt 2008), pp. 597-620.

Govind, S./Zolles, S., *The Anti-Tax Avoidance Directive*, in: *Lang*, M./et al. eds, *Introduction to European Tax Law on Direct Taxation* (6th edn Linde 2020).

Grant, R.M., *Strategic Planning in a Turbulent Environment: Evidence from the Oil Majors*, 24 Strategic Management Journal 6 (2003), pp. 491-517.

Graßl, B./Kemmer, J., *'Unshell': EU-Richtlinienvorschlag zur Bekämpfung substanzschwacher Gesellschaften*, Internationales Steuerrecht 7 (2022), pp. 226-235.

Green, R.A., *Future of Source-Based Taxation of the Income of Multinational Enterprises*, 79 Cornell Law Review 1 (1993), pp. 18-86.

Greinert, M./et al., *Folgen der DEMPE-Konzeption für die steuerliche Erfolgsabgrenzung bei der Nutzung von immateriellen Werten*, Unternehmensbesteuerung 9 (2020), pp. 523-531.

Großmann, K., *Doppelt ansässige Kapitalgesellschaften im internationalen Steuerrecht* (C.H. Beck 1995).

Grotherr, S., *Zweifelsfragen und Problembereiche aus der Anwendung des Risikokontrollansatzes bei der Verrechnungspreisanalyse*, Finanzrundschau (2021), pp. 1097-1110.

Gutmann, D./et al., *The Impact of the ATAD on Domestic Systems: A Comparative Survey*, 57 European Taxation 1 (2017), pp. 2-20.

Haase, F., *Substanz, Substanz, ist das Gebilde von Menschenhand*, Internationales Steuerrecht 18 (2016), pp. 767-770.

Hafkenscheid, R., *The BEPS Report on Risk Allocation: Not So Functional*, 24 International Transfer Pricing Journal 1 (2017), pp. 19-24.

Hahn, U., *Allgemeine Betriebswirtschaftslehre* (3rd edn Oldenbourg Wissenschaftsverlag 2018).

Hansmann, H./Kraakman, R., *Organizational Law as Asset Partitioning*, 44 European Economic Review 4/6 (2000), pp. 807-817.

Hansmann, H./Squire, R., *External and Internal Asset Partitioning*, in: Gordon, J.N./Ringe, W.-G. eds, *The Oxford Handbook of Corporate Law and Governance* (Oxford University Press 2018), pp. 251-274.

Hart, H.L.A., *Positivism and the Separation of Law and Morals*, 71 Harvard Law Review 4 (1958), pp. 593-629.

Hart, H.L.A., *The Concept of Law* (1st edn Clarendon Press 1961).

Haslehner, W./Kofler, G., *Three Observations on the Danish Beneficial Ownership Cases*, Kluwer Tax Blog (March 2019). Available at http://kluwertaxblog.com/2019/03/13/three-observations-on-the-danish-beneficial-ownership-cases/.

Haslehner, W./Pantazatou, K., *Assessment of Recent Anti-Tax Avoidance and Evasion Measures (ATAD & DAC 6)*, Publication for the Subcommittee on Tax Matters (FISC), Policy Department for Economic, Scientific and Quality of Life Policies, European Parliament (2022). Available at https://www.europarl.europa.eu/RegData/etudes/STUD/2022/703353/IPOL_STU(2022)703353_EN.pdf.

Haslinger, K., *Der Ort der tatsächlichen Geschäftsleitung als Tiebreaker nach Art 4 Abs 3 OECD-MA und seine in Diskussion befindlichen Reformen*, in: Lang, M. ed., *Die Ansässigkeit im Recht der Doppelbesteuerungsabkommen* (Linde 2008), pp. 191-206.

Haun, J./Käshammer, D./Reiser, H., *Das BMF-Schreiben vom 8.1.2007 zur Hinzurechnungsbesteuerung: eine erste Analyse*, GmbH Rundschau 4 (2007), pp. 184-188.

Heck, P., *Gesetzesauslegung und Interessenjurisprudenz*, 112 Archiv für die civilistische Praxis 1 (1914), pp. 1-318.

Heckemeyer, J.H./Overesch, M., *Multinationals' Profit Response to Tax Differentials: Effect Size and Shifting Channels*, 50 Canadian Journal of Economics 4 (2017), pp. 965-994.

Heckerodt, D., *Die deutsche Hinzurechnungsbesteuerung im Drittstaatenfall*, Internationales Steuerrecht 17 (2019), pp. 683-691.

Heckerodt, D./van Lück, N., *Die deutsche Hinzurechnungsbesteuerung im Drittstaatenfall*, Internationales Steuerrecht 22 (2020), pp. 857-866.

Heinrich, J., *Der 'Ort der Leitung' als Betriebstätte nach Art 5 Abs 2 OECD-MA*, in: Lang, M. ed., *Die Ansässigkeit im Recht der Doppelbesteuerungsabkommen* (Linde 2008), pp. 207-224.

Heinsen, O./Gsödl, M./Dietrich, M., *Reform der Hinzurechnungsbesteuerung: Zum geänderten Motivtest (§ 8 Abs. 2-4 AStG-RefE)*, Internationales Steuerrecht 19 (2020), pp. 729-735.

Helderman, L./et al., *A New Era in Determining Arm' s Length Compensation for Intangibles? A Comparative Overview of Existing and Possible Future Transfer Pricing Principles*, 20 International Transfer Pricing Journal 6 (2013), pp. 359-368.

Helderman, L./Sporken, E./Okten, R., *The Revised OECD Discussion Draft on Transfer Pricing Aspects of Intangibles*, 21 International Transfer Pricing Journal 1 (2014), pp. 3-8.

Hennart, J.-F., *Free-Standing Firms and the Internalisation of Markets for Financial Capital: A Response to Casson*, 36 Business History 4 (1994), pp. 118-132.

Hernández González-Barreda, P.A., *Holding Companies and Leveraged Buy-Outs in the European Union Following BEPS: Beneficial Ownership, Abuse of Law and the Single Taxation Principle (Danish CJEU Cases C-115/16, 116/16, 117/16, 118/16, 119/16 and 299/16)*, 59 European Taxation 9 (2019), pp. 409-421.

Hey, J., *Spezialgesetzliche Missbrauchsgesetzgebung aus steuersystematischer, verfassungs-und europarechtlicher Sicht*, Steuer und Wirtschaft 2 (2008), pp. 167-183.

Hey, J., *Harmonisierung der Missbrauchsabwehr durch die Anti-tax-Avoidance-Directive*, Steuer und Wirtschaft 3 (2017), pp. 248-265.

Holzinger, R., *Die Ergebnisabgrenzung bei verbundenen Unternehmen und Betriebsstätten post BEPS* (Linde 2020).

Hongler, P., *Justice in International Tax Law* (IBFD 2019).

Hoor, O.R., *The Revised OECD Transfer Pricing Guidance on Intangibles: A Critical Analysis*, Tax Notes International (23 April 2018), pp. 529-537.

Hoor, O.R., *The Concept of Substance in a Post-BEPS World*, Tax Notes International (12 August 2019), pp. 593-606.

Hoor, O.R./O'Donnell, K./Schmitz, S., *Using a Sledgehammer to Crack a Nut: The European Commission's Draft Directive to Tackle Shell Entities*, Tax Notes International (11 April 2022), pp. 225-246.

Horváth, P., *Controlling* (14th edn Vahlen 2020).

Huizinga, H./Laeven, L., *International Profit Shifting Within Multinationals: A Multi-Country Perspective*, 92 Journal of Public Economics 5/6 (2008), pp. 1164-1182.

International Underwriting Association, *BEPS Actions 8, 9 and 10: Discussion Draft on Revisions to Chapter I of the Transfer Pricing Guidelines (Including Risk, Recharacterisation and Special Measures)*, in: OECD ed., *BEPS Actions 8, 9 and 10: Revisions to Chapter I of the Transfer Pricing Guidelines (Including Risk, Recharacterisation, and Special Measures)* (2015), pp. 488-493.

Ismer, R., *History and Emergence of the Corporate Residence Concept in Europe: A Comparative Approach*, in: Traversa, E. ed., *Corporate Tax Residence and Mobility* (IBFD 2018), pp. 27-75.

Ismer, R./Blank, M., *Article 4*, in: Ismer, R. ed., *Doppelbesteuerungsabkommen* (7th edn C.H. Beck 2021).

Janssen, J.J.M./Sada Garibay, M., *What Should Be the Scope of the Beneficial Owner Concept?*, 48 Intertax 12 (2020), pp. 1087-1104.

Jensen, M.C./Meckling, W.H., *Theory of the Firm: Managerial Behavior, Agency Costs, and Ownership Structure*, 3 Journal of Financial Economics 4 (1976), pp. 305-360.

Jiang, Q., *Treaty Shopping and Limitation on Benefits Articles in the Context of the OECD Base Erosion and Profit Shifting Project*, 69 Bulletin for International Taxation 3 (2015), pp. 139-148.

Jochimsen, C./Gsödl, M., *Die geplante Reform des § 50d Abs. 3 EStG im Lichte der EuGH-Rechtsprechung zum Begriff des Nutzungsberechtigten und zum Missbrauch*, Internationales Steuerrecht 10 (2021), pp. 387-395.

Judge, W.Q/Zeithaml, C.P., *Institutional and Strategic Choice Perspectives on Board Involvement in the Strategic Decision Process*, 35 The Academy of Management Journal 4 (1992), pp. 766-794.

Jung, H., *Allgemeine Betriebswirtschaftslehre* (13th edn De Gruyter 2016).

Jungmann, C., *The Effectiveness of Corporate Governance in One-Tier and Two-Tier Board Systems*, 3 European Company and Financial Law Review 4 (2006), pp. 426-474.

Kaeser, C., *Article 29*, in: Wassermeyer, F. ed., *Doppelbesteuerung* (C.H. Beck August 2022).

Kahlenberg, C., *Cadbury-Test auch für Drittstaaten: Folgerungen aus der EuGH-Entscheidung in der Rs. X-GmbH für die anstehende AStG-Reform*, Der Betrieb 29 (2019), pp. 1590-1595.

Kahlenberg, C./Quilitzsch, K., *Das Ende der Hinzurechnungsbesteuerung in Drittstaatenfällen?*, Internationales Steuerrecht 4 (2021), pp. 135-140.

Kanduth-Kristen, S./Müller-Thomczik, S./Reiter, L., *Die Umsetzung der Hinzurechnungsbesteuerung gemäß ATAD in Deutschland und in Österreich: zentrale Aspekte im Rechtsvergleich*, Internationales Steuerrecht 14 (2021), pp. 533-545.

Kane, M.A., *Risk and Redistribution in Open and Closed Economies*, 92 Virginia Law Review 5 (2006), pp. 867-928.

Kane, M.A., *Milking Versus Parking: Transfer Pricing and CFC Rules under the Code*, 66 Tax Law Review 4 (2013), pp. 487-506.

Kane, M.A., *Transfer Pricing, Integration and Synergy Intangibles: A Consensus Approach to the Arm's Length Standard*, 6 World Tax Journal 3 (2014), pp. 282-314.

Kaplow, L., *Rules Versus Standards: An Economic Analysis*, 42 Duke Law Journal 3 (1992), pp. 557-629.

Karadkar, R., Action 6 of the OECD/G20 BEPS Initiative: The Effect on Holding Companies, 71 Bulletin for International Taxation 3/4 (2017).

Katz, R.L., *Skills of an Effective Administrator*, Harvard Business Review (1955). Available at https://hbr.org/1974/09/skills-of-an-effective-administrator.

Keidanren, Comments on the Revised Discussion Draft on BEPS Action 6 (Prevent Treaty Abuse), in: OECD ed., Follow-Up Work on BEPS Action 6: Prevent Treaty Abuse (2015), pp. 258-260.

Kessler, W./Müller, M.A., *Ort der Geschäftsleitung einer Kapitalgesellschaft nach nationalem und DBA-Recht*, Internationales Steuerrecht 11 (2003), pp. 361-369.

Kindler, P., *Niederlassungsfreiheit für Scheinauslandsgesellschaften?: Die 'Centros'-Entscheidung des EuGH und das internationale Privatrecht*, Neue Juristische Wochenschrift 28 (1999), pp. 1993-2000.

Kindler, P., *'Inspire Art': Aus Luxemburg nichts Neues zum internationalen Gesellschaftsrecht*, Neue Zeitschrift für Gesellschaftsrecht 23 (2003), pp. 1086-1090.

Kindler, P., *'Cadbury-Schweppes': Eine Nachlese zum internationalen Gesellschaftsrecht*, Praxis des Internationalen Privat- und Verfahrensrechts 3 (2010), pp. 272-278.

Kindler, P., *Unternehmensmobilität nach 'Polbud': Der grenzüberschreitende Formwechsel in Gestaltungspraxis und Rechtspolitik*, Neue Zeitschrift für Gesellschaftsrecht 1 (2018), pp. 1-7.

Kirk, M.B., *Legal Drafting: The Ambiguity of 'And' and 'Or'*, 2 Texas Tech Law Review 2 (1970/1971), pp. 235-254.

Klein, B./Crawford, R.G./Alchian, A.A., *Vertical Integration, Appropriable Rents, and the Competitive Contracting Process*, 21 Journal of Law and Economics 2 (1978), pp. 297-326.

Klug, U., *Juristische Logik* (4th edn Springer 1982).

Kofler, G., *Doppelbesteuerungsabkommen und Europäisches Gemeinschaftsrecht* (Linde 2007).

Kofler, G., *CFC Rules*, in: Lang, M./Alarcón García, G. eds, *Common Consolidated Corporate Tax Base* (Linde 2008), pp. 725-749.

Kofler, G., *Article 9*, in: Reimer, E. ed., *Klaus Vogel on Double Taxation Conventions* (5th edn Kluwer Law International 2021).

Köhler, S., *FG Münster: keine wirkliche wirtschaftliche Tätigkeit i.S.d. EuGH-Rs. Cadbury Schweppes (§ 8 Abs. 2 AStG) bei Outsourcing bestimmter Funktionen*, Internationale Steuerrundschau 4 (2016), pp. 119-124.

Köhler, S., *Ganz oder gar nicht(?): Substantiierte Gewinne durch die EU-Grundfreiheiten vor der Hinzurechnungsbesteuerung geschützt*, Internationale Steuerrundschau 12 (2018), pp. 453-460.

Köhler, S., *Hinzurechnungsbesteuerung bei Direktinvestitionen in Drittstaatenfällen grundsätzlich durch die Kapitalverkehrsfreiheit gesperrt*, Internationale Steuerrundschau 12 (2019), pp. 441-448.

Köhler, S., *BMF zu Gegenbeweis bei Hinzurechnungsbesteuerung: Gegendarstellung leider notwendig*, Internationale Steuerrundschau 6 (2021), pp. 201-213.

Köhler, S./Eicker, K., *Wichtige EuGH-Entscheidungen zur Hinzurechnungs- und Wegzugsbesteuerung Anmerkungen zu den EuGH-Urteilen vom 7. 9. 2006, 'N' und vom 12. 9. 2006, Cadbury Schweppes*, Deutsches Steuerrecht 42 (2006), pp. 1871-1875.

Köhler, S./Eicker, K., *Kritische Anmerkungen zum BMF-Schreiben 'Cadbury Schweppes' vom 8.1.2007*, Deutsches Steuerrecht 8 (2007), pp. 331-334.

Kokolia, E./Chatziioakeimidou, E., *BEPS Impact on EU Law: Hybrid Payments and Abusive Tax Behaviour*, 55 European Taxation 4 (2015), No. 4, pp. 149-156.

Kollruss, T., *EU Companies with Third State Dual Residency and the Freedom of Establishment: Unlawful Restriction by Secondary Legislation and Corresponding National Tax Law*, 55 European Taxation 9 (2015).

Koomen, M., *Transfer Princing in a BEPS Era: Rethinking the Arm's Length Principle – Part I*, 22 International Transfer Pricing Journal 3 (2015a), pp. 141-152.

Koomen, M., *Transfer Princing in a BEPS Era: Rethinking the Arm's Length Principle – Part II*, 22 International Transfer Pricing Journal 4 (2015b), pp. 230-244.

Kornikova, A.A., *Solving the Problem of Tax-Treaty Shopping Through the Use of Limitation on Benefits Provisions*, 8 Richmond Journal of Global Law and Business 2 (2008), pp. 249-286.

Korobkin, R.B., *Behavioral Analysis and Legal Form: Rules vs. Standards Revisited*, 79 Oregon Law Review 1 (2000), pp. 23-58.

Kortendick, A./Joisten, C./Ekinci, O., *Zur Anwendung der Hinzurechnungsbesteuerung: Folgerungen aus dem BFH-Urteil vom 13.6.2018: I R 94/15*, Betriebsberater 51/52 (2018), pp. 3031-3037.

Korving, J.J.A.M./Wisman, C., *ATAD Implementation in the Netherlands*, 49 Intertax 11 (2021), pp. 917-937.

Kostić, S.V., In Search of the Digital Nomad: Rethinking the Taxation of Employment Income under Tax Treaties OECD/UN/International, 11 World Tax Journal 2 (2019), pp. 189-225.

Kostikidis, S., *The Relationship Between the Taxation of Business Profits and Income from Immovable Property under Tax Treaties*, 76 Bulletin for International Taxation 3 (2022), pp. 142-157.

Kostikidis, S., *Nexus for Source Taxation of Mobile Individual Service Providers in Tax Treaties*, 2023 British Tax Review 2 (2023), pp. 164-192.

Kostikidis, S., *International Taxation of Holograms and Human Physical Presence in Tax Treaties*, 52 Intertax 1 (2024), pp. 38-46.

Kostikidis, S./Hintermayer, P., *On the Validity and Scope of Macro-Coherence*, 62 European Taxation 2/3 (2022), pp. 74-85.

KPMG, *Comments on the Discussion Draft on Revisions to Chapter I of the Transfer Pricing Guidelines (Including Risk, Recharacterization and Special Measures)*, in: OECD ed., *BEPS Actions 8, 9 and 10: Revisions to Chapter I of the Transfer Pricing Guidelines (Including Risk, Recharacterisation, and Special Measures)* (2015), pp. 524-547.

Kraft, G., *Seminar B: Form and Substance*, Internationales Steuerrecht 16 (2019), pp. 631-635.

Krasnobaeva, A., *The Objective Tests in Article 29 OECD MC*, in: Auer, D./ Dimitropoulou, C. eds, *Access to Treaty Benefits* (Linde 2021), pp. 395-419.

Kraus, V., *Value Creation and the Recognition of the Actual Transaction Undertaken*, in: Petruzzi, R./Tavares, R.J.S. eds, *Transfer Pricing and Value Creation* (Linde 2019), pp. 131-149.

Kreikebaum, H., *Strategisches Management* (8th edn Kohlhammer 2018).

Kuźniacki, B., *Strengthening CFC Rules in a Compatible Way with EU Law under BEPS Action 3 in Light of the European Commission's Proposal: A Critical Evaluation*, in: Danon, R. ed., *Base Erosion and Profit Shifting (BEPS)* (Schulthess 2016), pp. 125-171.

Kuźniacki, B., *Tax Avoidance Through Controlled Foreign Companies under European Union Law with Specific Reference to Poland*, 7 Accounting, Economics, and Law: A Convivium 1 (2017).

Kuźniacki, B., *The Limitation on Benefits Provision in BEPS Action 6/Multilateral Instrument: Ineffective Overreaction of Mind-Numbing Complexity: Part 2*, 46 Intertax 2 (2018a), pp. 124-139.

Kuźniacki, B., *The Principal Purpose Test (PPT) in BEPS Action 6 and the MLI: Exploring Challenges Arising from Its Legal Implementation and Practical Application*, 10 World Tax Journal 2 (2018b), pp. 233-294.

Kuźniacki, B., *X-GmbH v Finanzamt Stuttgart: Körperschaften – The Evolution of the EU Standard of Abuse of Tax Law and the Role of the Genuine Exchange of Tax Information Between Member States and Third Countries*, 84 Modern Law Review 1 (2021), pp. 1-19.

Lampert, S., *Doppelbesteuerung und deren Beseitigung*, in: Mössner, J.M./Baumhoff, H./Greif, M. eds, *Steuerrecht international tätiger Unternehmen* (5th edn Otto Schmidt 2018).

Landsiedel, S., *The Principal Purpose Test's Burden of Proof: Should the OECD Commentary on Article 29(9) Specify Which Party Bears the Onus?*, 13 World Tax Journal 1 (2021), pp. 83-115.

Lang, M., *CFC Legislation and Community Law*, 42 European Taxation 9 (2002), pp. 374-379.

Lang, M./Heidenbauer, S., *Wholly Artificial Arrangements*, in: Hinnekens, L./Hinnekens, P. eds, *A Vision of Taxes Within and Outside European Borders* (Kluwer Law International 2008), pp. 597-615.

Lavez, R.A., *The Implications of the Supreme Court of Canada's Decision in Alta Energy Luxembourg (2021) for the OECD Principal Purpose Test*, 76 Bulletin for International Taxation 6 (2022).

Lazarov, I., *(Un)Tangling Tax Avoidance under the Interest and Royalties Directive: The Opinion of AG Kokott in N Luxembourg 1*, 46 Intertax 11 (2018), pp. 873-884.

Leclercq, L., *Interacting Principles: The French Abuse of Law Concept and the EU Notion of Abusive Practices*, 61 Bulletin for International Taxation 6 (2007), pp. 235-244.

Lederman, L., *Statutory Speed Bumps: The Roles Third Parties Play in Tax Compliance*, 60 Stanford Law Review 3 (2007), pp. 695-743.

Lehfeldt, C., *§ 8 AStG*, in: Strunk, G./Kaminski, B./Köhler, S. eds, *Außensteuergesetz/ Doppelbesteuerungsabkommen* (Stollfuß 2016).

Lehmann, M., *Der Begriff der Rechtsfähigkeit*, 207 Archiv für die civilistische Praxis 2 (2007), pp. 225-255.

Lenaerts, K., *The Concept of Abuse of Law in the Case Law of the European Court of Justice on Direct Taxation*, 22 Maastricht Journal of European and Comparative Law 3 (2015), pp. 329-351.

Leukefeld, R., *Das Konzept der Substanz im Steuerrecht* (Dr. Kovač 2018).

Li, J., *Global Profit Split: An Evolutionary Approach to International Income Allocation*, 50 Canadian Tax Journal 3 (2002), pp. 823-883.

Li, J/Li, S., *Location-Specific Advantages: A Rising Disruptive Factor in Transfer Pricing*, 71 Bulletin for International Taxation 5 (2017), pp. 259-271.

Lipniewicz, R., *Place of Effective Management in the Digital Economy*, 48 Intertax 6/7 (2020), pp. 602-615.

Loomer, G., *Reformulating Corporate Residence: A Coherent Response to International Tax Avoidance* (Merton College 2011). Available at https://pdfs.semanticscholar.org/a1ca/1fc2aec3faa871178411ea4ea74906dd2469.pdf.

Luckhaupt, H./Overesch, M./Schreiber, U., The OECD Approach to Transfer Pricing: A Critical Assessment and Proposal, in: Schön, W./Konrad, K.A. eds, Fundamentals of International Transfer Pricing in Law and Economics (Springer 2012), pp. 91-121.

Lukjanenko, P., *LoB: Article X(3) of the OEC MC – Active Conduct of a Business*, in: Blum, D.W./Seiler, M. eds, *Preventing Treaty Abuse* (Linde 2016), pp. 207-230.

Maduro, M.P., *Interpreting European Law: Judicial Adjudication in a Context of Constitutional Pluralism*, 1 European Journal of Legal Studies 2 (2008), pp. 137-152.

Maisto, G., *The Impact of the European Convention on Human Rights on Tax Procedures and Sanctions with Special Reference to Tax Treaties and the EU Arbitration Convention*, in: Kofler, G./Maduro, M.P./Pistone, P. eds, *Human Rights and Taxation in Europe and the World* (IBFD 2011), pp. 373-396.

Maisto, G., Controlled Foreign Company Legislation, Corporate Residence and Anti-Hybrid Arrangement Rules, 68 Bulletin for International Taxation 6/7 (2014).

Maisto, G., *On the Difficulties Regarding the Formation of Customary Law in the Field of Taxation*, in: Weber, D. ed., *EU Law and the Building of Global Supranational Tax Law* (IBFD 2017).

Maisto, G./Pistone, P., *A European Model for Member States' Legislation on the Taxation of Controlled Foreign Subsidiaries (CFCs): Part 1*, 48 European Taxation 10 (2008), pp. 503-513.

Maisto, G./et al., *Dual Residence of Companies under Tax Treaties*, 1 International Tax Studies 1 (2018), pp. 3-84.

Maraia, J.-F., *Switzerland*, in: Maisto, G. ed., *Residence of Companies under Tax Treaties and EC Law* (IBFD 2009), pp. 795-816.

Marian, O., *Functional Model for Determining U.S. Corporate Tax Residence*, 54 Boston College Law Review 4 (2013a), pp. 1613-1666.

Marian, O., *Meaningful Corporate Tax Residence*, Tax Notes International (29 July 2013b), pp. 471-480.

Marian, O., *Corporate Tax-Residence in Territorial Systems*, 18 Chapman Law Review 1 (2014), pp. 157-184.

Marres, O./de Groot, I., *Combatting Abuse by Conduit Companies*, 61 European Taxation 8 (2021), pp. 329-342.

Martín Jiménez, A.J., *Domestic Anti-abuse Rules and Double Taxation Treaties: A Spanish Perspective – Part II*, 56 Bulletin for International Taxation 12 (2002), pp. 620-627.

Martín Jiménez, A.J., *Towards a Homogeneous Theory of Abuse in EU (Direct) Tax Law*, 66 Bulletin for International Taxation 4/5 (2012), pp. 270-292.

Martín Jiménez, A.J., *Tax Avoidance and Aggressive Tax Planning as an International Standard: BEPS and the 'New' Standards of (Legal and Illegal) Tax Avoidance*, in: Dourado, A.P. ed., *Tax Avoidance Revisited in the EU BEPS Context* (IBFD 2017), pp. 25-62.

Martín Jiménez, A.J., *Value Creation: A Guiding Light for the Interpretation of Tax Treaties?*, 74 Bulletin for International Taxation 4/5 (2020a), pp. 197-215.

Martín Jiménez, A.J., *Beneficial Ownership*, in: *Global Tax Treaty Commentaries* (IBFD July 2022a).

Martín Jiménez, A.J., *Is There an International Minimum Standard on Tax Treaty Shopping after BEPS Action 6? Some Recent Divergent Trends*, 14 World Tax Journal 3 (2022b), pp. 451-488.

McMechan, R., *Economic Substance and Tax Avoidance* (Carlswell 2012).

Meindl-Ringler, A., *Beneficial Ownership in International Tax Law* (Wolters Kluwer 2016).

Metzner, S., *Risikoallokation im internationalen Konzern* (Dr. Kovač 2016).

Meussen, G.T.K., *Cadbury Schweppes: The CJEU Significantly Limits the Application of CFC Rules in the Member States*, 47 European Taxation 1 (2007), pp. 13-18.

Miall, R., *Discussion Draft on Risk and Recharacterisation: The Importance of the Information Environment*, in: OECD ed., *BEPS Actions 8, 9 and 10: Revisions to*

Chapter I of the Transfer Pricing Guidelines (Including Risk, Recharacterisation, and Special Measures) (2015), pp. 708-709.
Mithe, A., *Critical Analysis of the Principal Purpose Test and the Limitation on Benefits Rule: A World Divided but It Takes Two to Tango*, 12 World Tax Journal 1 (2020), pp. 129-165.
Milewska, M., *A Mexican Perspective on Value Creation under the OECD's BEPS Approach to Transfer Pricing*, 24 International Transfer Pricing Journal 1 (2017), pp. 49-55.
Milogolov, N., *Treaty Between Russia and Netherlands: Arbitration Court Denies Treaty Benefits Because Recipient of Dividends Is Not Beneficial Owner*, Tax News Service (April 2020). Available at https://research.ibfd.org/#/doc?url=/data/tns/docs/html/tns_2020-04-01_ru_2.html.
Monsenego, J., *The Substance Requirement in the OECD Transfer Pricing Guidelines: What is the Substance of the Substance Requirement?*, 21 International Transfer Pricing Journal 1 (2014), pp. 9-23.
Monsenego, J., *Introduction to Transfer Pricing* (Wolters Kluwer 2015).
Mooij, H., *Netherlands Supreme Court Decides in Taxpayer's Favour Regarding the Application of Tax Treaties to a Fiscal Unity under Netherlands Domestic Tax Law*, 66 Bulletin for International Taxation 12 (2012), pp. 637-639.
Moreno González, S., *Implementation of the EU ATAD in Spain: Outstanding Issues of a Partial Transposion*, 49 Intertax 12 (2021), pp. 995-1012.
Mosquera Valderrama, I.J., *BEPS Principal Purpose Test and Customary International Law*, 33 Leiden Journal of International Law 3 (2020), pp. 745-76.
Müller, S., *Hinzurechnungsbesteuerung: Die Unionsrechtsmäßigkeit des Substanztestes*, GmbH Steuerberatung 9 (2021), pp. 283-289.
Musil, A., *§ 10 Abgabenordnung*, in: Hübschmann, W./Hepp, E./Spitaler, A. eds, *Abgabenordnung: Finanzgerichtsordnung* (Otto Schmidt October 2020).
Musselli, A., *Business Risk Allocation: The Outermost Boundary of the Arm's Length Principle and the Amazon Case*, 44 International Tax Journal 5 (2018), pp. 5-12.
Musselli, A./Musselli, A., *Observations on OECD Discussion Draft on Business Restructuring: Is the Notion of Control over Risk at Arm's Length?*, 16 International Transfer Pricing Journal 2 (2009), pp. 239-243.
Musselli, A./Musselli, A., *Rise of a New Standard: Profit Location in Countries of Important Intangible Functions Managers*, 24 International Transfer Pricing Journal 5 (2017), pp. 331-341.
National Foreign Trade Council, *Comments on BEPS Action Items 8, 9 and 10: Discussion Draft on Revisions to Chapter 1 of the Transfer Pricing Guidelines (Including Risk, Recharacterisation, and Special Measures)*, in: OECD ed., *BEPS Actions 8, 9 and 10: Revisions to Chapter I of the Transfer Pricing Guidelines (Including Risk, Recharacterisation, and Special Measures)* (2015), pp. 601-616.
Navarro, A., *Transactional Adjustments in Transfer Pricing* (IBFD 2017).
Navarro, A., *The Arm's Length Standard and Tax Justice: Reflections on the Present and the Future of Transfer Pricing*, 10 World Tax Journal 3 (2018), pp. 351-379.
Navarro, A., *Transfer Pricing*, in: Brauner, Y. ed., *Research Handbook on International Taxation* (Edward Elgar 2020), pp. 97-119.

Navarro, A., *The Multilateral Instrument (MLI) and Transfer Pricing*, 49 Intertax 10 (2021), pp. 803-817.

Navarro, A., *Complying with BEPS Substance Requirements Through Remote Personnel: Business Profit Allocation, the PPT and ATAD 3*, Max Planck Institute for Tax Law and Public Finance Working Paper 2023 – 013. Available at: Complying with BEPS Substance Requirements Through Remote Personnel: Business Profit Allocation, the PPT and ATAD 3 by Aitor Navarro: SSRN.

Navarro, A./Parada, L./Schwarz, P., *The Proposal for an EU Anti-avoidance Directive: Some Preliminary Thoughts*, 25 EC Tax Review 3 (2016), pp. 117-131.

Navisotschnigg, F., *The Beneficial Ownership Test*, in: Lang, M./et al. eds, *Tax Treaty Entitlement* (IBFD 2019), pp. 91-117.

Navisotschnigg, F., *Substance in International Tax Law* (Wolters Kluwer 2022).

Nielsen, L.F., *New Perspective on the Taxation of CFCs in Third Countries?*, 58 European Taxation 12 (2018), pp. 571-575.

Nikolakakis, A., *Aligning the Location of Taxation with the Location of Value Creation: Are We There Yet!?!*, 75 Bulletin for International Taxation 11/12 (2021), pp. 549-561.

Nyström, W., *Saving the ATAD CFC Regime Through Abuse of Law or the Rule of Reason*, 49 Intertax 3 (2021), pp. 223-236.

Obuoforibo, B.R., *Article 4*, in: Pasquale Pistone et al (eds) *Global Tax Treaty Commentaries* (IBFD October 2020).

Oehlrich, M., *Organisation* (Vahlen 2016).

Offermanns, R., *The Proposed Unshell Directive: The Luxembourg and Netherlands Approach*, 62 European Taxation 6 (2022).

Orlet, P./Schuch, J., *Directors' Fees and Remuneration of Top-Level Managerial Officials*, in: Lang, M./et al. eds, *The UN Model Convention and Its Relevance for the Global Tax Treaty Network* (IBFD 2017).

Padia, N./Maroun, W., *Determining the Residency of Companies: Difficulties in Interpreting 'Place of Effective Management'*, 5 Journal of Economics and Financial Sciences 1 (2012), pp. 119-134.

Panayi, C.H., *Double Taxation, Tax Treaties, Treaty-Shopping and the European Community* (Kluwer Law International 2007).

Panayi, C.H., *The United Kingdom*, in: Maisto, G. ed., *Residence of Companies under Tax Treaties and EC Law* (IBFD 2009), pp. 817-854.

Panayi, C.H., *The ATAD's CFC Rule and Its Impact on the Existing Regimes of EU Member States*, in: Pistone, P./Weber, D. eds, *The Implementation of Anti-BEPS Rules in the EU: A Comprehensive Study* (IBFD 2018), pp. 355-378.

Pankiv, M., *Post-BEPS Application of the Arm's Length Principle to Intangibles Structures*, 23 International Transfer Pricing Journal 6 (2016), pp. 463-476.

Parekh, S., *The Concept of 'Options Realistically Available' under the OECD Transfer Pricing Guidelines*, 22 International Transfer Pricing Journal 5 (2015), pp. 297-307.

Peng, C.(X.)/Lagarden, M., *DEMPE Functions and the RACI Concept: More Clarity or Confusion Ahead?*, 26 International Transfer Pricing Journal 1 (2019), pp. 3-11.

Peters, C., *On the Legitimacy of International Tax Law* (IBFD 2014).

Petruzzi, R., *The Arm's Length Principle: Between Legal Fiction and Economic Reality*, in: Lang, M./Storck, M./Petruzzi, R. eds, *Transfer Pricing in a Post-BEPS World* (Wolters Kluwer 2016), pp. 1-32.

Petruzzi, R./Holzinger, R., *Profit Attribution to Dependent Agent Permanent Establishments in a Post-BEPS Era*, 9 World Tax Journal 2 (2017), pp. 263-300.

Petruzzi, R./Myzithra, A., *Substance in Transfer Pricing in a Post-BEPS World and Beyond …*, 27 International Transfer Pricing Journal 6 (2020), pp. 430-447.

Picciotto, S., *International Taxation and Economic Substance*, 70 Bulletin for International Taxation 12 (2016), pp. 752-759.

Pichhadze, A., *Exposing Unaddressed Issues in the OECD's BEPS Project: What About the Roles and Implications of Contract Interpretation Law and Private International Law in the Transfer Pricing Arm's Length Comparability Analysis?*, 7 World Tax Journal 1 (2015), pp. 99-167.

Pichhadze, A., *Delineating the Terms of a Single Composite Transaction in Transfer Pricing: The Role of Step-Transaction Analysis in the Aggregation of Interrelated (Linked) Contracts*, 23 International Transfer Pricing Journal 3 (2016), pp. 179-199.

Picot, A., *Organisation* (6th edn Schäffer-Poeschel 2012).

Pinkernell, R., *Das Steueroasen-Dilemma der amerikanischen IT-Konzerne*, Internationales Steuerrecht 5 (2013), pp. 180-187.

Pistone, P., *Soft Tax Law: Steering Legal Pluralism Towards International Tax Coordination*, in: Weber, D. ed., *Traditional and Alternative Routes to European Tax Integration* (IBFD 2010), pp. 97-114.

Pistone, P., *International Tax Coordination Through the BEPS Project and the Exercise of Tax Sovereignty in the European Union*, in: Englisch, J. ed., *New Challenges to and from Constitutional and Legal Pluralism* (IBFD 2016).

Pistone, P./et al., *Abuse Through the Use of Shell Companies and Arrangements for Tax Purposes in the European Union: Feedback on the EU Consultation by the IBFD Task Force on EU Law*, 4 International Tax Studies 7 (2021), pp. 2-33.

Pistone, P./et al., *Abuse, Shell Entities and Right of Establishment: A Plea for Refocusing Current Proposals and Achieving Deeper Coordination Within the Internal Market*, 14 World Tax Journal 2 (2022).

Plakhin, Y., *The Place of Effective Management as a Tie-Breaker Criterion*, in: Hofstätter, M. ed., *Dual Residence in Tax Treaty Law and EC Law* (Linde 2009), pp. 81-98.

Polonska, T., *Cost Contribution Arrangements and Funding Activities*, 25 International Transfer Pricing Journal 2 (2018), pp. 92-115.

Ponticelli, D./Tronci, S., *The Non-Unique Notion of 'Control' in Transfer Pricing: Interpretation, Legislative Developments and Problematic Aspects from an Italian and International Perspective*, 28 International Transfer Pricing Journal 4 (2021).

Pörner, R., *Strategisches Management in den deutschen Dax-30-Unternehmen*, Working Paper (Fachhochschule für Technik und Wirtschaft Berlin 2003), pp. 1-28. Available at https://people.f3.htw-berlin.de/Professoren/Poerner/veroeffentlichungen/Strategisches_Management_DAX30.pdf.

Porter, M.E., *From Competitive Advantage to Corporate Strategy*, 65 Harvard Business Review 3 (1987), pp. 43-59.

Pötgens, F.P.G./Straathof, M.J.E., *Establishment and Substance of Intermediate and Other Holding Companies from an EU Law Perspective*, 44 Intertax 8/9 (2016), pp. 608-619.

Pötgens, F.P.G./et al., *The Impact of a Corporate Governance System on the Place of Effective Management Concept in Spain, France, the United Kingdom, the Netherlands, Germany and Italy: Part 1*, 54 European Taxation 9 (2014a), pp. 374-384.

Pötgens, F.P.G./et al., *The Impact of a Corporate Governance System on the Place of Effective Management Concept in Spain, France, the United Kingdom, the Netherlands, Germany and Italy: Part 2*, European Taxation (2014b), pp. 423-431.

Poulsen, M., *Treaty/Directive Shopping and Abuse of EU Law*, 41 Intertax 4, pp. 230-251.

Prasanna, S./Sollund, S., *Introduction to Transfer Pricing*, in: Lang, M./et al., *Fundamentals of Transfer Pricing* (Wolters Kluwer 2019), pp. 3-34.

Quek, H.L., *Economic Substance in U.S. Transfer Pricing Rule and the Regulation of Taxpayer Behavior*, Tax Notes International (24 January 2011), pp. 311-321.

Quilitzsch, C., *Die Hinzurechnungsbesteuerung* (Nomos 2013).

Radbruch, G., *Gesetzliches Unrecht und übergesetzliches Recht*, Süddeutsche Juristen-Zeitung 5 (1946), pp. 105-108.

Ramharter, L./Szudoczky, R., *Limitation on Benefits Clauses: Limiting the Entitlement to Treaty Benefits*, in: Lang, M./et al. eds, *Tax Treaty Entitlement* (IBFD 2019), pp. 55-89.

Ravelli, A./Strik, A., *Will Remote Working Mark the End of Substance Requirements?*, 63 European Taxation 6 (2023).

Richter, L./Kortendick, A./Ekinci, O., *Tatsächlich, wirklich oder doch wesentlich?: Die Exkulpationsklausel nach dem ATADUmsG im Lichte des Unionsrechts*, GmbH Rundschau 13 (2020), pp. 694-703.

Richter, T., *Die Bedeutung der Funktions- und Risikoanalyse im Rahmen der Verrechnungspreisdokumentation für Zwecke der Hinzurechnungsbesteuerung gem. §§ 7 ff. AStG: Zugleich Besprechung des BFH-Urteils v. 13.6.2018 – I R 94/15*, Internationale Steuerrundschau 9 (2019), pp. 336-344.

Rivers, J., *Proportionality and Variable Intensity of Review*, 65 Cambridge Law Journal 1 (2006), pp. 174-207.

Robert, E./Tof, D., *The Substance Requirement and the Future of Domestic Anti-abuse Rules Within the Internal Market*, 51 European Taxation 11 (2011), pp. 436-444.

Rosenzweig, A.H., *Source as a Solution to Residence*, 17 Florida Tax Review 6 (2015), pp. 471, 526.

Rotondaro, C., *The Application of Art. 3(2) in Case of Differences Between Domestic Definitions of 'Associated Enterprises'*, 7 International Transfer Pricing Journal 5 (2000), pp. 166-175.

Rudolf, M., *Treaty Shopping und Gestaltungsmissbrauch* (Otto Schmidt 2012).

Rust, A., *Die Hinzurechnungsbesteuerung* (C.H. Beck 2007).

Rust, A., *CFC Legislation and EC Law*, 36 Intertax 11 (2008), pp. 492-501.

Sasseville, J., *The Meaning of 'Place of Effective Management'*, in: Maisto, G. ed., *Residence of Companies under Tax Treaties and EC Law* (IBFD 2009), pp. 287-302.

Schade, D., *Die deutsche Anti-Treaty-Shopping-Regelung des § 50d Abs. 3 EStG* (Duncker & Humblot 2013).

Schauer, F., *The Tyranny of Choice and the Rulification of Standards*, 14 Journal of Contemporary Legal Issues 2 (2005), pp. 803-814.

Scheipers, T./Linn, A., *Substanzerfordernisse bei nachgeschalteten Zwischengesellschaften*, Internationales Steuerrecht 16 (2011), pp. 601-606.

Schlücke, K., *Hinzurechnung passiver Einkünfte nach § 8 AStG und Gegenbeweis: verdeckte Einlagen in Dreiecksverhältnissen*, Internationale Steuerrundschau 2 (2019), pp. 41-44.

Schmidtmann, D., *Anforderungen an die wirtschaftliche Substanz im Außensteuerrecht*, GmbH Rundschau 2 (2019), pp. 59-67.

Schön, W., *CFC Legislation and European Community Law*, British Tax Review 4 (2001), pp. 250-260.

Schön, W., *Attribution of Profits to PEs and the OECD 2006 Report*, Tax Notes International (4 June 2007), pp. 1059-1072.

Schön, W., Abuse of Rights and European Tax Law, in: Avery Jones, J.F. ed., Comparative Perspectives on Revenue Law (Cambridge University Press 2008), pp. 75-98.

Schön, W. *International Tax Coordination for a Second-Best World (Part I)*, 1 World Tax Journal 1 (2009), pp. 67-114.

Schön, W., *International Tax Coordination for a Second-Best World (Part III)*, 2 World Tax Journal 3 (2010a), pp. 227-261.

Schön, W., *Persons and Territories: On the International Allocation of Taxing Rights*, 2010 British Tax Review 6 (2010b), pp. 554-562.

Schön, W., *Transfer Pricing: Business Incentives, International Taxation and Corporate Law*, in: Schön, W./Konrad, K. eds, *Fundamentals of International Transfer Pricing in Law and Economics* (Springer 2012) pp. 47-67.

Schön, W., *Deutsche Hinzurechnungsbesteuerung und Europäische Grundfreiheiten*, 22 Internationales Steuerrecht 6 (2013a), Beihefter, pp. 3-23.

Schön, W., *Das System der gesellschaftsrechtlichen Niederlassungsfreiheit nach VALE*, Zeitschrift für Unternehmens- und Gesellschaftsrecht 3 (2013), pp. 333-365.

Schön, W., *International Taxation of Risk*, 67 Bulletin for International Taxation 6/7 (2014), pp. 280-294.

Schön, W., *Neutralität und Territorialität: Gegensätze oder Grundsätze des Europäischen Steuerrechts?*, in: Schön, W./Heber, C. eds, *Grundfragen des Europäischen Steuerrechts* (Springer 2015) pp. 109-164.

Schön, W., *Free Movement of Capital and Freedom of Establishment*, 17 European Business Organization Law Review 3 (2016), pp. 229-260.

Schön, W., *The Concept of Abuse of Law in European Taxation: A Methodological and Constitutional Perspective*, Max Planck Institute for Tax Law and Public Finance Working Paper 2019 – 18. Available at https://papers.ssrn.com/sol3/papers.cfm?abstract_id=3490489.

Schön, W., Interpreting European Law in the Light of the OECD/G20 Base Erosion and Profit Shifting Action Plan, 74 Bulletin for International Taxation 4/5 (2020a), pp. 286-302.

Schön, W., Rechtsmissbrauch im europäischen (Steuer-)Recht: Eine methodologische und institutionelle Perspektive – Teil 1, Europäische Zeitschrift für Wirtschaftsrecht 15 (2020b), pp. 637-646.

Schön, W., Is There Finally an International Tax System?, 13 World Tax Journal 3 (2021), pp. 357-384.

Schön, W., The Role of 'Commercial Reasons' and 'Economic Reality' in the 'Principle Purpose Test' under Art.29(9) OECD Model Tax Convention 2017, Max Planck Institute for Tax Law and Public Finance Working Paper 2022 – 03. Available at https://papers.ssrn.com/sol3/papers.cfm?abstract_id=4029573.

Schön, W., Internationale Steuerpolitik zwischen Steuerwettbewerb, Steuerkoordinierung und dem Kampf gegen Steuervermeidung, Internationales Steuerrecht 6 (2022b), pp. 181-191.

Schönfeld, J., The Cadbury Schweppes Case: Are the Days of the United Kingdom's CFC Legislation Numbered?, 44 European Taxation 10 (2004), pp. 441-452.

Schönfeld, J., Hinzurechnungsbesteuerung und Europäisches Gemeinschaftsrecht (Otto Schmidt 2005).

Schönfeld, J., Seminar C: Steuerliche Ansässigkeit von Kapitalgesellschaften, Internationales Steuerrecht 19 (2014), pp. 693-698.

Schönfeld, J., CFC Rules and Anti-Tax Avoidance Directive, 26 EC Tax Review 3 (2017), pp. 145-152.

Schönfeld, J., Aktuelle Entwicklungen zur Hinzurechnungsbesteuerung, Internationales Steuerrecht 11 (2019), pp. 397-401.

Schönfeld, J./Ellenrieder, B., Das Verhältnis von Primär- und Sekundärrecht: oder: Gibt es 'gegen Primärrecht immunisiertes Recht'?, Steuer und Wirtschaft 3 (2019), pp. 253-266.

Schönfeld, J./Wassermeyer, § 8 AStG, in: Flick, H./et al. eds, Außensteuerrecht (Otto Schmidt 2017).

Schotter, A./Beamisch, P.W., *Intra-Organizational Turbulences in Multinational Corporations*, in: Dörrenbächer, C./Geppert, M. eds, *Politics and Power in the Multinational Corporation* (Cambridge University Press 2012), pp. 191-230.

Schoueri, L.E., *Arm' s Length: Beyond the Guidelines of the OECD*, 69 Bulletin for International Taxation 12 (2015), pp. 690-716.

Schoueri, L.E./Galendi, R.A. Jr., *The Arm's Length Standard*, in: Brauner, Y., *Research Handbook on International Taxation* (Edward Elgar 2020), pp. 153-173.

Schröder, J., *Gesellschafter und Ort der Geschäftsleitung*, 20 Die steuerliche Betriebsprüfung 5 (1980), pp. 97-99.

Schuster, C./Steiner, N./Ullmann, R., *Funktionale Zuordnung nach DEMPE: Diskussion einer Einordnung und DEMPE-Schwelle*, Der Betrieb 4 (2022), pp. 148-156.

Schwarz, J., *Are Legal Rights Irrelevant for Transfer Pricing after BEPS Actions 8, 9 and 10?* (2015). Available at http://kluwertaxblog.com/2015/11/15/are-legal-rights-irrelevant-for-transfer-pricing-after-beps-actions-8-9-and-10/.

Schwarz, J., *Booth and Schwarz: Residence, Domicile and UK Taxation* (20th edn Bloomsbury Professional 2018).

Screpante, M., *Rethinking the Arm's Length Principle and Its Impact on the IP Licence Model after OECD/G20 BEPS Actions 8-10: Nothing Changed but the Change?*, 11 World Tax Journal 3 (2019), pp. 425-479.

Screpante, M., *The Arm's Length Principle Evolves Towards a 'Value Creation Functional (i.e., DEMPE) Formula Standard': A Barrier or a Gateway to Locational Business Planning?*, 48 Intertax 10 (2020), pp. 861-878.

Sepúlveda Ramirez, J.F., *Residence in Tax Treaties* (Leiden University 2016). Available at https://openaccess.leidenuniv.nl/bitstream/handle/1887/44535/Full_Doc._1._Cover_2._PhD._Residence_in_tax_treaties_05.10.2016_.pdf?sequence=1.

Sharma, S./Cardozo, J., *A Paradigm Shift of Residence Rules*, 28 Asia-Pacific Tax Bulletin 1 (2012), pp. 39-44.

Shaviro, D., *The Rising Tax-Electivity of U.S. Corporate Residence*, 64 Tax Law Review 3 (2011), pp. 377-430.

Simader, K., *Austria*, in: Maisto, G. ed., *Residence of Companies under Tax Treaties and EC Law* (IBFD 2009), pp. 339-374.

Smit, D.S., *Substance Requirements for Entities Located in a Harmful Tax Jurisdiction under CFC Rules and the EU Freedom of Establishment*, 16 Derivatives & Financial Instruments 6 (2014), pp. 259-265.

Smit, D.S., *The Anti-Tax Avoidance Directive (ATAD)*, in: Wattel, P.J./Marres, O./Vermeulen H. eds, *European Tax Law* (7th edn Wolters Kluwer 2019), pp. 485-538.

Squire, R., *Strategic Liability in the Corporate Group*, 78 University of Chicago Law Review 2 (2011), pp. 605-670.

Staringer, C., *Besteuerung doppelt ansässiger Kapitalgesellschaften* (Linde 1999).

Staringer, C., *Die Ansässigkeit aufgrund des Wohnsitzes, des ständigen Aufenthalts, des Ortes der Geschäftsleitung oder eines anderen ähnlichen Merkmals nach Art 4 Abs 1 OECD-MA*, in: Lang, M. ed., *Die Ansässigkeit im Recht der Doppelbesteuerungsabkommen* (Linde 2008), pp. 67-86.

Stewart, M., *Abuse and Economic Substance in a Digital BEPS World*, 69 Bulletin for International Taxation 6/7 (2015), pp. 399-409.

Stigler, G.J., *Smith's Travels on the Ship of State*, 3 History of Political Economy 2 (1971), pp. 265-277.

Stout, L.A., *The Mythical Benefits of Shareholder Control*, 93 Virginia Law Review 3 (2007), pp. 789-810.

Striefler, F./Kostikidis, S., *Fiktive Zinsen unter der Zins- und Lizenzgebührenrichtlinie: zugleich Anmerkung zu Viva Telecom Bulgaria*, Internationales Steuerrecht 20 (2022), pp. 759-766.

SwissHoldings, *Comments of SwissHoldings to the Discussion Draft on BEPS Action 6: Preventing the Granting of Treaty Benefits in Inappropriate Circumstances*, in: OECD ed., *BEPS Action 6: Preventing the Granting of Treaty Benefits in Inappropriate Circumstances* (2014), pp. 477-488.

Tavares, R.J.S., *The 'Active Trade or Business' Exception of the Limitation on Benefits Clause*, in: Lang, M./et al. eds, *Base Erosion and Profit Shifting (BEPS)* (Linde 2016), pp. 133-164.

Tavares, R.J.S./Bogenschneider, B.N., *The New De Minimis Anti-abuse Rule in the Parent-Subsidiary Directive: Validating EU Tax Competition and Corporate Tax Avoidance?*, 43 Intertax 8/9 (2015), pp. 484-494.

Tenore, M., *Taxation of Dividends: A Comparison of Selected Issues under Article 10 OECD MC and the Parent-Subsidiary Directive*, 38 Intertax 4 (2010), pp. 222-238.

Thiele, K., *Hinzurechnungsbesteuerung und Unionsrecht* (Dr. Kovač 2011).

Thömmes, O./Nakhai, K., *New Case Law on Anti-abuse Provisions in Germany*, 33 Intertax 2 (2005), pp. 74-79.

Töben, T./Birk, D. *Place of Management: An Analysis of German Law*, in: Jochum, H./et al. eds, *Practical Problems in European and International Tax Law* (IBFD 2016), pp. 499-540.

Torvik, O., *Transfer Pricing and Intangibles* (IBFD 2018).

Tracana, D., *The Impact of BEPS Actions 8–10 on Comparability Analysis in the Context of Attribution of Profits to Permanent Establishments*, 45 Intertax 5 (2017), pp. 411-416.

Traversa, E., *Corporate Tax Residence at the Crossroads Between International Competition and Convergence. Outlining the Debate*, in: Traversa, E. ed., *Corporate Tax Residence and Mobility* (IBFD 2018), pp. 4-25.

United States Council for International Business (USCIB), *USCIB Comment Letter on the OECD Discussion Draft on BEPS Actions 8, 9, and 10: Discussion Draft on Revisions to Chapter 1 of the Transfer Pricing Guidelines (Including Risk, Recharacterisation and Special Measures)*, in: OECD ed., *BEPS Actions 8, 9 and 10: Revisions to Chapter I of the Transfer Pricing Guidelines (Including Risk, Recharacterisation, and Special Measures)* (2015), pp. 842-853.

Useem, M./Zelleke, A., *Oversight and Delegation in Corporate Governance: Deciding What the Board Should Decide*, 14 Corporate Governance: An International Review 1 (2006), pp. 2-12.

Utz, S., *Ability to Pay*, 23 Whittier Law Review 4 (2002), pp. 867-950.

Valente Associati GEB Partners, *Comments to the OECD 'Discussion Draft on Action 6: Preventing the Granting of Treaty Benefits in Inappropriate Circumstances', March 14, 2014*, in: OECD ed., *BEPS Action 6: Preventing the Granting of Treaty Benefits in Inappropriate Circumstances* (2014), pp. 536-543.

Valta, M., *Das Internationale Steuerrecht zwischen Effizienz, Gerechtigkeit und Entwicklungshilfe* (Mohr Siebeck 2014).

Valta, M., *Zukunftsfragen der Ansässigkeitsbesteuerung*, in: Schön, W./Stark, J. eds, *Zukunftsfragen des Steuerrechts IV* (Springer 2022), pp. 55-85.

van den Hurk, H., *Tax Treaties and Abuse: The Effectiveness of the Principal Purpose Test and Some of Its Shortcomings*, 75 Bulletin for International Taxation 6 (2021), pp. 287-293.

Van Hulten, L.C./Korving, J.J.A.M., *Svig og Misbrug: The Danish Anti-abuse Cases*, 47 Intertax 8/9 (2019), pp. 793-800.

van Weeghel, S., *The Tiebreaker Revisited: Towards a Formal Criterion?*, in: Hinnekens, L./Hinnekens, P. eds, *A Vision of Taxes Within and Outside European Borders* (Kluwer Law International 2008), pp. 961-969.

van Weeghel, S., *Article 4(3) of the OECD Model Convention: An Inconvenient Truth*, in: Maisto, G. ed., *Residence of Companies under Tax Treaties and EC Law* (IBFD 2009), pp. 303-307.

van Weeghel, S., *A Deconstruction of the Principal Purposes Test*, 11 World Tax Journal 1 (2019), pp. 3-45.

Vanistendael, F., *From Abuse to Base Erosion, How Did it Come to This?*, in: Haslehner, W./et al. eds, *A Guide to the Anti-Tax Avoidance Directive* (Edward Elgar 2020), pp. 1-31.

Vann, R., *'Liable to Tax' and Company Residence under Tax Treaties*, in: Maisto, G. ed., *Residence of Companies under Tax Treaties and EC Law* (IBFD 2009), pp. 197-272.

Vann, R., *Taxing International Business Income: Hard-Boiled Wonderland and the End of the World*, 2 World Tax Journal 3 (2010), pp. 291-346.

Vega Borrego, F.A., *Limitation on Benefits Clauses in Double Taxation Conventions* (2nd edn Kluwer Law International 2017).

Verlinden, I./Ledure, D./Dessy, M., *The Risky Side of Transfer Pricing: The OECD Base Erosion and Profit Shifting Reports Sharpen the Rules on Risk Allocation under the Arm's Length Standard*, 23 International Transfer Pricing Journal 2 (2016), pp. 109-114.

Verlinden, I./De Baets, S./Parmessar, V., *Grappling with DEMPEs in the Trenches: Trying to Give It the Meaning It Deserves*, 47 Intertax 12 (2019), pp. 1042-1056.

Vogel, K., *Worldwide vs. Source Taxation of Income: A Review and Re-evaluation of Arguments (Part I)*, 16 Intertax 8/9 (1988), pp. 216-229.

Vogel, K., *Klaus Vogel on Double Taxation Conventions* (3rd edn Kluwer 1997).

von Brocke, K., *Kurzübersicht und Einordnung der 'UNSHELL'-Initiative*, Europäische Zeitschrift für Wirtschaftsrecht 4 (2022), pp. 197-200.

von Schanz, G., *Zur Frage der Steuerpflicht*, 9 Finanzarchiv 2 (1892), pp. 365-438.

Wacker, R., *Hinzurechnung passiver Einkünfte nach § 8 AStG und Gegenbeweis: verdeckte Einlagen in Dreiecksverhältnissen*, Internationales Steuerrecht 22 (2018), pp. 882-888.

Wardzynski, A., *The Limitation on Benefits Article in the OECD Model: Closing Abusive (Undesired) Conduit Gateways*, 68 Bulletin for International Taxation 9 (2014), pp. 471-479.

Watrin, C./Leukefeld, R., *Substanzanforderungen gegen missbräuchliche Gewinnverlagerungen und EU-Recht*, Deutsches Steuerrecht 43 (2018), pp. 2284-2290.

Weber, D., *Abuse of Law in European Tax Law: An Overview and Some Recent Trends in the Direct and Indirect Tax Case Law of the CJEU – Part 1*, 53 European Taxation 6 (2013), pp. 251-264.

Weber, D., *The New Common Minimum Anti-abuse Rule in the EU Parent-Subsidiary Directive: Background, Impact, Applicability, Purpose and Effect*, 44 Intertax 2 (2016), pp. 98-129.

Weber, D., *EU Beneficial Ownership Further Developed: A View from a Different Angle*, 14 World Tax Journal 1 (2022), pp. 51-74.

Weber, K./Zöller, D., *An die Substanz: zur Unionsrechtmäßigkeit der Hinzurechnungsbesteuerung im Drittstaatenfall*, Finanzrundschau 7 (2020), pp. 288-297.

Weggenmann, H./Nehls, D., *Article 29*, in: Ismer, R. ed., *Doppelbesteuerungsabkommen* (7th edn C.H. Beck 2021).

Weichenrieder, A.J., *Profit Shifting in the EU: Evidence from Germany*, 16 International Tax and Public Finance 3 (2009), pp. 281-297.

Wells, B./Lowell, C.H., *Income Tax Treaty Policy in the 21st Century: Residence vs. Source*, 5 Columbia Journal of Tax Law 1 (2013), pp. 1-39.

Werner, M., *Value Creation and the Accurate Delineation of the Transaction*, in: Petruzzi, R./Tavares, R.J.S. eds, *Transfer Pricing and Value Creation* (Linde 2019), pp. 93-130.

Weisbach, D.A., *The (Non)Taxation of Risk*, 58 Tax Law Review 1 (2004), pp. 1-58.

Weisbach, D.A., *The Use of Neutralities in International Tax Policy*, 68 National Tax Journal 3 (2015), pp. 635-651.

Wilkie, J.S., *The Definition and Ownership of Intangibles: Inside the Box? Outside the Box? What is the Box?*, 4 World Tax Journal 3 (2012a), pp. 222-249.

Wilkie, J.S., *Reflecting on the 'Arm's Length Principle': What is the 'Principle'? Where Next?*, in: Schön, W. ed., *Fundamentals of International Transfer Pricing in Law and Economics* (Springer 2012b), pp. 137-156.

Wilkins, M., *The Free-Standing Company, 1870-1914: An Important Type of British Foreign Direct Investment*, 41 The Economic History Review 2 (1988), pp. 259-282.

Williamson, O.E., *Public and Private Bureaucracies: A Transaction Cost Economics Perspective*, 15 Journal of Law, Economics & Organization 1 (1999), pp. 306-342.

Wittendorff, J., *The Transactional Ghost of Article 9(1) of the OECD Model*, 63 Bulletin for International Taxation 3 (2009), pp. 107-130.

Wittendorff, J., *Transfer Pricing and the Arm's Length Principle in International Tax Law* (Wolters Kluwer 2010).

Wittendorff, J., *OECD Revised Discussion Draft on Intangibles: A Step in the Right Direction*, Tax Notes International (30 September 2013), pp. 1325-1334.

Wöhe, G./Döring, U./Brösel, G., *Einführung in die allgemeine Betriebswirtschaftslehre* (26th edn Vahlen 2016).

Wright, D.R./et al., *The BEPS Action 8 Final Report: Comments from Economists*, 23 International Transfer Pricing Journal 2 (2016), pp. 99-108.

Zanotti, E., *Taxation of Inter-Company Dividends in the Presence of a PE: The Impact of the EC Fundamental Freedoms (Part One)*, 44 European Taxation 11 (2004), pp. 493-505.

Table of Cases

ECJ

ECJ (Advocate Generals' Opinions)

ECtHR

France

Germany

Ireland

Italy

Switzerland

The Netherlands

United Kingdom

USA

Official Documents

Australia

Australian Taxation Office, *Taxation Ruling 2014/6 – Income Tax: Transfer Pricing – the Application of Section 815-130 of the Income Tax Assessment Act 1997* (cited: 'ATO, TR 2014/6'). Available at: https://www.ato.gov.au/law/view/document?DocID=TXR/TR20146/NAT/ATO/00001, **21**

Australian Taxation Office, *Taxation Ruling 2018/5 – Income Tax: Central Management and Control Test of Residency* (cited: 'ATO, TR 2018/5'). Available at: https://www.ato.gov.au/law/view/document?DocID=TXR/TR20185/NAT/ATO/00001&PiT=99991231235958, **37**

Australian Taxation Office, *Practical Compliance Guideline 2018/9* (cited: 'ATO, PCG'). Available at: https://www.ato.gov.au/law/view/document?DocID=COG/PCG20189/NAT/ATO/00001#P26, **41, 80**

Board of Taxation, *Review of Corporate Tax Residency* (2020) (cited: 'Board, Review'). Available at: https://taxboard.gov.au/sites/taxboard.gov.au/files/2020-10/Signed%20-%20Final%20report%20-%20Review%20of%20Corporate%20Tax%20Residency.pdf, **35**

EU

Directive 2003/49/EC of the European Parliament and of the Council of 3 June 2003 on the common system of taxation applicable to interest and royalty payments made between associated companies of different Member States, OJ L157 (2003), as amended. Available at: https://eur-lex.europa.eu/legal-content/EN/TXT/?uri=CELEX%3A02003L0049-20130701, **8, 16**

Council Directive 2011/16/EU of 15 February 2011 on Administrative Cooperation in the Field of Taxation and Repealing Directive 77/799/EEC, OJ L 64 (2011). Available at: https://eur-lex.europa.eu/legal-content/en/ALL/?uri=CELEX:32011L0016, **193**

Council Directive 2016/1164 of 12 July 2016 laying down rules against tax avoidance practices that directly affect the functioning of the internal market, OJ L 193/1

(2016). Available at: https://eur-lex.europa.eu/legal-content/EN/TXT/?uri=uriserv:OJ.L_.2016.193.01.0001.01.ENG, **16**

Proposal for a Council Directive laying down rules to prevent the misuse of shell entities for tax purposes and amending Directive 2011/16/EU. Available at: https://eur-lex.europa.eu/legal-content/EN/TXT/?uri=CELEX:52021PC0565, **16**

Germany

Bundesfinanzministerium, 8 January 2007, IV B 4 – S 1351 – 1/07, BStBl. I (2007), p. 99, **214, 222, 223**

Bundesfinanzministerium, 17 March 2021, IV B 5 – S 1351/19/10002, Deutsches Steuerrecht 12 (2021), p. 732, **215, 217, 223**

India

Central Board of Direct Taxes, 24 January 2017, *Circular No. 6 – Guiding Principles for Determination of Place of Effective Management (POEM) of a Company* (cited: 'CBDT, Circular No. 6'). Available at: https://pdicai.org/docs/circular-06_2017_271201710597837.pdf, **42, 45**

League of Nations, The contents of the League of Nations' reports are available at: http://adc.library.usyd.edu.au/view?docId=law/xml-main-texts/brulegi.xml;database=;collection=;brand=default, **30, 31, 52, 53**

Bruins, G.W.J./et al., *Report on Double Taxation*, E.F.S.73. F.19 (1923), **30**

Technical Experts, *Report on Double Taxation and Tax Evasion*, F.212 (1925) (cited: 'LoN 1925'), **31**

Fiscal Committee, *Report to the Council on the Fourth Session of the Committee*, C.399.M.204. 1933.II.A. (1933)

OEEC, The contents of the OEEC documents are available at: https://www.taxtreatieshistory.org, **100**

WP2, *Report on the Concept of Fiscal Domicile* (October 1956) (cited: 'FC/WP2(56)1'), **31**

Working Party 2, *Report on the Concept of Fiscal Domicile* (May 1957) (cited: 'FC/WP2(57)1'), **35**

OECD

OECD, *The Impact of the Communications Revolution on the Application of 'Place of Effective Management' as a Tie Breaker Rule* – Discussion Draft (2001) (cited: 'OECD, TAG Discussion Draft'), **35**

OECD, *Action Plan on Base Erosion and Profit Shifting* (OECD 2013). Available at: https://www.oecd.org/ctp/BEPSActionPlan.pdf, **7**

OECD, *Addressing Base Erosion and Profit Shifting* (OECD 2013). Available at: https://www.oecd.org/ctp/addressing-base-erosion-and-profit-shifting-9789264192744-en.htm, **10**

OECD, *BEPS Project Explanatory Statement* (OECD 2015). Available at: https://www.oecd-ilibrary.org/docserver/9789264263437-en.pdf?expires=1617709855&id=

id&accname = ocid57015174&checksum = 187D9BEA8B4D2EB1A766E760D41B1A16, **152, 153**

OECD, *Designing Effective Controlled Foreign Company Rules*, Action 3 - 2015 Final Report (cited: 'OECD Action 3'). Available at: https://www.oecd.org/publications/designing-effective-controlled-foreign-company-rules-action-3-2015-final-report-9789264241152-en.htm, **14, 239**

OECD, *Countering Harmful Tax Practices More Effectively, Taking into Account Transparency and Substance* - 2015 Final Report (cited: 'OECD Action 5'). Available at: https://www.oecd-ilibrary.org/docserver/9789264241190-en.pdf?expires = 1605009795&id = id&accname = ocid57015174&checksum = F1431BD7B7CA3742138FA010385B0D1C, **117**

OECD, *BEPS Action 6: Preventing Treaty Abuse – Revised Discussion Draft* (22 May 2015), **34**

OECD, *Preventing the Granting of Treaty Benefits in Inappropriate Circumstances*, Action 6 - 2015 Final Report (cited: 'OECD Action 6'). Available at: https://www.oecd.org/tax/preventing-the-granting-of-treaty-benefits-in-inappropriate-circumstances-action-6-2015-final-report-9789264241695-en.htm, **13**

OECD, *Aligning Transfer Pricing Outcomes with Value Creation*, Actions 8-10 - 2015 Final Report. Available at: https://www.oecd.org/ctp/aligning-transfer-pricing-outcomes-with-value-creation-actions-8-10-2015-final-reports-9789264241244-en.htm, **12**

OECD, *Model Tax Convention on Income and on Capital* (2017). Available at: https://www.oecd.org/ctp/treaties/model-tax-convention-on-income-and-on-capital-condensed-version-20745419.htm, **7**

OECD, *Multilateral Convention to Implement Tax Treaty Related Measures to Prevent BEPS* (2017). Available at: https://www.oecd.org/tax/treaties/multilateral-convention-to-implement-tax-treaty-related-measures-to-prevent-BEPS.pdf, **33, 154**

OECD, *Explanatory Statement to the Multilateral Convention to Implement Tax Treaty Related Measures to Prevent Base Erosion and Profit Shifting* (2017). Available at: https://www.oecd.org/tax/treaties/explanatory-statement-multilateral-convention-to-implement-tax-treaty-related-measures-to-prevent-BEPS.pdf, **154**

OECD, *Prevention of Tax Treaty Abuse: Third Peer Review Report on Treaty Shopping* (2021) (cited: 'OECD, Peer Review Report on Treaty Shopping'). Available at: https://www.oecd-ilibrary.org/docserver/d6cecbb8-en.pdf?expires = 1617692804&id = id&accname = ocid57015174&checksum = C42B5E657057B4FC2FCA350977A318D6, **153, 154**

OECD, *Transfer Pricing Guidelines for Multinational Enterprises and Tax Administrations* (2022) (cited: 'OECD TPG'). Available at: https://www.oecd.org/tax/transfer-pricing/oecd-transfer-pricing-guidelines-for-multinational-enterprises-and-tax-administrations-20769717.htm, **12, 13, 21-23, 60, 86, 97-103, 105-109, 111-118, 120-138, 140-143, 158, 164, 238**

South Africa

SARS, *Interpretation Note 6, Resident: Place of Effective Management* (2002). Available at: https://www.sars.gov.za/wp-content/uploads/Legal/Notes/LAPD-IntR-IN-2018-12-Arc-12-IN6-Resident-Place-Effective-Management.pdf, **49**

SARS, *Discussion Paper on Interpretation Note 6 Place of Effective Management* (September 2011). Available at: https://cdn.ymaws.com/www.thesait.org.za/resource/resmgr/corporate_tax/71554_discussiondocumentpoem.pdf, **48**

SARS, *Interpretation Note 6 (Issue 2), Resident: Place of Effective Management (Companies)* (2015) (cited: 'SARS, Interpretation Note 6(2)'). Available at: https://www.sars.gov.za/AllDocs/LegalDoclib/Notes/LAPD-IntR-IN-2012-06%20-%20IN%206%20Resident%20-%20Place%20of%20effective%20management%20(companies).pdf, **42**

UK

HMRC, Statement of Practice 1 (1990). Available at: https://www.gov.uk/government/publications/statement-of-practice-1-1990, **42**

HMRC, *International Manual: Company Residence: Standard Treaty Tie-Breakers* (2016). Available at: https://www.gov.uk/hmrc-internal-manuals/international-manual/intm120085, **42**

USA

US Treasury, *Intercompany Transfer Pricing Regulations under Section 482* (1994) (cited: 'US Treas. Reg.'). Available at: https://www.irs.gov/pub/irs-apa/482_regs.pdf, **107, 108, 113, 114**

US Treasury, *Preamble to 2016 U.S. Model Income Tax Convention* (2016). Available at: https://www.treasury.gov/resource-center/tax-policy/treaties/documents/preamble-us%20model-2016.pdf, **155**

Index

H

I

L

M

N

O

P

R

S

SERIES ON INTERNATIONAL TAXATION

1. Alberto Xavier, *The Taxation of Foreign Investment in Brazil,* 1980 (ISBN 90-200-0582-0).
2. Hugh J. Ault & Albert J. Rädler, *The German Corporation Tax Law with 1980 Amendments,* 1981 (ISBN 90-200-0642-8).
3. Paul R. McDaniel & Hugh J. Ault, *Introduction to United States International Taxation,* 1981 (ISBN 90-6544-004-6).
4. Albert J. Rädler, *German Transfer Pricing/Prix de Transfer en Allemagne,* 1984 (ISBN 90-6544-143-3).
5. Paul R. McDaniel & Stanley S. Surrey, *International Aspects of Tax Expenditures: A Comparative Study,* 1985 (ISBN 90-654-4163-8).
6. Kees van Raad, *Nondiscrimination in International Tax Law,* 1986 (ISBN 90-6544-266-9).
7. Sijbren Cnossen (ed.), *Tax Coordination in the European Community,* 1987 (ISBN 90-6544-272-3).
8. Ben Terra, *Sales Taxation. The Case of Value Added Tax in the European Community,* 1989 (ISBN 90-6544-381-9).
9. Rutsel S.J. Martha, *The Jurisdiction to Tax in International Law: Theory and Practice of Legislative Fiscal Jurisdiction,* 1989 (ISBN 90-654-4416-5).
10. Paul R. McDaniel & Hugh J. Ault, *Introduction to United States International Taxation* (3rd revised edition), 1989 (ISBN 90-6544-423-8).
11. Manuel Pires, *International Juridicial Double Taxation of Income,* 1989 (ISBN 90-6544-426-2).
12. A.H.M. Daniels, *Issues in International Partnership Taxation,* 1991 (ISBN 90-654-4577-3).
13. Arvid A. Skaar, *Permanent Establishment: Erosion of a Tax Treaty Principle,* 1992 (ISBN 90-6544-594-3).
14. Cyrille David & Geerten M.M. Michielse (eds), *Tax Treatment of Financial Instruments,* 1996 (ISBN 90-654-4666-4).
15. Herbert H. Alpert & Kees van Raad (eds), *Essays on International Taxation,* 1993 (ISBN 90-654-4781-4).
16. Wolfgang Gassner, Michael Lang & Eduard Lechner (eds), *Tax Treaties and EC Law,* 1997 (ISBN 90-411-0680-4).
17. Glória Teixeira, *Taxing Corporate Profits in the EU,* 1997 (ISBN 90-411-0703-7).
18. Michael Lang et al. (eds), *Multilateral Tax Treaties,* 1998 (ISBN 90-411-0704-5).
19. Stef van Weeghel, *The Improper Use of Tax Treaties,* 1998 (ISBN 90-411-0737-1).

20. Klaus Vogel (ed.), *Interpretation of Tax Law and Treaties and Transfer Pricing in Japan and Germany*, 1998 (ISBN 90-411-9655-2).
21. Bertil Wiman (ed.), *International Studies in Taxation: Law and Economics; Liber Amicorum Leif Mutén*, 1999 (ISBN 90-411-9692-7).
22. Alfonso J. Martín Jiménez, *Towards Corporate Tax Harmonization in the European Community*, 1999 (ISBN 90-411-9690-0).
23. Ramon J. Jeffery, *The Impact of State Sovereignty on Global Trade and International Taxation*, 1999 (ISBN 90-411-9703-6).
24. A.J. Easson, *Taxation of Foreign Direct Investment*, 1999 (ISBN 90-411-9741-9).
25. Marjaana Helminen, *The Dividend Concept in International Tax Law: Dividend Payments Between Corporate Entities*, 1999 (ISBN 90-411-9765-6).
26. Paul Kirchhof, Moris Lehner, Kees van Raad, Arndt Raupach & Michael-Rodi (eds), *International and Comparative Taxation: Essays in Honour of Klaus Vogel*, 2002 (ISBN 90-411-9841-5).
27. Krister Andersson, Peter Melz & Christer Silfverberg (eds), *Liber Amicorum Sven-Olof Lodin*, 2001 (ISBN 90-411-9850-4).
28. Juan Martín Jovanovich, *Customs Valuation and Transfer Pricing: Is It Possible to Harmonize Customs and Tax Rules?*, Second Edition, 2018 (ISBN 978-90-411-6134-5).
29. Stefano Simontacchi, *Taxation of Capital Gains under the OECD Model Convention: With Special Regard to Immovable Property*, 2007 (ISBN 978-90-411-2549-1).
30. Michael Lang, Josef Schuch, & Claus Staringer (eds), *Tax Treaty Law and EC Law*, 2007 (ISBN 978-90-411-2629-0).
31. Duncan Bentley, *Taxpayers' Rights: Theory Origin and Implementation*, 2007 (ISBN 978-90-411-2650-4).
32. Sergio André Rocha, *Interpretation of Double Taxation Conventions: General Theory and Brazilian Perspective*, 2008 (ISBN 978-90-411-2822-5).
33. Robert F. van Brederode, *Systems of General Sales Taxation: Theory, Policy and Practice*, 2009 (ISBN 978-90-411-2832-4).
34. John G. Head & Richard Krever (eds), *Tax Reform in the 21st Century: A Volume in Memory of Richard Musgrave*, 2009 (ISBN 978-90-411-2829-4).
35. Jens Wittendorff, *Transfer Pricing and the Arm's Length Principle in International Tax Law*, 2010 (ISBN 978-90-411-3270-3).
36. Marjaana Helminen, *The International Tax Law Concept of Dividend*, Second Edition, 2017 (ISBN 978-90-411-8394-1).
37. Robert F. van Brederode (ed.), *Immovable Property under VAT: A Comparative Global Analysis*, 2011 (ISBN 978-90-411-3126-3).
38. Dennis Weber & Stef van Weeghel, *The 2010 OECD Updates: Model Tax Convention & Transfer Pricing Guidelines - A Critical Review*, 2011 (ISBN 978-90-411-3812-5).
39. Yariv Brauner & Martin James McMahon, Jr. (eds), *The Proper Tax Base: Structural Fairness from an International and Comparative Perspective— Essays in Honour of Paul McDaniel*, 2012 (ISBN 978-90-411-3286-4).
40. Robert F. van Brederode (ed.), *Science, Technology and Taxation*, 2012 (ISBN 978-90-411-3125-6).

41. Oskar Henkow, *The VAT/GST Treatment of Public Bodies*, 2013 (ISBN 978-90-411-4663-2).
42. Jean Schaffner, *How Fixed Is a Permanent Establishment?*, 2013 (ISBN 978-90-411-4662-5).
43. Miguel Correia, *Taxation of Corporate Groups*, 2013 (ISBN 978-90-411-4841-4).
44. Veronika Daurer, *Tax Treaties and Developing Countries*, 2014 (ISBN 978-90-411-4982-4).
45. Claire Micheau, *State Aid, Subsidy and Tax Incentives under EU and WTO Law*, 2014 (ISBN 978-90-411-4555-0).
46. Robert F. van Brederode & Richard Krever (eds), *Legal Interpretation of Tax Law*, 2014 (ISBN 978-90-411-4945-9).
47. Radhakishan Rawal, *Taxation of Cross-border Services*, 2014 (ISBN 978-90-411-4947-3).
48. João Dácio Rolim, *Proportionality and Fair Taxation*, 2014 (ISBN 978-90-411-5838-3).
49. Paulo Rosenblatt, *General Anti-avoidance Rules for Major Developing Countries*, 2015 (ISBN 978-90-411-5839-0).
50. Gaspar Lopes Dias V.S., *Tax Arbitrage through Cross-Border Financial Engineering*, 2015 (ISBN 978-90-411-5875-8).
51. Geerten M.M. Michielse & Victor Thuronyi (eds), *Tax Design Issues Worldwide*, 2015 (ISBN 978-90-411-5610-5).
52. Oktavia Weidmann, *Taxation of Derivatives and Cryptoassets*, Second Edition, 2024 (ISBN 978-94-035-2383-5).
53. Chris Evans, Richard Krever & Peter Mellor (eds), *Tax Simplification*, 2015 (ISBN 978-90-411-5976-2).
54. Reuven Avi-Yonah & Joel Slemrod (eds), *Taxation and Migration*, 2015 (ISBN 978-90-411-6136-9).
55. Alexander Bosman, *Other Income under Tax Treaties: An Analysis of Article 21 of the OECD Model Convention*, 2015 (ISBN 978-90-411-6610-4).
56. John Abrahamson, *International Taxation of Manufacturing and Distribution*, 2016 (ISBN 978-90-411-6664-7).
57. Frederik Boulogne, *Shortcomings in the EU Merger Directive*, 2016 (ISBN 978-90-411-6713-2).
58. Angelika Meindl-Ringler, *Beneficial Ownership in International Tax Law*, 2016 (ISBN 978-90-411-6833-7).
59. Andreas Waltrich, *Cross-Border Taxation of Permanent Establishments: An International Comparison*, 2016 (ISBN 978-90-411-6832-0).
60. Sergio André Rocha & Allison Christians (eds), *Tax Sovereignty in the BEPS Era*, 2017 (ISBN 978-90-411-6707-1).
61. Peter Antony Wilson, *BRICS and International Tax Law*, 2018 (ISBN 978-90-411-9435-0).
62. Louise Otis, Brigitte Alepin & Blanca Moreno-Dodson (eds), *Winning the Tax Wars: Tax Competition and Cooperation*, 2018 (ISBN 978-90-411-9460-2).

63. Marta Castelon, *International Taxation of Income from Services under Double Taxation Conventions: Development, Practice and Policy*, 2018 (ISBN 978-90-411-9594-4).
64. D.M. Broekhuijsen, *A Multilateral Tax Treaty: Designing an Instrument to Modernise International Tax Law*, 2018 (ISBN 978-90-411-9872-3).
65. John Abrahamson, *International Taxation of Energy Production and Distribution*, 2018 (ISBN 978-90-411-9101-4).
66. Leopoldo Parada, *Double Non-taxation and the Use of Hybrid Entities*, Second Edition, 2024 (ISBN 978-94-035-4666-7).
67. Richard Snoeij, *International Tax Aspects of Sovereign Wealth Investors: A Source State Perspective*, 2018 (ISBN 978-90-411-9431-2).
68. Aleksandra Bal, *Taxation, Virtual Currency and Blockchain*, 2019 (ISBN 978-94-035-0103-1).
69. Werner Haslehner, Georg Kofler, Katerina Pantazatou & Alexander Rust (eds), *Tax and the Digital Economy: Challenges and Proposals for Reform*, 2019 (ISBN 978-94-035-0361-5).
70. Eva Escribano, *Jurisdiction to Tax Corporate Income Pursuant to the Presumptive Benefit Principle: A Critical Analysis of Structural Paradigms Underlying Corporate Income Taxation and Proposals for Reform*, 2019 (ISBN 978-94-035-0640-1).
71. Jérôme Monsenego & Jan Bjuvberg (eds), *International Taxation in a Changing Landscape: Liber Amicorum in Honour of Bertil Wiman*, 2019 (ISBN 978-90-411-9234-9).
72. Kasper Dziurdź, *Non-discrimination in Tax Treaty Law and World Trade Law: The Impact of Formal, Substantive and Subjective Approaches*, 2019 (ISBN 978-94-035-0904-4).
73. Félix Daniel Martínez Laguna, *Hybrid Financial Instruments, Double Nontaxation and Linking Rules*, 2019 (ISBN 978-94-035-1074-3).
74. Jan Gooijer, *Tax Treaty Residence of Entities*, 2019 (ISBN 978-94-035-1301-0).
75. John Abrahamson, *International Taxation of Banking*, 2020 (ISBN 978-94-035-1094-1).
76. Richard Krever & François Vaillancourt (eds), *The Allocation of Multinational Business Income: Reassessing the Formulary Apportionment Option*, 2020 (ISBN 978-94-035-0614-2).
77. Ajit Kumar Singh, *Exploring the Nexus Doctrine in International Tax Law*, 2021 (ISBN 978-94-035-3363-6).
78. Galya Savir, *Regulation and Tax in Space*, 2021 (ISBN 978-94-035-3393-3).
79. Rita Julien, *Credit Method Compatibility and Constraints under EU Law: An Analysis of the Case Law of the CJEU*, 2022 (ISBN 978-94-035-2363-7).
80. Sergio André Rocha & Allison Christians (eds), *A Multilateral Convention for Tax: From Theory to Implementation*, 2022 (ISBN 978-90-411-9428-2).
81. Brigitte Alepin, Lyne Latulippe & Louise Otis (eds), *Coordination and Cooperation: Tax Policy in the 21st Century*, 2022 (ISBN 978-94-035-3740-5).
82. Chunyang Zhang, *The Role of Tax Law in Mergers and Acquisitions: A Chinese Perspective*, 2022 (ISBN 978-94-035-3741-2).

83. Florian Navisotschnigg, *Substance in International Tax Law: DEMPE Approach, Substantial Activity Requirement and Beneficial Ownership*, 2022 (ISBN 978-94-035-4895-1).
84. Mees Vergouwen, *The Effect of Directives Within the Area of Direct Taxation on the Interpretation and Application of Tax Treaties*, 2023 (ISBN 978-94-035-0907-5).
85. Rachna Matabudul, *Tax Treaty Dispute Resolution: Lessons from the Law of the Sea*, 2023 (ISBN 978-94-035-3407-7).
86. David Orzechowski-Zölzer, *The Taxation of Fees for Technical Services on the Basis of Article 12A UN Model Convention*, 2024 (ISBN 978-94-035-4297-3).
87. David Rüll, *The Resolution of International Tax Disputes: From the Established Mechanisms Towards an Institutionalised International Instrument*, 2024 (ISBN 978-94-035-2088-9).
88. Savvas Kostikidis, *Residence and Economic Substance of Subsidiary Corporations in International and European Tax Law*, 2024 (ISBN 978-94-035-3858-7).

www.ingramcontent.com/pod-product-compliance
Lightning Source LLC
Chambersburg PA
CBHW071240230926
51849CB00001B/174
* 9 7 8 9 4 0 3 5 3 8 5 8 7 *